tricontinental

HAVANA 1966

Documents of the First Solidarity Conference of the Peoples
of Africa, Asia, and Latin America

Published in February 2026 by
1804 Books, New York, NY

1804Books.com

This selection © 1804 Books, New York, NY
ISBN: 979-8-9990195-4-7
Library of Congress Control Number: 2026933114

Cover by Vivek Venkatraman

Table of Contents

Resolutions

Sub-Commission of Burning Issues

A Gathering that Will Never Be Forgotten

Vijay Prashad

When the revolutionaries came to Havana just after New Year's Day in 1966 for the Tricontinental Conference, they understood the power and danger of their meeting. The man who had helped organize it—Mehdi Ben Barka—left Havana in October 1965, arrived in Paris, and then disappeared later that month. The kidnapping and murder of Ben Barka remains a mystery, with accusations that it was not just the Paris police, but the Central Intelligence Agency (CIA), Moroccan intelligence services (DST), and the Israeli intelligence division (Mossad) that killed him. The fact that the West and its allies had such fear about Ben Barka's activities and therefore disappeared and killed him revealed to the participants that their meeting was not an ordinary one: it was built to overthrow imperialism, therefore it was to be expected that imperialism would fight its construction. In his closing speech given at Havana's Chaplin Theatre, Cuba's Prime Minister Fidel Castro assessed the murder of Ben Barka with clarity:

> . . . this repugnant, monstrous event demonstrated from the outset imperialism's interest in obstructing the conference, in making it fail. However, the results of this conference demonstrate that Ben Barka's blood was not shed in vain, and that Ben Barka's crime, his assassination—like the assassination of Lumumba, like the assassination of Aidit, like the assassination of Sandino—that with none of its horrible crimes, with none of its barbaric acts, imperialism will be able to stop the victorious march, the final liberation of the peoples.

Fidel made two important points in this section of his speech. First, that imperialism did not want to allow the Third World to develop in peace and build the sovereignty of their territories and the dignity of their peoples. Augusto César Sandino, the leader of the Army in Defense of the National Sovereignty of Nicaragua (EDSN) that sought to end the US occupation of the country (1912–1933) and to build a sovereign Nicaragua, was executed in 1934 by the National Guard and with US involvement; Patrice Lumumba, prime minister of the Democratic Republic of the Congo, was assassinated with the collusion of the CIA as well as Belgian and British intelligence in 1961; and Dipa Nusantra Aidit, leader of the Communist Party of Indonesia, was killed during the mass murder of a million communists as part of a CIA and Australian intelligence coup that resulted in a military dictatorship that lasted from 1965 to 1998. Fidel could have added the coup in 1964 against President João Goulart of Brazil that created a military dictatorship till 1985. Such imperialist violence had become commonplace in Africa, Asia, and Latin America—imperialist violence that denied its violence and blamed instead its victims for defending their rights to sovereignty and dignity.

Second, that despite this violence, the impact of the anticolonial struggles on the consciousness of the vast masses of the three continents could not be underestimated since their consciousness had been built by the wretchedness of colonialism and the bravery of the century-long anticolonial struggles that—for Latin America—had the armies of Simón Bolívar etched into their memory. In fact, the essence of the anticolonial struggles had been captured in a United Nations General Assembly resolution in 1960, which stated that "the process of liberation is irresistible and irreversible." The harsh nature of the violence was a result not of the weakness of the anticolonial struggles, but because of their effectiveness: their leaders had to be killed, their entire process had to be dismantled, and their ideologies had to be ripped out of society by the root. The coups in the Congo (1961), Ghana (1966), Brazil (1964), and Indonesia (1965) came as a result of the immense attractiveness of the processes set in place in each of these countries by political movements that straddled a range of political views, but which were rooted in anticolonial ambitions.

The irresistible and irreversible part of this Tricontinental dynamic became clear in 1974 when Portugal not only lost the national liberation wars across Africa (from Angola and Mozambique to Guinea Bissau) but these defeats led to the Carnation Revolution within Portugal against the fascist dictatorship of Estado Novo that had been set in place in 1933. These victories across Africa were the prelude to the Saur Revolution in Afghanistan in 1978; to the Nicaraguan Revolution of 1979 that was led by the Sandinistas (the FSLN), named after Sandino, whom Fidel named in his speech; and to the Grenadian Revolution of 1979. The dynamic of the Tricontinental can be seen in each of these revolutionary developments, and it can be seen further in the counterrevolutionary terror that they experienced (a mirror of the abduction and murder of Ben Barka).

What came after the Tricontinental Conference of 1966 was the establishment of the Organization in Solidarity with the Peoples of Asia, Africa, and

Latin America (OSPAAAL) in Havana (1966–2019), whose magazine—*Tricontinental*—was the main avenue for information about these revolutionary movements around the world, and whose posters made great gains in the battle of emotions against the commodification of life by capitalism. The solidarity that OSPAAAL built provides a great foundation for our own sense of solidarity with movements from Palestine to Cuba.

This volume, lovingly produced by Manolo De Los Santos, is part of the residue of solidarity—a genuine work of excavation from the archives that is necessary to be studied so that we have a better understanding of the Tricontinental Conference's origins and its history, but also so that we can deepen our praxis for the ongoing struggles to realize a world without imperialism.

— Vijay Prashad
Santiago, Chile

Echoes of Havana: The Tricontinental Conference

Manolo De Los Santos

In 1966, the world was ablaze with tension. The United States and its allies were openly confronting a growing number of countries charting a course toward socialism, national liberation movements were gaining momentum, and a revolutionary spirit filled the air. Amidst this global upheaval, Cuba, a crucial location in the Third World project, was about to host a landmark gathering: the First Solidarity Conference of the Peoples of Africa, Asia, and Latin America, famously known as the Tricontinental Conference.

A Revolution's Anniversary

The stage was set on New Year's Eve, 1965, as delegates from around the world joined Fidel Castro and thousands of Cubans for a celebratory dinner on Revolution Square, marking the seventh anniversary of the Cuban Revolution. This shared meal, under the watchful gaze of the monument to Cuba's anticolonial hero José Martí, laid the groundwork for the revolutionary discussions to come.

A few days later, at the opening ceremony in Pedro Marrero Stadium, a powerful *mística* captivated the attendees. Young Cuban volunteers and members of the Revolutionary Armed Forces performed a symbolic reenactment of Cuba's history of resistance to colonialism and imperialism. From the courageous Maroons who fought against their slave masters, to the barefoot heroes of the wars of independence, to the audacious campaign that emancipated Cubans from illiteracy, the performance paid homage to the island's insurgent spirit.

On a large screen, images of liberation martyrs like Augusto César Sandino, Nguyen Van Troi, and Patrice Lumumba flickered, their silent presence speaking volumes. As these images appeared, young, resolute soldiers marched in, carrying the flags of various liberation movements. This was a truly emotional representation of the unity of the three continents in their struggle, a unity that would be forged in the coming days.

Why Havana? Cuba's Role in the Tricontinental

The choice of Havana as the conference's host was no accident; it was a deliberate and symbolic act. Cuba, a beacon of a young revolution that triumphed through armed struggle just ninety miles from the epicenter of US imperialism, played an undeniably crucial role. Having achieved its own national liberation and embarked on building a socialist project, Cuba embodied the very synthesis of the two great contemporary currents of the world revolution that Mehdi Ben Barka, the Moroccan revolutionary, had clearly articulated: the socialist revolution and the national liberation revolution. Its unwavering defiance of the US economic blockade and relentless hostility served as a powerful example of revolutionary victory and resilience against seemingly insurmountable odds. Since 1959, Cuba had demonstrated its commitment to international solidarity, taking major political risks—for example, its solidarity with the cause of independence in Algeria served as a firm base of moral and material support for struggles across Africa, Asia, and Latin America.

The idea for such a conference had been brewing for some time, first raised during the Fourth Session of the Council of Solidarity of the Afro-Asian Peoples in Bandung in April 1961. This initiative gained momentum through the Afro-Asian Peoples' Solidarity Organization (AAPSO) and culminated in 1963 at the Third Conference of Solidarity of the Afro-Asian Peoples in Moshi, Tanzania, where Cuba's invitation to host was enthusiastically accepted. The preparatory committee, initially composed of twelve countries, expanded to include Latin American representatives from Mexico, Venezuela, Guatemala, Chile, Uruguay, and Cuba. A key organizer was Mehdi Ben Barka, president of the international preparatory committee, whose impassioned call—"Peoples of Africa, Asia, and Latin America: Move forward with your struggle!"—echoed throughout the Havana meeting despite his tragic kidnapping and assassination before the conference by Moroccan and French agents. The conference was strategically organized to also coincide with the seventh anniversary of the Cuban Revolution.

Expanding the Anti-Imperialist Front: Beyond Bandung

The Tricontinental Conference was a powerful continuation of a long tradition among anticolonial, anti-imperialist, Pan-Africanist, and communist forces who, despite differing tendencies, challenged the international structures of capitalism and white domination. Its roots stretched back to crucial gatherings like the 1927 League Against Imperialism and Colonial Oppression in Brussels, where early anticolonial thinkers like Jawaharlal Nehru (India), Josiah Gumede (South Africa), and Lamine Senghor (Senegal) laid foundational groundwork for future solidarity inspired by the anticolonial praxis of the Bolshevik Revolution and with the material support of the Communist International (Comintern).

Twenty-eight years later, the Bandung Conference of 1955 brought together newly independent nations from Asia and Africa, cementing principles of self-determination and Afro-Asian unity. President Sukarno of Indonesia would recall in his opening speech at the Bandung Conference of 1955: "At that Conference many distinguished delegates who are present here today met each other and found new strength in their fight for independence." However, the Tricontinental Conference expanded on Bandung's vision. It explicitly recognized the need for unity between socialist countries, the nonaligned movement, and national liberation movements, extending solidarity across the Atlantic to embrace Latin American revolutionary movements and taking a decidedly militant approach to decolonization. The conference aimed to build a distinct Third World project by coordinating the peoples of Latin America, Asia, and Africa to mount a final offensive on the system of domination imposed by the United States after World War II. This meant going beyond Bandung's principles of noninterference and nonalignment.

A Convergence of Revolutionaries

From January 3 to 15, 1966, Havana became the epicenter of a seismic shift in the global struggle for liberation. Over two weeks, the Tricontinental Conference convened 82 delegations from Africa, Asia, and Latin America, a historic assembly united by a common defiance of imperialism. This wasn't merely another international meeting; it was a declaration of war against imperialism, colonialism, and neocolonialism in all their forms.

A total of 512 representatives from 82 communist parties, progressive and socialist states, national liberation movements and popular organizations, alongside observers and guests, converged. This diverse attendance highlighted a crucial balance: while newly independent states and communist parties participated, significant emphasis was placed on the participation of national liberation movements, reflecting the conference's core focus on supporting those actively engaged in armed or political struggle. Cubans had pushed early in the preparation to make greater space for these movements, with over a third of the delegations coming from national liberation movements or left organizations from newly independent countries in the Third World.

The conference floor, buzzing with fervent debate, was held in the former Habana Hilton, now aptly renamed Habana Libre after its expropriation by the Cuban Revolution in 1960. What unfolded was a dynamic convergence of revolutionary thought and practice, reflecting the multifaceted and multilingual character of the anti-imperialist movement. Delegates included socialists, communists, revolutionary nationalists, and progressive forces, representing a broad spectrum of experiences, all contributing to a collective indictment of imperialist domination and a powerful blueprint for coordinated liberation efforts.

Key Voices and Shared Struggles

The plenary sessions opened with Dr. Osvaldo Dorticós Torrado, president of Cuba, whose passionate welcome resonated with the common plight of "underdevelopment"—a euphemism for the economic backwardness, hunger, illiteracy, and exploitation imposed by imperialism. Youssef El Sebai, secretary general of the Afro-Asian People's Solidarity Organization, then drew a thread of historical continuity, linking the burgeoning solidarity in Havana to the foundational spirit of the Bandung Conference.

From the front lines of heated conflicts, Nguyen Van Tien of the National Liberation Front of South Vietnam offered a searing account of US aggression, emphasizing Vietnam as the undeniable epicenter of the anti-imperialist struggle and detailing the brutal realities faced by his people. M. Gabriel Yumbu from Congo-Léopoldville laid bare the ruthless exploitation of his nation's immense natural resources by imperialist monopolies, articulating a desperate need for unity against the insidious development of neocolonialism in Africa.

Ibrahim Abu Sitta of Palestine broadened this critique, highlighting the struggle against Zionist aggression as an intrinsic part of the wider fight against imperialism and exposing Israel's role as a "military, economic, and cultural base" for Western colonialists. Wu Xueqian from China powerfully articulated the strategic necessity of revolutionary violence and people's war, asserting that US military superiority could be defeated. Khaled Mohieddin of the United Arab Republic (now Egypt) championed national liberation and the inherent right to armed struggle as a legitimate response to armed aggression.

Norman Pietri of Puerto Rico brought a stark reminder of direct colonialism, detailing the forced conscription of Puerto Rican youth into US imperialist wars, noting that Puerto Ricans, despite being only 1 percent of the US population, made up 3.5 percent of youths called to the ranks by the Johnson government, effectively imposing a blood tribute 3.5 times greater than that demanded of US citizens. Paul Lantimo of Haiti, echoing a long history of resistance, decried his nation's ongoing struggle against a subservient government.

Amidst these powerful speeches, the message brought by Amílcar Cabral of the African Party for the Independence of Guinea-Bissau and Cape Verde stood out for its acute ideological caliber. Cabral, acutely conscious of the problems and limitations inherent in national liberation movements, used his platform to offer a profound theoretical intervention. In what has now become a foundational text, he articulated the inseparability of national liberation and socialism, telling the delegates that "in our present historical situation—elimination of imperialism which uses every means to perpetuate its domination over our peoples, and consolidation of socialism throughout a large part of the world—there are only two possible paths for an independent nation: to return to imperialist domination (neocolonialism, capitalism, state capitalism), or to take the way of social-ism." Cabral also took stock of the independence struggles while connecting them to theoretical aspects of colonized societies. He argued that rigorous analysis and a clear ideological outlook were key for liberation movements, affirming that "it is usually said that national liberation rests on the peoples' right to freely choose their destiny, and the goal is national independence. . . . For us, the core of national liberation is built from the unassailable right of every people to have their own history." His insights challenged the delegates to move beyond superficial understandings of independence to embrace a deeper, more transformative revolutionary consciousness.

John K. Tettegah of Ghana, a radical trade unionist and close comrade of Kwame Nkrumah, passionately advocated for African unity as an indispensable bulwark against neocolonialism. Aruna Asaf Ali, a historic freedom fighter from India and the only woman to lead a delegation, spoke to the burgeoning global solidarity, emphasizing the urgent need to resist imperialist maneuvers that sought to divide newly independent nations. Robert Resha of South Africa painted a harrowing picture of apartheid, a "most brutal and barbaric system of racist and national oppression," and vehemently called for international sanctions against the racist regime.

Sharof Rashidov from the USSR affirmed robust Soviet support for national liberation movements, specifically condemning US aggression in Vietnam and highlighting Soviet material aid, including advanced weaponry. Osmany Cienfuegos of Cuba powerfully articulated Cuba's revolutionary line and the undeniable possibility of revolution even against the most formidable imperialist adversary. Ibrahim Isa of Indonesia described the fierce struggle against US imperialism and underscored the critical need for genuine revolutionary unity, revealing the brutal aftermath of a right-wing coup in Indonesia. Kim Wal Yong of the Democratic People's Republic of Korea condemned US occupation and called for broader support for the Vietnamese struggle. Luis Augusto Turcios Lima of Guatemala eloquently underscored the pivotal role of Indigenous peasants in the revolutionary process. Assayed Abdallah Bin Jehir El Alawi from the Yemen Arab Republic spoke of his nation's ongoing revolution. Salvador Allende of Chile urged Latin American peoples to intensify their struggle against the audacious Johnson Doctrine that asserted a US right to unilateral intervention.

Raúl Roa García, Cuba's foreign minister and president of the conference, delivered a powerful summation, encapsulating the gathering's success as a definitive "blow to the backbone of imperialism." Delegates concluded that to defeat US imperialism, national liberation movements and left and progressive organizations worldwide would have to embrace all forms of struggle, including armed struggle; create new forms of coordination; and build a new international order based on cooperation between the socialist bloc and emerging Third World nations.

Beyond Speeches: Building Solidarity and Connections

The conference was more than just formal speeches; it was fertile ground for bilateral conversations, personal connections, and acts of profound solidarity. On the sidelines, Vilma Espín, a historic fighter from the July 26th Movement and leader of the Federation of Cuban Women, met with women fighters from various delegations, including Florence Mophosho of South Africa. Their shared experiences fostered a powerful bond, a testament to the shared struggles of their movements.

A poignant moment underscored the tangible nature of solidarity: The Brazilian delegation, living under a military dictatorship and recognizing their nation's historical injustice in participating in the US-led military occupation of the Dominican Republic, formally handed their national flag to the Dominican delegation. This symbolic act of reparation transcended political rhetoric, offering a gesture of anti-imperialist unity.

The conference also celebrated individuals who embodied the spirit of resistance. Dan Thi Thanh, a young Vietnamese fighter renowned for bringing down American fighter planes, met Fausto Díaz, a Bay of Pigs veteran who had helped defeat the US-sponsored invasion of Cuba. Their handshake symbolized the interconnectedness of their struggles and shared victory against a common enemy. Even cultural figures were drawn to the revolutionary fervor; Josephine Baker, the renowned African American performer, antifascist fighter, and civil rights activist, defied her own country's policy of isolating Cuba to perform at the conference, a powerful statement of solidarity across racial and national lines.

At the close of the conference, Fidel Castro led delegates on a deeply symbolic visit to the Escambray Mountains. This region, once a battleground for counter-revolutionaries, had become a beacon of progress with new housing models and agricultural projects improving the lives of the peasantry. Throughout the visit, Amílcar Cabral stood at Fidel's side, the two leaders finding in each other not just political allies, but true intellectual and political peers, their conversations undoubtedly rich with strategic insights. Fidel, in his closing address, foresaw the conference's enduring legacy: "The united strength of revolutionary peoples will be much more powerful." He underscored the profound historical significance and reiterated Cuba's unwavering commitment of moral and material aid to national liberation movements. These diverse voices, though distinct, converged to articulate a shared understanding of the common enemy and a collective, unyielding resolve for liberation.

Challenges and the Birth of OSPAAAL

The conference established the Organization of Solidarity with the Peoples of Africa, Asia, and Latin America (OSPAAAL). Prior to this, OSPAAAL's precursor, the Afro-Asian Peoples' Solidarity Organization, had significant Soviet and

Chinese representation, often tied to the World Peace Council. The escalating Sino-Soviet rift deeply divided the organization and shaped the Tricontinental Conference's planning. However, incorporating Latin American movements offered a chance to move past these bilateral power struggles. During the first international preparatory committee meeting in Cairo in September 1965, the Soviet Union and China clashed over the representation of groups coming from Latin America, with both wanting their key allies to be the main representatives for each country. Cuba helped mediate a compromise in which solidarity committees representing all leftist, anti-imperialist, and liberation groups could participate under the direction of their respective communist parties of each country.

The mid-1960s were a crucible of upheaval marked by the Cold War's shadow, newly independent African nations navigating sovereignty, Latin American revolutions igniting hope and facing US intervention, and Vietnam becoming a symbol of Third World resistance. Yet, setbacks also abounded: CIA-backed coups toppled governments, and apartheid and Zionist occupation became further entrenched. The Tricontinental Conference emerged amidst this tumult, insisting that distant battles were interconnected fronts in a shared struggle.

Building the international unity of working-class and revolutionary forces has always posed considerable challenges. The Cubans sought to overcome the challenges and historical limitations of previous experiences, learning from the history of the First and Second Internationals and the Communist International. The Tricontinental Conference deliberately avoided imposing a singular model and structure for global solidarity. The Cubans skillfully navigated efforts to derail proceedings, primarily due to the Sino-Soviet split, and fundamental tactical differences among Latin American parties and national liberation movements.

The establishment of OSPAAAL, the permanent institution envisioned by the Tricontinental movement, faced three significant challenges, as detailed in an internal Cuban document written as a post-conference assessment. Firstly, there was the difficulty of forging a coherent anti-imperialist agenda. This agenda aimed to combat imperialism, colonialism, and neocolonialism while simultaneously championing genuine peace, universal disarmament, and peaceful coexistence. For many delegates, the most critical aspect was providing comprehensive, institutional support for achieving and defending national liberation, a concept broader than armed struggle.

Secondly, the movement struggled with developing an organization for active solidarity, one that could move beyond mere symbolic gestures or bureaucratic limitations.

Finally, the Sino-Soviet split presented a major obstacle. This open rift significantly weakened the socialist bloc and complicated negotiations, leading to polarized alignments among states, movements, and organizations across Asia, Africa, and Latin America. Both the USSR and China actively sought to influence the conference's program. Most discussions revolved around these three problems, with the Sino-Soviet split proving to be the most pervasive and divisive, even influencing responses to the other two challenges. Plenary sessions were extended, diverting time and energy from commission discussions where specific tasks were meant to be considered. Among the most important "burning issues" addressed were military occupations such as those in South Vietnam and the Dominican Republic, both sites of recent American military intervention.

The entry of Latin America and the Caribbean, with five national liberation movements and Cuba as the only state, changed the representation. The Cubans skillfully facilitated the conference by avoiding contentious plenary debates, instead pursuing bilateral talks with all actors, from the USSR and China to various African and national liberation movements and their key allies. This flexible approach, characterized by an unwavering dedication to consensus, allowed them to gain support from both sides of the Sino-Soviet split. This strategic flexibility has come to characterize Cuban foreign policy over six decades: the ability to forge diverse yet principled ideological and geopolitical alliances across the three continents.

The issue of armed struggle, though often highlighted by observers, was not a major point of contention within the conference. Most delegations already accepted its necessity where colonialism and imperialism were maintained by force. While the Soviet Union preferred a discourse of peaceful coexistence, many of the countries present, like Algeria, Cuba, and the Democratic Republic of Vietnam, had themselves emerged from violent struggles. Moreover, the conference included numerous delegations representing active or new armed liberation movements from across the globe. The disagreements often highlighted about armed struggle weren't because participants doubted its legitimacy; instead, some organizations and governments hesitated to rule out other political approaches, especially electoral participation in countries where conditions allowed for them. Support for this agenda came from the Soviet Union and China, both providing considerable material aid to a diversity of parties and movements throughout the Third World.

Enduring Legacy and a Call to Action

The decades following the conference witnessed both triumphs and setbacks, including the fall of the Portuguese empire in Africa, the collapse of Latin American dictatorships, and Vietnam's reunification. Though the socialist bloc's collapse in 1991 momentarily cemented US hegemony, the Tricontinental Conference's legacy has endured. Today, as new generations confront hyperimperialism, neocolonialism, fascism, and resurgent authoritarianism, the conference's legacy resonates—a reminder that liberation is neither singular nor static, but a collective, unyielding march.

The Tricontinental Conference's significance transcended immediate concerns like the Sino-Soviet split or debates on armed struggle. Its true legacy lay in its remarkable ability to fuse diverse socialist and national liberation currents into a cohesive and powerful force for the era's movements. It served as a vital platform for articulating a shared anti-imperialist agenda, fostering unprecedented bonds of solidarity, and establishing the foundation for coordinated action. The conference's resolutions, spanning economic, political, and cultural commissions, comprehensively addressed issues from economic exploitation to cultural penetration by US imperialism, providing a complete framework for liberation.

The creation of OSPAAAL and its Havana-based executive secretariat solidified the institutional structure for ongoing collaboration. OSPAAAL functioned as a hub for communication, an information clearinghouse, a space for analytical exchange, and a facilitator of bilateral relations, notably diverging from Comintern traditions by foregoing bylaws or regular summits. OSPAAAL became synonymous with the cultural production of the Third World. For over four decades, it shaped and disseminated a shared worldview of the Third World project to every corner of the globe through various avenues, including the *Tricontinental Bulletin*, radio programs via Radio Havana Cuba, iconic posters, and the theoretical journal Tricontinental. The establishment of committees dedicated to supporting liberation movements in Vietnam, Zimbabwe, Puerto Rico, and other hot spots further underscored the conference's commitment to tangible solidarity.

The conference also agreed to celebrate annually, from January 3 to 10, the International Week of Solidarity of the Peoples of Africa, Asia, and Latin America. Cuba's role as host and OSPAAAL's headquarters underscored Cuba's militant internationalism, exemplified by the contributions of close to four hundred thousand Cubans who served as soldiers, doctors, and teachers throughout Africa in support of national liberation movements. A crowning moment was the victory by the combined forces of Cuban, Angolan, SWAPO (Namibia), and MK (South Africa) troops at the Battle of Cuito Cuanavale in Angola against US-backed apartheid forces—a decisive blow to South Africa's white-minority regime.

Beyond its primary focus on the Third World, the Tricontinental Conference also had significant reverberations in the United States. While provoking strong condemnation from the US government, it simultaneously served as a source of inspiration for the radicalization of the civil rights revolution and the antiwar mass movement. These US movements drew vital connections, interweaving the fight against racial discrimination and the military-industrial complex with broader anti-imperialist principles. From its inception, the conference, despite its strong critique of the United States, purposefully included the cause of Black people in the US within its core platform. Preparatory materials clearly stated "support to the negro people of the United States in their struggle for the right to equality and freedom and against all forms of discrimination and racism" as a key agenda item. Although Robert F. Williams, an exiled militant activist in Havana, and performer Josephine Baker were the only African Americans officially listed as attendees, Williams notably helped draft the conference resolution on "The Rights of Afro-Americans in the United States." This resolution explicitly stated that while Afro-Americans were not geographically part of Latin America, Africa, or Asia, their specific oppression and ongoing struggle "merits special consideration and demands that the Tricontinental Organization create the necessary mechanisms so that these brothers in the struggle will in the future, be able to participate in the great battle being fought by the peoples of the three continents." This declaration not only conveyed the Third World's support for the Black Freedom Struggle but also explicitly integrated them into the Tricontinental. Ultimately, the conference advanced an anti-imperialist framework that inextricably linked anticapitalism with the fight against white supremacy.

The Tricontinental Conference's unprecedented character fostered a pervasive sense among attendees that the world was undergoing profound transformation, perceiving themselves at a pivotal historical moment necessitating fresh ideas and initiatives. Ongoing conflicts collectively fueled an image of a Third World ablaze, depicting an international revolution where the industrial proletariat of the West was overshadowed by armed peasants traversing the rural landscapes of the Global South. This represented a militant expansion beyond traditional communist and socialist parties, now encompassing national liberation movements and popular organizations not all rooted in the Leninist tradition. Cuban leaders envisioned the Tricontinental as a convergence point for representatives of left-wing and communist parties, national liberation movements, and socialist and socialist-leaning governments from across the Third World. A US Senate report described this gathering as "the most powerful gathering of pro-Communist, anti-American forces in the history of the Western hemisphere."

Today, as we mark this significant anniversary, the world finds itself navigating uncertain waters, facing the slow and dangerous decay of US hegemony, the violent resurgence of fascism, and the insidious advance of far-right politics across the globe. In such times, revisiting the spirit and documents of the Tricontinental Conference offers not just historical reflection, but a vital roadmap for contemporary liberation movements who must find the strength and clarity to combat our common enemy today.

This book, a compilation of original documents and speeches from the Tricontinental Conference, endeavors to bring to life the energy and profound ideas that permeated this historic gathering. Many of these documents and images, sourced directly from the conference itself, are seeing the light again after years in archives. The book's structure reflects the conference's comprehensive approach, with sections dedicated to political reports, messages, plenary speeches, and resolutions from various commissions. These documents offer invaluable insights into the strategic thinking, challenges, and aspirations of revolutionaries during this transformative period.

Young revolutionaries today should approach these historical documents not as mere academic discussion, but as a living, dialectical process that resists superficial slogans and rote repetition. Grasping the historical forces and material realities that shaped these movements, the intricate task of building solidarity and internationalism across diverse political and ideological cultures, and the steadfast dedication to confronting oppressive systems offers an indispensable blueprint for navigating current struggles. These records serve as a potent reminder that collective action, the pursuit of ideological common ground, and an unyielding commitment to the people as the subject of struggle are non-negotiable in the continuous battle for liberation against imperialism's enduring and evolving forms, particularly those championed by the United States.

Unfortunately, the postmodernist intellectualism of our current era often diminishes this period to one of naive idealism, unfulfilled aspirations, and failed guerrilla projects, all presumed to have been eclipsed by the pragmatism of a nonideological lens. Some would suggest that the materialist study of our past offers no insights into contemporary problems or how to address them. To achieve a more accurate understanding of the Third World project in relation to the socialist future our planet requires in order to survive, young revolutionaries must delve deeper into the specific contexts and reexamine the core strategic concepts of the Tricontinental's internationalism, appreciate its vision of unity, and evaluate them within their historical development.

This project is not an academic exercise but rather a direct result of my work with Tricontinental: Institute for Social Research and the International Peoples' Assembly, an initiative that brings together over two hundred revolutionary and left parties, trade unions, and people's movements of the planet, and stands as a worthy inheritor of the Tricontinental Conference's legacy. For several years, amidst the breaks of long meetings, challenged with the tasks of building internationalism in our times, and in transit through cities that resonate with the spirit of solidarity—Havana, Tunis, Accra, Caracas, Johannesburg, Shanghai, Niamey, and São Paulo—I have meticulously researched and edited these documents. This work has been a labor of love, fueled by the conviction that understanding these historical moments is crucial for navigating the challenges of today and building an internationalist movement of the oppressed and exploited rooted in the traditions of Leninism and national liberation Marxism.

I extend my deepest gratitude to all who have contributed to this endeavor. To Vijay Prashad and Tricontinental: Institute for Social Research, whose friendship, guidance, and unwavering commitment to the working-class project have been a constant source of inspiration. A special thanks to Yoerky Sánchez

Cuéllar, director of *Granma*, the official organ of the Communist Party of Cuba; Dilbert Reyes Rodríguez, former interim director of *Granma*; María Lourdes Batlle Ferreiro and Delfín Xiqués Cutiño, the dedicated archival specialists at *Granma*; Alberto Nuñez, director of *Bohemia* magazine; René González Barrios, director, Elier Ramirez Cañedo, vice director, and Evelia Zayas Chapman of the Centro Fidel Castro Ruz in Havana; all whose invaluable assistance provided access to these historical documents. Profound thanks to Abel Prieto Jiménez and Jaime Gómez Triana of Casa de las Américas and Ricardo Ronquillo and Rosa Miriam Elizalde of the Union of Cuban Journalists for their support and dedication to preserving the revolutionary heritage of Cuba. Finally, I extend my warmest thanks to my comrades whom I have had the honor of accompanying in this journey throughout the years: the staff of The People's Forum and the secretariat of the International Peoples' Assembly. This book is a testament to the enduring power of solidarity, the ongoing struggles of the Third World, and our unending belief in a socialist future.

TRICONTINENTAL, HAVANA 1966

Press Statement by
Mehdi Ben Barka (Morocco)

National Union of Popular Forces and President of
the International Preparatory Committee

This conference, which will unite the anti-imperialist organizations of Africa, Asia, and Latin America, is a historic event; it is historic because of its composition, because the two great contemporary currents of the World Revolution will be represented in this conference: the current which started with the October Revolution in the Soviet Union and which is the current of socialist revolution, and the parallel current of the revolution for national liberation.

The massive meeting of these two currents will take place in this conference on a three-continent scale.

This conference is also historic because it takes place in Cuba; because the Cuban Revolution is in effect the concretization of the union of these two historic currents of the World Revolution; because Cuba has known her revolution for national liberation and is now accomplishing her socialist revolution: Therefore, it was the country most indicated for the celebration of this meeting.

We believe that in the anti-imperialist struggle, over the last ten years, there are two peoples who have radically and unequivocally carried the banner. They are Vietnam and Cuba. This is both a way of paying tribute to Cuba and acknowledging the responsibility it assumes by being chosen as the first center of this meeting, which culminates the struggle of the three continents against imperialism. It will be a historic meeting.

We believe that in the anti-imperialist struggle, we must currently reevaluate our secondary differences and find appropriate formulas for our struggle, leaving no room for confusion or defeatism. Vietnam is an example that our solidarity must be expressed in two concerted ways: one positive, by committing to the struggle on our respective fronts against imperialism, in order to weaken it and prevent it from concentrating on Vietnam; and the other, by not taking any action claiming to resolve the Vietnam problem unilaterally and independently of those leading that struggle.

The role of our organization in coordinating the solidarity of our peoples consists precisely in defining the common strategy of our struggle against the imperialists and the modality of our common action.

(Fragments of the press conference held in Havana, Cuba, by Mehdi Ben Barka before traveling to Paris, France, where he was kidnapped and disappeared by imperialism to prevent the holding of the First Solidarity Conference of the Peoples of Asia, Africa, and Latin America.)

Antecedents and Objectives of the Movement of Solidarity of the Peoples of Africa, Asia, and Latin America

Political Report of the International Preparatory Committee

The twilight of the nineteenth century was characterized in Europe and in the United States by the development of the commercial and industrial bourgeoisie, as well as by the progress of technology, science, and culture for the benefit of the privileged minorities who retained and enjoyed the fruits of power. It culminated with the appearance of monopoly capital and the increase of financial capitalism. The imperative necessity of expanding existing markets, and the search for other markets to export capital accumulated at the expense of the toils of the peoples, determined—while the world was being distributed among the great powers— the strengthening and extending of the system of colonial rule, which had been set up in Asia, Africa, and Latin America—recently freed from the Spanish yoke—as well as the beginning of a colonial policy of monopolist domination which generated new forms of political and economic subordination. The colonial powers, formed after the great geographical discoveries of the fifteenth and sixteenth centuries—the first international adventure of the growing capitalist regime—and the subsequent advent of imperialism established a policy of aggression, exploitation, and plunder of the three continents.

As soon as the partition of Asia and Africa was completed by the European powers, the end of the last century and the beginning of this was characterized by the setting up of zones of influence in which colonial administrations took definite shape, that of repressive and governmental bodies, conceived and organized to put into force a permanent system of exploitation at the service of the metropolis. The ample natural resources and manpower of these continents made them both the mainstay of the European colonial powers and the pillars of the system of world imperialism.

The outstanding feature of the process of colonial exploitation in Latin America has been its evolution into new forms of neocolonial dependence, a phenomenon which originated earlier in that area than in Asia and Africa. There it appeared in its most acute and extended form only a few years ago, when many countries gained political independence.

The struggle for independence of most European colonies, and especially those of Spain in Latin America, culminated during the first three decades of the nineteenth century. Needless to say, the political principles, the economic ideas, social criteria, and the juridical standards which inspired this struggle came from the French Revolution and the North American Revolution, both traditional personifications of the beginning of universal domination of the bourgeoisie as a class, and the gradual geographic expansion of its political and economic hegemony in the underdeveloped regions of the world.

Because of the political, economic, and social backwardness to which they were submitted by colonial exploitation, the countries newly freed from Spain soon became a favorable field for economic penetration and monopolistic domination by European powers, especially by the United Kingdom. But after the Spanish-Cuban-North American war—which was the first imperialist war recorded in history and a sober preface to the plunder, robbery, and crime to be written from then on by Yankee imperialism—European influence in Latin America was progressively substituted by the new colonial system of the United States, aided and abetted in each country by the native oligarchy, which had seized power when the armed forces of Spain surrendered.

The political independence of Latin American countries was limited in reality to a nominal change of sovereignty which actually meant the strengthening of the semifeudal, social, and economic structure instituted by the colonial domination of Spain, with its corresponding class relations, hierarchy, and privileges.

The poverty-stricken, exploited, and affronted masses, from which were recruited the heroic and unselfish armies of Bolívar, San Martín, Sucre, O'Higgins, Paez, and Artigas, stayed harshly subjected by the regime of exploitation, oppression, discrimination, ignorance, and poverty which burdened them for four centuries and was made even worse by disguised impositions of the new colonial system and deceiving intoxicants of "representative democracy." The governments of these countries, servile administrators of the native oligarchy, and mere puppets of imperialism, represented for a great number of years before the world the dramatic farce of a constellation of politically independent nations, although progressively becoming new economic possessions of the United States.

It is important to note that in Latin America the process of substitution of direct forms of colonial exploitation took place at a time when the degree of development of social consciousness of the oppressed masses did not yet permit them to fight for definite objectives, define the class enemy, and separate the fiction of national independence from the reality of neocolonial servitude.

On the contrary, when at the end of the Second World War—in the midst of the emergence of progressive ideas resulting from the defeat of fascism and of international reactionary forces—the process of independence of most of the European colonies in Asia and Africa began, we are then in a totally different era, in which the death rattle of the old world in agony is intermixed with the birth cry of a new world. The principles, concepts, criteria, and standards sustaining the colonial system of imperialism are now confronted by principles, concepts, criteria, and standards which challenge it, both in theory and in practice. Their development and diffusion have extended so deeply and widely that they permeate and galvanize large sections of the exploited classes in the oppressed countries. The peoples of Africa and Asia are undoubtedly more mature and politically aware than the countries of Latin America were in a similar situation, possessing as they do a wealth of experience, accumulated in their struggles for national independence.

The following significant events have decisively contributed to widen, deepen, and invigorate the struggle of the peoples for their national liberation and for the progress of revolutionary ideas: The October Revolution, an event that changed the historic course of humanity and pointed the way to freedom and full justice to the peoples of the world; the Chinese Revolution; the upsurge of the world socialist system; the increasing struggles for independence from colonialism; the emancipation of many nations of Africa and Asia; and the Cuban Revolution, which gave birth to the first socialist state in America.

These events have tipped the balance in favor of progressive, democratic, socialist, and peace and freedom-loving forces, giving impetus to the liberation movements of the peoples and opening the way to national sovereignty for many countries of Africa and Asia. The colonial system of imperialism has disintegrated into pieces.

Under these new conditions and circumstances, the peoples of Asia and Africa are directing their efforts, with an ever clearer and firmer conscience, to obtain complete national freedom and to establish themselves as independent nations, both from the political and economic point of view. At the same time, the peoples of both continents already independent, or in process of emancipation, are becoming aware of the policy of imperialist expansion that the United States has begun to impose upon them after the Second World War, when it began to displace the old European colonial powers with such open insolence that it was soon unmasked before international public opinion as the pretended heir of its now less powerful allies, as well as the main support of the colonial system of imperialism, both in its old and its new manifestations. It blandished the monopoly of the atomic bomb for several years as a symbol and expression of universal predominance and as an arm of blackmail and aggression.

In line with this policy of expansion and hegemony, directed on one hand toward a more effective rule over and exploitation of the peoples and, on the other hand, toward the establishment of a menacing siege against the socialist nations, the government of the United States began to create a series of alliances and aggressive military pacts throughout the world.

Especially in the Far East, the North American imperialists, who dropped atomic bombs on Hiroshima and Nagasaki, have concluded aggressive military pacts with their new allies and puppets in Japan, South Korea, the Chinese territory of Formosa, the Philippines, and Thailand, occupying the Japanese territories of Okinawa and Ogasawara and establishing hundreds of military bases in these areas.

In 1950, in accordance with their policy of war and aggression, the United States imperialists began the invasion of Korea, developed an aggressive move to "contain China," and recently launched aggression in Vietnam and Laos. They are trying to extend the war all over Asia.

The United States imperialists, who continue to occupy the southern half of Korea, have turned it into a nuclear rocket base and are constantly carrying out war provocations along the military demarcation line in violation of the Armistice Agreement. Particularly in recent times, the United States imperialists are concocting a collusion between the Japanese reactionary government and the puppet clique in South Korea and enforcing the "conclusion" of a criminal "Japan–South Korea Treaty" thus blatantly opening a road toward the reinvasion and the overseas expansion into South Korea of Japanese militarism, which is being rapidly revived. Thus, with the revival of Japanese militarism as a lever, they are creating the aggressive North-East Asia Military Alliance and openly pushing forward its policy of aggression against Asian countries.

Now, taking advantage of the possibilities offered to them by oppression in Asia, the Japanese reactionary forces are rapidly infiltrating South Korea, and stepping up maneuvers of attacking the Democratic People's Republic of Korea, the People's Republic of China, and other Asian countries.

This does not only perpetuate the division of Korea and aggravate tension but also creates a serious situation threatening peace and security in Asia and the world.

The United States imperialists also deploy the Seventh Fleet, equipped with nuclear weapons, along the coast of Asia, trying to bring these weapons into Japan and other areas, thus resorting to nuclear blackmail and posing a danger of nuclear war.

This policy of expansion and hegemony of Yankee imperialism is directed chiefly against the peoples of Vietnam, Laos, Cambodia, and Korea. Accordingly, it has concluded with the puppet governments organized in the southern part of Vietnam and Korea, arbitrarily divided, separate, aggressive military agreements. Likewise, it has signed with the puppets of Taiwan—set up and backed by the North American Seventh Fleet—a similar military pact.

Faced with such a complicated and dangerous situation, the new states of Asia and Africa realize that it is a politically imperative necessity to unite their forces and bring about their solidarity for the joint defense of their independence and of the cultural and economic development of their peoples, threatened by distorting foreign influences. Thus, the historic conference of Bandung—in which the heads of state or government of twenty-nine nations of those two continents participated—was held in April 1955.

The Bandung Conference represented a vital landmark in the growing awareness of the peoples of Africa and Asia. It was the culmination of a movement of solidarity which had arisen in and had developed from the days of their fight for national freedom and independence, proclaiming the well-known principles of Bandung, of relevant importance for the anticolonialist movement. The Congress of the Peoples of Asia, assembled in New Delhi in March 1955, was an outstanding precedent to this conference.

During this same period the government of the United States maneuvered to prevent any possibility of union among the balkanized peoples of Latin America. It operated by resorting openly to force or by taking advantage of the servile and corrupt policy of the ruling oligarchies, which at the turn of the century had accepted the setting up of the Pan-American Union following the directives and under the control of the new rising empire. In 1948, this served as the base to create the Organization of American States, the sadly famous Yankee Ministry of the Colonies.

The previous year, in 1947, the United States, in accordance with its policy of expansion and hegemony, concluded with the governments of Latin America in Rio de Janeiro the infamous Treaty of Reciprocal Assistance for the defense of the hemisphere against imaginary aggressions from outside the continent. The real and only object of this treaty—so events have demonstrated—was to serve as a docile mechanism to enforce the United States foreign policy on this continent.

The contrast could not be more obvious. While on the one hand, in Bandung, the peoples of Africa and Asia were leading an anti-imperialist and anticolonialist struggle for closer unity and solidarity, on the other hand the majority of the governments of Latin America were betraying the aspirations and interests of their people and were tying themselves to imperialism in its common policy of exploitation and domination. At the same time, while the struggle against imperialism, colonialism, and neocolonialism fused into a single front in Asia and Africa, North American neocolonialism in Latin America strengthened and refined its system of political subjugation and economic profit with the connivance of the local oligarchies, thus creating complex and difficult situations for the struggle of the peoples for national liberation.

During their heroic struggle against Yankee imperialism, the peoples of Latin America had to suffer not only the draining of natural resources and the merciless exploitation of their labor force, but also direct military intervention of Yankee imperialism in their internal affairs. In 1898, coinciding with its appearance on the world scene, it intervened in the Cuban war against the Spanish colonial rule. It artfully stole away the independence of Cuba and occupied its territory, grabbed Puerto Rico and other islands in the Caribbean area, as well as the Philippines, and finally arrogated, by the imposition of a treaty, the right to intervene in the affairs of Cuba and to occupy a part of its territory in Guantanamo, where Yankee imperialism established a naval base against the will of the Cuban people.

In 1903, interfering with and acting against the political aspirations of the people of the isthmus of Panama, it imposed by force the adoption of a treaty guaranteeing the control, for its benefit, of international maritime transit between the Atlantic and Pacific Oceans, and at the same time giving it the right to establish a strategic military base to serve as a spearhead for its policy of expansion and domination in Latin America and in the world.

On various occasions and under different pretexts, Yankee imperialism has violated the sovereignty and territorial integrity of a large number of the countries of Latin America in order to maintain its economic privileges, to impose its policy of domination and to intimidate the people. Mexico, Guatemala, Cuba, Colombia, Nicaragua, Haiti, and the Dominican Republic—now the victim of an intervention more brutal and cynical than any previous one—have been the object of this hateful and rapacious policy.

In one way or another, and in the measure possible, the struggle of the peoples of Latin America for their national liberation followed its course with the same tenacity the peoples of Asia and Africa had shown while trying to weld their solidarity previous to, and above all, after the Bandung Conference.

The struggle of the people of Puerto Rico for independence clearly shows the character of Yankee imperialism. In a premeditated and persistent way, ever since North American imperialism, taking advantage of the collapse of the colonial rule of Spain, grabbed this isle of the Antilles, it has been exploiting the wealth and toil of the Puerto Rican people, and has been drowning in blood their outbreaks of rebellion. Yankee imperialism has been trying to destroy the cultural wealth of Puerto Rico and to adulterate its history by imposing on it an education contrary to its national tradition. To crush the people of Puerto Rico, Yankee imperialism maintains in the country an enormous military force and some of its bases there are equipped with atomic weapons. Puerto Rico constitutes an outdated remnant of the oldest and most predatory form of colonialism in our hemisphere.

The African liberation movement, developing simultaneously with the revolutionary movements of the post–Second World War era, dates more precisely with the Manchester Conference of 1945. This conference, organized and conducted by contemporary African leaders, formulated the strategy for political action of the struggle of the liberation movement of Africa. Characteristically, the tempo of the movement was to be determined by historical factors. The political divisions of the continent under the oppressive rule of the colonial powers had the effects of limiting the unity of purpose and action throughout the continent.

The revolutionary creed of the Manchester Conference—Positive Action—successfully implemented in the Gold Coast (now Ghana) completely swept aside British colonialism in this area in 1957. In East Africa, what was characterized as the Mau Mau Uprising was certainly the manifestation of the revolutionary upsurge initiated by the Manchester Conference of 1945. In view of the entrenched interests of the imperial masters in this part of Africa, the struggle here took on an intense confrontation no different from an armed struggle. On the other hand, the liberation movement in the former French colonial area, under the banner of the RDA (Rassemblement Démocratique Africain), became crucial in the liquidation of French colonialism.

Further accelerating the decolonization throughout the continent, the First All-African Peoples' Conference held in Accra, Ghana, in 1958 galvanized into one front the organizational efforts of the fighters for freedom directed to unleash a massive assault on the colonial regimes of Britain, France, Belgium, and Portugal. The achievements of the liberation movement since 1958 are brilliant landmarks of the struggle in Africa; Belgian colonialism in the Congo crumbled down as did the white-dominated Federation of Central Africa made up by the two Rhodesias and Nyasaland.

Like the All-African Peoples' Conference, the first meeting of the heads of state and government held later in Accra was simply to strengthen at a summit level the peoples' determination to wipe out imperialism by various means. But colonialism and imperialism die hard; the massive decolonization of the 1960s in Africa was a deceptive phenomenon. Neocolonialism only superseded traditional colonialism. And what are the characteristics of this new colonialism? The colonial power retaining military and economic interests continues to dominate the economic and political life of the ex-colony long after formal political independence. It must be understood, nevertheless, that this change in form from colonialism to neocolonialism does not imply a complete change in political tactics. Just as colonialism and imperialism for too long successfully employed policies of "divide and rule," so also does neocolonialism.

The astounding successes of the liberation movement in Africa are yet to be crowned with victory over neocolonialism. If the Organization of African Unity can survive the machinations of the neocolonial powers, Africa's ultimate victory will be won. But throughout its history the organization has become a victim of the diabolical policies of "divide and rule" engineered by the neocolonial powers. This implies an ever-growing need of intensifying the struggle until final victory is reached.

An analysis of the struggle in the African continent since the Second World War shows that it has been written by a heroic resistance of the peoples against foreign oppressors and exploiters. The African peoples at last have risen in arms against imperialism, colonialism, and neocolonialism. These struggles represent noble chapters in their history. These are some of the chapters:

1. The Egyptian revolution of 1952.
2. Positive action and the birth of the Republic of Ghana.
3. Guinea's open defiance of French colonialism.
4. The epic seven-year patriotic war of the Algerian people.
5. The heroic resistance of the Kenyan people.
6. The undaunted courage of the African peoples under the heels of apartheid and white domination.
7. The gallant struggle of the Africans in the so-called Portuguese colonies against Portuguese colonialism.

Out of these struggles new African states are being born. The emergence of sovereign African states, however, has coincided with the transformation of colonialism into neocolonialism. Hence the inevitable march of history has involved the African peoples in a mortal struggle with neocolonialism. The logical climax of this struggle gave birth to the Organization of African Unity. The First Conference of Independent African States in 1958 elaborated and proclaimed the goals and strategy of African unity. The strategy of African unity is that of total liberation and complete independence for Africa at a time when the crisis of imperialism is more acute. This is the theory and practice of African emancipation.

In present times when Africa's basic problem is to free itself from centuries of colonial subjugation, the concept of African unity is essentially directed against imperialism, colonialism, and neocolonialism. Africa's vital interests still are the end of colonialism, imperialism, and neocolonialism, the construction of a new economic, social, and political order and the safeguarding of world peace.

Inspired and guided by the principles formulated in Bandung, the unity movement of the Afro-Asian Peoples, having an outstanding precedent in the Congress of Asian Peoples held in New Delhi the previous year, is being consolidated, drawn together, and broadened.

A very important event in the history of the liberation movement took place in 1956. According to its program for political and economic liberation, the Egyptian Revolution nationalized the Suez Canal, an action that led to the tripartite aggression of Great Britain, France, and Israel, which was defeated by the struggle of the Egyptian people with the militant solidarity of the peoples of the world.

The victory of the Egyptian Revolution over the colonialist and imperialist powers was a great step forward in the struggle for liberation, as is clearly demonstrated by the fact that imperialism could not prevent it. The First Conference of Solidarity of the Afro-Asian Peoples held in Cairo, United Arab Republic, from December 1957 to January 1958, was the decisive point in the tasks of consolidating and organizing the solidarity of the Afro-Asian peoples.

The Organization for the Solidarity of the Afro-Asian Peoples was created in this first conference, and the permanent secretariat, which has been successfully working for the last eight years, was elected.

During the second conference held in Conakry, Guinea, the Afro-Asian Peoples' Solidarity Organization was more strongly consolidated, broadening its activities through the recently organized Afro-Asian Solidarity Fund.

The organization gained new strength and has solved many important problems in subsequent meetings; the Third Conference in Moshi, Tanzania, in 1963, and in Winneba, Ghana, in 1965.

These efforts, together with the creation of new independent states, mainly African, have strengthened the struggle and made it more effective.

The expression of this solidarity has been shown in a large number of agreements, resolutions, and practical measures adopted in the course of this vast movement, as well as in countless international conferences of various types.

The resolutions and recommendations, adopted by the economic seminar held in Algiers at the beginning of 1965, contributed to strengthen the fighting unity in this field and to define clearly the consequences of imperialist exploitation.

The Afro-Asian Peoples' Solidarity Organization held important conferences in various fields of Afro-Asian solidarity, as for example: the First Conference of Afro-Asian Youth in Cairo, UAR, in 1959; the First Conference of Afro-Asian Women in Cairo, UAR, in 1961; the First Conference of Afro-Asian Writers in Tashkent, USSR, in 1958; the Second Conference of Afro-Asian Writers in Cairo, UAR, in 1962, etc. It is especially necessary to emphasize the increasing unity among African countries, which in 1963 were already able to create the Organization of African Unity (OAU).

Similar objectives have also been reached in the regular meetings held by the heads of Arab states at a summit level during this period.

On the other hand, the conferences of heads of state and government of the non-aligned countries, especially at the second conference held in Cairo in 1964, in which the majority of the liberated countries of Asia and Africa, as well as Cuba and observers from Latin America participated, were very effective steps in the struggle for self-determination, independence, and sovereignty of the peoples, and for the unity of anti-imperialist forces, as well as in denouncing and rejecting aggressions and intervention by imperialist powers.

As a counterpart to this movement of solidarity, imperialism, colonialism, and neocolonialism have created their African OAS [Organization of American States] in the Malagasy Common African Organization (MCAO).

In the sphere of cultural and educational exchange, the outstanding event in the movement of solidarity was the holding of the athletic competition of the new emerging forces in Indonesia, in 1963, and the creation of the GANEFO [Games of the New Emerging Forces] organization.

In Latin America, the victory of the Cuban Revolution in 1959 was a turning point in the development of the anti-imperialist struggle, which showed itself in the strengthening of existing revolutionary movements, and in the widening and deepening of the fighting conscience of the masses. It can be affirmed that following this significant event, the strategy of Yankee imperialism in that part of the world was conditioned by the increasing strength of the Cuban Revolution, which shook the bases of the Yankee imperialist system in America and destroyed the myth of geographic fatalism. It revealed the new correlation of forces in the world and demonstrated the possibility of revolutionary struggle and victory of the peoples in this continent and further furnished a firm base for the struggles of the peoples of Africa, Asia, and Latin America for their self-determination, independence, and sovereignty.

These antecedents and circumstances, as a whole, made the broad and powerful Afro-Asian solidarity movement reach out toward Latin America, and examine similar experiences of the struggles and hardships of the three continents—all subjected to the same policy of exploitation, aggression, and intervention of the imperialist and colonialist powers—together with the peculiarities originating from various historical, economic, social, and cultural conditions.

The Second Declaration of Havana, approved in a General Assembly of the people of Cuba as of February 4, 1962, had already expressed the following: "What is the history of Cuba if not the history of Latin America? And what is the history of Latin America if not the history of Asia, Africa, and Oceania?" And "What is the history of these peoples but the history of the most merciless and cruel exploitation by imperialism in the entire world?"

The need for organizing the solidarity of the peoples of the three continents was first raised during the Fourth Session of the Council of Solidarity of the Afro-Asian Peoples, held in Bandung, in April 1961, the same month and year as the imperialist aggression at Playa Girón, crushed by the Cuban people in less than seventy-two hours. This resounding victory undoubtedly inspired the solidarity of the peoples of Asia, Africa, and Latin America with new stimulus, vigor, and drive.

At this meeting, attended for the first time in the history of the Afro-Asian solidarity movement, by an observer from Latin America in the person of a representative of the Cuban Revolution, the study of the possibilities for holding a conference of solidarity of the three continents was recommended. On the basis of this recommendation, the executive committee of the Afro-Asian Peoples' Solidarity Organizations in its meeting in Gaza, Palestine, in December of that same year, passed a resolution tending to prepare the convening of a conference of the peoples of Africa, Asia, and Latin America. In 1962, a Cuban delegation attended, as observers, the Second Conference of Afro-Asian Jurists that took place in Conakry, from the 15th to the 20th of October.

The First Latin American Conference for National Sovereignty, Economic Emancipation, and Peace, held in Mexico in 1961, unquestionably contributed to foster conditions for a Tricontinental Conference by declaring itself in favor of it.

During the Third Conference of Solidarity of the Afro-Asian Peoples celebrated at Moshi in 1963, decisive and concrete steps were taken. In this conference, also attended by a Cuban delegate as observer, an invitation from the prime minister of the Cuban revolutionary government, Major Fidel Castro, was extended. It offered Havana as the seat for the First Conference of Solidarity of the Peoples of Asia, Africa, and Latin America.

The Moshi Conference received the invitation with enthusiasm, set up the preparatory committee of the conference, and adopted a special resolution to this effect.

The preparatory committee should be formed by eighteen members or organizations from the following countries: Algeria, Guinea, Morocco, United Arab Republic, United Republic of Tanzania, South Africa, People's Republic of China, India, Indonesia, Japan, Union of Soviet Socialist Republics, and Vietnam. After the Fourth Conference of Solidarity of the Afro-Asian Peoples, at Winneba, Ghana, this later country was elected to replace Morocco, to which was given the chairmanship of the preparatory committee in the vigorous revolutionary personality of Mehdi Ben Barka. The Moshi Conference was a demonstration of the full support for the celebration of a Tricontinental Conference by all the movements and organizations that struggle against imperialism, colonialism, and neocolonialism, for complete national independence and for the peace and progress of the peoples of Africa, Asia, and Latin America.

The sixth meeting of the Council of Afro-Asian Solidarity in Algiers decided to convene the twelve African and Asian members in order to set up the conditions for the formation of the preparatory committee. Measures to carry this out were adopted at the meeting held in Cairo in April 1964, where the following Latin American countries were accepted as members of the preparatory committee: Mexico, Venezuela, Guatemala, Chile, Uruguay, and Cuba.

In the Fourth Conference of Solidarity held in Winneba, the historic decision was adopted to convene a meeting of the preparatory committee in Cairo, and to hold the First Conference of Solidarity of the Peoples of Asia, Africa, and Latin America in Havana, in the first days of January 1966, a date coinciding with the seventh anniversary of the Cuban Revolution. In the Cairo meeting, it was decided that the final list of participants would be determined through consultations with the chairman and the secretary general of the preparatory committee, with the African and Asian representatives of the Afro-Asian Peoples' Solidarity Organizations, and with the six representatives of Latin America.

The Cuban Revolution and the most representative organizations of the anti-imperialist struggle in Latin America have shown their solidarity with the Asian and African peoples in an active and consistent manner on different occasions, and especially on the most critical ones as, for instance, the Yankee imperialist intervention in South Vietnam and the subsequent aggression against the Democratic Republic of Vietnam; the Belgian–North American–British intervention in the Congo (Léopoldville); and previously, during the Algerian

War of liberation; with the people of Cyprus in their fight for self-determination and full sovereignty; as well as in the case of other African countries, numerous demonstrations of solidarity and assistance took place in Latin America. This solidarity was kept alive and vibrant throughout the development of the anti-imperialist struggles of the Afro-Asian peoples, especially during such times as the imperialist aggression in Korea in 1950, the war of French colonialism against the people of Vietnam, the Anglo-French-Israeli intervention in Egypt, the criminal policy of racial discrimination pursued in South Africa and other African states by the imperialists and in support of all the campaigns waged in both continents against imperialism, colonialism, and neocolonialism.

At the same time, the movement of solidarity of the Afro-Asian peoples with those of Latin America has expressed itself consistently, above all in the case of Cuba, which had its support in the struggle against Yankee imperialism. Similarly, the people of the Dominican Republic were backed when suffering the armed intervention of imperialism. The movement of Afro-Asian solidarity has also declared itself for the abolition of colonialism in Latin America, and in favor of the fight of the peoples of Puerto Rico, Guadeloupe, Martinique, and British Guiana for their national liberation. Likewise, it has expressed itself unequivocally for the elimination of North American military bases located in Latin America, for the end of all forms of racial discrimination in the United States and of the neocolonialist policy of oppressing Latin American countries, and also in support of their struggles against the policy of exploitation, aggression, and intervention of Yankee imperialism.

The movement of militant solidarity among the peoples of the three continents in a joint defense and unity for their struggles against imperialism, colonialism, and neocolonialism that was spontaneous at the outset, began, in consonance with the facts, to lay the bases for its organization and development into an undeniable living reality.

The celebration of this conference in Havana is an event of worldwide importance. For the first time, delegates of the anti-imperialist, anticolonialist militant organizations of the three continents meet. For the first time, the ideas tending to unify efforts toward the eradication of all forms of colonialism which imperialist and colonialist powers stubbornly insist on prolonging; to frustrate the aggressions of imperialism and of the reactionary forces of the three continents; to accelerate the liberation of the peoples; to assure their economic, social, and cultural development; to consolidate the movement of solidarity of Africa, Asia, and Latin America; and to maintain active and permanent the linking and coordination of all countries struggling to achieve or to maintain their independence, take a definite shape. All these joint efforts and the concrete measures to be adopted in order to materialize their solidarity in every sense, will help to strengthen and widen this fight even more, and will be a severe blow to the backbone of imperialism.

There is no more appropriate setting for the celebration of the Tricontinental Conference than the capital of Cuba, whose people, after having conquered by force of arms its full self-determination, independence, and sovereignty, resists unswervingly imperialist aggression in the form of brutal economic blockade; implacable political hostility; constant infiltration of spies, saboteurs, and subversive agents; mercenary invasion; provocations from the Yankee military base arbitrarily located on Cuban soil; piratical raids; and the real and permanent danger of a direct military attack.

This conference in itself constitutes, because of this circumstance, a powerful demonstration of support and solidarity from the Afro-Asian and Latin American peoples to Cuba and its revolution, and also to the peoples of the three continents that at this very moment are struggling for their freedom, and most of all, to those facing imperialism in Vietnam, Venezuela, the Dominican Republic, the Congo, Peru, Angola, Guatemala, Mozambique, the so-called Portuguese Guinea, Colombia, and so many other countries, fighting with weapons in hand and under the most dramatic conditions. Their sacrifice and heroism will enlighten its deliberations and resolutions, which will surely be implemented by effective and concrete measures of help and solidarity toward these fraternal peoples.

The First Conference of Solidarity of the Peoples of Africa, Asia, and Latin America is meeting at a time when the imperialists and the forces of reaction are unable to extinguish the flames of the movement of national liberation, or change the path taken by the countries that have achieved their independence. In view of all this, it is obvious that the imperialist system is in crisis and that its own internal contradictions are becoming more acute, lessening its capacity to maneuver. The powerful drive of world public opinion, which rejects the outdated pretensions of the colonialists and neocolonialists supplied and directed by the government of the United States, the military and ideological source of the forces now operating against the interests of the peoples, constitutes another dissolving factor for the warmongers and exploiters.

We all know the way imperialism operates. Its very reason for existence opposes national emancipation at every stage. Imperialism has never left a single ray of hope for the peoples of the world. The balance of its behavior is very evident: exploitation and discrimination; backwardness and poverty; cultural sterility and contempt for traditions and national dignity. This is its sole legacy. The unrestricted disposal of national wealth, the full development of the diverse ways of expression each country, the unblemished decorum and self-determination are fruits that the poisonous tree of imperialism does not bear. Nor could it be otherwise, because the very basis of imperialism, that is to say, the benefits obtained by the huge capitalist monopolies from both the manpower and the material resources of the peoples under their rule, would disappear if its principal aim were eliminated. This is its only goal. It has no other. Because of this, any concession that imperialism may seem to make, is not a rectification of conduct, but only a tactical withdrawal.

History, logic, and reason prove that in the long list of the deeds of imperialism there is not, and cannot be room for withdrawal. Military operations to conquer the peoples, or capitalist penetration to yoke them are two streams of the same torrent of mud and blood that for centuries has been flowing from colonialism. Brute force or the corrupting influence of money, threat and intimidation, economic blockade and diplomatic isolation, defamation and deceit are the weapons employed either separately or all together. In the long history of imperialist crimes, not a single step has been taken to favor the peoples. Nothing has been done that would imply a limitation of privileges; nothing has been said but to offend; nothing has been attempted but to sacrifice its victims and to increase the power of the metropolis.

The so-called tactic of "war of escalation" unleashed against the heroic people of Vietnam is the most recent manifestation of these aggressive actions.

The despoiled masses have resisted and rebelled against the wicked plunder to which they have been subjected. Never have they resigned themselves to poverty and humiliation, but instead, in their unceasing struggle for freedom, they have gained strength, increased their experience, and with a growing political knowledge have continued to pursue unity and solidarity in spite of distances in order to fight their oppressors. Every step forward toward freedom and independence has been won by popular rebellion. Not a single example can be cited in which the accomplishment was a consequence of the mercy or the repentance of the exploiters. These abandoned their positions only when existing conditions opened the way and the peoples, knowing how to take advantage of this, became makers of history. Faced with the thirst for justice of all the peoples, the voracity of the exploiters has turned into desperate actions, criminal interventions, bloody repressions, and in the long run, into defeat, and sooner or later the liberation movements, blandishing the indestructible arms of justice and assisted and encouraged by the moral force of conscientiousness, march unrestrainable forward to final victory.

Victory, however, is not the fruit of spontaneous generation. Breaking the barriers that prevented their development, the different societies of history slowly made their way through to progress, but the differences in available material resources, the accumulation of capital and the use of techniques applicable to production of goods for peace, or for war, the abysmal differences in the levels of knowledge imposed upon the poor masses by the wealthy classes, brought about the monstruous disproportion of today. It not only reflects the injustice of the imperialist system and of its colonial variants but also explains the backwardness of some peoples in relation to others in the liberation process. That is why it is a great responsibility of the Tricontinental Conference to determine correctly the forms, ways, and means to be followed in order to surmount these barriers which hinder the emancipation of the exploited classes, whether political, ideological, or cultural or in connection with every form of struggle, including armed struggle.

One objective lesson that should not be forgotten is the history of international relations. Sometimes taking on the title of "spheres of influence," at other times "balance of power," either "dollar diplomacy" or "the big stick"; sending aggressive expeditionary forces to other lands or in the case of alliances or doctrines, as the Monroe Doctrine, the truth is that the original purpose and the final result are the imperial domination of weaker countries, the distribution of the colonies, the exploitation of the riches and toil of other peoples. The revealing and denunciation of the thousand faces of imperialism and the unmasking of its tactics are important tasks in warning the people and orientating them correctly in the struggle to halt the aggressors.

Each people must decide its own destiny and must not be subject to a rule foreign to its vital interests, emancipation being an intimate part of the historic development of society. So long as the tutelage of one country over another still exists, the cycle which each nation must follow will be incomplete. It is also true that the internal organization of each society will reach its greatest development only when it has political and economic freedom as its base, and when this society enjoys autonomy of action in the world scene. These are historic axioms impressed upon the minds of the masses and there is no other way of applying them except by capturing the positions of imperialism. The imperialist system is today the main obstacle to progress.

Liberation is a right which the imperialists stubbornly fail to recognize. This inalienable right is born of the unjust nature of oppression. Eager to cover up their crimes, the imperialists and their oligarchic agents invent false legal arguments to justify the use of laws and agreements which they themselves took on, but which are no longer useful to their interests.

In the face of the growing struggle of the oppressed peoples to shake off the yoke of imperialist exploitation, the imperialists, especially the North Americans, use the incredibly cynical argument that this fight constitutes a foreign aggression, when it is their own bloody repressions that bring on a brutal armed intervention against the rights of peoples to independence and social progress.

This argument has been used by Yankee imperialism to try to justify its criminal intervention in Vietnam and the Dominican Republic. The House of Representatives of the United States, in a recent resolution, proclaimed the alleged right of the United States to intervene with its armed forces in any Latin American country in order to crush the revolutionary movement.

In opposition to this arbitrary norm of international conduct announced and carried out by imperialism, the conference must proclaim and carry out the right of each subjected country to solidarity; the right and the duty of all countries to assist, by all means within their power, those peoples who are fighting for their national liberation, in every corner of the world.

In our time we find appropriate conditions in Africa, Asia, and Latin America to purify the atmosphere of the poisonous fumes of colonialism, which keep millions of human beings economically asphyxiated and offended in their dignity. These conditions emerge from the actual modes of existence of Asians, Africans, and Latin Americans, from the history of their hardships and struggles and from the extraordinary impetus which the modern era has achieved in science, technology, and culture. The dramatic contrast between the conditions of the masses and the exploiting classes, together with the political clarification of their consciousness, are also powerful ingredients which today create exceptional circumstances for the ripening of the process of liberation.

In the light of these undeniable realities, one fact emerges strongly: Peoples must be followed in their march forward. If the fight for their liberation is a right of the peoples, this fight is also the inexcusable duty of all revolutionaries. Right paths must be opened along which the heroic people will move to the final attainment of its destiny. On whom does this glorious task fall? On whom does history impose such a great obligation? The revolutionary anti-imperialist vanguards of the three continents are the ones called upon to create the objective conditions wherever they are lacking, and to join the popular insurrection, wherever it has already begun. It is a task that cannot be evaded. Not only the prestige before the masses of the patriotic, revolutionary, and anti-imperialist parties and movements, but also their own reason for existing are committed to this implacable fight against the forces striving to hold back the advance of humanity.

The Tricontinental Conference, of course, faces a difficult and complex task. The meeting of the representatives of the revolutionary forces, of the national liberation movements and the mass organizations of Africa, Asia, and Latin America, is something of great significance and importance. The conference meets at a time that may be considered decisive, not only in the history of the peoples of Africa, Asia, and Latin America, but also in the history of all humanity, a moment of rapid advance of the national liberation movements against imperialism and both old and new colonialism, the fight for total national independence and world peace. These circumstances make the task easier, but do not free the way from obstacles.

During eight years of constant struggle of militant action and close cooperation, the representatives of Africa and Asia went from victory to victory, establishing brotherly bonds forged in the struggle for common interests and objectives which arose from a common inheritance and from similar historic conditions. The same factors make imperative the need for tighter fraternal cooperation among the three large continents. The struggle against imperialism, colonialism, and neocolonialism headed by North American imperialism and the achievement and consolidation of national independence of these three continents is the most urgent task of their peoples. Furthermore, national reconstruction and the establishment of the bases for new economic, social, and cultural structures in the emerging countries of Asia and Africa is now on the go, and these facts add new responsibilities.

The struggle to achieve an independent economy and emancipation from the economic yoke of the colonial powers, the struggle against the penetration of neocolonialism under different disguises in the newly independent countries is reaching new proportions. Nowadays this struggle on the economic front is apparently difficult and the future road of reconstruction depends on the victory of such a struggle.

The conference must prepare plans to give even more drive to the glorious battles which brighten the horizon of this promising situation. To carry out this task effectively, it is necessary to investigate and analyze exhaustively the multiple forms of the tortuous behavior of imperialism, to extract lessons from experience and to foresee its tactics in order to carry out a suitable activity which may shorten the struggle, striking in the most sensitive areas, keeping principles safe, and planning firm action which will not conclude until the extermination of the common enemy. The struggle for liberty and independence is really constituted by a series of episodes more advanced in some countries than in others, but already on a triumphal march. This struggle, endorsed by the blood of millions of heroes and martyrs, has a definite route.

The drawing together of the revolutionary movements of Asia and Africa has proven its extraordinary value, surpassing the test of time, surpassing barriers and difficulties, to emerge as a force which not only represents a contemporary historic reality but is also able to grow and join the revolutionary forces of Latin America to make possible the creation of what may one day be one of the greatest historic movements in the world.

The enemy maintains a policy of hostility in all geographic zones and the anti-imperialists must carry out actions which will be an adequate answer to this aggression on a world scale.

The importance of the struggle in some locations over others will never mean—nor will it justify—the abandoning, the weakening, or the cooling of the struggle in spots of a transitory, lesser urgency. The struggle is total and complete, without alternatives. The three continents must unite as one.

Within the context of the historical tricontinental movements, the consolidation of independence and national sovereignty of the peoples that have left behind the colonial and semicolonial bonds carry a seal of urgency in our deliberations. The new colonial form of exploitation known to Latin America for more than a century, and still known to Asia and Africa, is expressed in different ways. Imperialism, which uses all types of weapons in its eagerness for profit and control, must be opposed by watchfulness and ideological preparation. The masses must be equipped to fight against brutal aggression but also to unmask neocolonialism.

Neocolonialism implies not only the exportation of capital, economic penetration, intervention in internal affairs, political subversion, but also cultural corruption and the spread of deceptive and poisonous ideologies, with the intention of destroying national conscience. The independence and sovereignty of the peoples are not only guaranteed by sound governmental measures of internal order, to safeguard the volume of national wealth without foreign interventions, but also through the practice of international aid of the revolutionary governments and with increasing watchfulness over imperialism's intentions to twist the historical truth and separate the peoples from the knowledge of correct ideas which will lead them to clear reasoning of the destiny they must pursue.

Imperialism, headed by the United States in the present historical moment, with its confusing policy, its conspiracies, and its lack of scruples has created an atmosphere of violence affecting peace and world security. Yankee imperialism, by maintaining international tensions, by installing aggressive military bases throughout the world, and by imposing its will by force, with mockery of all principles of civil rights, is reaping the hatred of the peoples and is being rejected by all for its crimes and pillage. This same offensive conduct is accelerating its decomposition and worsening the crisis of the system. Coercion and threat, bribery and armed intervention, blockades and the contempt for the sovereignty of the nations resisting its penetration, gradually applied in different forms according to the thesis of escalation, are tactics imperialism resorts to in order to save itself.

We cannot accept the lesser step as an alternative for the following one. We cannot allow ourselves to be deceived or intimidated. The fight is unto death.

The peoples of the three continents must answer imperialist violence with revolutionary violence, not only to safeguard national independence, achieved at a high price, but also to obtain the liberation of the peoples fighting to shake off the colonial yoke. The peoples, subjugated and exploited by imperialism, are already becoming aware that under present historical, circumstances, where legal channels are closed by pressure and by the predominance of Yankee monopoly control and where imperialism and its lackeys carry out repressions and persecutions, the effective channel to reach victory is armed insurrection. Therefore, we must back and fully develop the various effective means of struggling, including armed struggle. Vietnam, Algeria, Cuba, give us enlightening examples that will persist in the annals of history as proof that nothing can bar the way of the peoples, no matter how small they are or how close they are to the imperialist and colonialist bastions, if these peoples insist on fighting unswervingly to achieve and defend their rights.

Support of the Cuban Revolution and the patriotic struggles of Latin American peoples is, doubtless, one of the focal points in the world process of the anti-imperialist movement, because it is the area which the United States government has reserved traditionally for its exclusive benefit, from which it extracts numerous resources to feed its interventionist colonial policy; because it has a decisive political significance in our era. Support of Cuba and the Latin American revolutionary movements means the strengthening of the most sensitive areas of the world where the peoples resist the bastion of world imperialism at their front door.

Yankee imperialism's global strategy is a vandalic action which today has its most outstanding manifestations in the aggression against the Vietnamese people and in the military occupation of the Dominican Republic. In both cases it demonstrates the barefaced ferocity and cynicism of those who threaten world peace and also the despair caused by the agony of the system.

In Vietnam, Yankee imperialism has unmasked itself once more before world opinion as the international gendarme and the number one common enemy of mankind. It has proven that its villainies know no limits by incessantly intensifying its aggressive war against the Vietnamese people, trampling on the inalienable national rights of the Vietnamese people, and committing all types of crimes including genocide, in flagrant violation both of the Geneva Agreements of 1954 on Vietnam and international law.

The Vietnamese people are suffering the worst manifestations of North American imperialism, which invades the Southern part of the country with a veritable Yankee expeditionary force and wages by air a cruel war of destruction against the northern part of the country. In Vietnam, the people witness, day by day, the murdering of their best men by Yankee bullets and bombs. Their peaceful villages, their schools, their hospitals, their industrial centers where population is heavily concentrated, their dams and hydraulic constructions are being bombed and destroyed by Yankee airplanes. At the same time that North American imperialism perpetrates its intolerable villainies against the people of Vietnam, it makes itself most repulsive as a result of its hypocritical and shameless propaganda about what it calls "unconditional negotiations."

On the other hand, the heroic and victorious resistance of the South Vietnamese people under the direction of the National Liberation Front against Yankee aggression, and the brilliant victories achieved by the people of North Vietnam, constitute an inexhaustible source of inspiration and encouragement for the peoples of Africa, Asia, and Latin America, inciting them to intensify, in all three continents and by all possible means; the struggle against imperialism, colonialism, and neocolonialism headed by Yankee imperialism.

That is why at this moment, the defense of Vietnam's just cause has become an essential matter and criterion for the revolutionary strategy of the peoples of Asia, Africa, and Latin America, for the socialist countries and for the progressive sectors and classes of capitalist nations.

Because of this, undoubtedly the present conference will devote special and preferred attention to the Vietnamese question. It is essential to continue mobilizing all revolutionary forces in the world and to continue giving all kinds of moral, political, and material support which might be necessary for the people of Vietnam. The present conference should adopt concrete and efficient measures in relation to the Vietnam problem. It is necessary at the same time to emphasize the unavoidable duty of all the revolutionary forces in the world to support openly the points stated by the National Liberation Front of South Vietnam and the government of the Democratic Republic of Vietnam for the solution of the Vietnamese problem, i.e., to demand from the United States government the respect for and the correct application of the Geneva Agreement of 1954; the immediate cessation of the war of aggression of Yankee imperialism in South Vietnam and the bombings against North Vietnam; the immediate withdrawal from South Vietnam of all US troops and war material in order to let the South Vietnamese people solve their internal problems by themselves.

The present conference considers the National Liberation Front of South Vietnam as the only and authentic representative of the South Vietnamese people and expresses its firmest conviction that, under the leadership of the NLF, the South Vietnamese people will undoubtedly obtain final victory.

Since the Second World War, the growing tide of the African revolution has wrested political power from the hands of the colonialists in a great part of the continent. However, with cunning, neocolonialist methods, they can still keep their economic, political, and military power.

In the southern part of Africa we find that domination is exercised by the vicious triumvirate of [Prime Minister of Rhodesia Ian] Smith, [Prime Minister of Portugal António de Oliveira] Salazar, and [Prime Minister of South Africa Hendrick [Verwoerd].

In these immense regions, domination still persists by a small white minority with which imperialist forces desperately try to contain the tide of progress.

The most powerful force maintaining the dominion by the white minority is South Africa, where 115 million pounds sterling are spent yearly in weapons; where 8,500 political prisoners languish in dungeons, and where oppression, for reasons of color alone, is the official policy of the state, supported by the most brutal military and police forces.

Verwoerd, however, depends for his existence on Great Britain, the United States, West Germany, powers which are members of NATO, and on Japan. Experience has shown that to the extent to which the fascist regime of Verwoerd is permitted to maintain its power over Africans and other nonwhite peoples, the well-armed regime of South Africa constitutes a very real and dangerous threat to the safeguarding of the independence of the African states and to world peace.

This conference must consider giving all material and moral help to the peoples of southern Africa, Angola, Mozambique, Zimbabwe, Southwest Africa, and South Africa in their hard and militant revolutionary struggle to overthrow the hated minority of the racist regimes and obtain their national independence.

Africa and the anti-imperialist forces cannot overlook the recent and illegal seizure of power by a racist minority in Southern Rhodesia. This fact, that is being universally condemned at the moment, is of the utmost importance to the struggle the entire African continent is carrying out.

The rising of a minority regime backed by imperialist powers further strengthens the "apartheid" regime based on hatred and racial discrimination. The destiny of the liberation struggle in southern Africa is linked to Rhodesia's struggle.

The Yankee invasion of the Dominican Republic is criminal and repulsive. In view of world reaction in the face of the aggression against the sovereignty and territorial integrity of the Dominican Republic, the imperialist aggressors pretend, with extraordinary impudence, to give a legal status to this sordid intervention. The patriotic reaction of the Dominican people, which deserves our most militant solidarity, has unmasked imperialism and has given an excellent example of courage and dignity.

It is the duty of this conference to denounce the presence of imperialism in South Africa and Zionist colonialism in Palestine, and it should call for the restoration of the legitimate rights of the Arab people and for their return to their usurped country.

This aspect is intimately bound with the fight against discrimination and racism, the ideological pillars of colonialism, and all forms of exploitation of man by man. It is because of this that the conference must strongly condemn racial discrimination, because imperialism tries to turn nations into slaves of the great monopolies.

In the Congo, Angola, Mozambique, in the so-called Portuguese Guinea and in the very heart of the United States, racism presents its most violent forms. However, this shows itself in all places where there are men who live at the expense of others.

That is how the indigenous masses of Latin America are exploited and discriminated against by the native oligarchies, agents of neocolonialism; how Latin Americans in general are despised by the settlers from the North regardless of their origins or physical characteristics, how the Negroes from Africa and from America are looked down upon as inferior, barbaric, and backward peoples; how the Asians were submitted to systematic humiliation by the colonialists' attempt to destroy their ties with their millennial history.

Against that policy of oppression and inequality and of division pursued by colonialism and neocolonialism, the only possibility is unity and equality between the peoples of the three continents. Against the violent action of the colonialists there is only one alternative: servitude or struggle; and it is under combat fire, in the common fight against the exploiter, where all the barriers, based on differences of color, customs, habits, and languages, will disappear in order that mankind may make history collectively.

Today in Zimbabwe (Rhodesia), the situation has reached a climax, especially after the unilateral declaration of independence by the racist government of the white minority. The British and Portuguese imperialists and the racists from Rhodesia and South Africa, with the help and cooperation of Yankee imperialism, are organizing a plot to turn the southern part of Africa into a bastion of neocolonialism, in order to dominate the rest of Africa from this base. This plot represents a serious danger to the independence of the whole African continent.

At this moment, it is important to carry out the battle for unity among Africa, Asia, and Latin America and the progressive forces of the world, so as to frustrate the plans of the imperialists, and especially in the Congo, where they are a threat to all the peoples of Africa, to give ample support to the Congolese people in their fight against the mercenary agents of the exploiters, and to offer material and moral support to the struggle of the peoples of the Portuguese colonies.

Hostilities in the African continent represent one of the most sensitive aspects in the general pictures of the fight against imperialism. This is closely related to the fight against discrimination and racial bias which the colonialists express with special virulence there.

In the Congo, Angola, Mozambique, in the so-called Portuguese Guinea, in Southern Rhodesia or the Union of South Africa, the fight against economic servitude goes hand in hand, in importance, with the defense of one of the basic human rights: the equality of all men. Racial discrimination, typical of imperialism, is manifest in the policy of "apartheid," and in the denial of civil rights to Negro citizens in the United States. Because of its inhuman foundations which deeply offend the dignity of all honest men, it is a subject of the highest priority in the agenda of the conference.

The First Conference of Solidarity of the Peoples of Africa, Asia, and Latin America should express its severest condemnation of the Paris kidnapping and almost certain murder of Mehdi Ben Barka, president of the preparatory committee, and one of the most prominent figures in the fight for national liberation in Africa. It is obvious that this abominable and dastardly act was planned and perpetrated by agents of imperialism and international reaction, both equally interested in obstructing the celebration of this great event of anti-imperialist and revolutionary solidarity. It is imperative that this criminal act be thoroughly investigated and solved, and that the material and intellectual authors be made responsible for their crime. Whatever the fate of comrade Ben Barka, it is only fair that the conference acknowledge his extraordinary contribution to the development and holding of this event.

Recent history corroborates, with utmost clarity, that Yankee imperialism is the greatest enemy of world peace; the fortress of colonialism and neocolonialism, the bastion of the forces of reaction, the public enemy number one of all the peoples of the world. Therefore, to fight for national liberation, self-determination, independence, and peace, fundamentally, means to fight without quarter against North American imperialism, which is responsible for the worsening of the international situation because of its policy of intervention, aggression, and subversion all over the world.

The strategy used by the revolutionary movements in their struggle against imperialism, colonialism, neocolonialism, and especially against Yankee imperialism (principal enemy of the peoples), demands a greater binding and tightening of the ties of militant solidarity among the peoples of Asia, Africa, and Latin America, the working classes and the progressive forces of capitalist countries in Europe, the United States and the socialist camp. This solidarity must be expressed in concrete actions of support of the peoples that are victims of imperialist aggressions, as in the case of Vietnam, where the movement of national liberation has the support of all the peoples of the world, while imperialist aggression has its unanimous rejection.

Imperialist strategy in Africa, Asia, and Latin America makes it imperative that the peoples of the three continents, together with those of the socialist world, maintain the closest solidarity and the utmost militant action in their fight against the common enemy. The aid of the peoples of the socialist camp is vital for the development of the liberation movements.

It is obvious that the militant solidarity of the peoples of the three continents is a necessity which cannot be postponed, dictated by the identity of problems and common aspirations. This solidarity is imposed by the dialectics of events, since the aggressive actions of imperialism have taken on a global character, threatening the self-determination, independence, sovereignty, and security of all the nations of the world.

Messages to the Tricontinental Conference

Ho Chi Minh

President of the Democratic Republic of Vietnam

The US imperialists' war of aggression in Vietnam is a typical example of the most cruel and barbaric acts of the imperialist aggressors. However, the Vietnamese people are fully determined to continue the war of resistance against the US imperialist aggressors and win new and even greater victories.

In their just struggle, the Vietnamese people count on the sympathy and support of the peoples of the socialist countries, the peoples of Asia, Africa, and Latin America, as well as the international public opinion as a whole, including progressive Americans.

The Vietnamese people, relying on their armed forces and the support of the peoples of the world, are determined to continue the struggle against the US imperialist aggressors and there is no doubt that they will achieve total victory.

The Tricontinental Conference currently meeting in the heroic land of Cuba has a political significance of extraordinary importance. It will make an active contribution to the strengthening of solidarity and mutual aid of the peoples struggling against imperialism and colonialism old and new, in defense of national independence and peace throughout the world.

Gamal Abdel Nasser

President of the United Arab Republic

With all the sympathy of the people of the UAR toward the combative peoples of Asia, Africa, and Latin America, with the faith our people have in the future of humanity and of mankind, and with hope placed in your historic meeting, I send to your conference from Cairo my greetings and consideration, as well as my best wishes and support for your work, wishing it success and a new step forward on the path of struggle.

We dreamed of uniting the peoples of Asia and Africa with those of Latin America in a common action that already has a common goal and follows the same path. When the peoples of Asia and Africa met at the Bandung Conference, their meeting constituted a historic event, a turning point in the development of events, and a materialization of the solidarity of the Afro-Asian peoples who took a firm stand against imperialism, exploitation, and aggression.

The results of this solidarity have been manifested repeatedly, from Bandung to the present day, and particularly in the Battle of Suez, which marked the dividing line between the dark ages in which strong states allowed themselves to impose their will through force, violence, destruction, and occupation, refusing to be held back by principles and respect for international values, and between the era of free peoples united by a common will, confronting the maneuvers and methods of imperialism with all their energies and the growing strength of solidarity.

The day has come when the representatives of the peoples of the three continents will gather in a single conference to carry out the same task, inspired by the same objectives, dedicated to the service of the people, the prosperity of humanity, and the dignity of man. They gather to enforce justice in international relations and to recognize the rights of each individual, to put an end to the mad race for the means of destruction, and to dedicate their efforts and capital to helping dispossessed peoples overcome the barriers set up by imperialism and compensate them for the theft of their goods and wealth.

It can be said that the day has come for the representatives of the peoples to gather together; it is another turning point in history, a new consolidation of the unity of the forces fighting for the sake of justice.

I do not mean to say that the path the peoples must follow is paved and that a conference or two will fulfill their hopes and cast imperialism and its methods and conspiracies into oblivion. I only mean to say that your conference is a starting point, but that the road that lies before us is long and arduous.

Imperialism remains clinging to its foundations, continuing to hold sway over the destinies of many peoples and attempting to turn their independence into a mirage. This new form of exploitation is a new problem that newly born states must confront.

There are those who continue to defend racial discrimination, those who establish plans to increase it, and create governments to consolidate it. The arms race terrifies the world, constantly inventing new means of destruction.

Our meeting today and our sincere desire that this meeting be one of the foundations of our solidarity, a commitment to cooperation in all areas, and the starting point of a common endeavor, heralds a new dawn in our world and will determine the destiny of many still subjugated peoples who place their hopes in us.

Allow me to take this opportunity of your meeting in revolutionary and free Cuba to greet the people of Cuba and the seventh anniversary of their victorious revolution. I would like to convey to you the wish of the people of the UAR to see the next Tricontinental Conference held in Cairo, in early January 1968, on the occasion of the tenth anniversary of the First Conference of Solidarity between the Peoples of the Two Continents in Cairo, at which the will of the Afro-Asian peoples was expressed and their solidarity strengthened, culminating in your current conference, which brings together all the anticolonialist forces of the peoples of the three continents.

I ask God to guide you on the path to ensuring the happiness of every human being.

Zhou Enlai

**Premier of the People's Republic of China
and Vice Chairman of the Communist Party of China**

On behalf of the government and people of China, I extend warm greetings to the Conference of Solidarity of the Peoples of Asia, Africa, and Latin America on the occasion of its convening in Havana. I hope that the conference will make a positive contribution to the cause of strengthening the revolutionary solidarity of the Asian, African, and Latin American peoples, promoting the struggle against imperialism, colonialism, and neocolonialism led by the United States, and defending world peace.

Kim Il Sung

Premier and Chairman of the Workers' Party of Korea

On behalf of the government of the Democratic People's Republic of Korea, on behalf of all the Korean people, and on my own behalf, I extend my warmest congratulations and greetings to your conference, held at a historic moment when the anti-US and anti-imperialist struggles are developing powerfully in Asia, Africa, and Latin America, and inflaming the peoples of Asia, Africa, and Latin America.

The peoples of Asia, Africa, and Latin America all share their history of having struggled against national oppression and exploitation under the yoke of foreign imperialists and colonialists.

The long-standing anti-imperialist struggle for national liberation waged by the peoples of these regions has dealt decisive blows to the imperialists' colonial system; a large number of nations have already won their national independence and are on the path to developing on their own resources; the peoples still under the yoke of colonialism are waging even more vigorous struggles to break the last chains of this odious colonialism.

The imperialists, led by the United States, are resorting to brutal armed intervention against the peoples' struggle for independence and liberation in order to extinguish the flames of the anti-imperialist and anticolonialist struggles that are emerging in Asia, Africa, and Latin America, and are embarking on a desperate, mad dash to strangle national independence.

The US imperialists are further expanding their piratical war of aggression against the Vietnamese people and intensifying their provocations and attacks against Laos and Cambodia.

The US imperialists continue to occupy the southern part of our country, hinder the unification of Korea, and wage a continuous war against the northern part of our republic.

However, the US imperialists, by reviving Japanese militarism, which in the past suffered a crushing defeat by invading vast territories in Asia and Oceania, with the illusion of establishing "a great sphere of co-prosperity in East Asia" and publicly paving the way for reinvasion to use it as a "shock force" in their aggression, seriously threaten peace in Asia and the world.

The US imperialists, who maintain their occupation of part of Cuba's territory, Guantanamo, constantly carry out aggressive and subversive activities against the Cuban Revolution and repress the struggles of the Dominican people through armed forces.

The imperialists, by brutally interfering in the internal affairs of African nations, maliciously maneuver to suppress the struggles of the peoples of this region to secure their sovereignty and independence, to achieve the complete liberation of Africa, and to eliminate racism.

However, none of the imperialists' desperate efforts will prevent colonialism from being ultimately overthrown; the struggles of the peoples of the three continents against imperialist aggression and plunder, and to achieve and safeguard national freedom and independence, will surely triumph.

The peoples of Asia, Africa, and Latin America demand even greater unity, solidarity, active mutual support, and encouragement in their common struggle against imperialism and colonialism led by US imperialism.

The Korean people will continue to march forward, as in the past, in solidarity with the peoples of Asia, Africa, and Latin America, in the anti-US and anti-imperialist struggle, and actively support and encourage these peoples in their just struggle. Convinced that your conference will contribute to further strengthening the solidarity of the peoples of Asia, Africa, and Latin America under the banners of the anti-Yankee and anti-imperialist struggle and to more actively encourage and support the struggle of all peoples of the three continents for freedom, national independence, and social progress, I sincerely wish you brilliant success in the work of your conference.

Speeches

Dr. Osvaldo Dorticós Torrado

President of the Republic of Cuba and Member of the Political Bureau of the Central Committee of the Communist Party of Cuba

Distinguished Delegates to the First Solidarity Conference of the Peoples of Asia, Africa, and Latin America;

Distinguished members of the Diplomatic Corps:

It is with singular joy that, in the name of the revolutionary government of Cuba, I fulfill the pleasant duty of bringing you the affectionate and joyful greetings with which our people receive the distinguished representatives of the peoples of Asia, Africa, and Latin America, who have come together in Havana on this exceptional occasion in a meeting of fighters for liberation. These first words of salutation do not spring from the necessity to fulfill a protocol procedure, nor from a duty of elementary official courtesy. It is, to the contrary, the sincerest interpretation of the unanimous feelings of the Cuban people. It is the testimony of the greetings of a people, whose personality and temperament have been forged in fighting, to the brothers of other countries who are also fighters for the same ideals of progress, liberty, and anti-imperialist struggle.

During these brief days, in which the preliminary work of the conference has demanded your presence amongst us, I know that you have had more than one opportunity to experience the warm welcome of our people and to appreciate the deep sentiments of joy which your presence has caused in our country. The people of Cuba are firmly convinced of the extraordinary importance of this event as another phase in the long and cruel struggle against poverty, ignorance, exploitation, and imperialism. Our people take deep satisfaction in greeting you today as the fighters in the front line of distant lands, but very close to our own ideals and hopes; our people who, after decades of frustration and slavery, won their struggle for liberation, the victory which we celebrated with you, only a few hours ago in the Revolution Square; the same people who won, one after another, the battles against internal counterrevolutionary attempts to destroy the achievements of the revolution; the same people who defeated the US imperialist mercenaries at Playa Girón; the same people with nerves of steel, unshakeable spirit, and fighting decisiveness who carried out their international duty with enthusiasm in the dramatic hours of the October crisis; the same working people who day by day create the spiritual and material riches of the new society they are building; the same happy people with whom you have enjoyed the festivities of the past hours. These heroic people, full of joy and hope for the future of their country and mankind, are the people in whose name, distinguished delegates, I greet and welcome you at this opening session.

It is a great honor for Cuba to have been chosen as the host country for this conference. We are convinced of the significance of this conference, of how much it means, and of how useful the tasks it undertakes may be from today on, the conclusions and declarations that will be agreed upon in following days, the solidarity and fighting spirit that will preside here and the encouragement and stimulus that this will mean for all the people of the world. The very fact that this is an opportunity for the most genuine representatives of the progressive and revolutionary movements of Asia, Africa, and Latin America to get together, and the fact that this conference affords the opportunity of conversation and reciprocal knowledge, constitutes sufficient foundation to give this event an importance of historic dimensions.

That is why the eyes of the world are upon this conference today. The struggling peoples of the three continents—those who have begun the fight for independence; those who have achieved formal independence and are moving along the road to true independence and those who are preparing themselves for the coming fight—all the peoples of Asia, Africa, and Latin America in these days are watching the development of this conference and are demanding that you fulfill your responsibilities and the hopes that these peoples have placed in this meeting, confident that this meeting will inevitably provide an opportunity for struggle and a proper occasion to find a common language: the revolutionary, fighting, and anti-imperialist language that millions of human beings who suffer, hope, and fight in these three continents have learned to speak.

But it is not only the peoples, the revolutionary and liberation movements who are today eagerly watching this conference. It is sufficient to look over the cables of the international news: this conference worries the peoples' enemies, the national oligarchies that serve the imperialists, their treacherous rules, and especially the imperialist circles. Therefore, it is the inescapable duty of the distinguished delegates to combine their efforts so that this may be a triumphant event. We should not fail to justify the faith that the peoples have placed in your work and decisions; nor should the imperialists, nor the other conspiring enemies of the people, be allowed to forget their alarm, their fear and indignation, when they learn the final results of this conference, its agreements, and the vigor which it will lend to international solidarity. What justifies a meeting of the representatives of the peoples of these three continents? What unites the millions of men and women of Asia, Africa, and Latin America? What are the common objectives that produce a meeting such as this? Different languages, diverse national characteristics, different races, a multiplicity of traditions, and various levels of economic and cultural development, are not obstacles for this meeting, nor for the unity of arms for which it was convened. It is simply that, regardless of the strategic and tactical methods which are the concern of each country, all the peoples represented here have their history, their present, and their future deeply committed to the struggle for total liberation and sovereignty; for progress, economic, and cultural development; for the ending of poverty and illiteracy; for the liquidation of the colonial and neocolonial forms of exploitation of the people; for the defeat of the imperialist enemy.

These are common objectives of the peoples of the three continents, of those who have succeeded in becoming independent nations and are fighting today to guarantee this independence and progress in the midst of imperialist bribery, aggression, and blackmail; and of those people who have achieved a formal independence and whose governments are abjectly submitted to imperialist interests, serving as guardians of exploitation and poverty within their respective countries; as well as those of the peoples who have not won even formal independence and are fighting for their true liberty or are preparing themselves for the struggle.

As an open and ill-disguised euphemism, the "underdevelopment" of the three continents has been spoken about, and even in the diplomatic language of the imperialists, the term has won legitimate usage. The people who meet in this conference know in a concrete and dramatic manner what "underdevelopment" means: economic backwardness, hunger, technical penury, illiteracy, sickness, political oppressions, the exploitation of national resources, direct or indirect domination by imperialism. The peoples who meet in this conference know that the problems of underdevelopment (even in the cases of nations that achieve their independence, and even those whose governments represent their ardent desires for liberation and progress) are not solved by the palliative measures, the institutions, and the technical instruments offered as solutions to the evils of underdevelopment in world forums and in specialized international conferences. We have attended these meetings many times. Very often they serve as platforms for the peoples to proclaim their truths. But we are not so naive as to believe that the problems of economic and cultural underdevelopment of the peoples can be debated and solved outside the limits of the great world antagonism, the division between oppressors and oppressed, and disregarding the fact that the ultimate cause of all manifestations of underdevelopment is none other than the survival of imperialist domination.

In a peoples' conference such as this, one basic truth becomes imperative: The definitive and complete elimination of underdevelopment can only be achieved by struggling against imperialism and totally defeating it.

The procedure for this fight, the ways to obtain such a victory are, of course, conditioned by the circumstances of each country and those prevailing in the world scene today.

So it is opportune at the inauguration of this conference to recount briefly the fundamental characteristics of the world today which will be dealt with at this meeting.

The new correlation of forces in the world permits liberation movements to grow vigorously in the three continents. The fighting vanguards of the people improve their ideological education, their revolutionary consciousness matures, and the movements of liberation grow and proliferate.

Temporary defeats suffered on some occasions are no more than the painful lessons learned by the peoples, so that they may enter the struggle once again. The important thing is to be convinced that the final victory belongs to the peoples, that when the will of the people is firm, there are no obstacles that cannot be overcome to achieve victory. In inaugurating this conference, we can point to the visible increase of the liberation movements: In the midst of hardship and difficult battles against the powerful enemy, some peoples have started the struggle, other peoples have gained victory, and many peoples are preparing to fight.

Nevertheless, it is true that imperialism, especially US imperialism, which has assumed in the history of our times the sad role of international gendarme, increases violence and intensifies the use of all the evil instruments of aggression against the people. From bribery and blackmail to the most brazen forms of violence and armed intervention, US imperialism, the center of world reaction and the foremost enemy of peace and progress, unscrupulously carries out within the framework of a perfectly defined world strategy, any number of openly criminal actions believing them to be useful to their fight for domination and survival. Therefore, as the peoples, filled with strength and bravery and increasing revolutionary consciousness, take the path of liberation, imperialism replies with all its weapons, employing all its potential and all its power. The armed mercenary intervention in the Congo, the armed intervention in the Dominican Republic, the formation of mercenary armies in Latin America, the constant threat against free revolutionary Cuba, the decision of the United States Congress in trying to legalize unilateral imperialist intervention in any country in the Americas, the establishment of a racist government in Southern Rhodesia, the brutal intensification of the most criminal forms of racial discrimination in South Africa, and finally the direct aggression by the armed forces of the United States in South Vietnam, and the bombing by United States planes of the Democratic Republic of Vietnam, are very definite expressions of the global strategy of imperialism today. In Asia, Africa, and in Latin America, the struggle against imperialism and for the liberation of the peoples is a struggle to the death.

Therefore, distinguished delegates, this conference is taking place in a historic moment when imperialism, all other means for subjugating the peoples having failed, imposes violence upon them, and there is no better place than in this conference to proclaim, without hesitation, the right of the people to oppose imperialist violence with revolutionary violence.

It is not our purpose, nor our mission upon opening this conference to define the line it should adopt. The position of Cuba on each of the topics on the approved agenda will be established during the course of the conference by the head of our delegation. Moreover, the resolutions and decisions of this meeting must be the spontaneous and democratic expression of the results of its deliberations and the fighting spirit that enlivens it. But I think I interpret the general feeling of the distinguished delegates, when I proclaim in this inaugural meeting a principle of universal value for all the liberation movements of the three continents. When imperialism and reaction close the doors to all legal forms of struggle, it is a right and duty of the peoples to respond to the armed violence of imperialism with revolutionary armed violence.

It is the responsibility of the vanguard of those peoples to create the subjective conditions when they are absent. When imperialism offers the peoples no other alternative, this is the only way of pursuing the struggle for liberation. In countries that have achieved their independence and that are trying to keep it, despite the stratagems and aggressions of imperialism, it is the duty of the leaders of those peoples to do more than preserve their own sovereignty and construct a new society promoting their independent economic and cultural development. The survival of these sovereign states and the guarantee of their future progress are also involved in the struggle taking place in the three continents against imperialist domination. But, furthermore, their duty of solidarity obliges the peoples that have achieved their independence, and their leaders, to pledge the necessary support, in such ways as may be necessary to the liberation movement. On this inaugural occasion, Cuba declares that it is a right and a duty of the peoples and governments of the countries that have achieved independence and begun building a new life, to give unrestricted support to the movements of liberation in Asia, Africa, and Latin America.

Being aware of this duty, the conference will consider it a fundamental obligation to express its solidarity and give its most determined support to the courageous people of Vietnam who are suffering today the most vandalic, criminal, and illegal aggression from US imperialism. That is why, when opening this conference, and while greeting from this platform the fighters who, in the most widely separated areas of the three continents, struggle today with weapons in their hands for the liberation of their peoples—in Latin American countries such as Venezuela, Peru, Guatemala, the Dominican Republic, Colombia; in the African Portuguese colonies or in the Congo (Léopoldville) or wherever there is a fighter or the readiness to fight—we reserve our word of highest honor for the heroic people of Vietnam. We offer our complete support to the positions adopted by the National Liberation Front of South Vietnam and by the government of the Democratic Republic of Vietnam as conditions for peace. And we reiterate on this occasion the firm decision of Cuba to support the heroic struggle of the people of Vietnam, in any way that may be necessary. As the first secretary of our party, comrade Fidel Castro, stated yesterday, we are also prepared to shed our blood for Vietnam.

Distinguished delegates: this conference is being held in a country that is still an anti-imperialist battlefield. On this soil, generous blood has been shed more than once fighting against US imperialism. The people who live here, creative and peaceful, the confident and happy people that you have met in these days, live in a permanent state of combat readiness. A short distance from the most aggressive imperialist country, the most savage and powerful enemy of the peoples, challenging its insolence and in historic denial of the thesis of geographic fatalism, we achieved our independence by a bloody war. From that revolutionary triumph, the first socialist country of the Americas was born. Despite the blockade, armed aggression and international conspiracy of US imperialism, our people are victoriously advancing upon the glorious road leading to the construction of a brilliant future. We are aware of our obligations to the peoples of the world, the importance of our humble example. We feel genuine pride at having achieved revolutionary triumph, and of having defeated Yankee imperialism on our own soil. This, however, does not justify vanity. We do not believe that we are the revolutionary center of the world. Our desire is to contribute modestly to meetings such as this, our experiences and above all our irrevocable determination for international solidarity.

Cuba is a small country, and we have only slightly more than seven million inhabitants. But on opening this conference, we wish to confirm once more before all of you with absolute clarity, that to the full extent of the means at our disposal, but with the militant and inexhaustible energies of our people, as Fidel Castro stated yesterday: "Any revolutionary movement, in any part of the world, can count on Cuba's unconditional and decided aid."

Today, more than ever, we renew that pledge of honor, giving our word as revolutionaries. All the efforts of the Cuban people today are dedicated to the construction of a new society. All that we have done in these seven years of revolution and all our work in the future, is for us a reason for revolutionary and creative passion. We deeply love our work and wish to protect it against all dangers. Our economic successes, our growing agriculture, our schools and our hospitals, our universities and our cultural centers, the new generation, which is being forged today, all this beautiful revolutionary reality which is Cuba, we love deeply. All this constitutes a priceless treasure for our people. But it is opportune, on this exceptional occasion, to firmly express our willingness to fulfill the commitments we have made to other peoples, even though we risk these achievements and these creations. If our duty of solidarity and support to liberation movements of the Asian, African, and Latin American peoples demands this sacrifice, our people will make the sacrifice. Cuba will not fail!

Distinguished delegates: I convey to you the expectation of the Cuban people for the success of this conference; their trust that every one of you, with absolute independence of judgement, will reach unanimous conclusions and militant decisions; their faith in that this first meeting of representatives of the peoples of the three continents will be an expression of the spirit of solidarity in the anti-imperialist struggle. The peoples expect a great deal from this conference. Consequently, your responsibility is a high one. It is now important to find the forms of a common language and common action against the imperialist foe. We ardently desire that this gathering will genuinely embody the aspirations for liberty of the peoples of Asia, Africa, and Latin America, the fighting spirit of these peoples, the encouraging support of all the progressive forces in the world, and the support of the socialist countries to the epic that these three continents are playing out.

On behalf of the Cuban people and the revolutionary government, I express our deep gratitude for your stimulating presence in our country, for the exceptional honor of sharing your company, for the distinction that has been given Cuba by selecting this, our country, as the seat of this meeting. And with renewed faith in the future of the peoples, in their invincible capacity for struggle, and in the certainty of the final defeat of imperialism, I declare that the First Solidarity Conference of the Peoples of Asia, Africa, and Latin America is hereby inaugurated.

Long live the struggle for the liberation of the Peoples of Asia, Africa, and Latin America!

Long live the heroic people of Vietnam!

¡Patria o Muerte! ¡Venceremos!

Youssef El Sebai
(United Arab Republic)

Secretary General, Afro-Asian People's Solidarity Organization

Mr. President;

Dear Friends and Brothers:

Allow me, on your behalf and in your name, to address our most sincere thanks and appreciation to Dr. Dorticós, president of the Cuban Republic, for the honor he gave us by inaugurating the opening session of the historical First Conference of Solidarity of the Peoples of Africa, Asia, and Latin America.

I would also like to address our thanks and fraternal greetings to the valiant people of Cuba, to their great party and to the outstanding leader of Cuba, brother Fidel Castro, for their welcome, hospitality, and the praiseworthy effort extended by them for their organization of this historical conference, and the opportunity they gave us for a most enjoyable and fruitful stay in their lovely capital.

Eight years ago, representatives of the revolutionary forces, the militant liberation movements, and the popular mass parties in Africa and Asia met in Cairo for the first time. That was a prominent landmark in the history of our two great continents, when the cornerstones of the great Afro-Asian Peoples' Solidarity Organization were laid down.

Now we meet in this historic conference, while our ranks are enlarged and strengthened by the revolutionary and mass organizations of our sister continent, Latin America, and where our militant solidarity has reached its natural and necessary apex of development.

Dear Brothers:

We are here to take action; positive, concrete, and effective action, against imperialism and colonialism in all their forms and manifestations and for full national independence and peace.

Let us all work, hand in hand, to achieve this action that is our duty.

I am sure we shall undertake action, in solidarity and close cooperation between ourselves, so as to fulfill our task with the greatest success and justify the confidence placed in us to continue the struggle until we attain full liberation; establish economic, social, and cultural reconstruction; and achieve prosperity and world peace.

Long live the solidarity of the peoples of Africa, Asia, and Latin America!

Nguyen Van Tien (Vietnam)

Member of the Central Committee of the National
Liberation Front of South

Mr. President and Members of the Presidency;

Dear Delegates;

Dear Friends:

It is a source of great joy and honor for us, delegates of the National Liberation Front of South Vietnam who have arrived here from the advanced trenches of struggle against the aggression of Yankee imperialism in Southeast Asia, to be able to attend this transcendental Conference of Solidarity of the Peoples of Africa, Asia, and Latin America held in Havana, the beautiful capital of heroic Cuba, the first territory on the American continent to free itself from Yankee domination and to defeat imperialist aggression and champion for all of Latin America.

In the current international situation, the presence at this conference of the fighting delegates of the national liberation movements and the heroic peoples of our three continents constitutes a splendid manifestation of the indestructible militant solidarity that unites the billions of men and women of Africa, Asia, and Latin America who have "said enough and have taken up the march," courageously fighting against imperialism, colonialism, and neocolonialism. It also constitutes a new development of tremendous importance, stimulating the struggle for national independence, and a most valuable contribution to the entire revolutionary movement of the peoples of the world.

On behalf of the people and the National Liberation Front of South Vietnam, we warmly welcome the holding of this Conference of Solidarity of the Peoples of Africa, Asia, and Latin America in heroic Cuba and wish our conference every success.

Allow us to extend our warmest greetings to the distinguished delegates and, through them, to the sister peoples of our three continents. We are very grateful to you for having reserved an appropriate place for the problem of Vietnam on the agenda of this conference. Allow us to enthusiastically greet and thank the Communist Party of Cuba, the revolutionary government, and the heroic people of Cuba, who, under the leadership of Prime Minister Fidel Castro, have created all the favorable conditions for this historic meeting and who have always provided unreserved support for the just patriotic struggle of the South Vietnamese people.

Allow us to extend our fraternal greetings to the delegations from the socialist countries, from international organizations, and to all our comrades and friends present here.

Dear Delegates and Friends:

Our peoples in Africa, Asia, and Latin America have suffered for long centuries under the cruel domination of imperialists and colonialists. It is precisely exploitation, the imperialist and colonialist yoke, and the common destiny of our peoples that have brought us closer together, even though we are geographically separated. It is also exploitation and the imperialist yoke that have motivated the unleashing of the great revolutionary forces of the peoples of our continents against imperialist and colonialist power.

The historic victories of the October Revolution and the Chinese Revolution, and the emergence of the world socialist system, have shifted the balance of forces in the world in favor of the revolution and have spurred the oppressed peoples of our continents to rise with an irrepressible drive to launch an offensive against the bastions of imperialism and colonialism. Twenty years after the end of World War II, more than fifty countries in Africa, Asia, and Latin America with over one billion inhabitants have achieved independence and sovereignty. Many other peoples are struggling bravely and patiently to liberate themselves. The world stage has radically changed. The global colonialist system is in complete disintegration, and this constitutes a great historic victory for the peoples of our continents, heralding the complete defeat of imperialism, colonialism, and the colonial slave regime.

However, in their agony, the imperialists and colonialists, with imperialism at the forefront, have never abandoned their maneuvers of aggression and domination against the peoples, and are desperately trying to maintain their system of colonial oppression and exploitation, employing new forms and means. South Vietnam, Laos, the Dominican Republic, the Congo (L), Palestine, Southern Rhodesia, Portuguese Guinea, Angola, South West Africa, South Africa, and many other countries on our continents are today victims of colonialism and imperialism.

The delegation of the National Liberation Front of South Vietnam believes that the most urgent problem facing the peoples of our continents today is to unite even more closely and continue our decisive struggle against imperialism, colonialism, and neocolonialism, especially against the most dangerous enemy of our peoples, American imperialism, to defeat its aggressive and enslaving policies, conquer our vital rights and our freedom, and defend peace.

For all these reasons, this conference assumes a great responsibility for the destiny of our peoples on the three continents. We have the firm resolve, the invincible force of solidarity. We have the experience of struggle. We are perfectly capable of mobilizing more powerfully still to the peoples of our continents to fulfill our historic task and achieve our great objective, which is to victoriously carry out the cause of national liberation in Africa, Asia, and Latin America.

Dear Delegates and Friends:

It was in this same historical framework, common to the peoples of our three continents and living under the same colonialist and imperialist domination, that our Vietnamese people rose up to wage a long and hard struggle against the French colonialists and the Japanese fascists. We carried out the victorious revolution of August 1945 and won independence, freedom, and democracy for our people. But the French colonialists, supported by the British and US imperialists, unleashed a new war of aggression against our homeland. For nine years, the entire Vietnamese people, under the clear-sighted leadership of President Ho Chi Minh, waged a heroic war of resistance, which culminated in the historic victory of Dien Bien Phu. The Geneva Accords on Vietnam, signed in July 1954, recognized the independence, sovereignty, unity, and territorial integrity of Vietnam and stipulated the holding of general elections throughout Vietnam within two years to reunify the country. It was a glorious victory achieved by the Vietnamese people, definitively ending the nearly century-long domination of French colonialism in our country. It was also an important contribution to the cause of national liberation of the peoples of Africa, Asia, and Latin America.

However, with their greed to take over the entire world, the Yankee imperialists have long sought to seize our country. During the Indochina War waged by the French colonialists, the Yankees provided the bulk of the military expenditures with the aim of replacing the French and prolonging and expanding the war in Vietnam and Indochina. But they failed in their criminal endeavor.

Barely after the Geneva Accords were signed in 1954, US imperialism dragged in several other imperialist and satellite countries to form the SEATO, which arbitrarily placed South Vietnam, Laos, and Cambodia within the "protection zone" of this aggressive military bloc. At the same time, US imperialism rushed to evict the French colonialists and turn South Vietnam into a new type of colony and a US military base, in complete violation of the Geneva Accords, and thus attempting to perpetuate the division of Vietnam, prepare for war, and gravely threaten peace in Indochina and Southeast Asia. From then on, US imperialism became the most perfidious and ruthless enemy of the people of South Vietnam. In South Vietnam, as in many other parts of Africa, Asia, and Latin America, for the past eleven years, US imperialism has carried out the extremely perfidious aggressive policy of Yankee neocolonialism:

From July 1954 to the End of 1961

During that period, through the dictatorial administration of its faithful lackey Ngo Dinh Diem which brandished the label of a "nationalist and independent government," through its military and economic "aid" and through its system of "military advisors," US imperialism was imposing its dominance in all aspects over South Vietnam.

Politically, the puppet administrative apparatus was completely in Yankee hands; economically, South Vietnam gradually became a market for surplus US goods; militarily, imperialism established hundreds of bases on our territory, forming, training, and commanding an entire mercenary army of hundreds of thousands of soldiers. The imperialists imposed the Yankee "way of life" on South Vietnam, poisoning our youth with the corrupt and slave-like culture of the so-called "free world."

US imperialism and the Ngo Dinh Diem dictatorship used every means to deceive and corrupt our people, while at the same time brutally repressing all progressive and patriotic people, suppressing all the most basic democratic freedoms. They exploited our workers to the core; they deprived our peasants of their lands; they stifled the development of national industry, agriculture, and commerce. In a word, the entire people of South Vietnam became victims of the Yankee–Diem regime.

The policy of imperialism and its lackeys was to accelerate the militarization of South Vietnam as much as possible and prepare for war; to seek every means to exterminate the patriotic movement of the South Vietnamese people; to use South Vietnam as a beachhead in Southeast Asia and a springboard for attacking North Vietnam; to threaten the socialist countries and to undermine the national independence movement of the peoples of Indochina and Southeast Asia.

Because of this imperialist policy, South Vietnam has become a vortex of increasingly acute contradictions between the peace-loving and independence-loving people on the one hand, and the imperialist aggressors and their traitorous lackeys on the other.

After the Geneva Accords were signed, for several years, the South Vietnamese people patiently waged a peaceful struggle, demanding from Yankee imperialism and its lackeys the correct implementation of the stipulations of the accords, the peaceful reunification of Vietnam, and demanding from the puppet authorities of South Vietnam the promulgation of democratic freedoms and improvements in the people's living conditions. But this peaceful struggle was violently suppressed and drowned in blood by the Yankees and their lackeys. They perpetrated extremely bloody massacres in Ngan Son, Chau Doc, Mo Cay, and other places, burying hundreds of people alive. They carried out so-called "denunciation of the communists" campaigns throughout the country, torturing and murdering tens of thousands of former participants in the previous patriotic resistance against the French colonialists.

They openly repressed the Saigon Peace Defense Movement and imprisoned its leaders, such as the lawyer Nguyen Huu Tho and the landowner Tu Bac Duoc; they murdered the jurist Nguyen Van Duong and arrested hundreds of patriotic intellectuals and students. Thousands of union activists and tens of thousands of workers were cruelly tortured. Many monks and Buddhist adepts were murdered. Driven to bankruptcy, many national bourgeoisie committed suicide. The Yankees and their lackeys annihilated all those who disagreed with them, even within the puppet government and the mercenary army. They established a nepotistic fascist regime entirely subordinated to the imperialist interests of the United States. To the legitimate aspirations of the people, Yankee imperialism and Ngo Dinh Diem responded with their weapons, their fascist laws, and their guillotines. The cries of pain of an entire people, from newborns to the elderly, shook all of South Vietnam. "The crimes committed by the Yankee–Diemists are incalculable; thousands of tons of paper, thousands of hours of work would not be enough to enumerate all these crimes." This was acknowledged by the American soldier Roque Matagulay, captured by the Armed Forces of Liberation in Phan Thiet province.

Faced with this situation, the South Vietnamese people could not stand idly by and watch the enemy exploit and murder at will. All social strata—intellectuals, students, religious leaders, bourgeoisie, and patriotic landowners—began to increasingly understand the true face of the Yankee imperialists and traitors, thus extinguishing any illusions that existed about these enemies of the homeland. It was for this reason that the popular strata of South Vietnam united and rose up to begin a struggle using all appropriate means to save the homeland and their homes. This patient and arduous struggle, carried out from the mountains to the countryside and cities for many years, has achieved great victories. This was achieved from the late 1960s onward; the period of stability of the temporary regime of the Yankees and lackeys disappeared to make way for the period of general crisis.

As a result of this vast patriotic movement, the National Liberation Front of South Vietnam was born, which launched a program of national unity and struggle to achieve independence, democracy, peace, and neutrality for South Vietnam and to advance toward the peaceful reunification of the country. This program consists of the following ten points:

1. Overthrow the colonial regime disguised as the American imperialists and their lackeys and establish a democratic national coalition government.
2. Establish a progressive regime of broad democracy.
3. Build an independent and sovereign economy, improve the living conditions of the people.
4. Reduce land rent and move toward solving the agrarian problem by returning the land to those who work it.
5. Build a culture and education of a national and democratic character.
6. Form an army for the defense of the homeland and for the protection of the people.
7. Establish equality of nationalities and gender equality. Protect the legitimate rights of foreigners in Vietnam and Vietnamese people abroad.
8. Implement a policy of peace and neutrality.
9. Reestablish normal relations between both parts of Vietnam and move toward the peaceful reunification of the country.
10. Fight against war of aggression and actively defend world peace.

This political line fully corresponds to the imperative need for social progress in South Vietnam.

Under the banner of the National Liberation Front, which called upon all the people to participate in the great task of national salvation, the revolutionary movement gathered unstoppable momentum and developed tempestuously. Throughout South Vietnam, the people carried out partial insurrections and organized guerrilla movements, dismantling the grassroots administrative apparatus of the pro-Yankee puppet government on a massive scale. The Yankee neocolonial regime faced inevitable collapse.

From 1962 to the End of 1964

Faced with the rapid decomposition of its neocolonialist regime in South Vietnam, Yankee imperialism realized that the puppet government and mercenary army lacked the capacity to confront the impetuous attacks of the South Vietnamese revolutionary people.

This caused the Yankees to change their strategy in South Vietnam, taking a more adventurous step in their policy of armed aggression against our people. In May 1961, the then vice president of the United States, Johnson, arrived in Saigon to sign a military pact with his lackey Ngo Dinh Diem. In February 1962, the United States established the Yankee Military Command in Saigon, led by General Paul Harkins, and increased the number of Yankee "advisors" from two thousand to more than eleven thousand in November 1962, so that together with the puppet army of almost half a million men, they could carry out an "undeclared war" called a "special war" against our people. This new type of war is also a war of "experimentation" to gain experience and use it to suppress the national liberation movement. With the aim of pacifying South Vietnam and annihilating the still very young revolutionary armed forces within a period of eighteen months, the Yankee imperialists developed the Staley–Taylor strategic plan of "lightning attack" and "quick wins."

They implemented new military tactics they considered "keys to victory," such as the "helicopter troop transport" tactic and the "amphibious vehicle troop transport" tactic. They mobilized large detachments of troops and carried out bloody "raking" operations against the newly liberated areas. They practiced the scorched-earth policy: burning everything, looting everything, and killing everyone. They applied many forms of torture and massacres reminiscent of medieval barbarism, but with modern means: They dismembered innocent children and threw them into the flames; they decapitated defenseless people, ripped open their stomachs, and removed their gallbladders, causing the people of South Vietnam ruin, destruction, mourning, and indescribable suffering.

Applying the experience of the British imperialists in Malaya and the French colonialists in Algeria, the Yankees and their lackeys carried out the vandalistic policy of the "strategic hamlets" which consisted of forcing the fourteen million inhabitants of South Vietnam to abandon their lands and their homes to live in sixteen thousand concentration camps baptized with the name of "strategic hamlets," thus turning South Vietnam into an immense prison of Yankee imperialism.

Without any regard for international law or the conscience of humanity, imperialism in South Vietnam resorted to chemical and bacteriological warfare on an ever-increasing scale. Tens of thousands of men, women, and children were killed or left in the lurch. Hundreds of thousands of hectares of rice paddies, orchards, crops, and vegetation were poisoned and razed to the ground. Furthermore, they dropped napalm bombs, phosphorus bombs, rockets, and other lethal instruments on our peaceful villages, schools, and hospitals, killing and wounding thousands of our children and schoolchildren. They attacked with cannon fire peaceful Buddhist demonstrations demanding freedom of belief and respect for the Buddhist flag on the anniversary of the birth of the venerable Buddha. Hundreds of Buddhist priests and followers were killed in cold blood and then thrown into rivers. They raped tens of thousands of our women, even young girls, old women, and Buddhist and Catholic nuns. The crimes perpetrated by the Yankees and their lackeys against our people, they wound the human conscience; no honest person in the world can remain indifferent to this situation and tolerate these crimes. With an uncontainable hatred for the enemy, with the iron determination to defeat the "Yankee special war," the people and the Armed Forces of Liberation of South Vietnam have overcome thousands of obstacles and difficulties, endured very difficult trials, and achieved great successive victories. Millions of people participated in political struggles to demand from the puppet authorities an end to terror, respect for freedom, and peace. In close coordination with the political struggle of the masses, the Armed Forces of Liberation have fought tens of thousands of heroic battles against the enemy. They successively defeated the Pentagon's famous helicopter and amphibious vehicle tactics. More than 80 percent of the concentration camps called "strategic villages" were destroyed by the people, and most of them were transformed into combat villages. Millions of peasants, the main force of the national liberation revolution, were liberated from the enemy's yoke and received more than two million hectares of land distributed by the National Liberation Front. The puppet army, the mainstay of Yankee imperialism's "special war," suffered heavy casualties, reaching over two hundred thousand men dead, wounded, and captured. More than three thousand Yankee officers and soldiers were put out of action. The failure of the "special war" increasingly sharpened the contradictions within the enemy, and on November 10, 1963, the Yankee masters physically liquidated their most faithful lackey, Ngo Dinh Diem, for being incapable. Since then, more than ten coups d'état and *"gorillazos"* have occurred, forcing imperialism to change its lackeys seven times. Despite everything, the puppet government remains completely powerless, unable even to control the people in the occupied cities, nor to exist for a single hour without the aid of Yankee bayonets and dollars.

The shameful failure of the Staley–Taylor plan and then the McNamara plan, as well as the dismissal of the number one general in the United States, Maxwell Taylor, marked the total bankruptcy of Yankee imperialism, both strategically and tactically in its "special war." At the same time, it was the bitterest defeat for the Yankees in their experimentation with an "antiguerrilla war." This failure has its deep roots in the inevitable bankruptcy of the neocolonialist policy of the United States, in the serious weakening of the entire new-type colonial system of North American imperialism in the face of the repeated devastating blows dealt to it by the peoples of the three continents in recent years.

From the Beginning of 1965 Until Now

In an attempt to escape their critical situation, the Yankee imperialists have taken even more dangerous steps in their military adventure: They have insolently extended the war to the Democratic Republic of Vietnam, an independent and sovereign country, waging a barbaric war of destruction against that country using American air force. At the same time, they have massively and rapidly introduced more and more Yankee combat troops into South Vietnam to intensify their criminal war of aggression. From twenty-five thousand Yankee aggressors at the end of 1964, today this number equals that of the French Expeditionary Corps in the Indochina War. The Yankee air force in South Vietnam now numbers 2,300 aircraft, the same number of planes used in the Korean War. In addition to American troops, an entire division of mercenary soldiers from the South Korean puppet regime and other military units from Australia and New Zealand are taking a direct part in the war of aggression in South Vietnam. Units of the US Seventh Fleet are currently anchored off the coast of Vietnam, considering "Vietnam and its maritime space as a combat zone" in flagrant violation of all international laws and the Geneva Agreements on Vietnam. The criminal war of aggression of US imperialism in South Vietnam has now become the largest and most vicious war in the world.

The fact that Yankee imperialism has increasingly intensified its aggressive war in South Vietnam and its bombing of the North, continued its aggression against Laos, and blockaded and threatened Cambodia demonstrates that it is trying to fan the flames of war throughout Indochina and Southeast Asia. Clearly, this is the most insolent and dangerous challenge not only to the people of Vietnam and the peoples of Indochina but also to the peoples of our three continents, to all freedom-loving, justice-loving, and peace-loving peoples of the world.

Dear Delegates and Friends:

The aggressive actions and maneuvers of Yankee imperialism against Vietnam have revealed to the peoples of the world its true image as an international gendarme, the leader of the warmongering imperialists and colonialists, the most dangerous enemy, not only for our people but also for all the peoples of our three continents and the world. Johnson and McNamara themselves have declared that a US withdrawal from South Vietnam would be equivalent to a withdrawal from all parts of the world. This clearly demonstrates that the Yankees want to maintain a foothold in South Vietnam, a key link in the chain of Yankee military bases and colonies. If they lose South Vietnam, it would be very difficult for them to hold on to other parts of our three continents.

Therefore, in the name of independence, peace, and the reunification of our homeland, in the name of the common interest of the peoples of our three continents and the world, allow us to declare from this platform that the people of South Vietnam are determined to spare no effort to fulfill their duty, which is to defeat the aggressive war of Yankee imperialism.

Under the clear leadership of the National Liberation Front of South Vietnam, over the past five years, the South Vietnamese people have achieved strategically important victories that guarantee the successful development of our struggle until final victory. Having started the struggle empty-handed, the South Vietnamese people have gone on to build the entire invincible structure of our current patriotic war, determining with their powerful political and military strength the future development of the situation in South Vietnam.

Today, the South Vietnamese people have a monolithic and extremely powerful political force that encompasses workers, peasants, youth, women, students, intellectuals, religious leaders, political parties and groups, national bourgeoisie, and patriotic figures. This hard-tested political army possesses valuable experience in political struggle and is constantly developing and consolidating. Wave after wave, this army has launched itself into the struggle, organizing rallies, demonstrations, and strikes involving tens and hundreds of thousands of people. With just and reasonable demands and appropriate forms of struggle, mass political struggles have, in most cases, succeeded in embarrassing the enemy and defending the legitimate interests of the people. In the political army, a place of special importance is given to South Vietnamese women, who with their courage, bravery, and intelligence have spread panic in the enemy ranks. The mass political struggle has transformed the enemy's "safe" rear into a front line of combat and the site of a powerful strategic offensive against the puppet and mercenary ranks. Prominent combat figures have been the workers Nguyen Van Troi, Tran Van Dang, Le Do, the Buddhist priest Thich Quang Duc, the student Le Hong Tu, the professor Le Quang Vinh, and others whose names today symbolize the heroism, patriotism, and spirit of sacrifice of our people.

On the other hand, the South Vietnamese Liberation Armed Forces, born of the people, have continued to grow and strengthen everywhere. The small armed propaganda groups and scattered guerrilla groups equipped with the most rudimentary weapons at the beginning have transformed through struggle into powerful popular armed forces composed of militia, regional units, and the regular army. The Liberation Armed Forces are currently capable of waging battles against the enemy not only at night but also in broad daylight, of waging not only lightning attacks but also battles lasting several days to several weeks. At Plei Me, our troops faced the Yankees and mercenaries for more than a month, fighting day and night under a rain of enemy bombs and bullets, surrounding them and inflicting more than four thousand casualties. There are guerrilla units like Ben Cat's that can annihilate entire enemy companies. Armed by high patriotism and revolutionary heroism, the more the Armed Forces of Liberation fight, the more experience and technique they acquire. They have written the most glorious pages of our liberation struggle against aggression, the brilliant victories of Ap Bac, Binh Gia, Van Tuong, Chu Lai, Plei Me, Bau Bang, Bien Hoa, Da Nang, and others.

The National Liberation Front of South Vietnam, availing itself of these ever-growing and increasingly powerful political and military forces, is leading a sacred war of resistance by all the people on all fronts against the war of aggression of US imperialism. The strategic line of the people and the revolutionary armed force of South Vietnam is to wage a long struggle, relying primarily on their own forces and considering the moral factor as decisive, mobilizing the entire people to develop in parallel the mass political struggle and the people's armed struggle, considering both forms as equally indispensable and decisive. Following this strategic line and fighting under the invincible banner of the National Liberation Front, our South Vietnamese people have achieved great successes over the past five years: They have annihilated 540,000 enemy soldiers, including dead, wounded, and captured, including nearly 20,000 US aggressor soldiers; it has shot down, destroyed, or damaged more than 2,390 aircraft and helicopters of all types; destroyed or damaged 1,922 military vehicles; sunk or damaged 912 boats and warships, including the aircraft carrier Card; raided nearly 2,000 enemy barracks and military posts; and captured more than 100,000 weapons of all types from the enemy. The mercenary army is in complete decomposition; more than 217,000 mercenary puppet soldiers have deserted its ranks in the last five years; cases of rebellion and mass desertion of even entire companies and battalions are becoming more frequent every day.

The Yankee imperialists believe that by intensifying and expanding their war of aggression, they could regain the military initiative, prevent the disintegration of the puppet army, achieve victories, annihilate the Liberation Army, subdue the South Vietnamese people, and achieve their military objectives.

However, the truth is that the more troops they brought into Vietnam from the South, the more the contradiction between our people and them became more acute, and the more national consciousness was awakened not only among the popular masses but also in the ranks of the administration and the puppet army.

Amidst the storm of war, a new life has sprung up in the vast areas liberated by the patriotic forces, which today cover more than 80 percent of South Vietnam and 10 million inhabitants. Significant political, social, economic, and cultural changes have taken place in these areas: The peasantry, the main force of the national liberation struggle has received two million hectares of land from the hands of the revolution and today has everything necessary to live a life without hunger or misery. Nearly four million men and women have joined the National Liberation Front. Nearly three million peasants have united to form mutual aid and collective work groups. Front Committees and People's Self-Administration Committees have been established at all levels, making the people the true masters of their lives and future. Schools, hospitals, infirmaries, and maternity wards operate in almost all liberated areas. The National Liberation Front has all the means of dissemination and propaganda: radio, news agencies, film studios, newspapers, magazines, and others. An immense and secure rearguard has been formed, stretching from the mountains to the coastal areas, encompassing the countryside and the cities, ensuring an inexhaustible source of human and material strength for the struggle. The liberated areas, where the people enjoy a free and healthy life, are a powerful attraction and a vision of their future for the people still suffering in the regions occupied by the enemy. The National Liberation Front of South Vietnam today is the true and sole representative of the South Vietnamese people. It is actually exercising all the functions inherent to a democratic state and is leading the victorious struggle of fourteen million men and women against Yankee aggression.

The people of South Vietnam also enjoy the unreserved support and invaluable moral and material assistance of their compatriots in the North, the socialist countries, the peoples of Asia, Africa, and Latin America, the other peoples of the world, including the American people, as well as many international and regional organizations.

To date, the National Liberation Front of South Vietnam has permanent representative missions in Cuba, Algeria, Czechoslovakia, the German Democratic Republic, Indonesia, the People's Republic of China, and the Soviet Union. In the near future, it will establish missions in Romania, Bulgaria, Poland, and other countries. More than thirty countries and national and international organizations have established committees of solidarity with Vietnam against Yankee aggression. The political organizations comprising the National Liberation Front have participated in sixty-six international and regional conferences and are executive members of ten international and regional organizations. Delegations from the National Liberation Front have visited many countries in Europe, Asia, and Latin America seventy-eight times. Recently, the revolutionary government of Cuba declared its formal and express recognition of the central committee of the National Liberation Front of South Vietnam as the sole and authentic representative of the South Vietnamese people and granted the National Liberation Front Mission in Havana the status of an official and permanent diplomatic mission. This is a highly significant event that further enhances the prestige of the National Liberation Front in the international arena.

While our people and the National Liberation Front of South Vietnam receive the solidarity and support of all peoples and progressive forces around the world, Yankee imperialism is increasingly isolated and condemned everywhere.

The Yankee rulers are knocking on every door, mobilizing support for their war of aggression. But everywhere they have been rejected or received coldly.

Militarily, since the end of World War II and the Korean War, Yankee imperialism has never suffered so many shameful defeats as it has today in Vietnam. Yankee military forces are powerful, but they are spread out across many parts of the world. The powerful national liberation movement of the peoples of our three continents is enormously weakening the Yankee empire. The more bogged down they are in South Vietnam, the less the Yankees will be able to carry out their plans of aggression elsewhere, and they will encounter greater difficulties in military personnel and transportation. Strategy and tactics based fundamentally on the superiority of weapons will never be able to subdue an entire people united and determined to fight. The Yankee expeditionary force is fighting not for a just cause but for the filthy interests of Yankee monopolies. Therefore, it is not chance to see the Yankee soldiers and officers completely demoralized by the surprising and devastating blows dealt by the people and the South Vietnamese Liberation Army.

In the economic sphere, despite a certain artificial prosperity created by increased war production, the United States is entering a new phase of acute crisis. The American gold reserve has rapidly diminished. Ever-increasing military spending is demanding higher taxes and causing inflation that devalues the American dollar. All of this has been reflected in the standard of living of the broad working masses of the American people. If the Yankees continue the war of aggression in Vietnam, they will face many insurmountable difficulties.

Under these conditions, the people of South Vietnam, with the experience they have gained in resistance against the French colonialists and the Japanese fascists, and that they have acquired in the struggle of these past eleven years against the Yankee aggressors and lackeys, will further intensify their efforts and will surely achieve total victory. The National Liberation Front of South Vietnam has solemnly and repeatedly declared before the people and international opinion that the people of South Vietnam have sufficient moral and material strength to defeat any army and any type of war that Yankee imperialism and its satellites wish to impose on us with the purpose of bringing our people to their knees. That if the Yankees do not renounce their military adventure and introduce up to three hundred thousand, four hundred thousand soldiers, or even more, this will never change the situation in their favor: The South Vietnamese people are determined to defeat them and will fight for five, ten, twenty more years until the Yankees abandon their aggressive policy and leave our territory.

If the Yankee imperialists continue to "escalate" their bombing of the Democratic Republic of Vietnam, the people of South Vietnam, along with their seventeen million compatriots in the North, will decisively cut off their hands. By attacking North Vietnam, the Yankees have offended the sacred sentiments of the people of South Vietnam. The Vietnamese homeland is one. American imperialism can never divide our homeland. The South Vietnamese people are determined to fight to liberate the South, defend North Vietnam, and move toward the reunification of all of Vietnam.

Dear Delegates and Friends:

While intensifying and expanding its war of aggression against our people, Yankee imperialism is carrying out a perfidious campaign of propaganda and slander aimed at deceiving world opinion and masking its warmongering actions.

They are endlessly repeating their hypocritical claims of "unconditional negotiations," while at the same time accelerating at a dizzying pace the dispatch of Yankee reinforcements to South Vietnam and their bombings in the north of our homeland. "Pray to God and keep swinging the hammer," such is the essence of the peace maneuver of President Johnson and the leaders of the United States. They are also shouting at the top of their lungs that they want "a cessation of hostilities," thereby attempting to paint a picture of what is plain, to confuse just with unjust, and to erase the dividing line that always exists between the aggressors on the one hand and the attacked on the other. In reality, by demanding "a total cessation of hostilities," the Yankees simply want to demand that our people lay down their weapons, cross their arms, and kneel before them, allowing them to carry out the occupation of South Vietnam and the division of our homeland, maintain the traitorous Saigon regime, and resume aggression whenever it suits them best. One might ask: The United States is separated from Vietnam by tens of thousands of kilometers. What right do the Yankee imperialists have to send and maintain their troops in our country? It is true that our people ardently love peace, but true peace cannot exist without true independence. For our freedom, independence, and sovereignty, our people will never give up the fight until they have expelled every last American aggressor soldier from our territory.

Mr. Johnson also said that our people "prefer the road to ruin and death to the road to the conference table." There is no slander baser and more shameless. Who, during these eleven years, have sown death and destruction in our country? Aren't they the Yankee imperialists? The South Vietnamese people love peace and freedom. But we are not afraid of sacrifices. We are determined to fight, to endure whatever sacrifices are necessary to achieve peace, independence, and true freedom for our people.

The shining example of the peoples of our three continents in their determined and patient struggles against imperialism, colonialism, and neocolonialism is a great lesson for our people. Our people and the National Liberation Front of South Vietnam draw lessons daily from the victorious struggles of the peoples of China, the Soviet Union, Korea, Cuba, Algeria, the most valuable experience and the most powerful stimulus, at the same time that we learn from our brothers in struggle from Venezuela, Peru, Guatemala, Colombia, the Dominican Republic, Angola, Congo (L), Mozambique, Portuguese Guinea, Aden, occupied South Arabia, South Africa, Southern Rhodesia, Laos, Cambodia, Japan, and other peoples. The people and the National Liberation Front of South Vietnam unreservedly support the just struggle of all these brothers, and we regard each of their victories as our own. We are certain that in the current world situation, when Cuba, ninety miles from the United States, has made its triumphant revolution and is building a happy and prosperous life; and when Algeria, a few miles from France, has been able to defeat an expeditionary force of seven hundred thousand soldiers, our people of the South Vietnam will also be able to perfectly defeat Yankee imperialism and win our freedom and the independence of our homeland.

The consistent and unwavering position of the National Liberation Front of South Vietnam, the sole legitimate representative of the South Vietnamese people, for the solution of the South Vietnamese problem is that US imperialism must end its war of destruction in North Vietnam, withdraw US and its satellite troops from South Vietnam, dismantle all its military bases, strictly and fully implement the 1954 Geneva Agreements, recognize the national and fundamental rights of the South Vietnamese people, and allow the South Vietnamese people to resolve their internal affairs. This just opposition of the National Liberation Front has been unanimously approved and supported by progressive opinion throughout the world.

Dear Delegates and Friends:

The victories achieved by the South Vietnamese people in the struggle against the Yankee imperialists and their lackeys cannot be dissociated from the sympathy, solidarity, and support of all the peoples of the entire world. The governments of many countries, many political and social organizations on our three continents and around the world have expressed with concrete actions their resolute support for the just patriotic struggle of the South Vietnamese people.

The royal government and the people of the Kingdom of Cambodia, both then and now, have generously and unwaveringly offered their sympathy and powerful support to the people and the National Liberation Front of South Vietnam. The Laotian people, close brothers of the South Vietnamese people, under the leadership of the Neo Lao Hak Sat, are always at our side in the struggle. The people of Indonesia have repeatedly raised their voices demanding the withdrawal of Yankee troops from South Vietnam. The peoples of Japan, Burma, Pakistan, Ceylon, Syria, and many other Asian countries have constantly organized a broad movement of solidarity with the South Vietnamese people. Many sailors from Japan, Australia, New Zealand, and other countries have refused to transport Yankee weapons and means of war to South Vietnam. The peoples of the Philippines, South Korea, Australia, and New Zealand have strongly protested against participation in the war of aggression in South Vietnam.

Throughout Africa, there is a powerful movement of struggle against the Yankee war of aggression and of solidarity with South Vietnam. The governments and peoples of Algeria, Mali, Guinea, Congo (B), the UAR, Tanzania, Ghana, etc., have expressed their support for the just struggle of the South Vietnamese people. Many political and mass organizations in various African countries, such as Congo (L), Angola, South Africa, South West Africa, Southern Rhodesia, Bechuanaland, Basutoland, Swaziland, and the Arab populations of Palestine, Aden, etc., have followed with deep sympathy and supported the patriotic struggle of the people of South Vietnam.

The Cuban people and revolutionary government are closely following the development of our long and arduous struggle and are prepared to provide us with any assistance, including weapons and men.

The peoples of Venezuela, Colombia, Guatemala, Peru, Argentina, Chile, Puerto Rico, Panama, Uruguay, Mexico, the Dominican Republic, and other Latin American countries, who share the same enemy as the people of South Vietnam, are waging a determined struggle against Yankee colonialism and firmly supporting the liberation movement of the South Vietnamese people. In Montevideo, the young student Jesús Rolán Rojas spat in Dean Rusk's face when the latter visited Uruguay, to express his disgust with the crimes committed by Yankee imperialists in Vietnam and Santo Domingo.

The governments and peoples of the Soviet Union, the People's Republic of China, and other socialist countries have always offered their most fraternal sympathy and most effective support to the National Liberation Front and the people of South Vietnam. They have always stood united with our people and have provided the most valuable assistance in the anti-imperialist struggle and for the independence and peace of South Vietnam.

Broad, progressive, and conscious sectors of the American people have increasingly raised their voices in protest against the Johnson administration's criminal policy of aggression in South Vietnam. Many young Americans openly expressed their categorical refusal to go to fight against the people of South Vietnam and publicly burned their draft cards. American students, youth, men, and women in many cities have organized powerful demonstrations, stopping trains to demand that the US government return their husbands, friends, and sons sent to the most senseless death in South Vietnam. Tens of thousands of citizens in the United States have participated in protest demonstrations and marches, carrying flags of the National Liberation Front of South Vietnam and chanting slogans demanding the withdrawal of US troops from Vietnam. Many American citizens have besieged military bases, ports, and military camps to prevent the recruitment and dispatch of troops to South Vietnam; they have gone on hunger strikes to protest the war of aggression and organized blood drives, fundraising campaigns to aid the South Vietnamese people, and written letters of encouragement to the people of South Vietnam. In the struggle for the common interest of the American and Vietnamese peoples, examples of self-sacrifice and heroism have emerged: Mrs. Alice Herz, the young Morrison, LaPorte, Jankowski, and others set themselves on fire to express extreme outrage against the US government, which has committed nameless crimes in Vietnam.

Many international and regional organizations, many cultural and social organizations from France, Great Britain, Italy, Belgium, Finland, Norway,

Switzerland, Canada, and other countries, and many eminent world figures, such as Lord Bertrand Russell, have issued statements, organized rallies, conferences, and adopted strong resolutions condemning the aggressive policy of Yankee imperialism in Vietnam. Many Western countries have coordinated their activities with the American people to protest the aggressive policy of the United States government against South Vietnam.

A vast and powerful united front of the peoples of the world has been formed in solidarity with the people of South Vietnam against Yankee aggression.

From the rostrum of this First Conference of Solidarity of the Peoples of Africa, Asia, and Latin America, allow us, on behalf of the fourteen million South Vietnamese and the National Liberation Front of South Vietnam, to sincerely express our gratitude for the warm support of the peoples of our three continents, the valuable support of the socialist countries, the sympathy and ever-stronger support of the American people, of international and regional organizations, and of the peace-loving and justice-loving peoples of the entire world.

The South Vietnamese people hold deep in their hearts their gratitude for the unreserved support they receive from the peoples of the world and consider it a source of invaluable encouragement to their struggle and a vital factor in achieving ultimate victory.

On this occasion, we reiterate the consistent position of the National Liberation Front, which is to support the struggle of the peoples of Asia, Africa, and Latin America for national independence and against imperialism, colonialism, and neocolonialism, led by Yankee imperialism.

We warmly salute the great victories achieved by the peoples of Africa, Asia, and Latin America in their long and difficult struggle for national independence, freedom, and social progress, and against imperialism, both old and new colonialism.

Dear Delegates and Friends:

Faced with inevitable defeat, US imperialism is taking increasingly dangerous and adventurous steps: It is ceaselessly intensifying and expanding its aggressive war in South Vietnam and continuing to escalate its destructive air war in North Vietnam. Under these conditions, the patriotic struggle of the South Vietnamese people will still be long and hard, but it will surely end in victory.

Let us make a fervent appeal to the First Conference of Solidarity of the Peoples of Africa, Asia, and Latin America, to the peoples of the three continents, the socialist countries, and of the world:

- Sternly condemn and strongly denounce the criminal war of aggression waged by Yankee imperialism in Vietnam; halt in time its activities of escalating the aggressive war in South Vietnam, as well as its destructive air war in North Vietnam; and expose Yankee imperialism's "unconditional negotiations" maneuvers.

- Fight decisively to demand that Yankee imperialism correctly implement the Geneva Accords on Vietnam; withdraw Yankee and satellite troops from South Vietnam, its military bases in South Vietnam; leave the South Vietnamese people the freedom to resolve their own internal affairs, without any foreign interference. The reunification of Vietnam must be resolved by the people of both parts of Vietnam.

- Intensify and further expand the movement of solidarity and political, moral, and material support for the liberation struggle of the South Vietnamese people, in appropriate ways and according to the capabilities of each country.

- Recognize and have recognized the National Liberation Front of South Vietnam as the sole authentic representative of the South Vietnamese people, providing it with all the political, diplomatic, moral, and material support within its reach.

- Organize struggles in conjunction with those of the South Vietnamese and American people to protest the deployment of troops to South Vietnam and to boycott the production and transportation of weapons to South Vietnam.

- Organize weeks of solidarity with the people of South Vietnam on July 20 and December 20 each year.

Dear Delegates and Friends:

The peoples of Africa, Asia, and Latin America are living in a time when imperialism and colonialism, old and new, led by Yankee imperialism, are in their final stages; a time when the struggle for national independence, peace, democracy, and social progress for the peoples of the three continents and the world is on the uninterrupted offensive and achieving important victories. The peoples of our three continents have sufficient strength to defeat imperialism and colonialism step by step, break link by link the chain of a system that is in complete decay, achieve national emancipation, and contribute to the defense of world peace. Our three continents have immense wealth; our people are very hardworking, and our strength of solidarity is invincible. We are determined not to let the imperialists and colonialists keep us in slavery. We are determined to advance!

This historic conference provides a good opportunity to consolidate the existing solidarity and friendship among the peoples of our three continents, to exchange experiences in the struggle for national emancipation and national construction, to coordinate our activities, and to encourage and assist each other in defeating imperialism and colonialism, both old and new. The delegation of the National Liberation Front of South Vietnam will spare no effort to contribute our modest part to the success of the conference.

Long live the unwavering fighting solidarity between the peoples of Africa, Asia, and Latin America!

Many thanks to the president of the conference and to all the delegates and friends.

M. Gabriel Yumbu
(Congo-Léopoldville)

Secretary General of the Supreme Council of the Congolese Revolution

Mr. President;

Excellencies;

Dear Fellow Delegates:

The Supreme Council of the Congolese Revolution, the governing body of the National Council for the Liberation of the Congo, takes this opportunity here to express its most sincere thanks to the organizers of this conference for the kind attention extended to it in inviting it to participate in the foundation of this historic meeting.

There are many reasons that impose upon oppressed peoples the sacred and unavoidable duty to use all means at their disposal to break the chains of slavery that still bind them, and this conference, at the opportune moment, comes to swell and consolidate the forces of the liberation and peace camp in the struggle against our common enemy: international imperialism, led by the United States.

The wise choice of Havana as the venue for this first conference lends it greater significance, since a retrospective look at the recent past allows us to perceive the heroic and triumphant struggle of the Cuban people against US imperialism, the leader of the criminal forces that are enemies of the peaceful and noble peoples of the world.

This Cuban victory, at the very gates of the imperialist bastion, is a great symbol, an invaluable stimulus for the Latin American peoples, as well as for all other oppressed peoples of the world, which has come to convince them of the possibility of their victory over the enemy through armed struggle. The Cuban people represent for all of us a model of heroism, selflessness, and hope, the champion of the Third World Revolution.

On behalf of the freedom fighters, militants of the National Council for the Liberation of Congo, the Supreme Council of the Congolese Revolution, pray to the brotherly people of Cuba, its Party, its great revolutionary leader, Prime Minister Fidel Castro, and the president of the republic, His Excellency Osvaldo Dorticós Torrado, may you receive the expression of his fraternal congratulations and wishes for prosperity and happiness.

Mr. President;

Excellencies;

Dear Comrade Delegates:

By initiating for the first time in the history of humanity this meeting, which allows representatives of popular organizations from the three continents to jointly consider their common unfortunate fate, we have organized an event of considerable global importance that has shaken the forces of evil gathered in the international reactionary camp.

Our warm congratulations to the members of the Conference of Solidarity of the Afro-Asian Peoples held in Winneba, Ghana, from May 9 to 16, 1965, who took the initiative and made the choice of the venue.

To assess the horror that the announcement of this conference caused imperialism, there is no more tangible proof than the cynical kidnapping of our brother Mehdi Ben Barka, president of the preparatory committee for this conference. This event, which unfortunately casts a pall over this day and worries those present here and the peoples they represent, compels us to grant this brother in combat the rank of hero and martyr of our common cause.

Since the end of the Second World War, the wind of freedom, blowing with unprecedented fury across our planet, has seen many peoples free themselves from the slavery, exploitation, domination, nameless misery, degrading humiliation, and ignorance to which they had been plunged by the exploiters, monopolists, and bourgeoisie, gathered within the bosom of international imperialism. These exploiters, ironically, and in the name of liberty, civilization, and a God made in their idealistic philosophical image, grimly persecute millions of people belonging to our three continents.

Our common enemy, international imperialism, led by the United States, has launched its war of domination to maintain the exploitation and impoverishment of the peoples of our three continents. In this war, it employs not only its formidable war machine, but also its philosophy of a social order formed by privileged classes holding a monopoly on the means of production. The imperialists dreamed, and still dream, of keeping millions of human beings in perpetual servitude and misery in the name of "bourgeois philosophical thinking about the eternal possession of the means of production."

Bourgeois philosophy grants the exploiting classes the right, in the name of God and the "superior race" they claim to represent, to keep the other races of humanity in servitude. Thus, American imperialism, the spearhead of global imperialism, arrogates to itself the right to bring aggression, devastation, genocide, moral depravity, poverty, and racism to our three continents. It does so in the name of God, in the name of piracy, applying the methods of the "good" filibusters of the Age of Adventure, in pursuit of riches that will allow them to seize, control, and regulate at will the standard of living of the humanity subjected to their domination.

The raw materials of our countries are used to fuel their war machine, which immediately turns against us to transform our people into slaughtered herds in the slaughterhouse of their criminal aggression.

By scrupulously implementing the resolutions adopted at the Winneba Conference, we have reached a decisive stage and achieved considerable progress in our common struggle against the enemy. The upcoming conferences, as foreseen by the 1966 Afro-Asian calendar, will allow us to better assess the shortcomings to be overcome, the balance of victories recorded, as well as the most promising future prospects for intensifying the struggle against imperialism, which threatens the existence of our peoples like tetanus threatens an infected human organism.

The Supreme Council of the Congolese Revolution nourishes the firmest hopes that the brothers in struggle in Latin America, Asia, and Africa will set to work to see the above decisions crowned, without any lukewarmness that could slow the momentum of the common struggle against a fiercely determined enemy, although obsessed by the idea of its inevitable defeat, which like a horrible specter haunts it, just as it does the victorious advance of the fighting revolutionary forces.

Our unity in action accelerates victory and reduces the countless miseries that imperialism inflicts on the peoples of our continents.

The United States government, after signing the 1954 Geneva Accords on the settlement of the Indochina problem, is deploying its genocidal aggression in that region of Asia, stirring the universal conscience.

To the cry of indignation of all humanity against the crime of a war unequal in means and forces, the enemy responds with a cynicism worthy of the filibusters and pirates of the Middle Ages, with an attitude that casts its shadow of shame over contemporary civilization. The reactionary forces of all the countries of the world, united within the imperialist clique, conspire against our peoples in the name of what they call law, but nothing other than the justification of the barbarism of prehistoric man.

The savage aggression of US imperialism against the peaceful Vietnamese people, the subversive actions they carry out continuously in this region of the world with absolute disregard for public opinion, reveal the bellicose nature and criminal character of US imperialism.

For us, this unjust war imposed on a people defending themselves, supported by their legitimate right to self-determination, independence, and sovereignty, constitutes a crime against humanity, reason, and law, and therefore against modern civilization.

With the unwavering determination to regain their rights and freedom, the Vietnamese people will surely triumph against the unleashed imperialist tide. The National Council for the Liberation of the Congo demands, with regard to the solution to the South Vietnamese problem, that the United States simply withdraw its aggressor troops from South Vietnamese territory.

We denounce the hypocritical attempts at preliminary talks aimed at confusing world public opinion, while they constantly increase their military forces, now estimated at more than two hundred thousand men, and they surrender to the senseless "escalation" warmonger in North Vietnam [sic].

We request that this conference recognize the National Liberation Front of South Vietnam as the sole legitimate representative of the South Vietnamese people, and that the organizations present here, representing the parties already in power in their respective countries, influence their governments to promote this recognition.

We stand by the South Vietnamese people, who can count on our full moral support. Their misfortune is our misfortune. We hope that all peace-loving and freedom-loving peoples of the world will support and sustain the just and heroic struggle of the South Vietnamese people until final victory.

We believe that deviating from this duty constitutes treason and a crime against humanity. We support the full implementation of the four points of the Government of North Vietnam and the five points of the National Liberation Front of South Vietnam regarding the regulation of the Vietnamese question.

In the African chapter, without ignoring the general situation, we emphasize that the specific cases of our countries, the Portuguese and British colonies, Rwanda, Cameroon, Senegal, and South Africa, deserve special attention, where we find ourselves facing the same enemy: international imperialism, led by the United States.

Mr. President;

Excellencies;

Dear Fellow Delegates:

As for the Congolese case, we will limit ourselves to highlighting the most notable events, so as not to waste your precious time.

Exactly twenty months have passed since the Congolese people decided to take up arms to wrest their rights and independence from the puppets imposed on our country, stripped of its core content.

The enemy, acting through a puppet government represented by [former President Joseph] Kasavubu, [Prime Minister Moïse] Tshombe, [President] Mobutu [Sese Seko], and their cronies, has presented our revolutionary struggle, through its propaganda, radio, and press, as one inspired from abroad. Who in the world, knowing the ferocious nature of American imperialism and its clique, can be surprised by this old procedure, used everywhere they intervene with their customary barbarity?

But, since the revolution is not an imported or exported commodity subject to sale and purchase, as imperialism would have us believe, we affirm that our people's decision to wage armed struggle stems from the humiliating conditions imposed on them by Yankee imperialism.

Dismayed by this unexpected situation, the rotten power installed in our country by imperialism against the will of the people has experienced hours of profound contradictions that have shaken it and caused serious political upheavals similar to those suffered by all puppet regimes in similar circumstances.

Under the irresistible revolutionary force, the puppets on the stage of power have been changed at an accelerated pace. To close the framework of this macabre political dance, a just penance deserved for the treatment of his homeland, a general driven and impelled by his common leaders has just exposed the man who was the main and original cause of all of Congo's misfortunes since its independence: Kasavubu.

This is how the old adage that crime never pays ("crime doesn't pay") has come to pass.

Is this a result that, therefore, leads to an appeasement solution to the thorny Congolese problem? Far from it; to be convinced, it is sufficient to refer to the declaration of the Supreme Council of the Revolution regarding this new form of conspiracy by US imperialism and its lackeys in the Congo.

The degradation caused by the establishment of a government run by the traitor Mobutu. A new military coup has put the puppets of the gang of puppets that constitute the de facto power in Léopoldville in a counterpoint.

Now the imperialist machinations of September 1960 have been reproduced, origin of the assassination of Patrice Émery Lumumba by the Kasavubu–Tshombe–Kalonji–Mobutu–Nendaka–Bomboko group, etc.

Congolese patriots have always affirmed that the Congolese problem cannot be resolved by changing individuals or as a result of a military coup d'état.

In Congo, the words: "parliament," "government," "president of the republic," "elections," "laws," "constitution," "army" have no meaning.

The government installed in Léopoldville is a creature of the United States, which pulls the strings at will. Thus, the frequent changes in the leadership of the so-called Congolese government, the events in which Adoula, Tshombe, Kimba, Mobutu, and their cronies have been involved, are far from over and stem from the same machinations of imperialism.

The contradictions that have recently emerged between Tshombe and Kasavubu, the two most docile horses in the American cavalry, characterize the neocolonialist regime built on betrayal, abuse of power, and crime.

Currently, faced with the victorious prospects of the Congolese people's armed revolutionary struggle, imperialism, reduced to a desperate situation as is happening in Vietnam and Santo Domingo, is expanding its criminal interference in the Congo's internal affairs.

As in the past, we proclaim that imperialist violence in our country will be faced with revolutionary violence. The National Liberation Council solemnly reaffirms before the world that it will never waver in its firm and resolute determination to tirelessly pursue its armed struggle until final victory.

In Addis Ababa, in April 1963, one of the greatest hopes of the African people: the creation of the Organization of African Unity.

Indeed, the OAU inscribed in golden letters in its constituent charter the consistent struggle against colonialism and imperialism in all their forms: thus translating the deep and legitimate aspirations of the African peoples.

In September 1964, at the suggestion of Mali, a special meeting was held in Addis Ababa, where resolutions were adopted that demonstrated, at one point, Africa's concern about the Congolese problem.

Firstly, the resolution stipulated that:

"The Congolese Government will be invited to immediately stop recruitment from any source and to re-embark those currently in the Congo as soon as possible, in order to allow for an African solution to the Congolese problem."

The activity carried out by the Organization of African Unity has not passed unnoticed by our organization, and in every report presented by this body, which claims to work for the liberation of the African continent from imperialist and colonialist shackles, we have expressed our point of view. Unfortunately, in the course of this work, there was never a single mention of the fight against neocolonialism.

We are aware that the current struggles in Vietnam, Santo Domingo, Congo-Léopoldville, Venezuela, Colombia, Peru, and Laos; the usurpation of the Arab national heritage in Palestine; the situation in South Arabia; and the latest challenge hurled at the African world by the situation in Southern Rhodesia—all constitute part of the undermining work of neocolonialism carried out by US imperialism in collusion with its Western accomplices. Since then, we have questioned the sincerity of those who loudly proclaim, with spectacular and moving declarations, that they are fighting against imperialism while vested with neocolonial power in their respective countries, against the will of the people and against democracy.

The National Council for the Liberation of Congo-Léopoldville will not stop fighting until it achieves the radical eradication of neocolonialism in the country.

We believe that, at the current Tricontinental Conference, neocolonialism will be reconsidered in the program of our peoples' struggle, on the same level as all other forms of domination and exploitation attempted by imperialism.

At the last session of the Organization of African Unity in Accra last October, our position on the outcome of these proceedings surprised many in African circles, and we were subjected to certain criticisms. The defiance, the temporary imperialist victory, and certain points of view held at the Accra summit by delegations from African puppet countries—aren't they reflected in the usurpation of power by the white minority in Southern Rhodesia, led by [Prime Minister] Ian Smith with the complicity of the British imperialists?

What practical effect has come from the unanimous decision of the African foreign ministers in Addis Ababa to break off diplomatic relations, in the face of the blatant mockery of the Black majority by the white minority in Southern Rhodesia? Can we consider the long-disguised hypocritical game played by certain puppets in Africa to be over? All Third World countries are today witnesses to the betrayal of the African struggle for emancipation and liberation from imperialist shackles by numerous African states.

What is the summary of these decisions, these meetings, these Platonic declarations? Can we admit today that Africa is liberated? Isn't the independence of certain African states marred by a real mystification and a certain aberration, in a positive sense?

We would like to express our point of view once and for all, without hesitation and avoiding any possible misunderstanding in the future.

Is the current struggle in the various regions of the world already mentioned actually directed against imperialism? Isn't neocolonialism another, even more odious form of imperialism and of the old colonialism? What result would we achieve in our common struggle against imperialism if we allowed all independent countries of the Third World to be transformed into neocolonies? Isn't this giving in with the right hand and then, through a skillful maneuver, taking it back with the left?

Some African countries, instead of encouraging us in our fight against neocolonialism, which is our common enemy, on the contrary, overwhelm us with all imaginable evils invented by the same enemy: some inventing misunderstandings in which they cooperate to worsen for reasons only they know, and others launching a defamatory campaign.

The Congo is a victim of imperialist aggression for two main reasons:

Imperialism is aware of the importance of our country's natural resources. Once freed from neocolonialist shackles, the Congo will be able to achieve an economic development capable of one day ranking it among the most powerful countries in Africa.

Economic development will lift the Congolese population out of the misery into which they have been plunged by colonial occupation and the current neocolonialism, personified by the de facto power currently imposed on us by Yankee imperialism and its Western allies.

We are aware that the liberation we pursue through our armed struggle is the only means and the only guarantee to achieve that goal. We will achieve it.

We do not judge anyone, but we expose the lamentable anachronistic situation we have experienced in our struggle, since we have been in contact with the outside world, starting with the barbaric intervention of the Belgian, English, and North American imperialist forces in Stanleyville.

We are unable to supply our forces operating inland (with war material, food, medicine, etc.). We have had many deaths so far, but we will not give up despite the difficulties caused by certain "friendly" African countries.

Is it possible to fight only with words? How could we fight the enemy, hungry and unarmed?

All aid received from powers friendly to the socialist camp is, to this day, for reasons unknown to us, blocked in certain African countries that call themselves "brothers." Does this embargo imposed on us, which we denounce before this international conference, constitute aid to the liberation of the Congo? Furthermore, barriers have been erected to prevent us from entering and remaining in the same countries, for the same unknown reasons, even though our presence does not constitute any threat to the security of those states.

Many of us have been subjected to punishment and imprisonment, without receiving any explanation.

While we gather here to study how to conduct the struggle against imperialism, colonialism, and neocolonialism, others among us are mulling over their intentions to torpedo the common enterprise to which they subscribe.

Mr. President;

Excellencies;

Gentlemen and Dear Comrades:

In the Congo, we don't have two languages for a friend; we have, in our idiosyncrasy, the courage to speak a sincere and unequivocal language in any circumstance.

We hope, thanks to your help during this conference, that you will intervene on behalf of the tricontinental solidarity that will be sealed and cemented here, to see your African friends abandon their previous attitudes, return to our side, and help us morally by granting us the freedom of movement that has been denied to us until now.

We would be ungrateful if we didn't make a special mention of gratitude to other African brothers and sisters who have done their best to help us at every turn, even at the risk of their own interests. We will never forget them. True friends are known in the darkest days of human history.

We wonder what prospects some responsible Africans imagine for the victory of the liberation struggle in the Congo. For our part, we believe, after having granted the sovereign people the full exercise of all their rights, that we can work within the international concert of peaceful nations, the socialist camp, to contribute to the achievement of objectives guided by all the oppressed and exploited peoples of the world: the relentless struggle against imperialism, colonialism, neocolonialism, racism, hunger, ignorance, and the full range of calamities that still afflict humanity, primarily in the Third World.

All the countries that have recognized the unspeakable regime of the murderous Mobutu have renounced all the OAU resolutions of Addis Ababa and Accra. These resolutions urged the Léopoldville puppet government to expel the mercenaries from the Congo. Panicked by this order, which would precipitate the regime's fall in the face of the unleashed revolutionary tide, US imperialism proceeded to disqualify the former pawn Kasavubu and replace him with a more docile Mobutu. Consequently, were we not right when we said, on the occasion of the African Summit meeting in Accra:

"In the Congo, the words 'government,' 'parliament,' 'president of the republic,' 'elections,' 'laws,' 'constitution,' 'army' have lost their meaning. The de facto power installed in Léopoldville is a 'puppet' of the United States of America that pulls the strings at will."

If the recognition of the Mobutu regime by some African member countries of the OAU is a policy intended to combat neocolonialism in Africa, we consider this policy truly foolish and cannot help but be perplexed. When we recount the calamities our country has endured since gaining its independence, our hearts ache when we briefly describe the unfortunate situation in the Congo, a victim of its own wealth.

In 1960, the imperialists, having seen the failure of all their colonial methods, were forced to grant us a theoretical independence that they intended to be political, not economic. The entire technical machinery of the conspiracy was mobilized to make P. E. Lumumba and all the Congolese people who were awaiting effective redemption fail. Denounced by Lumumba, the hero of our liberation, imperialism, through its Congolese lackeys, conspired against him to corner him to the fatal fate we now know. Today, in this hall, on behalf of the people we represent, we request the support of all those present here, in order to demand once again, before world opinion, that the UN provide the results of the investigation into the death of P. E. Lumumba and his companions and apply the punishment their murderers deserve.

For us, Congolese revolutionaries, the people's revolution had sounded its clarion call since the commission of that crime and had spread to its collaborators and followers during the period between Lumumba's death and the outbreak of the armed struggle.

To illustrate to you the true reason for the Congo's suffering and the determination of the American and Western imperialist vultures to rob the Congo of its freedom, we give you a brief picture of the extent of the penetration and massive exploitation of the international trusts in our country:

Economic data

Geologists, regarding our country, say it's a true "geological scandal." Not only because of the mineral resources, which are not exclusive to Katanga Province, but also because other riches abound in our country and have so far been exploited only for the benefit of imperialist tycoons.

A. Agricultural resources:
1-a) Food crops: cassava, corn, sorghum, rice, bananas, potatoes, peas, soybeans, peanuts; the latter grain is exported annually at the rate of:
- 5,715 tons in 1945
- 5,080 in 1946–1949
- 5,442 in 1950

2) Tree extracts:
a) Rubber: whose exploitation has made us suffer the most incredible exactions of forced labor accompanied by the whip, made of hippopotamus skin: Villages were mobilized to support the Allied war effort during 1939–1945 by supplying them with rubber and we have:
- 97 tons exported in 1941
- 322 tons exported in 1942
- 7,000 tons exported in 1943
- 11,250 tons exported in 1944

Since 1949, the United States and Belgium have accounted for all of our country's rubber production.

b) Copal: Our country is the largest producer of copal, a resin essential for the manufacture of lacquers and oily varnishes, with multiple industrial and military applications.

In 1950, the Congo exported:
- 6,392 tons of copal to the United Kingdom
- 3,709 tons of copal to Belgium
- 3,094 tons of copal to the United States

c) Wood: In inhumane conditions, our people, through forced labor, have been forced to contribute to supplying the imperialist powers with the woods essential for the construction of tools and hydraulic works: mahogany, ebony, limba, kambala, iroko, etc.

In 1950–1951, timber exports reached 135,651 tons to:
- Belgium
- The United Kingdom
- South Africa, from Malan to Verwoerd
- USA

d) Tropical Products:
- Sugar cane: which feeds the refineries of Belgium
- Pepper: 32,750 kg exported in 1950
- Quinoa
- Perfume plants (geranium, eucalyptus, etc.)

141 tons exported in 1950 to:
- Belgium, France, United States
- Insecticides
- Cocoa, coffee, tea, tobacco, kapok, jute, sisal, linen, cotton, raffia, henequen
- Oilseeds: sesame, copra, castor, areca
- Animal resources, mainly ivory

All these riches, produced in abundance, are plundered, as statistics show, for the benefit of the following countries: Belgium, France, West Germany, South Africa of the racists of Verwoerd, the United Kingdom, and above all the United States.

We find ourselves here, the ringleader and the acolytes of imperialism, who plot [missing line].

Currently, new machinations are being carried out to falsify the orientations of liberation struggles in order to deprive them of their revolutionary content.

The imperialists themselves recognize that the Congo's mineral wealth is extraordinary.

B. Mineral resources:
- Gold: the most important exploitation is carried out by Forminère
- Diamond: exploited by the Diamond Trading Company trust of London
- Tin: Congo is the fourth largest producer of this mineral after Malaysia, Bolivia, and Indonesia
- Uranium: 100 tons shipped to New York during the war to manufacture the deadly device dropped by US imperialism on Hiroshima
- Cobalt: 8,240 tons in 1960, world's leading producer

This very limited list does not mention rare and precious metals such as vanadium, tungsten, germanium, actinium, titanium, and beryllium.

Ours is a country of immense wealth exploited by imperialist monopolies that neocolonialist maneuvers seek to keep under the yoke of exploitation.

The beneficiaries of their wealth are joining forces to preserve their privileges and limit the scope of the changes demanded by the national liberation movement.

How could it be otherwise, as long as we know that the beneficiaries of the systematic plundering of our countries consider the status quo, or at least the limited or falsified scope of changes, necessary for the maintenance of colonial exploitation?

C. Beneficiaries of colonialist oppression:
The entire history of our country revolves around an acronym loaded with international financial resonance: the UMHK (Upper Katanga Mining Union).

It's a true empire within an empire. The Union Mineraçāo's concessions cover 34,000 km², an area larger than the whole of Belgium.

The mining union is the acolyte of the financial corporations that control mineral wealth, the media outlets of all of sub-Saharan Africa, a bastion of racism and monopoly capitalism. These are the charlatans with whom the Mining Union organizes a dance of millions to the detriment of the African people:
- [Taganyika] Concessions Limited
- British South Africa Company
- [De] Beers Consolidated Mines
- Rhodesian Anglo American
- Thokana Corporation
- [Chibuluma] Mines
- Roan Antelope Copper Mines
- Rhodesian Selection Trust
- American Metal Climax Incorporated
- Société Générale de Belgique

- Myfulima [Mufulira] Copper Mines

Once again, the structure of this consortium of beneficiaries of the plundering of our wealth reinforces our conviction that the United States of America is truly the main enemy of our people.

The United States of America has assumed an overwhelming responsibility for the process of disorganization and degradation of our country. After the tragic events in Katanga, perhaps they have not established a "delightful" American Committee to Aid the Combatants of Katanga, which includes figures such as Richard Nixon, Barry Goldwater, and the usual fauna of Moral Re-Armament and [the] John Birch Society.

It is with the financial complicity of the United States that the so-called "horrible" mercenary murderers were recruited. It is also with the blatant complicity of the United States that UN forces have carried out repressive operations against patriotic combatants. US diplomatic personnel in the Congo accompany the repressive forces before everyone's eyes.

It is certainly not because they feel an exceptional love for the Blacks of the Congo that the United States, a bastion of racism, supplies the Léopoldville puppets and the criminal UN operations with dollars and weapons.

The imperialists cling to their exorbitant privileges and are determined to prevent the necessary historical changes by all means. These privileges are enormous. As an example, according to the Central Bank's estimates, here are the profits of the Miners' Union:

Actual subscribed capital	$6,000,000
Frozen revaluation (4/12/1947)	$24,000,000
Premiums on the issuance of shares (10/12/46)	$12,000,000
Miscellaneous	$60,000,000
CAPITAL	$102,000,000

Which gives for the 1959 fiscal year, as a result of the exploitation, close to $88,000,000, that is, more than 60 percent of the capital.

At the height of the Congolese crisis, the UMHK issued victory statements announcing increased production. Amidst the euphoria and capitalist prosperity, our people have seen their poverty worsen, a situation that unites them with all Afro-Asian and Latin American countries. This unfortunate situation in our country has seriously affected all aspects of our life.

For example:

In 1958, there were 151 students in the Congo, most of whom were dedicated to the study of theology.

In 1960 we had only one native doctor.

According to 1957 statistics, there was one (nonnative) doctor for every 21,000 inhabitants in the Congo, compared to one for every 800 in Belgium.

In 1957 the mortality rate:

in Belgium 1.195%

in Léopoldville 8.32%

in Elisabethville 6.06%

in the industrial stronghold of UMHK 7.5%

in a typical environment where intensive medical action is carried out 17.79%

A similar situation exists regarding working conditions. As F. Bézy writes, demonstrating the cynicism of colonialist practices: "While a worker costs less than a dollar a day, a shovel and a pickaxe are a luxury, and it costs less to hire additional workers than to better equip those already working to increase their productivity."

In other words, the sweat of workers costs capitalists less than fuel for machines. The results of these practices become more apparent when comparing the wages received by African workers with those of European rentiers.

African workers			Europeans	
Year	Number	Salaries Received	Number	Admitted Income
1954	1,240,000	$220 million	32,000	$202 million
1958	1,102,270	$280 million	29,689	$206 million

The average wage of an African worker compared to that of a European in 1958 was in the ratio of 1 to 33. This disproportion, far from diminishing, worsens where capitalism, in order to preserve its acquired privileges, deploys all the resources of international monopoly capitalism, a corollary of the neocolonialism we all face.

This eloquent picture needs no comment to give you an accurate idea of the politics in the Congo, and the reasoning behind our determination to liberate our country and place this immense arsenal of wealth at the service of universal peace.

Today, as this conference is being held, fierce fighting is underway in the Congo, pitting patriotic forces against the barbaric imperialist hordes of Congolese mercenaries and puppets. The patriotic forces occupy a large area, if not the entire provinces of Kivu and Stanleyville, except for the major cities. In the provinces of [Coquilhatville] and Kasai, we occupy large areas, always excluding the major cities.

In the province of Léopoldville, Brother Pierre Mulele, who was the first to unleash armed struggle, occupies positions with which the enemy avoids all contact.

The significant blows we have dealt to the enemy are carefully concealed from world public opinion. They do this for strategic reasons and to maintain the morale of their troops, out of shame at having to confess their defeat to the world. This will change nothing, and we will continue forward until the final decision. All we ask is your support.

The enemy uses ultramodern conventional weapons supported by combat aircraft, composed of various types: T.28, DC.3, C.47, C.130, C.124, H.34, and B.26. In addition to their material superiority, they have a highly qualified force, including Rhodesian barbarians, South African Cuban counterrevolutionaries, the sinister OSA professionals, Israelis, and Belgian army personnel. We provide, as examples, the names of some of the leaders of these latter groups, who operate under the leadership of Mobutu's Congolese puppet army. The Colonels:

- Marlière: Mobutu's advisor
- Cook: Commander at Kamina Air Base. Commands the Belgian tactical airbase at Kamina
- Logiest: Head of the Belgian military technical assistance mission in the Congo.
- Lamouline: Fourth cyclist—one of the LIMA commanders—Second in the Fifth Mechanized Brigade
- Grailly: Second cyclist—one of the logistics team commanders in the Fifth Mechanized Brigade
- Bouzin: Air Force
- Mommart: Air and naval military attaché at the Belgian Embassy in the Congo
- F. [Vandewalle]: Former administrator of the *sûreté* in the Congo, manager of the consulate and then consul of Belgium in Elizabethville in 1961 and 1962, during the secession Katangese. Commander-in-chief of the operation called "Ommegang" of reconquest, by the Fifth Mechanized Brigade, of the territories that escaped the control of the Léopoldville government
- Liégeois: Fifth Ardennes Chasseurs—commander of the column known as "LIMA 1." Fifth Mechanized Brigade. Battles of Kabalo and Stanleyville
- De Coster: ANC column assistant—has operated in Bukavu, Uvira, and Bunia
- Lemercier: Added to the ANC columns operating on the left bank of the Watsa

In light of these reports, what material evidence can we provide of Belgium's direct involvement, alongside the United States of America, in the reconquest of the Congo?

For this reason, the Supreme Council of the Congolese Revolution considers it its duty to express its fraternal gratitude to the organizers of this conference for having associated it with the current work.

Until we are truly liberated from the chains imposed on us by the enemy, we will not consider ourselves a free people.

For us, those who do not exist cannot coexist with others who possess existence. On the day we are liberated, we will pose the problem of coexisting with all those who agree to exist in harmony with others.

We understand those who respect the fundamental rights of self-determination, the national sovereignty of others, and the territorial integrity of other states. We must declare that as long as imperialism tramples on the sacred principles of the right of the peoples of our three continents to freedom, prosperity, and happiness, we will remain hostile to them and act within the camp of those who fight for peace and equal rights for humanity in all areas.

Today, thanks to the Cuban people's revolution, we are here and speak as free men, regardless of the color of our skin. Therefore, we strongly condemn the imperialist blockade, exercised with the intention of cornering this friendly country into economic difficulties.

As far as we are concerned, we will be ready to provide our full support to cooperation with our oppressed brothers and sisters on the three continents to achieve this goal.

Imperialism executes monstrous conspiracy plans against the peoples of our continents, forming aggressive alliances, establishing military bases around the world, and proliferating weapons of mass destruction, despite universal protests. Wherever national liberation movements emerge, it proceeds to carry out barbaric repression against defenseless populations. This is how repression continues today in Latin America.

We affirm to all our Latin American brothers and sisters that the Congolese people stand by their side in the heroic struggle against the North American wolves. The day the Revolutionary Congo is able to do so, it will not hesitate to put every means at their disposal for the triumph of their cause.

The barbaric racist repression exercised by the United States against the Black people also does not escape the attention of our organization, which follows it with the greatest interest. The recent scenes of the massacre of Black people in Los Angeles have revealed to the world public the true form of American imperialism.

Our organization has strongly condemned the murders committed by Yankee forces against the Black population of the United States.

We are convinced that the organization that will emerge from this conference will allow us to muster the appropriate means to provide a solution to conclude our fight against the common enemy.

The enemy is intensifying its siege, not only against the world's progressive powers, but also against the liberation movements of our three continents. Thus, it is establishing its military bases in Third World countries to prevent the inevitable outbreak of liberation movements.

After having provoked a war of extermination among the tribes of Rwanda, he installed a neocolonialist regime in that country, subservient to his policy of domination. Four military bases equipped with the latest technical improvements are currently located:

- Ruhengeri
- B[u]gesera
- Byengwe [Bolenge]
- Kabira (Mutara)

Kamemba [Kamina] airbases made available to American aircraft operating against Congolese patriots. The [Kanombe] airbase (Kigali) has carried out the bombing of the provinces of North Kivu and Stanleyville.

The neocolonial regime of Rwanda has soaked the soil of that country in the blood of the victims of ferocious imperialist repression. The most infamous genocide that stirs human conscience, deportations, and the execution of Rwandan nationalist parliamentarians: These are the beneficial results of American civilization in Rwanda. And as a mockery of reason and human common sense, imperialism calls this protecting freedom in Africa.

We will maintain and support the heroic struggle of the Rwandan people against the aggression and barbaric neocolonial oppression established in that country.

The National Liberation Council supports the brotherly people of Angola in their heroic struggle against Portuguese colonialism. The brothers of the Popular Movement for the Liberation of Angola can count on our full moral support.

We are aware of the countless difficulties the Léopoldville puppet government is inflicting on our brothers and sisters in this liberation movement. But we are convinced of its ultimate victory.

We support the struggle of our brothers and sisters in Portuguese Guinea and Mozambique against the degrading colonialism in which they are still held.

We condemn the British colonialist policy in Rhodesia, which consists of eternally keeping the brotherly people of Zimbabwe under barbaric racist oppression, with Ian Smith as its enforcer.

We are convinced that the brotherly people of Zimbabwe will rise up as one to prevent this new form of slavery in the twentieth century.

And in that you can count on our full support.

We support the heroic struggle of the Venezuelan people against neocolonialism. We are certain that the blood of martyrs, such as Commanders Ponte Rodriguez and Argimiro Gabaldón, will not have been shed in vain and that, without a doubt, the final victory will belong to them.

Our people have followed the struggle of the people of the Dominican Republic with great interest. The US aggression against that territory in April 1965 eloquently illustrates the criminal designs of US imperialism, which has assumed the role of international policeman.

We hope to soon see the People's Republic of China take its seat at the UN, alongside all those who defend the rights, freedom, and justice of nations around the world. Representatives of Formosa island should simply be expelled from this international assembly, where their presence encourages neocolonialism in Asia. Formosa is the bastion of international imperialism in Asia, as Israel is in the Arab nation.

We hope that by the end of this conference, a solution will have been found to the problem of coordination among the liberation movements of the three continents, in order to unify our resources and experience, in order to reach a rapid conclusion to our struggle against the common enemy.

Our greatest wish is to be able, upon our return, to convey this decision as a greeting to our combatants and all our compatriots.

Mr. President;

Excellencies;

Dear Fellow Delegates:

We apologize for perhaps abusing your patience and precious time with our lengthy intervention, and we sincerely appreciate your kind attention.

Ibrahim Abu Sitta

Member of the Executive Committee of the Palestine Liberation Organization

Mr. President;

Combatant brothers:

It is a source of great pleasure for me to address the First Conference of the Peoples of Africa, Asia, and Latin America on behalf of the Palestine Liberation Organization, a symbol of the struggle of the Palestinian Arab people against the Zionist aggression against their homeland and their rights.

We feel that this great meeting at the present conference is proof of our peoples' full understanding of a primordial truth: the indivisible unity of our struggle. We all aspire to a common goal: to achieve freedom and peace based on justice for all the peoples of the world. It is a single struggle. We all face a common enemy: Western imperialism, led by the United States. I can also say that it is a single and indivisible struggle because we have the same means and methods of action: armed struggle.

Another source of great satisfaction is being here in Cuba, symbolized by the hero and courageous leader, Dr. Fidel Castro, the example we must follow in our struggle, both in its aims and its means. The victorious Cuban Revolution is living proof that the constant and stubborn struggle against colonialism leads to no other path but victory. Our meeting here in Cuba, a few dozen kilometers from our common enemy, means that we have the strength to challenge our enemy in his own home.

At this conference, the Palestine Liberation Organization appreciates having had the privilege of sharing the ideas of other delegations and taking part in their problems. We are proud to be able to benefit, at this conference, from the experiences of the glorious people of South Vietnam, who are fighting against

American aggression with dazzling heroism that earned the admiration of our people and the appreciation of the peoples of the entire world.

We would also like to express our support and deep admiration for all the combatants in Angola, Mozambique, Rhodesia, as well as those in Colombia, Peru, and Venezuela.

In saluting the peoples who achieved victory in their struggle for freedom, independence, and progress, we believe it is our duty to enlighten you about our own experience.

What happened in Palestine in 1948 is identical to what happened in Southern Rhodesia in 1965. A minority of intruders subjugated the majority of the country's legitimate inhabitants, with the difference that what happened in Palestine was more brutal, fanatical, and unjust. The Arab people of Palestine were forcibly expelled, leaving behind their cities, towns, and farms. All this was possible thanks to the actions of imperialism and its lackey, Israel.

Our people's experience with US imperialism has special characteristics that highlight the brutality of imperialism and its perfidy. We do not confront imperialism face to face, but behind the mask of Zionism and the Israel it created to serve its aims. The intimate relationship between Israel and imperialism was not always clear in the minds of the people of the world. For its part, US imperialism concealed this truth in order to more effectively utilize Israel in Asia, Africa, and Latin America. We believe it is our duty to emphasize this point and expose the connection between Israel and US imperialism. Western colonialism created Israel to serve as a base from which to stifle liberation movements in the Arab nation and maintain its monopoly on oil resources in the region. Israel soon became a base for American colonialism, not only against the liberating forces of the Arab world, but also against revolutionary forces in Asia, Africa, and Latin America. In reality, Israel can be considered a military, economic, and cultural base for Western colonialists.

As a strategic base, Israel was used in 1948 to expel the Palestinian people from their homeland; in 1956, against the glorious Egyptian revolution; and to protect imperialist interests in the Suez Canal during the blatant tripartite aggression. In 1963, Israel served to crush the revolutionary forces of the Congo and to back imperialism's number one agent in Africa, Moise Tshombe. In 1964, Israel sent weapons to the reactionary government of Portugal, for use against the revolutionary movements in Angola and Mozambique. Today, Israel sends shipments of medicines and equipment as gifts to the American imperialist forces in South Vietnam. It also leases its entire fleet to the United States government to transport military equipment to South Vietnam; and Israel, in its entirety, has now become an arsenal installed in the Middle East to combat liberation movements in Asia and Africa.

Israel is also an economic base for Western imperialism. The Israeli economy has become the center of global monopolies. Exploitative global imperialism, no longer able to direct its monopolies directly to Asia and Africa, found in Israel the ideal instrument for its economic infiltration into these continents. Today, most of Israel's financial institutions, businesses, and institutions are closely linked to similar North American institutions. The examples are numerous and it is pointless to list them here.

To defend the interests of these monopolies, the United States government showed particular interest in strengthening and consolidating Israel and defending its economy. In 1962, loans and grants offered by the US government to Israel reached $1.5 billion, in addition to $500 million from the sale of securities in Israel that year, in the United States.

On the other hand, Israel was able to raise more than $1 billion through the Jewish fundraising agency. To facilitate this operation, the United States allowed these donations to be deducted from income taxes.

As the ideological basis of imperialism, Israel is attempting to infiltrate countries in Asia, Africa, and Latin America, advocating imperialist ideas and plans. To this end, it has founded two institutes, one for Asia and Africa, and one for Latin America. The first, the Afro-Asian Institute for Labor Affairs and Cooperative Studies, has as its vice president George Meany, president of the American Federation of Labor and Congress of Industrial Organizations. The board of directors of this institute is made up of leaders of the American labor movement, and the American Federation of Labor pays more than 50 percent of the institute's budget. The second is called the Israeli Information Center in Latin America; the United States disseminates its ideas and propaganda in Latin America through its main offices in Jerusalem and Argentina.

It is clear, then, that Israel constitutes one of the most dangerous and damaging forms of imperialism and neocolonialism.

In this way, the Israeli threat is not directed only toward the Arabs of Palestine, its immediate victims, nor toward the Arab nation as a whole but also toward the continents of Asia, Africa, and even Latin America. This threat poses a grave danger to all military, economic, and cultural spheres, and therefore our conference must take appropriate measures to counter it.

We aspire and strongly demand that Israel be condemned and that all nations and progressive forces in the world sever all political, economic, and cultural ties with this "state."

Every progressive ideology is radically opposed to racism, neofascism, and "chauvinism," as well as to exploitation and aggression, concepts that constitute the basis of the Zionist movement and what is called the "state" of Israel.

The Palestine Liberation Organization is convinced that solidarity among the peoples of the three continents cannot be limited to words. This solidarity cannot be effective or positive unless the means are provided to turn these words into actions.

Our solidarity must be one of action, because every victory achieved against the forces of imperialism and colonialism anywhere in the world is, at the same time, our own victory. Likewise, our triumph against international Zionism, personified in Israel, is the triumph of all revolutionary and progressive forces around the world.

Wu Xueqian

Director General of the International Liaison Department of the
Central Committee of the Communist Party of China

The Chinese delegation hails the convocation of the Afro-Asian Latin American Peoples' Solidarity Conference. We wish to extend our cordial greetings to the anti-imperialist fighters from the three continents and to thank our Cuban friends, the hosts of this conference, for their hospitality.

Together with the Cuban people, we celebrated the seventh anniversary of the victory of the Cuban revolution. The Cuban revolution and the revolutionary spirit manifested in the two Havana Declarations have given encouragement to the Latin American peoples in their struggle for liberation. The Chinese people consistently support the Cuban people in their just struggle against US imperialism and for the defense of their motherland and their revolutionary accomplishments.

Our conference is being held at a time when a struggle, the intensity of which is unparalleled in history, is going on between the peoples of Asia, Africa, and Latin America on the one hand, and imperialism, colonialism, and neocolonialism headed by the United States on the other.

Ever since World War II, the national liberation movement in Asia, Africa, and Latin America have scored great victories. In all three continents, the political consciousness of the people has been unprecedentedly heightened, and the revolutionary movement has gathered increasing momentum. Throughout the world, the soaring flames of the national liberation movement are spreading, the chains of imperialist colonial oppression are being broken, and imperialist domination is being shaken to its very foundation.

Faced with the revolutionary storm of the people of the three continents, imperialism, however, refuses to meet its doom. US imperialism is promoting neocolonialism at the same time as it is backing the old colonialists, thus playing the role of international gendarme in suppressing the national liberation movement. The United States is doing its utmost to place Asia, Africa, and Latin America completely under the domination of the Dollar Empire.

The United States has established thousands of military bases and stationed almost a million troops in Asia, Africa, and Latin America. It carries on subversion and unleashes war of aggression everywhere.

US imperialism forces Latin American countries to conclude unequal treaties with it and has set up an Inter-American Peace Force designed to put down revolution. In the past twenty years, the US Central Intelligence Agency has engineered forty-five counterrevolutionary coups in Latin America.

US imperialism has openly declared that it would resort to force to suppress "all unacceptable regimes" in the three continents. In the past twenty years, it has unleased over ten large-scale military operations and aggressive wars to suppress the national liberation movement.

The United States spent six billion US dollars and armed eight million Chiang Kai-Shek bandit troops to wage civil war against people in China. It is still occupying the Chinese territory of Taiwan.

Under the banner of the United Nations, the United States launched a sanguinary war of aggression in Korea.

It has backed the Philippine reactionaries in putting down the patriotic Hukbong Mapagpalaya ng Bayan (People's Liberation Army) by armed force.

It sent its troops to Laos and sparked off its war of aggression in Indochina.

The US Sixth Fleet landed its troops in Lebanon to suppress the national liberation movement in the Near and Middle East.

The United States twice sent its troops to the Congo (Léopoldville) to throttle her national independence, in this way thrusting the dagger of aggression into the heart of Africa.

It organized a mercenary army to overthrow the patriotic regime of Guatemala.

It openly directed the counterrevolutionary bandits in their armed invasion of Cuba at Playa Girón.

Under the cover of a so-called advisory group, US troops are taking a direct part in the suppression of the patriotic armed struggle in Venezuela.

US aggressor troops occupying the Panama Canal savagely massacred the Panamanian people when they started a patriotic uprising.

The United States went so far as to send more than forty thousand aggressor troops to suppress a patriotic armed uprising in the Dominican Republic, a country with a population of only three million.

At present, US imperialism is conducting an inhuman war of aggression in Vietnam. In order to carry out aggression against south Vietnam with its population of fourteen million, the United States has sent an expeditionary force of two hundred thousand men and employed all the latest types of weapons except for the atom bombs. The US air bandits are making round-the-clock air raids on North Vietnam.

The road US imperialism is following today is precisely the old road taken by Hitler. US imperialism is the mainstay of colonialism in our time. It is the most vicious and the chief enemy of the peoples of Asia, Africa, and Latin America.

US imperialist's frenzied armed suppression of the national liberation movement has taught the people of Asia, Africa, and Latin America to realize ever more clearly that the most effective weapon to defeat US imperialism and all reactionaries and to win liberation is to use revolutionary violence against counter-revolutionary violence and wage people's war of aggression [against] armed suppression by US imperialism and its lackeys. People's war has fully demonstrated its power in the national liberation struggles of China, Korea, Vietnam, Cuba, and other countries, and it is again demonstrating its power today in the struggle of the Vietnamese people against US aggression and for national salvation.

Relying on the high political consciousness of all combatants, their courage and spirit of sacrifice on the support of the broad masses of the people, the South Vietnamese people's armed forces have engaged the US aggressor troops in close-quarter fighting, night operations, and bayonet battles, wiping them out by whole battalions and regiments and shattering them to pieces. Fired by profound hatred against the enemy, the army and people in North Vietnam have also severely punished the invading US bandit airmen. The vaunted "US naval and air superiority" has broken down and its "peace talk" intrigues have also gone bankrupt one after another.

Why is it that the leading imperialist power of the world has been so badly beaten by the Vietnamese people? The answer is quite clear, this is determined by the nature of the war itself.

The Vietnamese people are fighting a patriotic and just war, a genuine people's war. The thirty million Vietnamese people rising up to fight the enemy, with resolve and indignation, constitute an irresistible force.

As to the US imperialists, they are fighting a hopeless war of aggression. They are fighting an unjust cause with virtually no support. They have fallen into the flames of the anti-US struggle of the Vietnamese people which they themselves kindled. They have thus revealed their true features as a paper tiger.

In order to save itself from defeat, US imperialism is sending more troops to South Vietnam and is preparing to expand the war to Laos, Cambodia, Thailand, and China as well. Of late, US imperialism has been actively putting up a smokescreen of "peace talks" and shamelessly creating news of peaceful negotiations. This is precisely a prelude to its new military adventures. Escalation, deception, failure, escalation again, deception again, failure again until complete defeat, this is the logical development and the inevitable sequel of the war of aggression against Vietnam by the US imperialists.

As a fraternal neighbor closely linked with the Vietnamese people like the lips and teeth, the 650 million Chinese people firmly support the Vietnamese people in their just struggle against US aggression and for national salvation and firmly support the four-point proposition of the Democratic Republic of Vietnam and the five-part statement of the National Front for the Liberation of South Vietnam. The Chinese people have long been prepared. Should US imperialism insist on going further along the road of war expansion and having another trial of strength with the Chinese people, the Chinese people will resolutely take up the challenge and fight to the end. Come what may, the Chinese people will unswervingly side with the fraternal Vietnamese people and contribute all our efforts to defeat of US imperialism until final victory.

The Vietnamese people have pinned down and wiped out a large number of US imperialist troops and upset US plans for aggression and war. The victories of the Vietnamese people have greatly inspired the fighting will of all oppressed peoples and slapped the imperialists' arrogance, and they constitute the greatest support for the national liberation in the countries of Asia, Africa, and Latin America and a great contribution to the cause of safeguarding world peace.

The struggle of the Vietnamese people is the focus of the anti-imperialist struggle of the peoples of the world today. Therefore, to support the Vietnamese people should be the most important task of our conference. We must firmly support the Vietnamese people in their struggle to defend the North, liberate the South, and reunify their motherland. The four-point proposition of the Democratic Republic of Vietnam and the five-part statement of the National Front for the Liberation of South Vietnam are the only solution to the Vietnam question, the most essential point of which is that the US aggressors must get out of Vietnam, lock, stock, and barrel.

The victories of people's war in Vietnam once again demonstrate that the decisive factor in war is man and not weapons of whatever type. It is the law of national liberation war that the newborn forces will overcome the old decaying forces, the weak overcome the strong, the oppressed nations fighting with rifles and hand-grenades will overcome the imperialists equipped with the most modern weapons.

US imperialism is everywhere brandishing missiles and nuclear weapons to frighten the people. Nuclear weapons may appear terrifying, but actually they are not so formidable. The spiritual atom bomb of the oppressed peoples is thousands of times more powerful than the material atom bomb of US imperialism. Should US imperialism dare to use nuclear weapons, it can in no way conquer the fighting people and will inevitably find itself utterly isolated and accelerate its own destruction.

Recently the famous British philosopher Bertrand Russell has also pointed out: "When the people of Peru, Guatemala, Colombia, Vietnam, Thailand, the Congo, Venezuela, Cameroon, the United States, Britain, all the people, demonstrate and struggle and resist, nuclear power is of no avail. It will destroy its user."

The people of Asia, Africa, and Latin America are aware that war will cause suffering, sacrifices, and devastation to the people. But the far greater suffering, sacrifices, and devastation will befall on the people if they submit to imperialist enslavement and subjugation and do not resist the armed aggression and suppression of imperialism and its lackeys by people's war. As the Havana Declaration says: "Revolutionaries cannot sit in the doorways of their homes to watch the corpses of imperialism pass by . . . Each year by which America's liberation army may be hastened will mean millions of children rescued from death, millions of minds freed for learning, infinitudes of sorrow spared the peoples."

At present, people's wars are being waged in more than twenty countries in Asia, Africa, and Latin America, against imperialism headed by [the] USA and its lackeys.

Every one of these battlefronts represents a rope tied around the neck of US imperialism. This armed-to-the-teeth monster is now being surrounded ring upon ring by the oppressed peoples.

The "global strategy" of US imperialism has made itself the enemy of the people of the whole world. Its battlefronts are so extended, its rear so remote, and its armed forces so scattered that it finds itself in an inextricable predicament. Its position is so bad that it is being beaten everywhere, and total defeat is awaiting it.

At present, a broad mass movement on an unprecedented scale against the US policy of aggression in Vietnam is unfolding in the United States itself. Demonstrators from more than one hundred cities converged in a torrent of wrath on Washington. The ruling circles of the United States, which have always used the banners of the "defense of freedom and democracy" to deceive the American people are no longer able to do so. The awakening American people are directing their struggle against the Johnson administration's policy of aggression abroad and closely linking it with the struggle against oppression, exploitation, and racial discrimination by monopoly capital at home. This is a great event of historic significance for the American people's movement. It can be said with certainty that with every escalation the US government makes in its war of aggression, the revolutionary struggle of the American people will advance a big step forward. The great American people will finally be the real masters of the United States of America.

US imperialism is beset with tremendous difficulties both at home and abroad and is facing an imminent and deep crisis in all spheres. Under these circumstances, the people of Asia, Africa, and Latin America must strengthen their struggle and give US imperialism no breathing spell. Like all forces of reaction, US imperialism will not fall unless it is felled. It is therefore necessary for us to start still more powerful movements, wage people's war on a still greater scale, tighten the rope around the neck of US imperialism, and bring about its final defeat.

We, the Chinese people, determinedly stand side by side with anti-imperialist fighters of Asia, Africa, and Latin America, and together we shall overcome all obstacles and fight for final victory.

The Chinese people pay respects to their comrades-in-arms from the Latin America. We resolutely support the peoples of the Dominican Republic, Venezuela, Peru, Colombia, Guatemala, and other countries in their armed struggle against US imperialism and its lackeys; resolutely support the peoples of Puerto Rico, Guianas, Martinique, and Guadalupe in their struggle for national independence; and resolutely support all the peoples of Latin America in their mass movements for national liberation and democracy and freedom.

The Chinese people pay respects to the anti-imperialist fighters from Africa. We resolutely support the Zimbabwe people in their struggle against the reactionary white racist regime of Ian Smith and for national independence; resolutely support the people of the Congo (Léopoldville) in their patriotic armed struggle; resolutely support the peoples of the so-called Portuguese Guinea, Mozambique, and Angola in their armed struggles against the Portuguese colonialists; resolutely support the people of South Africa and South West Africa in their just struggle [against] racial discrimination and oppression and for national liberation; and resolutely support the peoples of Basutoland, Swaziland, Bechuanaland, French Somaliland, and all other African peoples still under colonial rule in their struggle for national independence.

The Chinese people pay respects to the Arab people. We resolutely support the Arab people in their just struggle against Israel, tool of US imperialism, and for the restoration of the legitimate rights of the Palestinian people.

The Chinese people pay respects to their brothers from Asia. We resolutely support the Laotian people in their just and patriotic struggle against US intervention and aggression, resolutely support the Cambodian people in their just struggle against US imperialist armed provocations and aggression, in defense of national sovereignty and independence. We resolutely support the Indonesian people in their just struggle against imperialism, colonialism, and neocolonialism, against the persecution of democratic and progressive forces by the right-wing forces, and for the defense of independence and democracy. We resolutely support the people of Thailand in their just struggle against US imperialism and its lackeys and resolutely support the peoples of North Kalimantan, Malaya, and Singapore in their struggle against imperialism and its running dogs.

In particular, we pay respect to our close neighbors, the Korean brothers and the Japanese brothers. The Japan–South Korea Treaty, which has been single-handedly created by US imperialism, is a grave step toward a new war of aggression in Asia. The Chinese people resolutely support the peoples of Korea and Japan in their struggle against the Japan–South Korea Treaty, resolutely support the Korean people in their just struggle for the reunification of their fatherland, and resolutely support the Japanese people in their great struggle against US control and occupation of Japan and the revival of Japanese militarism.

Who are our enemies and who are friends? This question is of crucial importance to the national liberation movement. We have consistently advocated that the people of Asia, Africa, and Latin America unite and form the broadest possible united front with the people of the socialist countries and all the peoples subjected to US imperialist aggression, control, interference, and bullying, including the American people itself, to fight against imperialism headed by the United States.

Chairman Mao Tse-Tung has said: "In waging struggle against imperialism, victory can be achieved by taking the correct line, relying on the workers and peasants, uniting with the broad masses of revolutionary intellectuals, the petty bourgeoise and the national bourgeoise who oppose imperialism, as well as all the patriotic anti-imperialist forces, and maintaining close links with the masses."

At a time when the people's struggle against imperialism aggression is very acute, it is necessary for us to unite with all the genuine anti-imperialist forces to oppose imperialism, colonialism, and neocolonialism headed by the United States. There are some people who maintain that they stand for "united action" to wage a "common struggle against the enemy." But their actual deeds cannot but oblige us to raise the following questions: With whom do they really take united action? And unity against whom?

Why do they regard US imperialism, the mortal enemy of the people of our three continents, as their principal ally, proclaiming that their policy of all-round cooperation with the United States will never change?

Why do they sabotage people's wars and why do they preach here and there that "a tiny spark can cause a world conflagration"?

Why did they collaborate with the United States and vote for the sending of a UN force to suppress the struggle of the people of the Congo (Léopoldville)?

Why did they collaborate with the United States in having the United Nations adopt a "ceasefire" resolution on the question of the Dominican Republic?

Why did they collaborate with the United States in defending the British imperialist policy of supporting and encouraging the reactionary white racist government of Ian Smith in Southern Rhodesia and warmly applaud Wilson in the United Nations?

Why did they collaborate with the United States in plotting for a permanent UN force to serve as a ready tool for the suppression of national liberation war?

Why do they serve US imperialism time and time again in its "peace talk" intrigues on the Vietnam question? Why did they sit together with the "representatives" of the Chiang Kai-Shek gang and the puppet cliques of South Korea and South Vietnam to discuss the establishment of the "Asia Development Bank" in order to implement Lyndon Johnson's plan for the so-called development of Southeast Asia, which is designed to coordinate with the US war of aggression in Vietnam?

Why do they vociferously clamor for "united actions" on the question of giving aid to Vietnam and at the same time utilize this question to make fabrications and calumnies against China?

Why do they assure US imperialism that all is quiet on the Western front, so that US troops can be shifted from West Germany to South Vietnam?

If they really oppose US imperialism in action, change their erroneous line of collaboration with the United States for world domination and cease and desist from the mistakes they make disrupting the national liberation movement and opposing socialist countries, we would, of course, unite and take united actions with them.

We hope that through democratic discussion and full consultation this conference will strengthen unity against imperialism and contribute to the common cause of the peoples of the three continents.

We propose that the conference adopt resolutions firmly supporting all the peoples of Asia, Africa, and Latin America in their just struggles for national liberation, democracy, and freedom, backing the American people's just struggle against the Johnson administration's aggression in Vietnam and standing by our American Negro brothers in their just struggle against racial discrimination and for democratic rights.

Friends, we are living in a great era in which the peoples of Asia, Africa, and Latin America fight for liberation and to be masters of their own countries. The people are fighting and advancing. Let us join hands, sweep away all the obstacles in our advance, and greet the advent of a new Asia, a new Africa, and a new Latin America without imperialism, without colonialism, and without neocolonialism!

People of the world, unite to defeat imperialism!

Khaled Mohieddin
(United Arab Republic)

Secretary of the Press Committee of the Arab Socialist Union

Brothers and Colleagues:

On behalf of the United Arab Republic delegation, I would like to convey our fraternal greetings and deep gratitude to the valiant people of Cuba, to their party and national committee, and to their great leader, Fidel Castro, for the hospitality we have enjoyed in their beautiful capital and for the precision they have displayed in organizing this historic conference. We are indeed grateful for the opportunity they have afforded us.

Our meeting here in the First Conference of Solidarity of the Peoples of Asia, Africa, and Latin America, is in itself a realization of a hope long cherished by us. We stand together, a mighty force against colonialism in all its forms and manifestations; a force working for the achievement and safeguarding of real national independence; for cultural, economic, and social reconstruction; for the realization of sufficiency, justice, and prosperity for our peoples; and for the establishment of peace throughout the world.

We are meeting at a time which is a turning point in the history of Afro-Asian Latin American peoples. National liberation movements and revolutionary development are surging ahead, against colonialism and neocolonialism for the consolidation of the structure of our societies and for safeguarding peace based on justice—which are essential objects of the struggle waged by our peoples.

Representatives of the revolutionary forces of liberation and of popular parties in Africa and Asia met for the first time in the history of our peoples eight years ago in Cairo. The Cairo Afro-Asian Solidarity Conference, held in January 1958, was the natural outcome of the historic Bandung Conference. The Bandung spirit and resolutions acquired a vast revolutionary and popular concept at the Cairo Conference, particularly after the great victory scored by the people of Egypt against the armed imperialist aggression. The solidarity of Afro-Asian peoples acquired a concrete and positive form that effectively contributed to the repelling of the imperialist aggression, and the upsurge of the Egyptian people, under the revolutionary leadership of Gamal Abdel Nasser. It was this upsurge which resulted in two major victories: the nationalization of the Suez Canal and the completion of a socialist structure. The triumph of the Egyptian revolution, supported from the very outset by Afro-Asian Solidarity over imperialist aggression, was one of the historic factors that contributed to the great liberation movement throughout the whole African continent.

In eight years of perpetual struggle, militant action, and close cooperation, the Afro-Asian countries have scored many victories. Their representatives at the Afro-Asian Peoples' Solidarity Organization have established obstacles in the way of imperialist forces, have consolidated bonds of fraternity forged in the struggle for common aims against a common enemy, the struggle emanating from a common heritage and similar historical circumstances.

It is these common aims and heritage that make it imperative for the peoples of the three continents to develop solidarity and close fraternal cooperation.

While the Afro-Asian Solidarity continued with its struggle against colonialism and neocolonialism, the peoples of Latin America were also carrying out a fight against all forms of colonialism, valiantly confronting tyrannic imperialism . . . the imperialism of the United States. The choice by valiant Cuba of the path of socialism was a clear proof that the people can impose their will and challenge the very existence of imperialism.

As you are all aware, comrades, neocolonialism has basically concentrated its influence on Latin America. This led to the necessity of tightening the blockade which our people have imposed on the imperialists and of unifying the efforts of the three continents in their common struggle against the common enemy.

If the Himalayas, the Indian Ocean, and the great Sahara could not stand in the way of solidarity among the peoples of two continents, how can the Atlantic Ocean bar the undauntable wave of international solidarity?

Here we are today in heroic Cuba crowning a full cycle of solidarity, fraternity, and common struggle and about to embark on a new phase which aims at crushing all aggressive imperialist forces.

Our aggressor is one and the same in Vietnam in Asia; the Congo, Zimbabwe, and the Portuguese colonies in Africa; and the Dominican Republic in Latin America, whose people are subjected to an armed aggression.

The solidarity of Afro-Asian Peoples has been able to weather all storms, and to forge successfully ahead—until it has now emerged as a historic reality of our times, as a force which is capable of development and expansion until it has now enveloped the new revolutionary forces of Latin America. This expansion will, no doubt, make it one of the most powerful movements in world history.

Dear brothers, we fully believe in the right of people to liberty, to independence, and their freedom to choose their system of government. We believe that they have to defend and safeguard this right with all the means at their disposal. We must accept the principle that the armed struggle is no more than a means of confronting armed aggression.

The spread of popular armed struggle as a reaction to the domination of imperialism and its puppet governments is the manifestation of the important change which has taken place in the balance of power, and at the same time a proof that all peoples fully realize that the era of imperialism is approaching its end.

This, however, is not to say that we should ignore other means of struggle against imperialism. There are in fact numerous ways and means which differ according to conditions, circumstances, and the balance of power. The important provision is that all these means should aim at enabling the people to assert their will and choose their way in full liberty.

We denounce the increasing tendency among the imperialists of resorting to force and, herewith, we affirm the determination of our peoples to counter this tendency by all means. We express our full support to the great liberation struggle of Vietnam. We support the armed struggle of the South Vietnamese people to achieve complete national independence, self-determination in full liberty and without any foreign interference, and the reunification of their homeland; we demand that aggressive air raids on the Democratic Republic of Vietnam be immediately stopped, and that the Geneva Agreement of 1954 be implemented to the letter. We uphold the demands of the National Liberation Front of South Vietnam, which we consider the sole and true representative of the South Vietnamese people, and we support the stand of the Democratic Republic of Vietnam in the solution of the Vietnamese issue. We demand the withdrawal of all foreign forces and the liquidation of all military bases from the soil of valiant South Vietnam. We consider the imperialist pretense of calling for negotiations while at the same time persisting in air raids and expanding the scope of war in South Vietnam but a vile imperialist maneuver. We strongly condemn the US aggression on North and South Vietnam and consider it a serious threat to all the achievements of the Afro-Asian Latin American peoples. We are fully confident that the victory of the South Vietnamese people against aggression would be a major achievement which would help all the liberation causes in the future and become an encouraging example to be followed.

We support the struggle of the Dominican people to safeguard their national independence and repel the North American aggression. We support the struggle led by Latin American peoples to liquidate all forms of traditional imperialism and neocolonialism by all means, including the armed struggle whenever this is necessary. We support the struggle of Colombia, Guatemala, Venezuela, and other peoples of Latin America who are waging a revolutionary fight against imperialism; we are convinced that this struggle will enrich the revolutionary experience in Africa and Asia in as much as the revolutionary experience in these two continents has enlightened the experience of Latin America.

The heroism of the Cuban people and their valiant resistance to North American imperialism, the most powerful in our times, although Cuba is at their doorsteps is a source of great admiration and an inspiration for all the peoples who find in it encouraging example, which makes them more determined to persist in the struggle and resistance to all forms of imperialist pressure.

We believe that the question of lifting the economic blockade enforced on Cuba should prominently figure in the topics to be dealt with during this conference. The heroic struggle of the peoples of Latin America against imperialist intervention and the economic exploitation of the US, and further against world monopolies, has the complete support of our people and of all Afro-Asian peoples. It is in fact very closely linked with the struggle of all peoples to eradicate colonialism in all its forms. We consider it a sacred duty that has to be carried out unflinchingly by our peoples.

We insist on the full implementation of the UN declaration on the granting of independence to the colonized regions and peoples. We uphold the right of peoples to choose their path to independence and for the attainment of their legitimate rights, in a manner keeping with the dictates of their special conditions and their history!

We believe in the effective role the UN can play: We believe in the importance of strengthening it and developing its organs, in the necessity of fighting imperialist intervention within the organization, and the enhancement of the role the revolutionary and popular forces could play in it. Only in this way can it develop into a strong front against aggression, for the safeguarding of peace, and for the defense of peoples' rights. In this connection, we demand that the People's Republic of China recovers its legitimate seat in the UN.

In face of the increasing tendency of the imperialist states to use brute force in the international domain, we should intensify our struggle against their military bases from which they launch aggression. Military bases still menace our region, in Aden, Libya, Saudi Arabia, and Cyprus.

We are continually struggling for the immediate liquidation of these bases, and especially Israel, which is used as a tool in the hands of neocolonialism to menace, not only the Arab world, but the Middle East and all Afro-Asian countries.

With the establishment of the Organization of African Unity, and the initiative taken by the African states in a number of problems, the struggle of the African peoples has acquired new dimensions. For the first time in history the idea of armed support for the national forces in their anti-imperialist struggle is conceived. The face of Africa is changing; its states are not satisfied with gaining independence themselves, but they are persistently struggling to wrench the independence of the rest of African territories even by the use of arms as a legitimate means of ensuring the rights of people.

The decisive and united stands taken by Africa demonstrates the real meaning of solidarity. Indeed, the significant stand regarding the case of Rhodesia illustrates to the world at large that Africa will not rest arms folded before any aggression.

Africa believes in peace based on justice . . . believes in the struggle to realize this justice. Its stand, vis-a-vis the revolutionaries of the Congo, Angola, and Rhodesia, is the best implementation of this principle. Africa is well aware that peaceful coexistence is also a means of realizing this justice, of ensuring the rights of people, and of liquidating all forms of imperialist influence.

The struggle of peoples against colonialism is closely linked with the cause of peace: It is, indeed, part of the struggle for peace. Consequently, the link between the revolutionary forces struggling against colonialism and the forces struggling for peace is both organic and essential for the safeguarding of a world where justice, peace, and prosperity prevail.

Peaceful coexistence does not mean surrendering to acts of aggression and usurpation. In this context, the stand against the white minority in Rhodesia which is attempting to usurp the land from its original owners who have lived there for thousands of years, is in itself part of the legitimate struggle and is necessary for establishment of peace and peaceful coexistence.

The first fundamental right of man is to be the sole master of his land, not to be challenged in this right by any power, however strong it may be.

In view of this, our people deem it necessary to adopt a decisive and effective stand against the white usurpers in Rhodesia. In the same way, our people and Arab brethren stand against the Zionist usurpers who through deception have sneaked, and with imperialist arms have succeeded, in usurping land from its original owners, cruelly expelling them from their homes.

Justice, friends, is indivisible, and the aggressive usurper who is dispersing the original people in Rhodesia is the same aggressor who has dispersed the original people of Palestine.

The silence of world public opinion in the face of the Palestine tragedy gave the aggressors the opportunity to repeat the crime in another place. Had the world conscience shown any reaction to the first aggression, there would have been no chance for its repetition.

We are the Africans closest to understanding the nature of the people's struggle in Southern Rhodesia. In essence, it is a repetition of the conspiracy of Israel. An alien minority backed by imperialism and by the forces of economic exploitation and racial discrimination claims rights in the homeland of another people. Protected by colonialism, it lays hands on the national wealth, seizes actual power to the extent of proclaiming an independence that is faked, unleashes a reign of terror against the people, and denies them all rights to a free and dignified existence on their own land.

Our stand in the face of the imperialist menace and racial discrimination is dictated by our experience in this region of the Afro-Asian world. If we condemn the illegitimate domination of a racial minority in Rhodesia and the deprivation of the African people of Zimbabwe from their own rights in their country, it is because we know from our own experience what this domination is like. Racial Zionist colonialism has usurped Arab Palestine and set up a bridgehead there, infringing on the rights of its people, dispersing them, and leaving more than a million refugees to destitution under the cruelest conditions in camps. Zionist colonialism in Palestine, similar to racial colonialism in Rhodesia, is organically tied up with imperialism and neocolonialism. It is up to all the peoples of Africa, Asia, and Latin America to counteract this danger, which menaces their independence and freedom. The struggle of the people of Palestine to recover their home is a legitimate one which deserves the total support of the peoples of the three continents as well as all peace- and justice-loving peoples in the world.

Colonialism in our region, using its puppet Israel to menace the liberties of the peoples in the Arab East and their progress, resorts to terrorism, repression, and war to consolidate colonialist invasion of the "occupied" South Yemen. The people of that area are waging a heroic armed struggle against British colonialism to recover their freedom, independence, and the right to determine their own destiny.

We support the struggle of the Arab people in the occupied South Yemen, and we call for its financial and military support, for the rejection of imperialist projects that seek to create a faked independence. We also support the struggle of the people of Oman and their right to rid themselves of the military bases in accordance with the UN resolutions.

We vehemently condemn the Zionist imperialist conspiracies in the south of Sudan.

We condemn the military bases from which imperialism launches its attacks against the occupied South Yemen and other Arab and Middle Eastern countries. These bases are used as a springboard for aggression against the rights and independence of the people of the whole area.

We demand the abrogation of all aggressive treaties; we denounce imperialist military bases wherever they are in our continents, and demand their liquidation in Asia, especially in Japan, South Korea, South Vietnam, and Southeast Asia; in Africa, where preparations are underway to transform the Mauritius and Seychelles islands into imperialist military bases; and in some regions of Latin America.

We support the right of the peoples in the three continents to territorial integration and their realization of their complete sovereignty. We support the right of the peoples of Korea and Vietnam to the reunification of their homelands.

We wholly back the African peoples battling against colonialism and waging valiant struggle to wrest their independence and freedom and to do away with racial discrimination. We support the Congo (Léopoldville) in its valiant struggle against the imperialist forces and world monopolies that plunder the resources of the country and resort to the most barbarous measures of repression and extermination, either through flagrant interference or under the cover of neocolonialism.

We support the struggle of Angola, Mozambique, so-called "Portuguese" Guinea against racial discrimination and the brutal Portuguese; the struggle of French Somaliland; the struggle of the people of South Africa and Zimbabwe against colonialism and the settler minority.

We support the resolutions of the African Summit Conference, the Arab Summit Conference, the First and Second Conferences of the Non-Aligned Movement, the UN Conference for Trade and Development in Geneva because we believe that they can play an important role in the general strategy of the anti-colonial struggle of peoples and for construction. The principal burden, however, lies on the liberated and struggling peoples who have to continue the struggle until the final defeat of colonialism, the eradication of all forms of exploitation, and the establishment of a society of dignity, justice, and prosperity.

Fellow Freedom Fighters:

Our attitude is clear and decisive:

- Unwavering faith in peace based on justice; unflinching struggle to liquidate colonialism and neocolonialism, military bases, economic monopolies that plunder the resources or the peoples; continuous action for peaceful coexistence, so that humanity would not live at the mercy of nuclear accumulation and dissemination, and as a preliminary step toward disarmament and consecration of this tremendous energy wasted in the military field to the service of progress and prosperity; unceasing efforts to alter conditions of foreign trade to guard against the majority of the peoples being exploited and robbed by the technically advanced minority as a result of the historical colonialist plunder.
- Condemnation of racial discrimination as another form of slavery in the modern times.
- Firm adherence to nonalignment, which in essence is the freedom to stand by one's principles and the positive undertaking to serve peace and freedom and the rejection of all considerations that may reflect any semblance of dependency or bias.

Furthermore, our people are ever ready to act, are actually acting in the international domain, on the basis of a positive movement which rejects isolation and self-preoccupation.

They believe that peace is indivisible, freedom is indivisible, prosperity is indivisible; that the human society is an integrated whole where the individual and the whole are in need of each other, on the basis of equality, mutual respect, common interests, and human fraternity.

Freedom Fighters:

We know that imperialism and colonialism can never voluntarily change their inherent aggressive nature and can never accept defeat. They resort to any tactics ranging from wily and deceptive maneuvers of penetration to flagrant and brutal actions of aggression. As long as imperialism and its collateral aspects of neocolonialism and reaction survive, our peoples will suffer exploitation, humiliation, misery, and stagnation. We know that we possess immeasurable riches and powers, unlimited capacities for creation and production. We are determined to eliminate forever this contradiction and no force in the world will hinder us from finally wresting our freedom and independence, from winning peace, and from coming into our own.

Our program of action becomes clear:
We must continue our struggle to do away with the last entrenched forces of imperialism and old colonialism by every means we can, including armed warfare if necessary. This struggle is not only the duty of our brother countries still enslaved by these forces; it is our own struggle in every part of the three continents.
We must carry on a vigilant and unremitting struggle against all neocolonialists' tactics and machinations. We must foil these attempts wherever they are made and specially in newly independent countries in Africa and Latin America.
We must exert all our creative efforts to safeguard our national independence against direct or indirect violation of our sovereign rights of free and unhampered self-determination.
We must foil all aggressive war policies of the imperialists and defend world peace established on justice, equality, and equal opportunity for all the peoples the world over.
We must wage a ruthless and determined struggle against all forms of racial discrimination, apartheid, and reducing any community to a second-rate status in any part of the world. We know that at the root of these discriminatory policies lies exploitation and domination.
We must put an end to the exploitation of man by man and we must establish national economies ensuring full and equal opportunities for all. We must further the common cooperation between the Afro-Asian Latin American countries and between them and other anti-imperialist and anticolonialist countries.

We must struggle for the liquidation of all foreign military bases in the three continents and we must act against the policies of military pacts so as to ensure lasting world peace.

We must continue the struggle for the ban on the use, production, tests, and stockpiling of nuclear weapons; for the complete destruction of all existing nuclear weapons; for the liquidation of all means of their production; and for disarmament.

We must extend fraternal and unreserved assistance to the liberation movements in Africa, Asia, and Latin America; organize, train, and provide with all forms of assistance liberation movements in our countries or in the brotherly countries of the three continents, and in particular armed struggle, anywhere the people find it necessary.

We must act with all means in our hands, which are unlimited—against the policies of economic isolation, blockade, or boycott imposed by the imperialist or colonialist powers against countries struggling for their liberation or striving to build their economies on the bases they find appropriate and in keeping with the aspirations of their peoples.

We must lay down broad policies of economic planification both in the internal, regional, or international spheres on the bases of equality and mutual interests. We must mobilize our resources, natural and human, for the economic development of our countries and genuine economic independence in the framework of close cooperation and mutual advantage amongst ourselves and with all anti-imperialist and anticolonialist countries, taking into consideration the principle of self-reliance.

We must effect appropriate agrarian reforms in our countries, in the form that fits the particular conditions of each country and within the framework of the abovementioned economic development and cooperation.

We must work for the speedy formation of national cadres in every field of activity and production.

We must promote solidarity throughout the three continents in all spheres of creative activities between economic, scientific, social, educational, artistic, and cultural organizations and professional groups. We must enhance common action among trade unions, youth, and women's movements, between jurists, writers, and artists movements.

Inspired by our similar conditions and common heritage, we must continue to revive and build up our great cultural foundation and contribute to the progress of the whole of mankind through our rich potentialities of civilization.

Fellow Brothers in the Struggle:

The struggle of our peoples to liquidate the vestiges of colonialism and to give independence its genuine significance meets strong resistance from colonialism and its world monopolies. The realization of the ultimate content of independence implies more nutrition, housing, education, and insuring economic and social rights for the peoples. Here appears the counteraction of the world monopolies to this genuine progress for the profits that they reap from our territories are thus endangered, and therefore they continually seek to obstruct this progress by various means.

The elimination of their influence is necessary for our progress. Our United Arab Republic has a tremendous experience in this direction. The attempt to obstruct the construction of the High Dam by the withdrawal of the International Bank was met with the nationalization of the major imperialist concern, the Suez Canal Company. Following the 1956 tripartite aggression, we eliminated all imperialist pockets in our economy, and it became all ours. This enabled us later, in 1961, to proceed to actual transition toward socialism. Our people, with their own efforts and the assistance of friendly states have succeeded in realizing the first five-year plan: an annual 7.5 percent increase in our national income, a very high increase for any developing country. Perhaps the experience of the High Dam in Aswan is the best evidence to this. Nevertheless, the domination of the world monopolies still obstructs our efforts to develop our own economy in the same way as it does with all newly independent states in the three continents. Action for the establishment of equitable and just economic relations, particularly in the field of raw materials and the products of the developing states, [and] the eradication of monopolistic hold over the destinies of the people [are aims] which should receive great attention from us, and which should become an integral part of our political program in the three continents.

Dear Brothers;

Dear Freedom Fighters:

Our peoples expect from us positive action in both stages: the stage of achieving our genuine and complete freedom, and the stage of achieving cooperation, development, reconstruction, peace, and brotherhood in our future.

We assert our firm determination to rise up to the expectations of our peoples.

We assert our firm determination to carry out these tasks, to persist in our struggle until we triumph over imperialism and colonialism in all their forms; to achieve, consolidate, and safeguard complete national independence and liberation in all fields; to promote and expand the Afro-Asian Latin American Solidarity Movement; to realize and safeguard world peace; and build up a future world where justice, prosperity, and peace prevail.

President Gamal Abdel Nasser has invited the Second Afro-Asian Latin American Peoples' Solidarity Conference to convene in Cairo at the beginning of 1968 in commemoration of the tenth anniversary of the First Afro-Asian Peoples' Solidarity Conference held in Cairo in 1958.

We express here the enthusiastic support of the people of the United Arab Republic to this proposal and we hope that we will meet in the capital of our country.

Long live the solidarity of the peoples of Africa, Asia, and Latin America!

Norman Pietri (Puerto Rico)

Pro-Independence Movement

Comrade President, Comrade Delegates:

The Puerto Rican delegation, composed of the representatives of the pro-independence movement, expresses fraternal thanks on behalf of our people for the invitation to participate actively in this conference of authentic revolutionary and anti-imperialist content. We are also grateful for the hospitality of the Cuban government and people, who so faithfully interpret the spirit of the very necessary international solidarity among peoples. We, supporters of Puerto Rican independence, reciprocate to the Cuban people by remaining loyal to the founders of the joint struggle of Cuba and Puerto Rico for their independence.

The occupation of Puerto Rico signified at that time, as it does today, that an entire Latin American nation had come to be governed directly from the capital of an empire which subjected a nation of three million inhabitants to colonial servitude and, at the same time, exposed the rest of the Latin American peoples to the constant threat of direct imperialist military aggression from Latin American lands. Therefore, in Latin America, Puerto Rico is what Southern Rhodesia and South Africa are on the African continent and Taiwan (Formosa) is in Asia.

As a matter of fact, 14 percent of the national territory of Puerto Rico is occupied by nine immense US military bases designed to strengthen Yankee domination in Puerto Rico, as well as to serve for attacks against Cuba and the peoples who may rise up in arms against imperialism. Imperialism has everything in those gigantic bases—long-range guided missiles, superbombers loaded with atomic bombs, nuclear submarines at the Roosevelt Roads base, and special antiguerrilla troops. From this stems the imperative need to win national independence in order to promote conditions conducive to the total eradication of Yankee military installations in Puerto Rico and the threat they represent to the rest of the Latin American continent.

Puerto Rico, up in arms, has proclaimed its independence on two occasions, the last of which was fifteen years ago. In 1950, the revolution was drowned in blood when there was unleashed an imperialist repression that still imprisons in the United States and Puerto Rico a good number of patriots, many of whom are sentenced to life imprisonment. Dr. Pedro Albizu Campos, the chief leader of independence, fell victim to the repression, dying in San Juan, Puerto Rico, some months ago after suffering twenty-five years of imprisonment. The delegation of the pro-independence movement requests solidarity with our struggle to obtain the release of Puerto Rican political prisoners.

Comrade delegates, according to the laws imposed by the US Congress on our people, we Puerto Ricans are legally Yankee citizens. Like North Americans, we are prohibited by law from traveling to Cuba and other socialist countries under pain of five years' imprisonment in the United States. This is an attempt to isolate the Puerto Rican liberation movement from the rest of the world, particularly from the revolutionary example of Cuba. Also, by colonial order, tens of thousands of Puerto Ricans are obliged to serve in the Yankee armed forces and to participate in the imperialist aggressions against Korea, Panama, and now the Dominican Republic and Vietnam.

The Puerto Rican pro-independence movement resolutely supports the Vietnamese people in their struggle against Yankee aggression. In repudiating the Yankee aggression, we place all the blame on the US government for the consequences of applying to Puerto Rico the Yankee compulsory military service law, which sentences Puerto Rican youths to wage a dirty war in Vietnam, to invade the Dominican Republic or any other fraternal nation, or to serve prison sentences if they refuse to participate in such inhuman actions.

One thousand Puerto Ricans are recruited every month by the US armed forces. It is noteworthy that although the population of Puerto Rico is 1 percent of the US population, more than 3.5 percent of the youths called to the ranks by the Johnson government are Puerto Ricans, which means imposing on the Puerto Rican people a tribute of blood 3.5 times greater than that required of the US people themselves. The Puerto Rican pro-independence movement is currently engaged in an intense mass campaign against military service, exhorting Puerto Rican youths to resist the Yankee pretension of having Puerto Ricans and Vietnamese fighting in opposing camps.

Puerto Rico is a country superexploited by imperialism, or as is said euphemistically, underdeveloped. Imperialism obtains cheap labor in our country and enjoys an internal market monopoly, with miserable living conditions, a high unemployment rate, and so forth prevails. One million Puerto Ricans, one-third of our population, have been forced to leave our country in the largest exodus in the history of the American continent, emigrating to the United States where they are victims of discrimination and exploitation as are the US Negro people, whose struggle for equality has the firm and resolute support of the Puerto Rican people. In addition to all this, 80 percent of capital investments in Puerto Rico are made and directly controlled by Yankee monopolists.

The Puerto Rican worker, who lives under the inflationary framework of the US economy, earns one-third as much as the US worker. However, the cost of living for our worker is 30 percent higher than that of an inhabitant in New York City. The United States has the national economy of Puerto Rico under its direct and complete control. The national territory has been converted into an immense base for military aggression against Latin America, particularly against Cuba, Santo Domingo, Haiti, Venezuela, Colombia, the Guianas, Guadalupe, Martinique, and the rest of the Caribbean countries. The Yankees are in charge of Puerto Rican foreign relations, radio communications, banking, press, education, and mail. The US Congress is the supreme legislative power over the Puerto Rican people who, deprived of sovereignty, have not been able to exercise the inalienable right of self-determination.

Puerto Rican culture has been constantly attacked by imperialism which has unsuccessfully attempted to take our language, Spanish, from our people, but has been unable to stop Puerto Rico from being what it is, a Latin American people and nation. Trying to deceive world public opinion, Yankee imperialism has tried to conceal its brazen colonial intervention in Puerto Rico by baptizing our country with the name of "Free Associated State," without its really being a state, free, or associated. Now it is trying, by means of a committee created by the US president, which consists of seven North Americans and six lackey Puerto Ricans, to mock the anticolonial offensive unleashed in the world. Toward that end, it is pressuring the anticolonial committee of the United Nations, the so-called Committee of 24, to not consider the colonial case of Puerto Rico, despite the efforts of the anti-imperialist governments represented in that organization.

During the meeting of heads of governments held in Cairo in 1964, it was unanimously agreed to demand of the Committee of 24 the examination of the case of Puerto Rico as a US colony. The Cuban government reiterated this request before the committee only two months ago. We know that Yankee pressure has prevented the discussion of the matter. We do not expect the United Nations to create our independence. We well know what that organization is and the correlation of forces existing therein.

Puerto Rican independence will undoubtedly be achieved through our popular struggle, but we are interested in having the Committee of 24 take our case into consideration or unmask itself as an instrument created by imperialism, [there] not to help the peoples in their liberation struggle, but to deceive them, giving them false illusions of solidarity and delaying their attainment of freedom. Puerto Rico is much more than the only classic Yankee colony in America and much more than a Yankee military base. Puerto Rico is also the model presented by imperialism in Latin America.

Comrade delegates, Yankee imperialism has turned Puerto Rico into the anti-Cuba example. Imperialism's Peace Corps operates from our country, as does the neocolonial apparatus of the Alliance for Progress and the recently created Caribbean Corporation for the neocolonization, by the empire, of the Dominican Republic, Haiti, Guadalupe, Martinique, the Guianas, and the rest of the Caribbean area, which is when the contradictions between imperialism and the struggling peoples have become most acute in America.

We feel that the Puerto Ricans and the peoples of the three continents represented here must unite their efforts and coordinate their struggle, creating toward this end an organization capable of making more radical and increasing the revolutionary struggle and putting the agreements of this conference into practice.

Comrade delegates, receive the revolutionary greetings of the supporters of independence of Puerto Rico.

Long live the first Tricontinental Solidarity Conference!

¡Patria o Muerte! ¡Venceremos!

Paul Lantimo (Haiti)

Unified Democratic Front of National Liberation (FDULN)

Brother Delegates of the Countries of Asia, Africa, and Latin America:

In the name of the oppressed people of Haiti, the delegation from the Unified Democratic Front of National Liberation warmly salutes the peoples of the countries of Asia, Africa, and Latin America that are struggling against international imperialism for the sake of economic and political independence, social progress, and peace. The Front transmits its message of vivid encouragement to the people of Congo (Léopoldville), South Africa, the peoples of Colombia, Venezuela, Peru, Guatemala, and Laos, who struggle heroically against imperialism and the retrograde governments of their respective countries. The Haitian delegation sends a special greeting to the Dominican people and assures them of the complete solidarity of the Haitian people in their struggle against the Yankee troops. Finally, admiration is expressed for the valiant people of Vietnam who at this moment deal serious blows to imperialism and its lackeys. By landing numerous troops in Vietnam and intimidating the people, American imperialism thought that the situation would be placed in their favor. Mr. Johnson and the Pentagon militarists were grossly mistaken. In Vietnam, it is the people that have the initiative—North American imperialism will be crushed sooner or later. Today, confronted with the willful intensification of imperialist aggression, the delegates of the progressive and revolutionary movements of Asia, Africa, and Latin America are reunited so that conditions for decisive response from all the peoples may be planned. Oh, how the imperialists tremble!

Brother Delegates: The people of our country have already lived in the memory of revolutionary feats. In 1791, under the leadership of Toussaint Louverture and Jean-Jacques Dessalines, and utilizing intercolonialist rivalries, the French slave yoke was broken, the war of independence was victoriously sustained, and the Napoleonic armies were thrown out of the country. This was in 1804.

But in the conditions of that epoch in which growing international capitalism leaned upon the colonial slavery in Africa and America (and thus determined the future of humanity), it was extremely difficult for a small country to develop an independent economy. The capitalist countries imposed upon us a sort of economic blockade and refused us credit and technical equipment so vital to us after a dozen years of devastating war. Leaning upon the military chiefs and the enormous import-export commerce in foreign hands, they succeeded in making our country into a semi-colony, thus condemning the Haitian masses to misery.

This situation became worse in the first part of the century. Yankee imperialism, taking advantage of the rivalries between the European powers following the first world wars, sent their marines to our territory and occupied our country for nineteen years (1915–1934). The American imperialists utilized their presence in our country to outstrip their English, German, and above all, French rivals. They directly controlled our banks and our finances. They established a custom house management that bequeathed the foreign trade to their monopolies, they installed a judicial system according to their fancy, and an administration and military that permitted them to control the economic and political life of our country, which continued after their departure. They imposed on us the purchase of their oil and their coffee prices; they expropriated our peasants in the Northeast, in the Artibonite Valley, and the West for the installation and working of their sugar and sisal refineries, and for the extraction of copper and bauxite, which instead of being processed in the country, is exported to the US. By robbing us of our mineral riches and ferociously exploiting the labor of our people, imposing their trade and their prices, North American domination succeeded in aggravating and accelerating the internal crisis of the regime.

North American imperialism ended its occupation of Haiti in 1934. But it has left behind itself its slaughterhouses and a system conforming to its interests. The government of [François] Duvalier is its present representative and faithful servant.

Put into power by the Haitian army with the benediction of the State Department, Duvalier has not ceased to maintain for it an internal and external reactionary policy. He has supported and maintained: a free rein for the investments of imperialist capital; sabotage of the national effort in economy; fiscal policy that crushes agricultural producers, starving the mass of workers and middle classes; intolerance and persecution of syndical and democratic organizations leaving the oppressed classes to the mercy of their masters, the feudal lords, and the state; total support for US foreign policy; notorious support to the imperialist intervention of the Congo, North American intervention in the Dominican Republic, and to the policy of US hostility against Cuba.

But North American imperialism and its flunky Duvaliers cannot maintain domination of our people much longer. Already there have been outward signs of a crisis. The phenomenon of the insolvency of state has reappeared in dramatic manner: Entire ranks of public employees and employers do not receive their semimonthly and monthly salaries and/or they collect it with great delay—this situation places them in the hands of usurers. Certain enterprises of production controlled by the state (essential oil factories nationalized in 1959, central confectioner of Cayes) are in constant deficit. The morality and state credit are bankrupt; the national, secondary, and university teaching have lost their prestige because of the meddling of the *"tonton macoutes"* among professors, who in part are provoked into departing for Canada or Africa (on the other hand, harm done to the low-income citizens provokes and increases the prestige of private schools). In the custom houses and post offices, pillages of foreign packages have been organized with the immense anger of citizens and especially businessmen. Justice has entirely disappeared.

All conflicts are settled under the pressure of a *"tonton macoutes"* who heap abuses on all classes. The political prisoners are executed or else they rot in prison, completely cut off from the outside. An unimaginable terror is thrown down over the cities and countryside. The families of Benoit Riobe in Port-au-Prince, Guy Sansaricq in Jérémie, and many others were assassinated in broad daylight because of police denunciation and without any other foundation. On the Haitian-Dominican border areas, hundreds and hundreds of peasants were machine-gunned and thrown to the pit and graves simply for having sold or supplied the Haitian rebels with food who fought in the mountains at that time. In short, all levels of political and military authority are controlled by sinister persons, who owe no allegiance to any class, and who are ready to complete, if it is ordered of them, all the sorrowful tasks, and in case of necessity commit the most dishonest and cruel acts. The Haitian crisis thus became more visible, clear for all the world to see. But this was worse, because now a principal, decisive sphere of action must be passed, the power sphere of the reactionary classes. The state is discovered to be incapable of satisfying the appropriate elementary obligations to the classes that sustain it. Their debts are inflated indefinitely to the detriment of the bank, or some big businessmen, and certain imperialist companies. And now the state is faced with the necessity of utilizing extraordinary methods of taxation that are simply exigences of investment of this or that sum of money or opportunity. Thus, more and more the machinery of the state functions in the interest of one reactionary group against another. From that results an aggravation of the contradictions inside the exploited classes. It becomes vital for each group to directly take over the state machinery for themselves. In the long electoral campaign that was ferociously fought between the different traditional political sectors, the winning Duvalierist gangs used the state machinery not only against the people—which was to be expected—but also against the other gangs of reaction. Public liberties do not even exist.

In summary: The incredible misery of the working masses, the weakness of the regime as a result of the hostility between the different reactionary gangs, the blind and ferocious repression, and disappearance of all liberties for the people has created a new situation that permits new forces to advance steadily in the country.

The Duvalier government did not fall from the sky. It is the expression of the crisis of the regime and of world imperialism. Because the reactionary classes have been and always will be impotent in solving crisis, only the revolutionary action of the people will be sufficient to change the situation.

Up to now the Haitian masses have developed combat under different forms. The workers, students, and professionals have sustained important syndical and political battles despite the repression. During 1961, students organized a powerful strike which took an immediate political character and endangered the power of Duvalier. The peasants have often undertaken violent manifestations in order to defend themselves against the expropriation or the abuses of the *"tonton macoutes."* Likewise, on three or four occasions groups of patriots took the initiative of armed action that failed because of the authors' political inexperience and their isolation from the people.

The new opposition constantly organizes itself on a superior level: It supports portions of the vanguard, it does not yet entrust to itself the role of liberators, it works together on the basis of a program or any way on the basis of ideas; it turns its back on the past and looks toward the future, condemning the imperialists, the big businessmen, and the feudal lords; it desires to lean upon the masses, to conscientiously support and guide them in assault: for these reasons this front has been established—the United Democratic Front of National Liberation.

It is a front which agrees to solve the present revolutionary situation. Our work is to unify the action of all Haitian revolutionaries and put an end to the division within our ranks in order to lead the masses in armed struggle against Duvalierism. We are convinced of the future demolition of the Duvalierists (by the popular forces), the bulwark of imperialist domination in Haiti. The popular forces will lead radical change in the structure of the regime and will strike a strong blow against imperialism.

The demolition of Duvalierism and the regime which sustains it constitute our particular contribution to the struggle of the peoples of Santo Domingo and of Vietnam, to struggles of the peoples of the world against international imperialism, against North American imperialism. Brother Delegates: When the North American imperialists occupied our country, the Haitian people heroically resisted Yankee aggression. Our valiant peasants, under the leadership of Charlemagne Péralte and Benoît Batraville, entrenched themselves in the mountains and molested the US military. But due to lack of a revolutionary vanguard and isolation from other countries, they were eventually annihilated and their leader Charlemagne Péralte was captured then shot after being appended to a wooden cross. Since then, the times have changed. On Dominican soil and in Haiti, determined and shining vanguards work in order to unite both peoples against their principal enemy—US imperialism. Besides, the socialist countries and revolutionary movements of other countries are determined to aid our two peoples. Imperialism cannot take action on their whim. Recently, US imperialism disembarked troops in Santo Domingo, but it is incapable of imposing its peace; it is incapable of dominating the popular resistance. The Dominican people will conquer US imperialism.

The North American imperialists have cynically affirmed, since the events of Santo Domingo, their will and right to land their troops where they please.

But the Haitian and Dominican peoples learn their lesson of history. And now on Dominican territory workers and patriots have begun to get along with the people that struggle against North American imperialism.

The Haitian and Dominican peoples, under their respective vanguards and leaning upon brother peoples, are obliged to cooperate and they will cooperate in order to make the imperialists pay dearly for the humiliations of yesterday and today. They must wage a long and difficult struggle. But closely united with and aided by brother peoples, they will fling the North American imperialists into the sea and annihilate, internally, the puppets that support Yankee imperialism.

Brother Delegates: The Haitian people must meet above all else the battle against North American imperialism. But we are jointly liable with the struggle of all the peoples against the other imperialists and we want to extend our hands especially to the West Indian people who struggle against French, British, and Dutch imperialism. Since all the imperialist[s] have an understanding amongst themselves to maintain their colonies in the Caribbean, the Caribbean people must unify their action against international imperialism headed by the USA. We propose that the Tricontinental Conference should adopt a practical resolution with that perspective. Equally, as they come to their accursed agreement on their passing divergences on less essential questions, they are determined to smother the peoples' struggle for social progress, peace, and socialism. It is in response to this that the peoples of Asia, Africa, and Latin America united in common action against international imperialism. Because of that we desire that the Tricontinental Conference make a resolution by which to establish a permanent organization to coordinate the struggle of the peoples of Africa, Asia, and Latin America.

Down with the imperialists!

Long live the Caribbean peoples!

Long live the peoples of Africa, Asia, and Latin America!

Amílcar Cabral

**Secretary General of the African Party for the
Independence of Guinea-Bissau and Cape Verde**

Mr. President,

Dear Comrades in Struggle:

The peoples and nationalist organizations of Angola, Cape Verde, Guinea, Mozambique, and São Tomé and Príncipe sent their delegations to this conference for two main reasons:

First: Because we want to be present and take an active part in this transcendent event in the history of humanity.

Second: Because it was our political and moral duty to bring to the Cuban people, at this doubly historic moment, the seventh anniversary of the revolution and the First Tricontinental Conference, concrete proof of our fraternal and combative solidarity.

Allow me, therefore, Mr. President, on behalf of our peoples in struggle and on behalf of the militants of each of our national organizations, to extend my warmest congratulations and fraternal greetings to the people of this tropical island on the seventh anniversary of the triumph of their revolution, for the holding of this conference in their beautiful and hospitable capital, and for the successes they have achieved on the path to building a new life, whose essential objective is the full realization of the aspirations for freedom, peace, progress, and social justice of all Cubans.

I particularly greet the central committee of the Communist Party of Cuba, the revolutionary government, and its exemplary leader, Commander Fidel Castro, to whom I express our wishes for continued success and a long life in the service of the Cuban homeland, for the progress and happiness of its people, and for the service of humanity.

If any of us came to Cuba with doubts in our mind about the solidity, strength, maturity, and vitality of the Cuban Revolution, these doubts have been removed by what we have been able to see. Our hearts are now warmed by an unshakeable certainty which gives us courage in the difficult but glorious struggle against the common enemy: No power in the world will be able to destroy this Cuban Revolution, which is creating in the countryside and in the towns not only a new life but also—and even more important—a New Man, fully conscious of his national, continental, and international rights and duties. In every field of activity, the Cuban people have made major progress during the last seven years, particularly in 1965, Year of Agriculture.

We believe that this constitutes a particular lesson for the national liberation movements, especially for those who want their national revolution to be a true revolution. Some people have not failed to note that a certain number of Cubans, albeit an insignificant minority, have not shared the joys and hopes of the celebrations for the seventh anniversary because they are against the revolution. It is possible that others will not be present at the celebrations of the eighth anniversary, but we would like to state that we consider the "open door" policy for enemies of the revolution to be a lesson in courage, determination, humanity, and confidence in the people, another political and moral victory over the enemy; and to those who are worried, in a spirit of friendship, about the dangers which many be involved in this exodus, we guarantee that we, the peoples of the countries of Africa, still completely dominated by Portuguese colonialism, are prepared to send to Cuba as many men and women as may be needed to compensate for the departure of those who for reasons of class or of inability to adapt have interests or attitudes which are incompatible with the interests of the Cuban people. Taking once again the formerly hard and tragic path of our ancestors (mainly from Guinea and Angola) who were taken to Cuba as slaves, we would come now as free men, as willing workers and Cuban patriots, to fulfill a productive function in this new, just, and multiracial society, and to help and defend with our own lives the victories of the Cuban people. Thus, we would strengthen both all the bonds of history, blood, and culture which unite our peoples with the Cuban people, and the spontaneous giving of oneself, the deep joy, and infectious rhythm which make the construction of socialism in Cuba a new phenomenon for the world, a unique and, for many, unaccustomed event.

We are not going to use this platform to rail against imperialism. An African saying very common in our country says: "When your house is burning, it's no use beating the tom-toms." On a tricontinental level, this means that we are not going to eliminate imperialism by shouting insults against it. For us, the best or worst shout against imperialism, whatever its form, is to take up arms and fight. This is what we are doing, and this is what we will go on doing until all foreign domination of our African homelands has been totally eliminated.

Our agenda includes subjects whose meaning and importance are beyond question, and which show a fundamental preoccupation with struggle. We note, however, that one form of struggle which we consider to be fundamental has not been explicitly mentioned in this program, although we are certain that it was present in the minds of those who drew up the program. We refer here to the struggle against our own weaknesses. Obviously, other cases differ from that of Guinea; but our experience has shown us that in the general framework of daily struggle this battle against ourselves—no matter what difficulties the enemy may create—is the most difficult of all, whether for the present or the future of our peoples. This battle is the expression of the internal contradictions in the economic, social, cultural (and therefore historical) reality of each of our countries. We are convinced that any national or social revolution which is not based on knowledge of this fundamental reality runs grave risk of being condemned to failure.

When the African peoples say in their simple language that "no matter how hot the water from your well, it will not cook your rice," they express with singular simplicity a fundamental principle, not only of physics, but also of political science. We know that the development of a phenomenon in movement, whatever its external appearance, depends mainly on its internal characteristics. We also know that on the political level our own reality—however fine and attractive the reality of others may be—can only be transformed by detailed knowledge of it, by our own efforts, by our own sacrifices. It is useful to recall in this tricontinental gathering, so rich in experience and example, that however great the similarity between our various cases and however identical our enemies, national liberation and social revolution are not exportable commodities; they are, and increasingly so every day, the outcome of local and national elaboration, more or less influenced by external factors (be they favorable or unfavorable) but essentially determined and formed by the historical reality of each people, and carried to success by the overcoming or correct solution of the internal contradictions between the various categories characterizing this reality. The success of the Cuban Revolution, taking place only ninety miles from the greatest imperialist and antisocialist power of all time, seems to us, in its content and its way of evolution, to be a practical and conclusive illustration of the validity of this principle.

However, we must recognize that we ourselves and the other liberation movements in general (referring here above all to the African experience) have not managed to pay sufficient attention to this important problem of our common struggle.

The ideological deficiency, not to say the total lack of ideology, within the national liberation movements—which is basically due to ignorance of the historical reality which these movements claim to transform—constitutes one of the greatest weaknesses of our struggle against imperialism, if not the greatest weakness of all. We believe, however, that a sufficient number of different experiences has already been accumulated to enable us to define a general line of thought and action with the aim of eliminating this deficiency. A full discussion of this subject could be useful, and would enable this conference to make a valuable contribution toward strengthening the present and future actions of the national liberation movements. This would be a concrete way of helping these movements, and in our opinion no less important than political support or financial assistance for arms and suchlike.

It is with the intention of making a contribution, however modest, to this debate that we present here our opinion of the foundations and objectives of national liberation in relation to the social structure. This opinion is the result of our own experiences of the struggle and of a critical appreciation of the experiences of others. To those who see in it a theoretical character, we would recall that every practice produces a theory, and that if it is true that a revolution can fail even though it be based on perfectly conceived theories, nobody has yet made a successful revolution without a revolutionary theory.

Those who affirm, in our case correctly, that the motive force of history is the class struggle would certainly agree to a revision of this affirmation to make it more precise and give it an even wider field of application if they had a better knowledge of the essential characteristics of certain colonized peoples, that is to say peoples dominated by imperialism. In fact, in the general evolution of humanity and of each of the peoples of which it is composed, classes appear neither as a generalized and simultaneous phenomenon throughout the totality of these groups, nor as a finished, perfect, uniform, and spontaneous whole. The definition of classes within one or several human groups is a fundamental consequence of the progressive development of the productive forces and of the characteristics of the distribution of the wealth produced by the group or usurped from others. That is to say that the socioeconomic phenomenon "class" is created and develops as a function of at least two essential and interdependent variables—the level of productive forces and the pattern of ownership of the means of production. This development takes place slowly, gradually, and unevenly, by quantitative and generally imperceptible variations in the fundamental components; once a certain degree of accumulation is reached, this process then leads to a qualitative jump, characterized by the appearance of classes and of conflict between them.

Factors external to the socioeconomic whole can influence, more or less significantly, the process of development of classes, accelerating it, slowing it down, and even causing regressions. When, for whatever reason, the influence of these factors ceases, the process reassumes its independence, and its rhythm is then determined not only by the specific internal characteristics of the whole, but also by the resultant of the effect produced in it by the temporary action of the external factors. On a strictly internal level the rhythm of the process may vary, but it remains continuous and progressive. Sudden progress is only possible as a function of violent alterations—mutations—in the level of productive forces or in the pattern of ownership. These violent transformations carried out within the process of development of classes, as a result of mutations in the level of productive forces or in the pattern of ownership, are generally called, in economic and political language, revolutions.

Clearly, however, the possibilities of this process are noticeably influenced by external factors, and particularly by the interaction of human groups. This interaction is considerably increased by the development of means of transport and communication which has created the modern world, eliminating the isolation of human groups within one area, of areas within one continent, and between continents. This development, characteristic of a long historical period which began with the invention of the first means of transport, was already more evident at the time of the Punic voyages and in the Greek colonization, and was accentuated by maritime discoveries, the invention of the steam engine, and the discovery of electricity. And in our own times, with the progressive domestication of atomic energy it is possible to promise, if not to take men to the stars, at least to humanize the universe.

This leads us to pose the following question: Does history begin only with the development of the phenomenon of "class," and consequently of class struggle? To reply in the affirmative would be to place outside history the whole period of life of human groups from the discovery of hunting, and later of nomadic and sedentary agriculture, to the organization of herds and the private appropriation of land. It would also be to consider—and this we refuse to accept—that various human groups in Africa, Asia, and Latin America were living without history, or outside history, at the time when they were subjected to the yoke of imperialism. It would be to consider that the peoples of our countries, such as the Balantes of Guinea, the Coaniamas [Kwanyamas] of Angola, and the Makondes of Mozambique, are still living today—if we abstract the slight influence of colonialism to which they have been subjected—outside history, or that they have no history.

Our refusal, based as it is on concrete knowledge of the socioeconomic reality of our countries and on the analysis of the process of development of the phenomenon "class," as we have seen earlier, leads us to conclude that if class struggle is the motive force of history, it is so only in a specific historical period. This means that before the class struggle—and necessarily after it, since in this world there is no before without an after—one or several factors was and will be the motive force of history. It is not difficult to see that this factor in the history of each human group is the mode of production—the level of productive forces and the pattern of ownership—characteristic of that group. Furthermore, as we have seen, classes themselves, class struggle, and their subsequent definition, are the result of the development of the productive forces in conjunction with the pattern of ownership of the means of production. It therefore seems correct to conclude that the level of productive forces, the essential determining element in the content and form of class struggle, is the true and permanent motive force of history.

If we accept this conclusion, then the doubts in our minds are cleared away. Because if on the one hand we can see that the existence of history before the class struggle is guaranteed, and thus avoid for some human groups in our countries—and perhaps in our continent—the sad position of being peoples without any history, then on the other hand we can see that history has continuity, even after the disappearance of class struggle or of classes themselves. And as it was not we who postulated—on a scientific basis—the fact of the disappearance of classes as a historical inevitability, we can feel satisfied at having reached this conclusion which, to a certain extent, reestablishes coherence and at the same time gives to those peoples who, like the people of Cuba, are building socialism, the agreeable certainty that they will not cease to have a history when they complete the process of elimination of the phenomenon of "class" and class struggle within their socioeconomic whole. Eternity is not of this world, but man will outlive classes and will continue to produce and make history, since he can never free himself from the burden of his needs, both of mind and of body, which are the basis of the development of the forces of production.

The foregoing, and the reality of our times, allow us to state that the history of one human group or of humanity goes through at least three stages. The first is characterized by a low level of productive forces—of man's domination over nature; the mode of production is of a rudimentary character, private appropriation of the means of production does not yet exist, so there are no classes, nor, consequently, is there any class struggle. In the second stage, the increased level of productive forces leads to private appropriation of the means of production, progressively complicates the mode of production, provokes conflicts of interests within the socioeconomic whole in movement, and makes possible the appearance of the phenomena "class" and hence of class struggle, the social expression of the contradiction in the economic field between the mode of production and private appropriation of the means of production. In the third stage, once a certain level of productive forces is reached, the elimination of private appropriation of the means of production is made possible, and is carried out, together with the elimination of the phenomenon "class" and hence of class struggle; new and hitherto unknown forces in the historical process of the socioeconomic whole are then unleashed.

In politico-economic language, the first stage would correspond to the communal agricultural and cattle-raising society, in which the social structure is horizontal, without any state; the second to feudal or assimilated agricultural or agro-industrial bourgeois societies, with a vertical social structure and a state; the third to socialist or communist societies, in which the economy is mainly, if not exclusively, industrial (since agriculture itself becomes a form of industry) and in which the state tends to progressively disappear, or actually disappears, and where the social structure returns to horizontality, at a higher level of productive forces, social relations, and appreciation of human values.

At the level of humanity or of part of humanity (human groups within one area, of one or several continents) these three stages (or two of them) can be simultaneous, as is shown as much by the present as by the past. This is a result of the uneven development of human societies, whether caused by internal reasons or by one or more external factors exerting an accelerating or slowing-down influence on their evolution. On the other hand, in the historical process of a given socioeconomic whole each of the abovementioned stages contains, once a certain level of transformation is reached, the seeds of the following stage.

We should also note that in the present phase of the life of humanity, and for a given socioeconomic whole, the time sequence of the three characteristic stages is not indispensable. Whatever its level of productive forces and present social structure, a society can pass rapidly through the defined stages appropriate to the concrete local realities (both historical and human) and reach a higher stage of existence. This progress depends on the concrete possibilities of development of the society's productive forces and is governed mainly by the nature of the political power ruling the society, that is to say, by the type of state or, if one likes, by the character of the dominant class or classes within the society.

A more detailed analysis would show that the possibility of such a jump in the historical process arises mainly, in the economic field, from the power of the means available to man at the time for dominating nature, and, in the political field, from the new event which has radically changed the face of the world and the development of history, the creation of socialist states.

Thus we see that our peoples have their own history regardless of the stage of their economic development. When they were subjected to imperialist domination, the historical process of each of our peoples (or of the human groups of which they are composed) was subjected to the violent action of an exterior factor. This action—the impact of imperialism on our societies—could not fail to influence the process of development of the productive forces in our countries and the social structures of our countries, as well as the content and form of our national liberation struggles.

But we also see that in the historical context of the development of these struggles, our peoples have the concrete possibility of going from their present situation of exploitation and underdevelopment to a new stage of their historical process which can lead them to a higher form of economic, social, and cultural existence.

The political statement drawn up by the international preparatory committee of this conference, for which we reaffirm our complete support, placed imperialism, by clear and succinct analysis, in its economic context and historical coordinates. We will not repeat here what has already been said in the assembly.

We will simply state that imperialism can be defined as a worldwide expression of the search for profits and the ever-increasing accumulation of surplus value by monopoly financial capital, centered in two parts of the world; first in Europe, and then in North America. And if we wish to place the fact of imperialism within the general trajectory of the evolution of the transcendental factor which has changed the face of the world, namely capital and the process of its accumulation, we can say that imperialism is piracy transplanted from the seas to dry land; piracy reorganized, consolidated, and adapted to the aim of exploiting the natural and human resources of our peoples. But if we can calmly analyze the imperialist phenomenon, we will not shock anybody by admitting that imperialism—and everything goes to prove that it is in fact the last phase in the evolution of capitalism—has been a historical necessity, a consequence of the impetus given by the productive forces and of the transformations of the means of production in the general context of humanity, considered as one movement, that is to say a necessity like those today of the national liberation of peoples, the destruction of capital, and the advent of socialism.

The important thing for our peoples is to know whether imperialism, in its role as capital in action, has fulfilled in our countries its historical mission: the acceleration of the process of development of the productive forces and their transformation in the sense of increasing complexity in the means of production; increasing the differentiation between the classes with the development of the bourgeoisie, and intensifying the class struggle; and appreciably increasing the level of economic, social, and cultural life of the peoples. It is also worth examining the influences and effects of imperialist action on the social structures and historical processes of our peoples.

We will not condemn nor justify imperialism here; we will simply state that as much on the economic level as on the social and cultural level, imperialist capital has not remotely fulfilled the historical mission carried out by capital in the countries of accumulation. This means that if, on the one hand, imperialist capital has had, in the great majority of the dominated countries, the simple function of multiplying surplus value, it can be seen on the other hand that the historical capacity of capital (as indestructible accelerator of the process of development of productive forces) depends strictly on its freedom, that is to say on the degree of independence with which it is utilized. We must however recognize that in certain cases imperialist capital or moribund capitalism has had sufficient self-interest, strength, and time to increase the level of productive forces (as well as building towns) and to allow a minority of the local population to attain a higher and even privileged standard of living, thus contributing to a process which some would call dialectical, by widening the contradictions within the societies in question. In other, even rarer cases, there has existed the possibility of accumulation of capital, creating the conditions for the development of a local bourgeoisie.

On the question of the effects of imperialist domination on the social structure and historical process of our peoples, we should first of all examine the general forms of imperialist domination. There are at least two forms: The first is direct domination, by means of a power made up of people foreign to the dominated people (armed forces police, administrative agents, and settlers); this is generally called classical colonialism, or colonialism as indirect domination, by a political power made up mainly or completely of native agents; this is called neocolonialism.

In the first case, the social structure of the dominated people, whatever its stage of development, can suffer the following consequences: (a) total destruction, generally accompanied by immediate or gradual elimination of the native population and, consequently, by the substitution of a population from outside; (b) partial destruction, generally accompanied by a greater or lesser influx of population from outside; (c) apparent conservation, conditioned by confining the native society to zones or reserves generally offering no possibilities of living, accompanied by massive implantation of population from outside.

The two latter cases are those which we must consider in the framework of the problematic national liberation, and they are extensively present in Africa. One can say that in either case the influence of imperialism on the historical process of the dominated people produces paralysis, stagnation, and even in some cases regression in this process. However this paralysis is not complete. In one sector or another of the socioeconomic whole in question, noticeable transformations can be expected, caused by the permanent action of some internal (local) factors or by the action of new factors introduced by the colonial domination, such as the introduction of money and the development of urban centers. Among these transformations we should anticipate a progressive loss of prestige of the ruling native classes or sectors, the forced or voluntary exodus of part of the peasant population to the urban centers, with the consequent development of new social strata; salaried workers, clerks, employees in commerce and the liberal professions, and an instable stratum of unemployed. In the countryside there develops, with very varied intensity and always linked to the urban milieu, a stratum made up of small landowners. In the case of neocolonialism, whether the majority of the colonized population is of native or foreign origin, the imperialist action takes the form of creating a local bourgeoisie or pseudobourgeoisie, controlled by the ruling class of the dominating country.

The transformations in the social structure are not so marked in the lower strata, above all in the countryside, which retains the characteristics of the colonial phase; but the creation of a native pseudobourgeoisie which generally develops out of a petty bourgeoisie of bureaucrats and accentuates the differentiation between the social strata and intermediaries in the commercial system (compradors), by strengthening the economic activity of local elements, opens up new perspectives in the social dynamic, mainly by the development of an urban working class, the introduction of private agricultural property and the progressive appearance of an agricultural proletariat. These more or less noticeable transformations of the social structure, produced by a significant increase in the level of productive forces, have a direct influence on the historical process of the socioeconomic whole in question. While in classical colonialism this process is paralyzed, neocolonialist domination, by allowing the social dynamic to awaken (conflicts of interests between native social strata or class struggles), creates the illusion that the historical process is returning to its normal evolution. This illusion will be reinforced by the existence of a political power (national state) composed of native elements. In reality it is scarcely even an illusion, since the submission of the local "ruling" class to the ruling class of the dominating country limits or prevents the development of the national productive forces.

But in the concrete conditions of the present-day world economy this dependence is fatal and thus the local pseudobourgeoisie, however nationalist it may be, cannot effectively fulfill its historical function; it cannot freely direct the development of the productive forces; in brief it cannot be a national bourgeoisie. For as we have seen, the productive forces are the motive force of history, and total freedom of the process of their development is an indispensable condition for their proper functioning.

We therefore see that both in colonialism and in neocolonialism the essential characteristic of imperialist domination remains the same: the negation of the historical process of the dominated people by means of violent usurpation of the freedom of development of the national productive forces. This observation, which identifies the essence of the two apparent forms of imperialist domination, seems to us to be of major importance for the thought and action of liberation movements, both in the course of struggle and after the winning of independence.

On the basis of this, we can state that national liberation is the phenomenon in which a given socioeconomic whole rejects the negation of its historical process. In other words, the national liberation of a people is the regaining of the historical personality of that people, its return to history through the destruction of the imperialist domination to which it was subjected.

We have seen that violent usurpation of the freedom of the process of development of the productive forces of the dominated socioeconomic whole constitutes the principal and permanent characteristic of imperialist domination, whatever its form. We have also seen that this freedom alone can guarantee the normal development of the historical process of a people. We can therefore conclude that national liberation exists only when the national productive forces have been completely freed from every kind of foreign domination.

It is often said that national liberation is based on the right of every people to freely control its own destiny and that the objective of this liberation is national independence. Although we do not disagree with this vague and subjective way of expressing a complex reality, we prefer to be objective, since for us the basis of national liberation, whatever the formulas adopted on the level of international law, is the inalienable right of every people to have its own history, and the objective of national liberation is to regain this right usurped by imperialism, that is to say, to free the process of development of the national productive forces.

For this reason, in our opinion, any national liberation movement which does not take into consideration this basis and this objective may certainly struggle against imperialism, but will surely not be struggling for national liberation.

This means that, bearing in mind the essential characteristics of the present world economy, as well as experiences already gained in the field of anti-imperialist struggle, the principal aspect of national liberation struggle is the struggle against neocolonialism. Furthermore, if we accept that national liberation demands a profound mutation in the process of development of the productive forces, we see that this phenomenon of national liberation necessarily corresponds to a revolution. The important thing is to be conscious of the objective and subjective conditions in which this revolution can be made and to know the type or types of struggle most appropriate for its realization.

We are not going to repeat here that these conditions are favorable in the present phase of the history of humanity; it is sufficient to recall that unfavorable conditions also exist, just as much on the international level as on the internal level of each nation struggling for liberation.

On the international level, it seems to us that the following factors, at least, are unfavorable to national liberation movements: the neocolonial situation of a great number of states which, having won political independence, are now tending to join up with others already in that situation; the progress made by neocapitalism, particularly in Europe, where imperialism is adopting preferential investments, encouraging the development of a privileged proletariat and thus lowering the revolutionary level of the working classes; the open or concealed neocolonial position of some European states which, like Portugal, still have colonies; the so-called policy of "aid for undeveloped countries" adopted by imperialism with the aim of creating or reinforcing native pseudobourgeoisies which are necessarily dependent on the international bourgeoisie, and thus obstructing the path of revolution; the claustrophobia and revolutionary timidity which have led some recently independent states whose internal economic and political conditions are favorable to revolution to accept compromises with the enemy or its agents; the growing contradictions between anti-imperialist states; and, finally, the threat to world peace posed by the prospect of atomic war on the part of imperialism. All these factors reinforce the action of imperialism against the national liberation movements.

If the repeated interventions and growing aggressiveness of imperialism against the peoples can be interpreted as a sign of desperation faced with the size of the national liberation movements, they can also be explained to a certain extent by the weaknesses produced by these unfavorable factors within the general front of the anti-imperialist struggle.

On the internal level, we believe that the most important weaknesses or unfavorable factors are inherent in the socioeconomic structure and in the tendencies of its evolution under imperialist pressure, or to be more precise in the little or no attention paid to the characteristics of this structure and these tendencies by the national liberation movements in deciding on the strategy of their struggles.

By saying this we do not wish to diminish the importance of other internal factors which are unfavorable to national liberation, such as economic underdevelopment, the consequent social and cultural backwardness of the popular masses, tribalism, and other contradictions of lesser importance. It should however be pointed out that the existence of tribes only manifests itself as an important contradiction as a function of opportunistic attitudes, generally on the part of detribalized individuals or groups, within the national liberation movements. Contradictions between classes, even when only embryonic, are of far greater importance than contradictions between tribes.

Although the colonial and neocolonial situations are identical in essence, and the main aspect of the struggle against imperialism is neocolonialist, we feel it is vital to distinguish in practice these two situations. In fact the horizontal structure, however it may differ from the native society, and the absence of a political power composed of national elements in the colonial situation make possible the creation of a wide front of unity and struggle, which is vital to the success of the national liberation movement. But this possibility does not remove the need for a rigorous analysis of the native social structure, of the tendencies of its evolution, and for the adoption in practice of appropriate measures for ensuring true national liberation. While recognizing that each movement knows best what to do in its own case, one of these measures seems to us indispensable, namely, the creation of a firmly united vanguard, conscious of the true meaning and objective of the national liberation struggle which it must lead. This necessity is all the more urgent since we know that with rare exceptions the colonial situation neither permits nor needs the existence of significant vanguard classes (working class conscious of its existence and rural proletariat) which could ensure the vigilance of the popular masses over the evolution of the liberation movement. On the contrary, the generally embryonic character of the working classes and the economic, social, and cultural situation of the physical force of most importance in the national liberation struggle—the peasantry—do not allow these two main forces to distinguish true national independence from fictitious political independence. Only a revolutionary vanguard, generally an active minority, can be aware of this distinction from the start and make it known, through the struggle, to the popular masses. This explains the fundamentally political nature of the national liberation struggle and to a certain extent makes the form of struggle important in the final result of the phenomenon of national liberation.

In the neocolonial situation the more or less vertical structure of the native society and the existence of a political power composed of native elements—national state—already worsen the contradictions within that society and make difficult if not impossible the creation of as wide a front as in the colonial situation. On the one hand the material effects (mainly the nationalization of cadres and the increased economic initiative of the native elements, particularly in the commercial field) and the psychological effects (pride in the belief of being ruled by one's own compatriots, exploitation of religious or tribal solidarity between some leaders and a fraction of the masses) together demobilize a considerable part of the nationalist forces. But on the other hand the necessarily repressive nature of the neocolonial state against the national liberation forces, the sharpening of contradictions between classes, the objective permanence of signs and agents of foreign domination (settlers who retain their privileges, armed forces, racial discrimination), the growing poverty of the peasantry and the more or less notorious influence of external factors all contribute toward keeping the flame of nationalism alive, toward progressively raising the consciousness of wide popular sectors and toward reuniting the majority of the population, on the very basis of awareness of neocolonialist frustration, around the ideal of national liberation. In addition, while the native ruling class becomes progressively more bourgeois, the development of a working class composed of urban workers and agricultural proletarians, all exploited by the indirect domination of imperialism, opens up new perspectives for the evolution of national liberation. This working class, whatever the level of its political consciousness (given a certain minimum, namely the awareness of its own needs), seems to constitute the true popular vanguard of the national liberation struggle in the neocolonial case. However it will not be able to completely fulfill its mission in this struggle (which does not end with the gaining of independence) unless it firmly unites with the other exploited strata, the peasants in general (hired men, sharecroppers, tenants, and small farmers), and the nationalist petty bourgeoisie. The creation of this alliance demands the mobilization and organization of the nationalist forces within the framework (or by the action) of a strong and well-structured political organization.

Another important distinction between the colonial and neocolonial situations is in the prospects for the struggle. The colonial situation (in which the nation class fights the repressive forces of the bourgeoisie of the colonizing country) can lead, apparently at least, to a nationalist solution (national revolution); the nation gains its independence and theoretically adopts the economic structure which best suits it. The neocolonial situation (in which the working classes and their allies struggle simultaneously against the imperialist bourgeoisie and the native ruling class) is not resolved by a nationalist solution; it demands the destruction of the capitalist structure implanted in the national territory by imperialism, and correctly postulates a socialist solution.

This distinction arises mainly from the different levels of the productive forces in the two cases and the consequent sharpening of the class struggle.

It would not be difficult to show that in time the distinction becomes scarcely apparent. It is sufficient to recall that in our present historical situation—elimination of imperialism which uses every means to perpetuate its domination over our peoples, and consolidation of socialism throughout a large part of the world—there are only two possible paths for an independent nation: to return to imperialist domination (neocolonialism, capitalism, state capitalism), or to take the way of socialism. This operation, on which depends the compensation for the efforts and sacrifices of the popular masses during the struggle, is considerably influenced by the form of struggle and the degree of revolutionary consciousness of those who lead it. The facts make it unnecessary for us to prove that the essential instrument of imperialist domination is violence. If we accept the principle that the liberation struggle is a revolution and that it does not finish at the moment when the national flag is raised and the national anthem played, we will see that there is not, and cannot be national liberation without the use of liberating violence by the nationalist forces, to answer the criminal violence of the agents of imperialism. Nobody can doubt that, whatever its local characteristics, imperialist domination implies a state of permanent violence against the nationalist forces. There is no people on earth which, having been subjected to the imperialist yoke (colonialist or neocolonialist), has managed to gain its independence (nominal or effective) without victims. The important thing is to determine which forms of violence have to be used by the national liberation forces in order not only to answer the violence of imperialism, but also to ensure through the struggle the final victory of their cause, true national independence. The past and present experiences of various peoples, the present situation of national liberation struggles in the world (especially in Vietnam, the Congo, and Zimbabwe) as well as the situation of permanent violence, or at least of contradictions and upheavals, in certain countries which have gained their independence by the so-called peaceful way, show us not only that compromises with imperialism do not work, but also that the normal way of national liberation, imposed on peoples by imperialist repression, is armed struggle.

We do not think we will shock this assembly by stating that the only effective way of definitively fulfilling the aspirations of the peoples, that is to say of attaining national liberation, is by armed struggle. This is the great lesson which the contemporary history of liberation struggle teaches all those who are truly committed to the effort of liberating their peoples.

It is obvious that both the effectiveness of this way and the stability of the situation to which it leads after liberation depend not only on the characteristics of the organization of the struggle but also on the political and moral awareness of those who, for historical reasons, are capable of being the immediate heirs of the colonial or neocolonial state. For events have shown that the only social sector capable of being aware of the reality of imperialist domination and of directing the state apparatus inherited from this domination is the native petty bourgeoisie. If we bear in mind the aleatory characteristics and the complexity of the tendencies naturally inherent in the economic situation of this social stratum or class, we will see that this specific inevitability in our situation constitutes one of the weaknesses of the national liberation movement.

The colonial situation, which does not permit the development of a native pseudobourgeoisie and in which the popular masses do not generally reach the necessary level of political consciousness before the advent of the phenomenon of national liberation, offers the petty bourgeoisie the historical opportunity of leading the struggle against foreign domination, since by nature of its objective and subjective position (higher standard of living than that of the masses, more frequent contact with the agents of colonialism, and hence more chances of being humiliated, higher level of education and political awareness, etc.) it is the stratum which most rapidly becomes aware of the need to free itself from foreign domination. This historical responsibility is assumed by the sector of the petty bourgeoisie which, in the colonial context, can be called revolutionary, while other sectors retain the doubts characteristic of these classes or ally themselves to colonialism so as to defend, albeit illusorily, their social situation.

The neocolonial situation, which demands the elimination of the native pseudobourgeoisie so that national liberation can be attained, also offers the petty bourgeoisie the chance of playing a role of major and even decisive importance in the struggle for the elimination of foreign domination. But in this case, by virtue of the progress made in the social structure, the function of leading the struggle is shared (to a greater or lesser extent) with the more educated sectors of the working classes and even with some elements of the national pseudobourgeoisie who are inspired by patriotic sentiments. The role of the sector of the petty bourgeoisie which participates in leading the struggle is all the more important since it is a fact that in the neocolonial situation it is the most suitable sector to assume these functions, both because of the economic and cultural limitations of the working masses, and because of the complexes and limitations of an ideological nature which characterize the sector of the national pseudobourgeoisie which supports the struggle. In this case it is important to note that the role with which it is entrusted demands from this sector of the petty bourgeoisie a greater revolutionary consciousness, and the capacity for faithfully interpreting the aspirations of the masses in each phase of the struggle and for identifying themselves more and more with the masses.

But however high the degree of revolutionary consciousness of the sector of the petty bourgeoisie called on to fulfill this historical function, it cannot free itself from one objective of reality: the petty bourgeoisie, as a service class (that is to say that a class not directly involved in the process of production) does not possess the economic base to guarantee the taking over of power. In fact, history has shown that whatever the role—sometimes important—played by individuals coming from the petty bourgeoisie in the process of a revolution, this class has never possessed political control. And it never could possess it, since political control (the state) is based on the economic capacity of the ruling class, and in the conditions of colonial and neocolonial society this capacity is retained by two entities: imperialist capital and the native working classes.

To retain the power which national liberation puts in its hands, the petty bourgeoisie has only one path: to give free rein to its natural tendencies to become more bourgeois, to permit the development of a bureaucratic and intermediary bourgeoisie in the commercial cycle, in order to transform itself into a national pseudobourgeoisie, that is to say in order to negate the revolution and necessarily ally. In order not to betray these objectives the petty bourgeoisie has only one choice: to strengthen its revolutionary consciousness, to reject the temptations of becoming more bourgeois and the natural concerns of its class mentality, to identify itself with the working classes and not to oppose the normal development of the process of revolution. This means that in order to truly fulfill the role in the national liberation struggle, the revolutionary petty bourgeoisie must be capable of committing suicide as a class in order to be reborn as revolutionary workers, completely identified with the deepest aspirations of the people to which they belong.

This alternative—to betray the revolution or to commit suicide as a class— constitutes the dilemma of the petty bourgeoisie in the general framework of the national liberation struggle. The positive solution in favor of the revolution depends on what Fidel Castro recently correctly called the development of revolutionary consciousness. This dependence necessarily calls our attention to the capacity of the leader of the national liberation struggle to remain faithful to the principles and to the fundamental cause of this struggle. This shows us, to a certain extent, that if national liberation is essentially a political problem, the conditions for its development give it certain characteristics which belong to the sphere of morals.

We will not shout hurrahs or proclaim here our solidarity with this or that people in struggle. Our presence is in itself a cry of condemnation of imperialism and a proof of solidarity with all peoples who want to banish from their country the imperialist yoke, and in particular with the heroic people of Vietnam. But we firmly believe that the best proof we can give of our anti-imperialist position and of our active solidarity with our comrades in this common struggle is to return to our countries, to further develop this struggle and to remain faithful to the principles and objectives of national liberation.

Our wish is that every national liberation movement represented here may be able to repeat in its own country, arms in hand, in unison with its people, the already legendary cry of Cuba:

¡Patria o Muerte! ¡Venceremos!

Death to the forces of imperialism!

Free, prosperous, and happy country for each of our peoples!

¡Venceremos!

John K. Tettegah (Ghana)

Member of the Central Committee of the Convention
People's Party and Secretary General of the All-African
Trade Union Federation

On behalf of the People's Convention Party, our party's secretary general, and our leader Dr. Kwame Nkrumah, the Ghanaian delegation greets the people of Cuba and their leader, Dr. Fidel Castro, on the occasion of the seventh anniversary of the Cuban Revolution. We express our sincere gratitude for the hospitality that the people and government of Cuba have extended to our delegation since its arrival in the beautiful city of Havana.

The unparalleled example of revolutionary Cuba, fearlessly building the society it has chosen at the side of the imperialist colossus, has been an inspiration to the subjugated peoples of the world. There is no doubt that Cuba will continue to be an inspiration to the many in Africa, Asia, and Latin America who are continually fighting against imperialism, colonialism, and neocolonialism. We in Ghana firmly support them in their just struggle against the imperialist monster of the United States of America.

We rejoice today that the solidarity of the peoples of Africa and Asia, born ten years ago in the historic city of Bandung, has been extended to include our brothers and sisters in Latin America, with whom we face common enemies and dangers. The inspiration that began in Bandung lives on in our hearts today, and we note with deep sorrow the reality that Latin America is making common cause with us across the great oceans, against the common enemy.

We congratulate the international preparatory committee, which has worked hard to make this conference a reality. However, we note with great regret the absence of our comrade, brother, and fighter, Mehdi Ben Barka, a man whose indomitable spirit will continue to shine through our deliberations.

Comrades and brothers, we are gathered here in a spirit of camaraderie and solidarity, and it will do us no good to disrupt and destroy the unity for which we are fighting.

Today, imperialism has intensified its campaign of murder, plunder, and terror throughout our three continents. It is using the strategy of armed conflict, economic blockades, and a vile campaign against our peoples. But the more aggressive imperialist weapons become, the firmer our resolve and determination to fight will be.

We salute the heroic people of Vietnam who have stood up to the armed might of the United States and won resounding victories in their just struggle for freedom and national independence. Their example serves as a spur to us, and their great heroism is an eloquent testament to a people's willingness to pay the highest price to obtain their freedom.

We salute the government and people of North Vietnam in their just struggle against US military threats and their determination to refuse to be blackmailed by those who are plundering their homeland with fire and sword. The quality of their steadfastness is a testament to their will to maintain the freedom they won with blood and tears.

We salute the combatants of Santo Domingo, Venezuela, Colombia, Guatemala, Costa Rica, Panama, Laos, Angola, Mozambique, the so-called Portuguese Guinea, Congo-Léopoldville, Zimbabwe, and all those who have taken up arms to liberate themselves forever from the imperialist monster. Imperialism is being cornered everywhere, and the solidarity being forged here will seal the fall of the dying monster.

We support the people of Japan fighting against US nuclear threats; we support all the combatant peoples who have taken up arms, those who know that the price of freedom is small, yet are determined to continue their struggles until final victory. The entire world trembles with struggle. Colonialism, the foundation of imperialism, trembles and threatens to bring down the rotten edifice. Their empires retreat before the pressure of the people. While their empire crumbles, they try to prop it up with economic blockades, puppet governments, spies, and nominal independence granted so that the former masters retain the instruments of power. Neocolonialism emerges, like the adopted child of dying imperialism.

But we know that the people are alert, ready for sacrifice, ready to maintain their rights, their freedom, and their independence at all costs. The more imperialism develops its devices, the more effective the people's weapons become, and the more intense their struggles become.

This is the time to close our ranks, to strengthen our solidarity and unity. We in Ghana are ready to play our part in this great task of redeeming our people from the agony of imperialism, rebuilding our nations, eliminating disease, illiteracy, and ignorance—a task for a better world of justice and freedom.

We condemn the US for its aggressive war in South Vietnam and its armed provocations in North Vietnam. We demand that the US withdraw its troops from both countries, and that all bases in Southeast Asia be withdrawn as soon as the US complies with the 1954 Geneva Treaty. We condemn US proposals for unconditional negotiations. We insist that the Vietnamese people resolve their problems alone and unify their homeland.

We condemn the Labour government of Harold Wilson for using blackmail, supporting and allowing the establishment of the bandit minority clique in Zimbabwe, joined by Salazar and Verwoerd, arch-fascists and enemies of the African peoples.

We condemn the political maneuvering carried out by some at the UN in defense of the fascist Verwoerd, who continues to abuse the African masses.

But it must be made clear that those interested in fighting for their homeland must unite their ranks and consolidate their struggle against the enemy so that their victory over the enemy is complete. We in Ghana will continue to provide material and moral support until they achieve final victory.

For us, unity in Africa is an indispensable factor against our common enemy. It is also essential for you in Asia and Latin America. This growing unity will solidify our forces in their final advance toward victory.

My delegation came to Havana with concrete proposals regarding the steps to be taken for our people's victory over the common enemy. We will present these in the various committees. We have not come on a pleasure trip, or on a country excursion, nor have we come to make lengthy resolutions. We have come here to advance the work begun in Winneba. With unity and solidarity, the movements of our peoples on the three continents will go from victory to victory. Solidarity means equality and mutual trust. There is no force on earth that can subjugate us; because victory is ours.

We wish the Tricontinental Conference every success.

Aruna Asaf Ali

Indian Association for Afro-Asian Solidarity

Mr. Secretary General, Fellow Delegates, Observers, and Friends:

The Indian delegation has traveled thousands of miles and crossed two continents to reach this beautiful capital of the heroic Cuban people. We have done so because we wish to bring to this great meeting the congratulations and greetings of goodwill from the 470 million people of India. We are here also to join the Cuban people and their steadfast leaders, who have courageously lit the torch of freedom for two hundred million Latin Americans. Our beloved leaders, the late Pandit Nehru, were inspired by these same sentiments when, during the UN heads of state meeting, he proposed meeting with Fidel Castro, despite the fact that the dominant reactionary circles in North America did not approve of such a meeting on their own soil. The Indian people, on the other hand, were rejoicing and jubilant.

During our short stay in Havana, we have seen that the people are cheerful, vigilant, and disciplined; we have also enjoyed your unprecedented and boundless hospitality. On behalf of our delegation, I would like to express our sincere gratitude for the warmth and affection we have received.

Friends, as I speak to you here at this noble and historic Tricontinental Conference, from one corner of our vast country to the other, the Indian people are observing "Havana Week" in response to the call of the Fifth National Conference on Afro-Asian Solidarity, held in Kanpur from December 17 to 19. They are therefore with us in spirit, proclaiming in practice their desire that this conference achieve its aims.

We trust that this Havana Conference will lay the foundation for the creation of a common movement of solidarity among the peoples of the three continents that will propel humanity's march toward peace and progress.

We, members of the Indian Delegation, are proud that the seed of this massive solidarity gathering was sown in New Delhi in 1955, the year in which the Asian Conference was held. Since those beginnings, the solidarity movement has grown steadily, transforming from a mighty river into a mighty ocean, whose waves lap the shores of three continents and embrace the overwhelming majority of humanity. The fact that the USSR and the socialist states of Eastern Europe, representatives of organizations such as the World Peace Council, and international workers', women's, students', and youth organizations are with us here to give their resolute support to this powerful movement, enhances its capacity as an anti-imperialist force.

We have been entrusted with the task of making every effort to unify and consolidate the movement that this conference represents. We must concentrate on matters that unify the peoples of the three continents and resist all attempts, from any corner of the world, to foment controversies that might divide or frustrate solidarity.

The Afro-Asian solidarity movement has worked for a decade to achieve its goals. We trust that this ever-expanding movement, which now encompasses the peoples of Latin America, will open new horizons for the struggle against imperialism, colonialism, and neocolonialism, as well as for world peace.

I would now like to address certain aspects of the situation we face. Naturally, this conference must salute and extend its unanimous support to the Cuban people. Despite the economic blockade and acts of piracy emanating from Washington, undeterred by the danger from the Guantanamo base, despite the threat from the American colossus, and right on its doorstep, the Cuban people have established a bastion of revolutionary progress in this part of the hemisphere.

Secondly, I would like to extend our unanimous support to the heroic Vietnamese people, who, under the banner of the Liberation Front, are waging a tireless struggle against US military might. Every puppet imposed on them by imperialism failed before it began. The war of plunder and pillage waged in Vietnam by US imperialism has shaken the conscience of humanity, and even in the United States itself, there is a growing movement demanding the withdrawal of US troops from Vietnamese territory. Without a doubt, this conference will call for a worldwide and effective struggle to end the bombing of North and South Vietnam, demand recognition of the Liberation Front, the withdrawal of all US troops from these territories, and respect for the Geneva Conference Agreements. Allow us to declare once again that the Vietnamese people must be the sole masters of their land and the shapers of their own destiny.

The Conference must also denounce the cruel intervention in Santo Domingo by the US armed forces. It is necessary to make US imperialism understand that there is a growing wave of indignation and hatred against colonialism and neocolonialism, and that our people are not willing to allow any country, no matter how powerful, to try to impose its will on them.

Desperation is preparing similar measures in southern Africa. In Zimbabwe, the fascists have established a white, racist dictatorship; this regime, with its policy of apartheid and its forced occupation of southwest Africa, continues to oppress the people there. The actions of Portuguese imperialism in Angola, Mozambique, and so-called Portuguese Guinea reveal a carefully plotted conspiracy to use South Africa as a base for the restoration of imperialism.

Similarly, the military base that England and the US imperialists intend to establish in the Indian Ocean constitutes a grave threat to the security of South Asia and East Africa. The people and government of India strongly oppose these machinations, since underestimating these imperialist maneuvers against the Afro-Asian peoples and humanity in general could pose a very serious danger to us.

Friends, this conference must raise its unanimous voice against all such threats and outline guidelines for the peoples' struggle against imperialism; it must extend its militant support to the peoples in Aden and Cyprus who oppose the imperialists and fully support the Arab people in their conflict in Palestine.

It is also urgent to consider the problem of the threat posed by the stockpiling of nuclear devices. Effective measures to prevent the proliferation of these devices must be an integral part of the struggle against imperialism: prohibition of nuclear testing, the liquidation of all foreign military pacts and bases, and the struggle for general disarmament and world peace. The peoples of these three continents cannot allow military bases and nuclear devices to remain in the hands of those who could lead the world to disaster and death. The conference cannot but unanimously and resolutely urge the peoples to intensify their struggles for peace and the independence of their respective countries.

Faced with the growing solidarity of popular movements, the imperialists exploit any difference of color, religion, or social, political, or ideological status for their purposes. And they also exploit, to divide free nations, the difficulties they face in overcoming the colonial structure of their economies and in building new independent structures.

The economic blockade, as in the case of Cuba, politically conditioned aid, the fomenting of discord, and attempts to intervene as arbitrator in the disputes that arise are widely recognized as imperialist maneuvers.

The historic Bandung Conference warned against these maneuvers of imperialism and declared that the free nations of Asia and Africa must base their mutual relations on principles of peaceful coexistence, noninterference in the internal affairs of other nations, economic cooperation based on equality and mutual benefit, and the peaceful settlement of all differences. The Bandung principles must not be forgotten.

Friends: Neither this powerful wave of solidarity among peoples nor the birth and economic development of the nations liberated from imperialism would have been possible without the existence of the socialist bloc, which in many ways helps strengthen the ranks of anti-imperialism. For example, the socialist market is in itself the most powerful factor assisting liberated nations moving toward independent economic development; and, throughout the world, under-developed and developing countries cannot but feel grateful to the USSR, which not only remains militarily alert against imperialism, but also contributes to the economic development of the liberated nations.

We would also like to refer here to the Tashkent meeting between the leaders of two neighboring nations: India and Pakistan. This initiative, taken by the Soviet Union, strongly urges the parties involved to strictly observe the Bandung principles. India has always advocated a peaceful solution to this dispute, and our prime minister came to Tashkent inspired by this same sentiment.

The world we encompass from this forum of the three continents reveals an encouraging panorama, despite the many problems and difficulties faced by the different peoples. Throughout the world, whether Black or white, Chinese or mixed race, the masses are uniting as never before against imperialism, for national independence, and for social justice. We are all fervently dedicated to these noble, sacred, and invincible goals.

We all here support Fidel Castro's proclamation proclaiming 1966 as the Year of Solidarity.

Long live the Tricontinental Conference!

Long live the solidarity of the peoples against imperialism!

Long live the awakening of humanity!

Robert Resha (South Africa)

**Member of the National Executive Committee of the African
National Congress**

Dear President and Friends:

On behalf of my delegation, I have the honor to convey to the heroic people of Cuba and its revolutionary leader, Fidel Castro, a warm and fraternal greeting from the fourteen million inhabitants of South Africa who today live oppressed and struggle for their liberation. We wholeheartedly thank the people of this island for having demonstrated to us and to the entire world how the will and determination of a small country succeeded, right at the doors of the most powerful of imperialist powers, the United States of America, in freeing itself from the yoke that oppressed it. The victory of the Cuban people serves as an inspiration to the peoples of the world in their struggle to achieve liberation and uphold human dignity. It was no coincidence that the first Tricontinental Conference, comprised of progressive and anti-imperialist forces from around the world, was held in "CUBA, FREE TERRITORY OF AMERICA."

We consider this Tricontinental Conference to be an important step in consolidating the militant unity of all anti-imperialist, anticolonialist, and anti-neocolonialist forces. In this era of national liberation and socialist revolutions, we have gathered here to accelerate the defeat of imperialism's worldwide offensive, as evidenced by its cruelest aggressions in Vietnam and its brutal intervention in Santo Domingo. The fact that this event is being held at such a time is an expression of the historic need for positive and militant action by all revolutionary forces. We therefore urge this conference to cooperate in mobilizing the new forces emerging daily in Asia and Africa, the peoples fighting against the neocolonialism in Latin America, to socialist countries, and to progressive and working-class movements around the world. It is for these reasons that Vietnam must be defended, and the US imperialists must be expelled from Asia, Santo

Domingo must be freed from Yankee intervention, and Latin America from the clutches of dollar imperialism.

The national liberation revolution is spreading across the African continent, and through it, a large number of our countries have achieved sovereignty and independence. Faced with this revolutionary outbreak, the imperialists are attempting to continue exploiting Africa's human and natural resources for their own benefit. England, France, the United States of America, and other NATO forces have established a vast network of military, air, and naval bases on and near our continent. Some of these bases are in the Congo and are being used by Belgian and American interventionists to suppress the national liberation movement of the Congolese people.

To carry out their strategic plans in Africa, the imperialists count on South Africa as a bastion to halt the African Revolution and to preserve the enormous profits they continue to extract from our continent. For this reason, the British government is frantically trying to maintain the status quo in Rhodesia at all costs, preventing the African majority based on the principle of individual suffrage from taking power. The British imperialists understand perfectly well the need to maintain the rule of the white minority in Southern Rhodesia; they know that the victory of freedom in Zimbabwe would be a devastating blow against the forces seeking to keep Africa chained and under new forms of slavery. It is absolutely essential that this conference cooperate in the execution of such an urgent task as the expulsion of the illegal Smith regime and demand the release of the thousands of political prisoners and detainees, and that it also give its most effective moral and material support to the people of Zimbabwe in their just struggle for independence and freedom.

We salute our brothers and sisters in the Portuguese territories of Africa who are waging an armed struggle against the Portuguese colonialist fascists, who, together with Smith of Rhodesia and Verwoerd of South Africa, have allied themselves in a military-economic pact that enjoys the full support of international imperialism.

Comrades, let me now turn to the problem of South Africa, the stronghold and headquarters of imperialism throughout southern Africa, with imperialist support of 1.5 billion pounds sterling in investment, with the participation of England, the United States, West Germany, France, and Japan; which is rapidly becoming an important military and industrial center and a springboard for imperialist domination in southern Africa and the entire African continent.

South Africa is a country with vast resources. It has a large mining and industrial complex. It produces 43 percent of all minerals on the African continent and two-thirds of the world's gold production. It consumes as much electricity as the rest of the African continent. It accounts for 30 percent of the continent's total national income. In 1963, South Africa's known capital investments reached 240 million pounds sterling, of which 154 million pounds were invested in Southern

Rhodesia and Northern Rhodesia (now Zambia). It is this enormous wealth that provides investors with "the highest returns in the world," according to the vice president of the Newmont Mining Corporation. Mining this wealth, extracted from the blood and sweat of the African people, provides the white minority of three million people with the highest standard of living in the world. This gave rise to what is currently the most brutal and barbaric system in the world: apartheid.

This is what apartheid means to us:

- LACK OF LAND – Eighty-seven percent of South Africa's best land belongs to and is for the exclusive use of the white minority, which constitutes 20 percent of South Africa's total population, while the 13 percent of the worst land belongs to the African people. African reserves are nothing more than forced labor zones.

- POLITICAL RIGHTS – whether executive or legislative are for the exclusive benefit of the white minority.

- TRAFFIC LAWS – control the movement and residence of the African population. They are required to carry a document at all times; failure to do so incurs a penalty punishable by imprisonment. In ten years, nearly four million people (one in four) have been imprisoned for this reason.

- AFRICAN TRADE UNIONS – are not legally recognized, therefore workers' strikes are illegal. Only whites have the right to skilled labor. The average wage of white workers compared to that earned by Africans in the mining industry is 15-to-1, and in secondary industries, 5-to-1.

- NATIONAL INCOME – In 1959, the per capita income of the white population was 425 pounds sterling per year, that of Africans was 39 pounds sterling, and that of Indians (Hindus) and mixed-race people 54 pounds sterling.

- EDUCATION – The South African government spends 64 pounds annually on the education of each white child and 9 pounds on that of an African child. According to Dr. Verwoerd, who was formerly minister of education, the natives are being educated to make them understand from childhood that they are not equal to Europeans . . . and that there is no place for them in the white community, except for certain types of work.

- INFANT MORTALITY – is the highest in the world for African children (400 out of every thousand) and the lowest in the world for white children (27 out of every thousand).

In short, "apartheid" means a life filled with misery, hunger, the degradation of human dignity, and the total denial of human rights. Our people are fighting against this diabolical system through demonstrations, protest campaigns, and general strikes—led by the African National Congress and its allies, the Indo–South African Congress, the Congress of Democrats, and the South African Congress of Trade Unions. Any resistance by our people has been brutally and cruelly repressed by state police terror. All organizations deemed dangerous to the regime have been outlawed in one way or another.

The Sharpeville massacre of Africans in 1960 and the military crackdown in response to nationwide demonstrations and strikes in 1961 marked a turning point in the struggle against white supremacy. Thus, on December 16, 1961, a new phase in the struggle emerged, consisting of systematically organized acts of sabotage aimed primarily at destroying government property, installations, and communications. These acts were organized by the Umkhonto we Sizwe (Spear of the Nation), the military branch of the outlawed African National Congress. In a proclamation to the entire country, Umkhonto we Sizwe declared that "the patience of the people is not inexhaustible. There comes a time when only two paths remain: submit or fight, and that time has come in South Africa."

There are more than eight thousand political prisoners with sentences ranging from five years to life imprisonment. Among those sentenced to life imprisonment on Robben Island are some of the most well-known popular leaders, including Nelson Mandela. More than fifty people have been sentenced to death. The courageous African National Congress and trade union leader Vuyisile Mini, renowned author of countless songs about freedom, ascended the scaffold shouting the patriotic slogan of the national liberation movement, *"Amandla Ngawesthu"* (Power to the People).

South Africa has become a vast prison, subjecting nonwhite Africans to daily police persecution and intimidation. It continues to arrest and detain opponents of the apartheid policy in all communities. Recently, Abram Fischer, a member of one of the most prominent Afrikaner families, was arrested. Fischer is one of South Africa's leading lawyers and successfully defended political leaders in the famous Treason Trial. At the Rivonia Trial of Nelson Mandela, Walter Sisulu, and other leaders, Fischer handled their defense and participated in other political trials as well. After being charged under the Suppression of Communism Act, he continued to fight against apartheid and white supremacy underground.

The fascist white government of Verwoerd has put its police and military forces on a war footing in a desperate attempt to suppress the underground political movement and trained numerous detachments in counterguerrilla warfare. Army units have been equipped with the most modern weapons supplied by NATO powers. The fascist Verwoerd government has recruited OAS [Organization of American States] military personnel, Hitlerite German generals, and former officers from Malaya and Kenya in South Africa to direct the training of the white army and police forces.

No type of repression, police brutality, torture, or the use of military force will be able to prevent our people from achieving their established revolutionary aspirations in the Freedom Charter.

This charter declares that South Africa belongs to its people, Black and white alike, that no government can claim authority unless it is supported by the will of the people, that our people have been stripped of their inalienable rights, and therefore we pledge to fight together without regard for sacrifice until the following democratic changes are achieved:

- A POPULAR GOVERNMENT
- EQUAL RIGHTS FOR INHABITANTS (NATIONAL GROUPS)
- THE PEOPLE MUST HAVE A PARTICIPATION IN THE COUNTRY'S WEALTH
- THE LAND SHOULD BE GIVVEN TO THOSE WHO WORK IT
- EQUAL RIGHTS BEFORE THE LAW FOR ALL CITIZENS
- ENJOYMENT OF HUMAN RIGHTS FOR ALL CITIZENS EQUALLY
- SOCIAL SECURITY FOR ALL
- EQUAL OPPORTUNITIES FOR ALL CITIZENS TO STUDY AND IMPROVE CULTURALLY
- GUARANTEE HOUSING, STABILITY, AND WELL-BEING FOR ALL CITIZENS
- FOR AN ENVIRONMENT OF PEACE AND FRATERNITY

In his call for unity of action among all democratic forces that support the revolutionary demands of the Freedom Charter, Nelson Mandela said: "To achieve these demands, it is necessary to launch a campaign for mass organization on a large scale . . . If the United Congress Front is developed and strengthened, the Freedom Charter will become a dynamic, active instrument, and we will be able to remove all obstacles on the way to achieving the South Africa we have longed for all our lives."

Frightened by the revolutionary content of the Freedom Charter and the widespread approval it received from the people, the South African government imprisoned 156 leaders of the national groups and put them on trial for treason. The "Treason Trial," as it was called, lasted five years, and in the end, the court was forced to acquit them. This trial inspired the masses to further efforts.

The people are prepared to face the bloody and difficult days that lie ahead. Inspired by the heroism of their imprisoned leaders, and led by the underground African National Congress, a courageous youth is being forged that masters the various techniques of armed struggle. The people have understood that there is no alternative but to prepare the forces that opportunely confronted reaction, using the only language the latter understands. Relying on their determination and courage, and on the sacrifices made in the struggle, our people are accelerating the overthrow of fascist white domination.

Comrades, the Verwoerd regime constitutes a grave threat to the peace, stability, and security of Africa and the world. In collusion with Smith and Salazar, Verwoerd strives to maintain all of South Africa as a reserve for white minority rule and as a base for imperialist reaction. Undoubtedly, the racist regime of South Africa has become the most important bastion of the international forces that daily conspire to eliminate the gains achieved by the peoples of the African continent over the past ten years.

Aware of the threat posed by South Africa's policy, the United Nations has appealed to the General Assembly and the Security Council to take action and place severe sanctions against South Africa, such as the severance of diplomatic relations, economic sanctions, and embargoes on arms and oil. Sixty-four member states support these decisions, but Great Britain, the United States, France, West Germany, and Japan refuse to impose these sanctions on South Africa. Their benefits are of vital importance. To implement these important UN decisions, we urge that maximum pressure be exerted on these countries that maintain and support white domination in South Africa.

The African National Congress of South Africa calls for support on a larger scale internationally and actively, the isolation of South Africa, and the imposition of sanctions against that country in all aspects: political, economic, social, and cultural. The imperialist powers must be forced to impose an embargo on arms and oil and to sever trade and diplomatic relations with the South African regime. The peace fighters in our country call for moral and material support in their revolutionary struggle to overthrow the fascist Verwoerd regime.

Mr. President, we would be departing from our duty if we did not highlight the active assistance that we receive from our brothers in the independent African states and from our faithful friends in the USSR, the GDR, and other socialist countries. We therefore wish to express our deep gratitude for the enormous sacrifices made for the cause of our struggle by the peoples of Tanzania, the UAR, Algeria and Tunisia, as well as other African states.

On the international front, we support the anti-imperialist and anticolonialist struggle of the peoples of Latin America against US imperialism, especially the heroic struggle of the Cuban people, who are at the forefront of the struggle against Yankee imperialism, a struggle that encompasses Venezuela, the Dominican Republic, Peru, Guatemala, Colombia, Nicaragua, Haiti, Uruguay, Puerto Rico, and all the Latin American peoples, including the struggle of Black people in the United States of America.

We condemn the imperialist oppression of the Arab people of the Middle East and the sinister machinations of Zionism in Palestine. We demand that they be ordered to be restored to the Arab people, their legitimate rights to the territory of Palestine, and we ask that they be supported in their struggle to recover their usurped homeland.

We stand on the side of the heroic struggle of the African people for the reconstruction of their continent and support the peoples of so-called Portuguese Guinea; Angola; Mozambique; the Canary Islands; Zimbabwe; South West Africa; the British High Commission for the Territories of Basutoland, Swaziland, and Bechuanaland; the Comoros Islands; and the Congo (Léopoldville).

We support the anti-imperialist struggle in Asia, where Yankee domination takes various forms, such as in Cambodia, Laos, South Korea, North Kalimantan, and the entirety of Southwest Asia. We condemn SEATO, ANZUS, and the Japan–South Korea Treaty.

As far as the whole of Vietnam is concerned, we condemn the US aggression against the Democratic Republic of Vietnam and against South Vietnam. We reject the false propaganda of the United States regarding unconditional negotiations as a solution to the conflict. US domination in Asia and the Far East. We give our unconditional support to the just struggle of the Democratic Republic of Vietnam and the National Liberation Front of South Vietnam. We call for an immediate solution to the Vietnamese conflict based on their demands.

For our part, we reiterate our commitment within the framework of this historic and transcendental conference, that we, on behalf of the people of South Africa, will continue to wage our militant revolutionary struggle with unwavering determination, using the forms of struggle dictated by historical necessity, until we achieve victory, crush the domination of the white minority, and free our people from the clutches of imperialist tyranny.

The African National Congress and the people of South Africa have no illusions about the sacrifices required in the struggle to defeat the fascist and imperialist forces. In this determination to fight until victory, we are inspired by the Great October Revolution, the Chinese Revolution, and the Cuban and Algerian Revolutions, and we pledge to fight until victory is achieved.

WE DO NOT DOUBT THE SECURITY OF OUR FINAL VICTORY.

Comrades, in conclusion, on behalf of the African National Congress, I wish this first and only Tricontinental Conference every success in its noble and important efforts to foster the militant unity of the peoples of Asia, Africa, and Latin America, together with that of the socialist countries and the democratic peoples of the rest of the world, against imperialism, colonialism, neocolonialism, and for national independence, against imperialist military pacts and bases, and for world peace.

Long live the solidarity of the peoples of Africa, Asia, and Latin America!

Long live the just cause of national independence and the freedom of all peoples!

Long live peace and progress!

Amandla!

Sharof Rashidov

First Secretary of the Central Committee of the Communist Party of Uzbekistan and Candidate Member of the Politburo of the Communist Party of the Soviet Union

Dear Friends!

On behalf of the Soviet people, we cordially greet the participants of this historic conference of representatives of the peoples of Asia, Africa, and Latin America who are struggling against imperialism and colonialism, for freedom, independence, peace, and social progress. I am happy to convey the fraternal greetings of the peoples of the Soviet Union to the freedom-loving Cuban people. We all know what great efforts must be made to prepare such meetings as these. And, from the bottom of our hearts, we thank the government and the people of Cuba for their fraternal hospitality and everything they have done toward the convocation of this conference.

It is a notable fact that the forum of the peoples of the three continents has convened in Havana at a time when the Cuban people, together with all of progressive mankind, are marking the seventh anniversary of the victory of the glorious Cuban revolution. We can see with our own eyes the great successes achieved by the Cuban people in creating a new social system, and their achievements in peaceful construction and in strengthening the defenses of their free motherland. Free Cuba—the first socialist state on the American continent—symbolizes the invincibility of a people fighting for liberation from the oppression of imperialism, and for socialism. We congratulate our dear Cuban friends on their great revolutionary day—Liberation Day—and wish them fresh successes in building a socialist society. On this solemn day, the entire Soviet people declare once more: "We are always with you, dear Cuban brothers, we are with you both in times of difficulty and in times of rejoicing, in the common work and in the common struggle for the victory of socialism."

I would like, first of all, to stress that the Soviet delegation has arrived at this conference with the aim of giving all-round assistance to the unification of the anti-imperialist forces of the three continents in order to provide greater impetus to our common struggle against imperialism, colonialism, and neocolonialism— led by the US capitalists. Our stand is clear to all, and we have no intention of indulging in polemics. The rostrum of the conference must be a rostrum of unity and not of splits.

We are participating in a major event in the history of the national liberation struggle of the peoples of Asia, Africa, and Latin America. The anti-imperialist struggle, with its demands for the unshakable unity of its fighting forces, has brought the peoples of our continents to a realization of the urgent necessity for an even greater consolidation, and an even greater coordination, of our struggle against our common enemy—imperialism and, first and foremost, US imperialism. The peoples of Asia, Africa, and Latin America are reaching out their hands to one another, in a concerted desire for joint action; for the sake of militant solidarity and revolutionary friendship. The Soviet delegation warmly supports the proposal that an organization of tricontinental solidarity be set up at this conference.

Our epoch is a great epoch. The bulwarks of the system built on exploitation and violence, on national oppression and social inequality, are collapsing one after another. The disintegration of the colonial system of imperialism is a vivid expression of the great universal and historical process of the liberation of the peoples from all kinds of oppression. But we must not forget even for a moment that colonialism—a mortally wounded and dying predatory animal—is not yet completely wiped out and is trying to prolong its criminal life. By hook or by crook, it is attempting to cling on to Angola, Mozambique, "Portuguese" Guinea, the Spanish possessions in Africa, the south of the Arabian Peninsula, Aden, North Kalimantan, islands in the Caribbean Sea, the Pacific, and other areas. We declare from this high rostrum: There must be no place for colonialism on earth; it must be completely wiped off the face of our planet. The right of the peoples to wage the struggle for the complete liquidation of colonialism and neocolonialism with all available means is sacred.

The Soviet people have always supported the wars waged by the peoples, the armed struggle of the oppressed peoples, and renders them all-round support and aid. It took the colonialists several centuries to set up the colonial system. But to undermine it and then to crush it took only a few decades of joint struggle—the victory of the Great October Socialist Revolution, the rout of fascism in World War II, the victories of the Chinese revolution and the national liberation movements in Asia, Africa, and Latin America. The rapidity of the historic struggle which is doing away with the colonial system is conditioned by the courage and heroism of the oppressed peoples themselves, by the might and unity of action of all the anti-imperialist forces. The setting up of the solidarity movement of the peoples of Asia and Africa was an important landmark in the anti-imperialist struggle. This movement, which was born in the battles against imperialism, in fraternal unity with the world movement for peace and security of the peoples; and in alliance with the forces of democracy and socialism; has become in the course of eight years a mighty force of our time. It has become an important factor in mobilizing and organizing the anti-imperialist forces and in their growth and strengthening. One of its strongest aspects was that it did not become inward-looking. It was striving to go beyond the framework of the countries of the two continents and strengthened its ties with the entire worldwide anti-imperialist front and, in particular, with the peoples of Latin America.

The aspiration of the peoples of Latin America for solidarity and unity also has a long and glorious tradition. The great patriots of Latin America, Simón Bolívar, José de San Martin, José María Morelos, and others, dreamed of this unity as far back as in the days of the struggle for independence. The same noble aims inspired the thinker and fighter José Martí, the glorious son of the Cuban people. Martí's belief that, in struggling for their freedom and independence, the countries of the American continent should support everything which brings the peoples nearer together and oppose everything which divides them, sounds prophetic. These words of the great Cuban revolutionary are most topical today. Reaction many a time raised obstacles in the way of the consolidation of the liberation movement of the three continents. But, despite all the machinations of the colonialists, our unity has become a real factor, which is proved by the present conference.

The winning of national independence by the majority of the peoples of Asia and Africa, and the revolutionary upsurge in many countries of Latin America, have brought nearer together the content and tasks of the liberation movements on the three continents. This is what forms the real foundation for the genuine solidarity which has been dictated by life itself and which has become the main motto of the First Conference of the Three Continents.

We express our gratitude to the people of the United Arab Republic and President Gamal Abdel Nasser for the invitation to hold a second Tricontinental Solidarity Conference in Cairo.

Dear friends, we meet together at a time when the international situation has become greatly intensified; losing their positions, the imperialists are resorting to extreme reactionary measures, including armed intervention, in order to block the way to the national and social liberation of the peoples. Despite the contradictions which exist between them, the imperialist powers are bound by mutual interests in their aggressive actions against the freedom-loving peoples. They are striving to coordinate their efforts and to jointly work out plans for the struggle against socialism and the national liberation movements. NATO is the main headquarters of the imperialist plotters and the foundation of imperialism's worldwide military-strategic system.

The role played in NATO by West German imperialism, which has become one of the main accessories of the USA in the struggle against the world liberation forces, is getting greater and greater. The FRG [Federal Republic of Germany] is closely cooperating with Portugal and the South African racialists, ships them armaments, grants large loans, and concludes secret agreements with Israel directed against the Arab countries. The main danger emanates from US imperialism, the leading force of the entire imperialist camp.

In Asia, the piratical policies of imperialism have been especially vividly expressed in the criminal aggressive war waged by the USA against the heroic people of Vietnam. The United States is subjecting the cities and villages of the Democratic Republic of Vietnam to barbaric air raids, destroying the civilian population, burning the crops, destroying industrial enterprises and communications. The Soviet people resolutely condemn the aggression of the USA against the Vietnamese people and express their solidarity with the heroic struggle against the modern barbarians.

All over the Soviet Union, crowded meetings and demonstrations of working people are being held, at which millions of workers, collective farmers, office workers, and intellectuals are expressing their indignation and are protesting against the shameful and dirty war waged by US imperialists in Vietnam. The Soviet Union is supplying the fraternal people of Vietnam with the most modern weapons for meeting US aggression. We are doing everything in order that the deliveries of Soviet military equipment—aircraft, rockets, artillery, ammunition, and so on—will get into the hands of the Vietnamese freedom fighters as rapidly as possible. The heroic soldiers of the DRV [Democratic Republic of Vietnam] have shot down more than eight hundred US aircraft since the beginning of the piratical raids on the peaceful cities and villages of Vietnam.

Recently, *Time* magazine published in New York the lamentations of Major John Godeon, a USAF [US Air Force] pilot, who said that they were shot at all altitudes. When flying low, they encountered small arms fire and AA guns; higher up, they were fired at with rockets; and at very high altitudes, they were attacked by MiG [Mikoyan-Gurevich] fighters. We Soviet people are happy that the military equipment which the workers of the land of Soviets are producing at their enterprises with such great enthusiasm also helps the cause of the victory of our Vietnamese brothers over the aggressor.

The Soviet people believe that peace in Vietnam can be achieved in conformity with the program put forward in the statement of the National Front for the Liberation of South Vietnam of March 22, 1965, and the resolution adopted by the National Assembly of the DRV. I would like to inform the present conference that on December 9, 1965, the Supreme Soviet of the USSR declared that it completely shares this position of the DRV government and the National Front for the Liberation of South Vietnam. The Supreme Soviet of the USSR has called upon the parliaments and governments of all countries, in their turn, to make the necessary efforts in order to cause the United States of America to stop its aggression in Vietnam and give the Vietnamese people the opportunity to settle their internal affairs by themselves.

The US imperialists, by indulging in hypocritical verbiage about talks, are trying to lull world public opinion and to turn attention away from the fact that they are expanding their aggression. The Soviet people believe that it is necessary to unite all efforts in rendering real and effective assistance to the people of Vietnam, in order for solidarity with the Vietnamese people to be more effective. The Soviet delegation is making a proposal to launch throughout the world a broad campaign for rendering moral and material assistance to the struggling people of Vietnam. We propose that an international fund be set up. The Soviet people will make a tangible contribution to such a fund.

The development, all over the world, of a mighty mass protest against the dirty war waged by the US imperialists in Vietnam, the demand[s] that it be immediately stopped and the armed forces of the USA and its allies be recalled from Vietnam and a settlement be reached on the basis of the Geneva Agreements—all this must become the practical aim of the mass struggle waged by millions upon millions of honest people in all countries of the world. Expanding the scale of its military operations, the USA has intensified its military activities against Laos. USAF planes are bombing and strafing the areas controlled by the patriotic forces of Laos. And the troops of the Saigon puppets, instigated by the Pentagon, are at the same time making bandit raids into the territory of Cambodia. The ruling circles of Thailand are going deeper and deeper into the struggle on the side of reaction and imperialism. These facts go to prove that the USA is intending to spread the flames of war all over the Indochinese Peninsula.

To rebuff the high-handed US aggressors in southeast Asia is the present and urgent task of all the anti-imperialist forces. If today progressive mankind does not stop the international piracy being committed by the United States in Vietnam, if it does not block the way to armed interference in the internal affairs of countries and peoples which are striving for freedom and independence, then tomorrow the same fate may await any other country or any other nation in the world. The aggression of US imperialism in Vietnam is a brazen challenge to the entire national liberation movement and to all the free peoples of the world.

The Vietnamese people are not alone. They are fighting for a just cause, and we are firmly confident that they will be victorious.

The imperialists are also trying to stifle the liberation movement in Africa. Intervention and interference in the affairs of the Congo, the economic and political support given to the Portuguese colonialists and the South African and Rhodesian racialists, the organization of plots against the lawful governments of African states which have taken to the road of independent development, and the instigation of conflicts between them with the aim of undermining African unity—such is a far from complete list of the criminal actions being committed by the imperialists on the African continent.

Recently, the colonialists have committed a new crime against the peoples of Africa. With the connivance and actual support of Great Britain and the USA, the racialist clique of Ian Smith declared the so-called independence of Rhodesia with the aim of perpetuating there the colonial order, which is based on the inhuman oppression of the four-million-strong people of Zimbabwe by a racialist minority. The usurpation of power by the racialists in Rhodesia is aimed at strengthening that outpost of imperialism in Africa. It is nothing other than the beginning of a sinister plan directed at preserving the domination of the colonialists and racialists in the southern and central parts of the African continent. The ruling circles of Great Britain cannot slough off their guilt for this crime against the people of Zimbabwe and against all the peoples of Africa.

The Soviet government, unswervingly striving for the complete liquidation of colonialism and racialism, has resolutely condemned the new crime of the imperialists in Africa and has declared that it will not recognize the racialist regime which has usurped power in Rhodesia. The Soviet government has once again confirmed its readiness to cooperate with the African states in rendering all-round joint support to the people of Zimbabwe in their just struggle for genuine national independence.

US imperialists openly interfered in the affairs of the Dominican Republic and sent troops there in order to prevent by armed force the Dominican people from deciding their own destiny. But the Dominican people are carrying on their selfless struggle, which will lead to the triumph of their just cause. We declare that the Soviet people side firmly with the Dominican patriots. The Soviet Union, together with all the peoples of Latin America, Asia, and Africa, resolutely demands that the troops of the USA and the other interventionists be immediately recalled from the Dominican Republic.

The imperialists are openly encouraging and supporting coup d'états which lead reactionary pro-imperialist regimes to power. Under the false pretext of combating communism, they want to legalize intervention and interference in the internal affairs of Latin American countries. The shameful resolution adopted by the House of Representatives of the US Congress is an attempt to justify this most crass violation of the basis of international law. The plans for setting up "inter-American armed forces" have the same aim.

The Soviet people are deeply in sympathy with the courageous struggle waged by the peoples of Latin America who are striving to defend their national sovereignty and to bring about their national and social dreams. We express our fraternal solidarity with the armed struggle being waged by the Venezuelan, Peruvian, Colombian, and Guatemalan patriots for freedom against the stooges of imperialism. We are in solidarity with the struggle being waged by the peoples of British, French, and Dutch Guiana and the Antilles against the colonial regimes, and also with the struggle waged by the people of Puerto Rico. We express the firm conviction that the struggle waged by these peoples will lead them to their coveted goal—national independence.

We are completely in solidarity with the liberation movement of the peoples of South Arabia, Aden, and Oman, and with the just struggle waged by the people of North Kalimantan for their national independence. We are in solidarity with the people of Korea who are struggling for the recall of the foreign troops from South Korea and for the unification of their native land. We condemn the collusion between the South Korean puppets of the USA and the Japanese imperialists, which is aimed against the people. We are in solidarity with the Japanese people who are demanding the liquidation of US military bases and who are taking a stand against the military treaty with the USA. We are in solidarity with the people of Cyprus who are fighting for the strengthening of national independence and sovereignty, against the intrigues of NATO, and for the liquidation of imperialist military bases.

The Soviet people are in solidarity with the struggle waged by the Arab peoples for the inalienable and lawful rights of the Palestinian Arabs. They resolutely condemn the subversive activities of the Zionist circles in Israel, which are directed against the national liberation movement and which serve the interests of international imperialism.

We are in solidarity with the struggle waged by the peoples of Angola, Mozambique, "Portuguese" Guinea, the Congo, "French" Somalia, Mauritius, and "Spanish" Guinea. We support the courageous people of South Africa who are carrying out, in the difficult conditions of repression, an inflexible struggle against racialism and for national freedom and democracy. We support the struggle waged by the peoples of South and South West Africa, Bechuanaland, Swaziland, and Basutoland against racialism and colonialism and the criminal policy of apartheid.

Dear friends, at present, when the old colonial regimes have been liquidated in most countries of Latin America, Asia, and Africa, the colonialists are resorting to new forms of prolonging imperialist oppression and slavery. Neocolonialism is arriving to replace colonialism. Neocolonialism is not a myth; it is an active force which has now become the main threat for the liberated countries. Its aim is to keep—with new methods and in modified forms—the liberated peoples in economic bondage by pulling new "invisible" chains on them, which are no lighter than were the previous ones.

In order to achieve these aims, the imperialists have created a rich arsenal of most diverse weapons. They are: the military and political groupings connected with NATO, such as SEATO, CENTO, and others, which are backed by imperialist powers; the unequal bilateral agreements of military, political, and economic character; the setting-up, with the help of military coups, bribery, and blackmail, of regimes favorable to the imperialists; and deep economic penetration in various forms with the aim of securing the domination of the foreign monopolies.

The struggle of the developing countries for their economic independence is becoming one of the most important aspects of the national liberation movement. The winning of political independence cannot mechanically of itself liquidate the economic positions which imperialism has at its disposal. These positions are characterized by the domination of the monopolies which have usurped the natural resources of the majority of countries in Asia, Africa, and Latin America, by the backward agrarian structure of the economy of the liberated countries, which they have inherited from the colonial past, by their subjected situation in the world capitalist division of labor, and by their extreme dependence on the export of raw materials and import of the most important kinds of industrial goods.

By relying on reactionary and pro-imperialist regimes, by subjugating the economy of the former colonies and semi-colonies, the neocolonialists are striving for all they are worth to channel the socioeconomic development of the countries in Asia, Africa, and Latin America in a direction which would conform to the interests of the imperialist monopolies and not to the interests of the peoples of those countries.

It is absolutely clear that, in the obtaining situation, the expansion of economic cooperation, mutual assistance, exchange of experience, and coordination of the economic efforts of the countries of the three continents against imperialism have become urgent problems. The working-out and the implementation of a common policy as regards foreign private investment, the conditions for selling of the most important raw materials and foodstuffs, and the problems of customs, currency, and financial affairs enhances the most rapid achievement of economic independence.

Friends, our delegation represents the public and the peoples of the Union of Soviet Socialist Republics, the country of victorious socialism which is now building the material and technical basis of communism. Socialism is winning more and more the minds and the hearts of millions of people. Many nations of Europe, Asia, Africa, and Latin America are marching under the banner of socialism and are waging a struggle for the implementation of its ideals. We are deeply convinced that socialism is the near future of all the peoples of the world.

Following the behests of Lenin, the Soviet Union is consistently working for universal peace and security for all nations. We believe that relations between sovereign states with different social systems must be built on the foundation of peaceful coexistence. At the same time, it is clear that there does not and cannot exist any kind of peaceful coexistence between the oppressed peoples and their oppressors—the colonialists and the imperialists—and between the imperialist aggressors and their victims. The struggle for peace is inseparably connected with the struggle against colonialism, against imperialist aggression, and against all forms of oppression.

Fidelity to the ideals of freedom and independence, and consistent struggle against all sorts of oppression, enslavement, and injustice, form the foundation of the world outlook of the Soviet people and constitute the basis of our state policy. Throughout all its history, the Soviet state, following the behests of the great Lenin, has been rendering all-round support to the peoples who are struggling against colonialism and imperialism for their own national and social liberation. The peoples who rise to the great act of combating imperialism, no matter in what corner of the globe this may take place, can be assured that the Soviet people will always be at their side.

By its might, the Soviet Union is keeping in check the main forces of the imperialist powers and is thus considerably facilitating the conditions in which the peoples are waging the struggle for freedom, independent development, and social progress. In their turn, the Soviet people highly value the revolutionary support which the progressive forces in the other countries of Asia and in the countries of Africa and Latin America have been rendering them for many decades.

At all the international forums, including the United Nations Organization, the Soviet Union has been acting in close concert and complete mutual understanding with the delegates of the peoples of Africa, Asia, and Latin America which are waging the struggle against imperialism and has consistently defended the cause of freedom and independence of those peoples.

Cooperation and mutual assistance between the Soviet Union and the other countries of Asia, and the countries of Africa and Latin America, is varied in form. These forms embrace various spheres of life—politics, economics, science, and culture. We are happy that the industrial enterprises which were built with the participation of the Soviet Union are becoming front-ranking enterprises in the young national states, that with our cooperation the power of the mighty rivers in Asia and Africa is harnessed to the service of man, and that thousands of highly qualified experts are being trained in our universities who, after their return home—to the countries of Asia, Africa, and Latin America—will become active participants in national renaissance in the former colonies and semi-colonies and will become active fighters for social progress.

More than six hundred enterprises of national economy and about one hundred educational establishments which the USSR has already built or is now building in the developing countries, several score of thousands of experts trained in the USSR, support in military equipment of peoples and countries which are struggling for their independence against the attacks of imperialism—

such is the practical contribution made by the Soviet people to the great cause of liberation and national renaissance of the former colonies and semi-colonies.

The imperialists are well aware how great a force is the solidarity and unity of the peoples of Asia, Africa, and Latin America. That is why they are striving to incite contradictions and arguments, and chuckle with pleasure when these contradictions and arguments become conflicts and when they manage to hinder the settling of these conflicts.

It is necessary to mete out a resolute rebuff to these intrigues of imperialism and neocolonialism. The consolidation of all the revolutionary forces of our time—the peoples of the socialist countries, the peoples which are waging the national liberation struggle, and the international democratic and labor movement—is of decisive importance in achieving this end. The profound unity of aims and the interest in mutual assistance forms the basis of the consolidation of those three powerful anti-imperialist forces. They are the main forces with which we wish to be in alliance in order to act in complete unity. Our common aim is freedom, independence, peace, democracy, and social progress. Our common enemy is world imperialism, and first of all, world imperialism led by the imperialism of the USA. We must counterpose the cunning machinations of imperialism directed at splitting our movement with the historically tested weapon—the strengthening of the solidarity, cohesion, and fighting capacity of our great movement.

As comrade Fidel Castro, the leader of revolutionary Cuba, so aptly put it: "Disunity in the face of the enemy has never been a revolutionary or a clever strategy."

We must make the aspiration for unity the basis of the tricontinent solidarity movement and must constantly strengthen our unity around the main aim of the movement—the struggle against imperialism, colonialism, and neocolonialism, for freedom, peace, independence, and social progress.

Our conference must unite the two mighty streams of the anti-imperialist forces into one single movement of the people of the three continents which will have as its banner the militant spirit of Havana. In order to consolidate this unity, the Soviet delegation supports the proposal to set up at this conference an Organization of Tricontinent Solidarity.

To mark the First Conference of Solidarity of the Peoples of Asia, Africa, and Latin America, the Soviet delegation also proposes that there be introduced and annually held from January 3 to 10, an international week of solidarity of the three continents in the struggle against colonialism, neocolonialism, and imperialism.

The Soviet delegation earnestly appeals to all the national organizations and their movements represented at this conference to unite in the struggle for this great goal. Let our conference be a new stage on this road. Let it multiply and strengthen the unity of our ranks and impart new force to the liberation struggle throughout the world.

Osmany Cienfuegos

**Minister of Construction, Head of International Relations of the
Central Committee of the Communist Party of Cuba, and Chair of
the Cuban Delegation**

The Cuban Delegation greets all the anti-imperialist fighters attending this conference as true representatives of the fraternal peoples of Africa, Asia, and Latin America, comrades in the struggle to obtain a better future for mankind.

As President Dorticós states in the opening session, it has been a singular honor for the Cuban people to have our country chosen as the site for such a supremely important event.

Your presence during the celebration of the seventh anniversary of the Cuban Revolution will remain a pleasant memory for our people, for having shared these joyful days at the very doorstep of the common enemy, Yankee imperialism, with fighters of the three continents who have also been hard hit by the crimes and greed of the colonialists and neocolonialists.

We know that from this historic occasion we must draw the utmost experience and reach the most effective conclusions as to the goals we are pursuing: the struggle for national liberation, the merciless battle against imperialism.

In organizing the conference, our party aimed to provide the ideal conditions and facilities so that this meeting would give a new impulse, new strength, vigor and experience, to the liberating struggle of the people of the three continents, the open combat against Yankee imperialism and against every system of imperialist, colonialist, and neocolonialist exploitation.

Cuba's revolutionary line has been sufficiently expressed in the development of its policy since the very beginnings of the revolution. This revolutionary line has been set forth in the First and Second Declarations of Havana, which constitute irrevocable program documents of our people. The Second Declaration of Havana states:

> That which Cuba can give to the peoples and has already given
> is its example. And what does the Cuban Revolution show? That
> revolution is possible. That the peoples can carry it out, that in the

present-day world there are no forces capable of holding back the liberation movement of the peoples.

Revolution is possible because it is imposed by the miserable conditions in which our people live. The shameful imperialist and colonialist exploitation have created adequate conditions on the three continents for the development of the liberation movement and popular revolt.

Analyzing the conditions of imperialist, colonialist, and neocolonialist exploitation and the living standard of our people suffices to make clear that the situation is more than ripe for rebellion, for revolution.

Thus far not a single liberated people have won their liberation in any other way than revolution. It is said that experience is the best teacher, and this is indeed the case. This conference should benefit by the experience of those triumphant peoples, of those people who have won their victory, of those who as in Vietnam today are showing that no one can oppose with lasting success the heroic action and unshakable determination to obtain independence and liberation.

Not a single example can be cited to the contrary.

As to the concrete conditions of the underdeveloped countries applied to the social and economic realities and fighting tactics, we must declare as an incontrovertible fact that our people find themselves in a favorable situation on the road to their independence. Allow us to quote again the Second Declaration of Havana, which offers a realistic analysis in this respect when it states:

> When armies organized and equipped for conventional warfare, which are the force by which the exploiting classes stay in power, confront the irregular warfare of the peasants on their home ground, they are rendered absolutely impotent. They lose ten men for each revolutionary fighter who falls; they succumb rapidly to demoralization when having to face an invisible and invincible cadre, who gives them no opportunity to display their military academy tactics and their war fanfare, which they so boastfully brandish to suppress the workers and students in the cities.

Many are the tasks and issues which must be covered by our conference.

One of the problems of greatest interest to the conference is the idea of setting up a tricontinental organization to promote the solidarity of the peoples of Asia, Africa, and Latin America. Various opinions are being debated as to the best means of reaching this objective. Whatever the solution, we must reach it after full and profound discussion in which all of these opinions will be carefully studied. Moreover, the solution must correspond to the interests of the popular liberation movements, to these interests only.

We must ask ourselves what kind of organization we desire and for what purpose. We must find the path leading to an organization which it its form and content will be effective in giving drive to the revolutionary struggle of the peoples.

It must be an organization of fighting peoples, with enough flexibility and the capacity for action to assist the peoples of the three continents in the development of the national liberation movement and anti-imperialist struggle. We must give to the concept of solidarity an active, dynamic, and militant content.

The organization should conform to this objective, both in form and in content.

Some opinions have advanced regarding the maintenance of the Afro-Asian Solidarity Organization and the parallel creation of the Tricontinental Organization with a seat, at the suggestion of some of the delegations, in Havana. The selection of Cuba as the seat would undoubtedly be an honor to us but our position is not conditioned by any aspirations of a nationalist nature that might create obstacles. If the conference should decide to establish one sole organization to unify the anti-imperialist efforts of Asia, Africa, and Latin America with Cairo as a seat, Cuba would back that decision, but in this case its vote would be conditioned. This is indeed a matter in which we are fundamentally interested in seeing the designation of a representative of the heroic Vietnamese people as president, since this country is today the center of the most ferocious, criminal, and inhuman of all imperialist aggressions and around which should be centered the solidarity and the will to fight of the peoples of the three continents and of the whole world, as well as an expression of the character and tone of this conference.

The list is already long of peoples fighting arms in hand against one or another form of imperialist, colonialist, neocolonialist, or racist oppression. The list is headed by the heroic people of Vietnam who inspire our firmest solidarity; the peoples of Santo Domingo, Laos, Venezuela, the Portuguese colonies of Guinea and Cape Verde, Angola and Mozambique, of the Congo (Léopoldville), of Guatemala, Peru, and Colombia.

The most oppressed and virtually enslaved peoples of Rhodesia and South Africa are demanding their rights with ever-greater energy. The movement of Negroes in the United States for human dignity is growing. The small but admirable people of Puerto Rico are not faltering in their efforts to preserve their Latin American nationality in order to be able to join as a free country the fraternal peoples of this continent.

Cambodia has warned of its resolve to fight against the aggressors if the imperialists extend the war to its territory.

The Arabs of Palestine demand the restoration of their usurped rights.

The people of Panama are insisting on their sovereignty over the territory that was seized from their country which is paying with the generous blood of its sons for this rightful aspiration. British Guiana, Guadeloupe, Martinique are not resigned to the colonial status which still shamefully prevail on their territories.

As there so many peoples who are still suffering under the colonial yoke, direct or indirect, this list of peoples who are struggling, demanding, insisting, fighting, is growing and will go on growing until the time when, with the help of all the revolutionary peoples of the world, this planet can truly call itself a territory free of imperialism.

So that this day may come, all of our peoples must struggle, and we must all try to be first in solidarity and effort. This is the aspiration and purpose of our country and our people.

At this moment in which this Conference of Solidarity of the Peoples of Asia, Africa, and Latin America is taking place, with resounding success, we must all voice our severest condemnation of the kidnapping in Paris and almost certain assassination of the president of the preparatory committee, Mehdi Ben Barka, one of the most outstanding figures in the struggle for national liberation in Africa. It is evident that this abominable deed was devised and perpetrated by agents of imperialism and reaction, both interested in obstructing this manifestation of anti-imperialism and revolutionary solidarity.

It is absolutely necessary that this criminal act be elucidated and the responsibility of governments and powers that have participated in it be exposed.

Whatever may have been the fate suffered by comrade Ben Barka, it is right that the conference recognizes his extraordinary contribution to the development and culmination of this event.

The paths of unity among the peoples are the paths of revolution. There is no true popular unity without revolution. The question is how to achieve this unity. There is only one way: making revolution. How to make revolution? We must set ourselves an immediate objective: to frame strategy and tactics to achieve this objective, incorporate the highest number of forces to achieve that objective. What matters is that tactics unleash and develop the action and unity of the people and it be effective in the struggle against the enemy.

This, fellow delegates, is the experience of our revolution, learnt in the struggle and confirmed by success and by the monolithic unity of the Cuban people. This example is displayed by all successful revolutions.

Today all peoples have a very clear objective: defense of the principles of national sovereignty, of self-determination of states, the right of peoples to make revolution, aid to those peoples by all means within our reach.

Progressive humanity has in its hands today an uncommon strength, which if united around these objectives will step-by-step triumph over imperialism and defeat it.

Even though the conditions for the victory of revolution exist, revolution is not born spontaneously. The duty of revolutionaries is fundamental, and this duty is fulfilled in the action, in the fight, in the open struggle against imperialism, national oligarchies, colonialism, neocolonialism, feudalism, and great landownership.

"The duty of every revolutionary is to make the revolution."

The delegation of Cuba participates in the work of the conference with the full conviction that millions of human beings on our three continents shall not be defrauded, who after centuries of suffering the most abominable crimes, the crudest and most unjust exploitation of their labor, of bearing the most painful offences against their dignity, are irrevocably determined to win forever their complete liberation.

"This great humanity has said, '*Enough!*' and has begun to move and the march of these giants shall not be stopped, until they achieve their true independence!"

Ibrahim Isa (Indonesia)

Dear Friends:

This week, Havana, Cuba, a free territory in Latin America, is once again the center of attention. People from one end of the world to the other, especially in Asia, Africa, and Latin America, are following this historic Tricontinental Conference with great attention and high hopes. It is therefore our sacred duty to do everything within our power and ability to make this significant conference a success. We must not fail to fulfill the wishes and aspirations of our peoples.

Before moving on to the topic to be discussed at this conference, allow me, first of all, to extend warm greetings from the revolutionary forces of Indonesia to the heroic and courageous people of Cuba and to all the delegations participating in this conference. At the same time, we wish to express our sincere gratitude to our Cuban friends for their hospitality and excellent organization.

Dear Brothers and Friends:

We are here to strengthen and consolidate our forces and strengthen our ranks. We have come here to expose our enemies and reaffirm our determination to fight to the end against imperialism, colonialism, and neocolonialism led by the United States imperialists. In a word, we want principled unity directed against the enemy of the peoples of the world, imperialism led by the United States. We must take all actions conducive to this end and oppose all measures that confuse or hinder it by exposing them to all the peoples of the world.

We are meeting in a situation very favorable to the world's revolutionary forces. A constantly growing revolutionary situation is developing in Asia, Africa, and Latin America. In this highly revolutionary part of the world, the imperialists are receiving blow after blow. AAA (Africa, Asia, and Latin America) is the weakest bastion of imperialism. It is, therefore, in these areas where the struggle against the imperialists is most important. It is therefore not surprising that it is in these regions of Asia, Africa, and Latin America where the struggles in their highest forms, that is, armed struggles, are being carried out.

The struggles of the peoples of Asia, Africa, and Latin America have shaken the foundation of imperialism. This constitutes a great aid to the struggles of other progressive peoples in Europe, North America, and Australia. It is, therefore, the international duty of all revolutionaries and progressives to support the struggles of the peoples of all three continents.

Today, the fiercest and most decisive struggle against public enemy number one, US imperialism, is taking place in Vietnam. A glorious war is being waged by the people of Vietnam. The Vietnamese people, using all the tactics and resources of a people at war, are dealing a mortal blow to the US imperialists, despite the troops it has sent or will send to South Vietnam. Its policy of escalation, false peace, escalation, and false peace again has been widely denounced before the masses and peoples of the entire world.

With their glorious struggle, the people of Vietnam are greatly contributing to the global struggle against imperialism and for world peace. We have a sacred duty to politically and materially support the struggle of the Vietnamese people. This conference must launch another major campaign of support for Vietnam; support and insist on the four points proposed by the DRV (Democratic Republic of Vietnam) and the five points contained in the NLF (National Liberation Front of South Vietnam) declaration.

US imperialism is committing crimes all over the world, unleashing wars and aggression, fomenting subversion, exercising dominance, and encouraging infiltration in Laos, Japan, Thailand, Cambodia, Indonesia, the Philippines, Congo, Cuba, the Dominican Republic, and other countries in Asia, Africa, and Latin America. Last year, the Johnson administration publicly announced its doctrine of truncating the independence and freedom of all countries, suppressing national liberation movements and all revolutionary movements through war and aggression.

The aggressive nature of the US imperialists will never change. Like a furious bulldog, they will attack and devour peoples, whether provoked or not. Therefore, there is no alternative but to fight, exterminate them, or be exterminated sooner or later. A decision must inevitably be made.

The people of Vietnam have clearly demonstrated that the US imperialists can be defeated, no matter how difficult it may seem. A just people's war is the best response to imperialist domination and aggression. Armed struggles against neocolonialism are currently being waged in Venezuela, Santo Domingo, Portuguese Guinea, Congo, Mozambique, Colombia, North Kalimantan, Laos, Guatemala, Malaysia, and other parts of the world. There is no doubt that these struggles will be crowned with success. Likewise, the struggles of the peoples of Kashmir; Puerto Rico; British Guiana; Guadeloupe; Martinique; Japan; South Korea; Malaya, including Singapore; Angola; Southern Rhodesia; Basutoland; Swaziland; Aden; South Arabia; and Palestine will be victorious. The struggle undertaken by the people of Thailand when they took up arms caused fear and indecision among the US imperialists and their lackeys. This struggle of the Thai people is a just struggle.

This conference must support all these peoples in their struggle against neo-colonialism led by US imperialists.

The world situation has shown us that the peoples of the three continents are engaged in revolutionary struggles. As stated in the Havana Declaration:

> The duty of every revolutionary is to make revolution. We know that in America and throughout the world, the revolution will be victorious. And that the Cuban revolution demonstrates that revolution is possible, that the people can make it, that in today's world there are not enough forces to prevent popular movements.

Given this situation, it is undoubtedly the duty of the participants in this conference to consolidate the struggle and the true unity of the revolutionary forces. May this true unity of the revolutionary forces be directed against the true common enemy: the American imperialists and their lackeys.

Dear Friends and Brothers:

In a situation where imperialism, led by the United States, is resorting to every means to pursue its warlike, aggressive, subversive, and dominating policy, it is all the more important for us to understand the content of true revolutionary unity. It is in this regard that I wish to inform you about the recent drastic changes in Indonesia. The division between Indonesia's revolutionary and reactionary forces has recently become more evident. All of us have been asked the question of whom this movement should join. The answer has already been given: that it should join the revolutionary forces.

Since October 1965, right-wing and reactionary elements within Indonesia's military circles, in close collaboration with and instigated by international imperialism led by the United States and through the CIA, have been attempting to seize control of power in Indonesia, one way or another. A regime of terror, discrimination, and racism plagues the Indonesian people and nation. To date, more than one hundred thousand people have been arrested, including many popular leaders, steadfast fighters for independence and against neocolonialism. Those detained are subjected to the most brutal and inhuman treatment, demonstrating the fascist nature of those currently in power. More than three hundred Indonesian journalists have been arrested, imprisoned, fired, and terrorized, while the circulation of newspapers and magazines has been banned.

In the name of "revolutionary actions," they are uniting all counterrevolutionary elements and carrying out all kinds of counterrevolutionary actions. In the name of the "revolution," they are fomenting the counterrevolution. In the name of the "Left," they are turning the situation to the Right. In the name of suppressing the September 30th Movement, they are repressing communism, and under the banner of anticommunism, they persecute all democrats, regardless of whether they are nationalist, religious, or communist.

Under the pretext of eliminating the September 30th Movement, Indonesian reactionaries, supported by reactionary military circles, are carrying out coups step by step, using the most treacherous methods. It is interesting to see how, in his effort to reach a solution to the September 30th political problem, President Sukarno said: "If you agree with me, keep me in power. If you don't, throw me out." This statement was directed at the rightists.

US imperialism and its accomplices are aware that a united, strong, and progressive Indonesia represents a great danger to them, and are therefore doing everything possible to eliminate this movement. The current acts of violence and counterrevolutionary actions against our country's patriotic forces and the anticommunist campaign are part of these imperialist plans.

Dark clouds are covering the skies of our homeland. But this is only a temporary phenomenon. The democratic forces of our country are powerful and sufficient. Moreover, our people are hardened in struggle. There is no power that can defeat the people, and there is no power in the world that can give victory to the rightists.

The revolutionary nationalists, religious figures, and communist revolutionaries, united with the ranks of the four armed forces of the Republic of Indonesia, are strengthening the bonds of unity, which have every right to defend and protect the gains of the revolution achieved over these past twenty years. The time will come when these rightists will be trampled underfoot by the law of the revolution.

Dear Friends and Brothers:

We, the representatives of the patriotic and revolutionary forces of Indonesia, have the duty to expose the situation and counterrevolutionary activities in Indonesia. This is not an internal problem; it is a problem for all progressives and revolutionaries in Asia, Africa, Latin America, and around the world. What has happened in Indonesia can happen in any other country on our three continents. There is no neutrality in this matter. One has to decide: ally oneself with the revolutionaries or the rightists. Exposing this situation is also necessary to clarify who we should unite with and who we will fight against. It is necessary for this solidarity movement to insist on its revolutionary principles. Only by insisting on these revolutionary principles can this movement continue to expand and advance by leaps and bounds.

Let us unite to crush the warlike and aggressive policies of the imperialists, led by the United States. We will continue the struggle against imperialism's policy of nuclear blackmail. We must support the strengthening of the defense capabilities of the socialist countries. Nuclear weapons in the hands of the socialist countries are necessary for the defense of world peace.

Let's better expose the repulsive face of the imperialists who use the United Nations as their instrument for world domination and to deceive the peoples of the world.

Let us continue our struggle, trusting above all in our own strength and insisting on the principle of self-reliance.

We are going to expose the so-called foreign "aid" of imperialism, which is an instrument to dominate the economy and politics of independent countries.

Dear Friends and Brothers,

The Indonesian delegation will exert its utmost efforts at this conference to contribute to its success. We must strive to ensure that this conference deals a decisive blow to imperialism and promotes the anti-imperialist struggle on all three continents.

We have come with the same objectives and have prepared them to reach agreements after consultations. The principle of unanimity must be maintained by all means. Only by insisting on these principles can we firmly unite the revolutionary forces of Asia, Africa, and Latin America.

Thank you so much.

Kim Wal Yong (Democratic People's Republic of Korea)

Member of the Central Committee of the Workers' Party of Korea

Dear Mr. President;

Dear Delegates:

Taking this opportunity, I would first like to extend my warmest greetings to the heroic Cuban people, our comrade in arms and close brother fighting against the common enemy, US imperialism, and to Prime Minister Fidel Castro.

I take this opportunity to wholeheartedly thank the Communist Party of Cuba, the revolutionary government, and the preparatory committee of this conference for inviting the Korean delegation.

I would also like to extend our warmest greetings to our brothers and sisters from Asia, Africa, and Latin America who are meeting with us.

We are extremely pleased that this historic gathering for the powerful anti-imperialist march of the peoples of three continents is being held in Cuba, the first free territory of the Americas, ninety miles from Yankee imperialism.

Today, the Cuban people are destroying the malignant aggressive maneuvers of US imperialism, firmly defending the revolutionary achievements and successfully accelerating socialist construction. The glorious path of the heroic Cuban people constitutes the revolutionary banner of the Latin American peoples and provides the strength of inspiration to all peoples fighting for freedom and independence.

The Korean people rejoice in all the successes achieved by the brotherly Cuban people as if they were their own.

I wish the sister people of Cuba even more brilliant victories in the subsequent struggles against the incessant aggression of Yankee imperialism and for the acceleration of socialist construction under the leadership of the Communist Party of Cuba and the revolutionary government headed by comrade Fidel Castro.

Dear Delegates:

This conference is being held at a time when the gigantic wave of revolution is sweeping across Asia, Africa, and Latin America, and all oppressed peoples are waging a courageous struggle for freedom and independence under the banner of national liberation.

Today, in Asia and Africa, the banner of freedom, liberation, sovereignty, and self-reliance flies high thanks to the long and arduous struggle against foreign aggressors, and the anti-imperialist struggle in various forms, including armed struggle, is raging in Latin America. In this way, the odious imperialist and colonial system is completely disintegrating.

But the imperialists, led by Yankee imperialism, are trying to find a way out of their destruction through policies of aggression and war, and are maneuvering more desperately than ever against the socialist countries and trying to stifle the national liberation struggle of the peoples.

The US imperialists, the main bastion of world reaction, are strengthening their aggressive and warlike manipulation everywhere and are increasingly embarking on the path of provocative adventurism, "local war," and "total war," fanning a frenzy of nuclear blackmail and anticommunist war behind the deceptive facade of "peace."

US imperialism is particularly directing its aggressive baton toward Asia, Africa, and Latin America to try to extinguish the flames of the anti-imperialist and anticolonial struggle that are raging in these regions, committing cruel armed interventions in the people's struggle.

The US imperialist aggressors, who are suffering shameful defeat after shameful defeat in Vietnam, have taken off their false masks and embarked on the path of further expanding the aggressive war by greatly increasing their troops and armed forces, even introducing troops from other puppet countries, and are blindly frantically trying to spread the flames of war throughout Indochina and Asia.

The US imperialists have established numerous military bases in Japan, occupied Okinawa, turning it into a staging ground for their aggression against Asia, and are continuing their relentless provocative activities against the People's Republic of China by occupying Taiwan.

Yankee imperialism is actively supporting racists, barbarously repressing the national liberation struggle of the Congo and the peoples of Africa, and threatening the independence and security of the Arab peoples by arming Israel.

The US imperialists continue their dirty plan of cruel intervention in internal affairs and sabotage in various areas of Latin America, including the Dominican Republic, and they incessantly commit barbaric armed attacks.

Truly, the American imperialists have not ceased their aggressive war in Asia, Africa, and Latin America for a single day, nor has there been a single day in which they have not shed the blood of the people.

All the facts clearly demonstrate that Yankee imperialism is the main force in the war, the international gendarme, the main bastion of neocolonialism, and the common enemy of the peoples of Asia, Africa, and Latin America.

The US imperialists have been occupying southern Korea for twenty years now, bringing countless calamities and suffering to the South Korean people.

The US imperialists have seized power on all fronts: political, economic, and military in South Korea, and have turned it into a complete colonial and military base.

US imperialism and its puppet, the Park Chung Hee clique, are savagely murdering patriots in South Korea who demand the unification of the country. They have completely dissolved democratic mass organizations and political parties, thus completely destroying the freedom and rights of the people.

US imperialism, which has completely destroyed South Korea's national economy, has driven the people into extreme poverty and the abyss. Yankee imperialism, frantically violating the Korean armistice agreement, is introducing large quantities of nuclear weapons and rockets into South Korea, thus turning South Korea into a launching pad for aggression against the Asian continent and also incessantly raising an outcry against the North Korean side.

The occupation of South Korea by Yankee imperialism and its policy of colonial slavery are the cause of all the suffering and misfortunes of the South Korean people, the main obstacle to the unification of Korea, and the cause of the danger of war in Asia.

Above all, recently, the criminal South Korea–Japan Treaty was maneuvered between the Park Chung Hee puppet clique of South Korea and the Satō government of Japan, despite the firm protests of the peoples of Japan and Korea, thus creating the most serious phase in the situation in Korea and Asia in general.

This "treaty" is a treaty of aggression and war fabricated as a link in its aggressive plan against Asia, under the manipulation of Yankee imperialism.

The US imperialists are frantically trying to maintain their shaky system of colonial rule in South Korea and Asia by uniting Japanese militarist forces with the South Korean puppet clique through the South Korea–Japan Treaty to fabricate the Northeast Asia Military Alliance[*] and trying to position the Japanese militarists as a "shock brigade" for their aggression against Asia.

This is a dangerous maneuver aimed at expanding the war in Asia against the socialist countries of Asia and crushing the people's struggle for national liberation.

Currently, the Japanese militarists, clinging to Yankee imperialism, are embarking on the path of overseas expansion and large-scale penetration into South Korea.

They take over the supply and training of all kinds of equipment for the South Korean puppet army, seize important South Korean lines, and are further accelerating direct military collaboration relations with South Korea.

---

[*] The formal name of this alliance is the Northeast Asia Treaty Organization, but leaders in the conference named it as such to highlight its true objectives.

Above all, today, the Japanese militarists and the South Korean puppet clique are actively participating in US imperialism's aggressive war against Vietnam.

Tens of thousands of South Korean puppet soldiers have already been sent to South Vietnam, Japanese territory is being used as a base for US imperialist aggression against Vietnam, and Japanese war materials, transportation, and even military personnel are under US control.

As demonstrated by secret plans such as Operation Three Arrows and Operation Flying Dragon, which have already been exposed to the world, the Japanese militarists, together with the United States, have made strict preparations to carry out the attack operation against the Democratic People's Republic of Korea, the People's Republic of China, and other Asian countries, and are carrying out large-scale military exercises.

The Japanese militarists, who in the past brought enormous calamities to the peoples of Asia by provoking the Pacific War, after having occupied Korea and attacked China, today reappear on the world stage as the enemy of the peoples of Asia, as the disturber of the peace of the Far East and of the world, conspiring with Yankee imperialism.

If these dangerous machinations of Yankee imperialism and Japan are not destroyed, not only will the division of Korea be perpetuated and South Korea become a double colony of the US and Japan, but all the peoples of the Far East and Asia, including those of Japan, will also fall into great misfortune.

Today the fight against Yankee imperialism, and to thwart its aggressive machinations by removing the mask of the Japanese militarists, is an urgent task to defend peace in Asia and the world.

The Korean people have waged a firm and consistent struggle against the criminal South Korea–Japanese Treaty.

The South Korean people, youth, and students have fought against it on a massive scale, sacrificing their lives and rejecting the barbaric and bloody repression of troops and police under circumstances as dangerous as permanent martial law.

Now in South Korea, the mass struggle for the right to live, for democracy, and against the South Korea–Japan Treaty continues vigorously.

In Japan, too, the gigantic struggle of progressive political parties, social organizations, and the broad masses of the people is being waged against Yankee imperialism and the South Korea–Japan Treaty and militarization, as well as against fascism.

The Korean people strongly support this just struggle of the Japanese people and stand in firm solidarity with their struggle.

The Korean people, as the government of the Democratic People's Republic of Korea has repeatedly stated, will never recognize the criminal South Korea–Japan Treaty that goes against the will and interests of the people.

To eliminate the misfortune of the Korean people and consolidate peace in Asia, the aggressive troops of US imperialism must withdraw from South Korea and the peaceful unification of the country must be achieved.

The entire Korean people will continue to fight perseveringly to unify the country by expelling US troops, without any intervention from foreign forces and independently.

I take this opportunity to express our gratitude to the people of Asia, Africa, and Latin America who actively support the struggle of the Korean people.

At the same time we call on this conference to take strong measures to oppose the occupation of South Korea by Yankee imperialism to frustrate the South Korean–Japanese Treaty and destroy the manipulation and the plan of the "Northeast Asia Military Alliance" and to destroy the external aggressive maneuvering of Japanese militarism.

Dear Delegates:

The most important task facing the peoples of Asia, Africa, and Latin America today is to fight to thwart the aggressive maneuvers of Yankee imperialism, to achieve national freedom and independence, and to defend peace. Fighting against Yankee imperialism is precisely the fight for freedom, independence, progress, and peace. If the fight against American imperialism is abandoned, we cannot speak of the victory of any revolutionary cause, nor of independence, peace, or progress.

The peoples of Asia, Africa, and Latin America must fight firmly against American imperialism and do everything possible to expose and thwart its machinations of aggression and war.

Above all, supporting and backing the just struggle that the Vietnamese people are heroically waging in the first forefront of the anti-imperialist struggle is a sacred duty of the peoples of the socialist countries, Asia, Africa, and Latin America, as well as of the progressive peoples of the world.

Today, the struggle of the Vietnamese people against the aggressors of US imperialism constitutes the focus of the anti-imperialist struggle of the peoples of the world.

The Vietnamese people are fighting heroically not only for the complete liberation, unification, and independence of their homeland, but are also shedding their blood to defend the socialist bloc and for peace in Asia and the world.

We must unconditionally and firmly support the solid and unwavering position of the brotherly Vietnamese people to fight to the bitter end against the aggressors of Yankee imperialism and do everything possible to support their struggle.

The Korean people, who consider the struggle of the Vietnamese people as their own and are willing to share life or death with them, will spare no support or aid of any kind, including weapons, for the struggle of the Vietnamese people. They are filled with the firm resolve to participate at any time as volunteers should the National Liberation Front of South Vietnam so request.

We fully support the four points of the government of the Democratic Republic of Vietnam and the five points of the National Liberation Front of South Vietnam, which propose just measures for resolving the Vietnam issue.

We categorically condemn Johnson's false machinations on the issue of Vietnam of the "peaceful solution" and the "unconditional conversation" and we strongly demand that the Yankee imperialists immediately cease the aggressive war in Vietnam and that [they] withdraw immediately with [their] soldiers and [their] genocidal weapons.

This Conference must take decisive measures to support and assist, both materially and spiritually, the struggle of the Vietnamese people, to expose all kinds of deceptive maneuvers and to stop this aggression.

The Korean delegation proposes to organize at this Conference the Three Continents Solidarity Committee with Vietnam to more vigorously assist and support the struggle of the heroic Vietnamese people.

Dear Delegates:

The Korean people actively support the Laotian people's struggle for peace and neutrality and the Cambodian people's struggle for sovereignty and territorial integrity.

The Korean people support the struggle of the Indonesian people against "Malaysia," an instrument of neocolonialism by the US and British imperialists, and express their active solidarity with the courageous struggle of the people of North Kalimantan.

The Korean people express their full support and solidarity with the people of Congo (L) who are fighting heroically with weapons in hand and actively support the heroic struggles for freedom and liberation of the peoples of Angola, Mozambique, Portuguese Guinea, Basutoland, Swaziland, Bechuanaland, French Somalia, and South West Africa.

The Korean people express their full and active solidarity with the struggle of the people of Zimbabwe and the peoples of all Africa against the machinations of the Smith clique's illegal and unilateral independence of Southern Rhodesia, and also express their solidarity with the peoples of Southern Africa who are struggling against racial discrimination.

The Korean people actively support and encourage the struggle of the Arab peoples to defend their independence and sovereignty against the aggression of the Israeli imperialists, and the struggle of the Palestinian people for the liberation of their homeland.

Furthermore, we actively support the beloved patriotic struggle of the peoples of South Yemen.

The Korean people express their active solidarity with the peoples of Latin America who are fighting against Yankee imperialism and reactionary domination within the country.

The Korean people actively support the courageous struggle of the Dominican people against the armed intervention of Yankee imperialism and for true independence, and actively support the struggle of the people of Panama, just as they actively stand in solidarity with the peoples of Venezuela, Guatemala, Peru, Colombia, and other countries waging a courageous armed struggle.

We send our active support to the peoples of all countries in Asia, Africa, and Latin America who are fighting against imperialism, colonialism, and neocolonialism.

Dear Delegates:

The common task of the peoples of Asia, Africa, and Latin America is to fulfill the sacred task of national liberation by raising the revolutionary banner ever higher.

The peoples of countries under the colonial yoke must open the way to freedom and liberation by further expanding the struggle and liquidating the abominable system of imperialism and colonialism.

In circumstances where the imperialists repress the national liberation struggle of the peoples with weapons, they have the right to fight with weapons in hand against the oppressors.

The peoples of the liberated countries must fight tenaciously to defend the independence they have already achieved, to achieve national prosperity and social progress, to build an independent economy and culture by thoroughly eliminating colonial vices and against the penetration of neocolonialism.

In terms of achieving the common cause posed to the peoples of Asia, Africa, and Latin America, the most important thing is to further strengthen unity and collaboration under the firm anti-imperialist and anticolonial banner.

If the peoples of Asia, Africa, and Latin America wage a persistent common struggle, uniting firmly, they will achieve even greater and new victories and make great contributions to world peace and humanity.

The Korean people will always march hand in hand with the peoples of Asia, Africa, and Latin America who are fighting against imperialism and neocolonialism and will make continuous efforts to strengthen unity and solidarity with them.

Dear Delegates:

We are at the moment of a great revolutionary turning point in which the peoples of Asia, Africa, and Latin America have risen up and rejected the old system.

We are convinced that this Havana Conference will contribute to the struggle for the liberation of Asia, Africa, and Latin America by strengthening the unity and cohesion of the peoples of three continents in the fight against imperialism, colonialism, and neocolonialism, led by the Yankee empire.

Long live the solidarity of the peoples of Asia, Africa, and Latin America!

Down with imperialism, colonialism, and neocolonialism led by Yankee imperialism!

Long live the Tricontinental Conference!

Luis Augusto Turcios Lima (Guatemala)

Commander of the Rebel Armed Forces

Comrades in struggle from Asia, Africa, and Latin America: Allow me first to express, on behalf of my country's people, a revolutionary and militant greeting to the heroic brotherly people of Cuba on the occasion of the seventh anniversary of their glorious revolution—the initial milestone of the Latin American revolution.

I also wish to convey the heartfelt gratitude of the delegation I lead for the solidarity and warm welcome extended by the Cuban people en masse to the representatives of the peoples of Asia, Africa, and Latin America. We have deeply felt the combative and fraternal solidarity of the Cuban people as our own.

Comrade delegates: The delegation I represent brings to this important conference the voice of a country whose very name is an indictment against US imperialism: Guatemala. Yet we arrive filled with confidence, for we know that in our era, the path to victory remains open to all peoples—large or small—fighting for national liberation, economic independence, and political and social freedom, provided they resolutely take up the struggle and rely on the unwavering solidarity of all other peoples.

The remnants of colonialism, imperialism, and neocolonialism are irrevocably condemned to be swept from our three continents and the entire world by the global revolutionary movement, in which anti-imperialist and liberating forces form the decisive majority.

In our small country, Guatemala, we are experiencing in full force the situation imposed on Latin American peoples by imperialism's efforts to prevent Cuba's revolutionary example from spreading across the continent. This reality, marked by the desperate offensive of internal reactionary forces, the imposition of military tyrannies, and violent repression, is by no means a sign that imperialism can block the revolution's path. For us, the struggle will be long and arduous, but we are certain it will culminate in the people's definitive victory.

The Guatemalan revolution, which began under different circumstances with the democratic revolution of 1944 and was uprooted by the 1954 Yankee intervention, learned through painful experience the necessity of a new path. Bitter lessons from our own history and the example of Cuba's revolutionary war guided us to the correct path: In Guatemala, the only viable route for revolution is armed struggle—the revolutionary war forced upon us by the enemy's oppression.

This war has already begun and is growing with increasing popular participation. As stated in the declaration of the provisional revolutionary leadership center of the Rebel Armed Forces (FAR): "With no possibility of peaceful or legal struggle, the revolutionary forces have taken the only path left to our people: to counter counterrevolutionary violence with revolutionary violence, to clear the way for the Guatemalan revolution with weapons in hand, and to organize and advance the people's revolutionary war. Under current historical conditions, our revolution will not pass through electoral ballots."

The people cannot wait for the enemy regime to collapse at their feet, torn apart by its internal contradictions. In reality, the neocolonial strategy of Yankee imperialism, endured by our people for over half a century, is a silent war waged with weapons of exploitation, misery, hunger, illiteracy, racial discrimination, and systematic repression—often institutionalized for convenience.

There were never true possibilities for freedom during periods of deceptive, illusory legality. The process has always followed a vicious cycle: superficial reforms, false democratic hopes, limited shifts in power, followed by imperialist pressure, threats, intervention, and a return to repression, military rule, and coups. This history has repeated for decades, leaving real power in the same hands, preserving imperialist domination, and perpetuating the people's oppression under the most ruthless exploitation—a neocolonial farce disguised as formal independence.

To all this, we have declared: "Enough!" We have reached the brink and resolved to end this silent war in which only the people suffer casualties. The revolutionary war, the people's war, has already begun. Though we know we will endure great suffering, death, and destruction for a long time, we are determined not to halt until the people seize power. We cannot deceive ourselves or the people: popular victory demands a high price.

To wage this struggle, the Rebel Armed Forces (FAR) were formed—the political and military instrument the Guatemalan people need to lead the war. Our organization grows, nourished by the people: peasants, workers, students, and other popular sectors. By envisioning revolutionary war as a movement advancing from the countryside to the city, we have defined the peasantry as the revolution's principal force. Peasants overwhelmingly strengthen the FAR, from clandestine political and support networks to guerrilla ranks.

The Guatemalan peasantry is predominantly composed of Indigenous masses—national groups of glorious Mayan descent, heirs to the continent's most remarkable pre-Columbian civilization. Colonialist ideology, to facilitate the subjugation of this extraordinary people, imposed the distortion of Indigenous culture and racial discrimination. For centuries, Indigenous peoples were deemed inferior, backward, and incapable of progress. Even past revolutionaries succumbed to this ideology, dismissing Indigenous masses as a "dead weight" for revolution. Yet guerrilla struggle has proven that Indigenous peasants are not an obstacle but the revolution's decisive force.

No people, however oppressed, cannot be mobilized by armed liberation struggle under a correct line. Our rural reality and revolutionary path enable the mobilization of these peasant masses, not based on their level of consciousness but on the severity of their exploitation.

The most advanced expression of our struggle lies in the establishment of the first guerrilla zones, particularly the Edgar Ibarra Guerrilla Front. Formed over two years ago, this front is now definitively consolidated. It survived and thrives by winning and organizing peasant support. It endures because it has forged a core of guerrilleros with unshakable revolutionary conviction and indomitable sacrifice. Their morale is rooted in understanding the war's protracted difficulty, confidence in ultimate victory, and recognition of the enemy's entrenched power—and its ultimate weakness against an armed people. In the guerrillas, a new armed people and a new Guatemalan are emerging. This is why US-trained and equipped army offensives, even with Central American military units, have failed against us.

Yet the enemy, unable to strike guerrillas directly, savagely attacks peasants: murdering, burning homes, destroying villages, raping women, mutilating, and torturing. These atrocities, far from intimidating the people, fuel their resolve.

But the people do not let these depredations—over a decade of counter-revolutionary terror—go unpunished. Popular justice in Guatemala is inexorable. Many executioners and henchmen have been held accountable by FAR units.

In cities and towns of "resistance zones," our special units carry out sabotage, harassment, and agitation against the regime, US corporations, exploiters, and reactionaries. Other FAR units enforce forced taxation, including kidnappings. We openly proclaim this: Exploiters must return the wealth stolen from the people to fund the revolutionary war.

Our strategy, accounting for enemy plans, anticipates potential direct intervention by US imperialist forces. We foresaw this even before the Yankee invasion of the Dominican Republic, which confirmed our fears.

By expanding the revolutionary war nationwide, we prepare for this future phase—ideologically and morally above all. The examples of heroic Vietnam and the brave Dominican Republic guide this preparation.

A people with inner strength, determination to win at all costs, and solidarity from fighting peoples can resist imperialism. Cuba's revolution is a shining example. This conference's significance lies in reinforcing such solidarity.

Solidarity is not only a revolutionary duty but a historical necessity in our common struggle against imperialism. It unites Asia, Africa, and Latin America beyond cultural or historical ties. From this basic bond, all else flows.

The foremost expression of solidarity is struggle itself. Every action, blow, and battle against imperialism is effective solidarity. Cuba's unyielding anti-imperialist stance ninety miles from the US, under brutal blockade, epitomizes internationalism. Vietnam's heroic fight is the highest contribution to global anti-imperialist solidarity.

Vietnam lives in our hearts. Our combatants are taught this solidarity. Many guerrilleros, though illiterate or barely Spanish speaking, know of Vietnam's heroism. In tribute, we renamed a village in our guerrilla zone "Nuevo Viet Nam," honoring peasants who resisted enemy repression.

We express total support for all peoples under colonial or imperialist oppression, especially those waging armed struggle: Laos, Cambodia, Congo, Mozambique, Angola, Portuguese Guinea, Venezuela, Santo Domingo, Peru, Colombia, Indonesia, Zimbabwe, and Brazil.

Anti-imperialist struggle requires maximum solidarity—it determines humanity's future. This struggle is inseparable from the world. There can be no peace while our peoples fight relentlessly and imperialism, humanity's chief enemy, remains undefeated.

We need socialist countries' support—a decisive anti-imperialist bastion—and solidarity from European workers, progressive forces, and the US people to destroy imperialism.

The Guatemalan delegation to this First Tricontinental Solidarity Conference declares our people's unreserved support for the social progress, economic independence, and cultural defense of Asian, African, and Latin American peoples.

This historic conference deals imperialism a mortal blow. Let it institutionalize tricontinental solidarity through a body that channels, coordinates, and efficiently applies all anti-imperialist means, ensuring our peoples' efforts are not dispersed or lost.

As the Second Havana Declaration states: "This great humanity has said '*Enough*!' and begun to march." We are certain it will not halt until crushing the enemy.

Long live the Solidarity of the Peoples of Africa, Asia, and Latin America! Death to Imperialism!

Assayed Abdallah Bin Jehir El Alawi (Yemen Arab Republic)

Afro-Asian Solidarity Committee

It is a great day, the day of the meeting of this conference of the peoples of the three continents, a day that all humanity should salute: We should be proud to see the representatives of the peoples of the most remote parts of the world, gathered in Havana, in order to join hands to fight and free ourselves from imperialism, colonialism and neocolonialism.

The peoples of the three continents have met in the territory of heroic Cuba. This illustrious meeting constitutes a far-reaching historic event. It represents a turning point of extraordinary importance in the struggle for world peace and the liquidation of the imperialist regime. It is a recognition and a crowning achievement of Cuba's heroism.

Comrades:

From the heights of this tribune, in this historic hall, before these delegations whose faces express firmness, will, determination, and solidarity, from this beautiful city, capital of this heroic country, in the shadow of the statue of its first liberator, José Martí, and enjoying the hospitality of its current leader, the illustrious Fidel Castro, I greet the revolutionary people of Cuba, the people of the first free territory in the Americas, on behalf of the revolutionary people of Yemen. I also thank you for your generous hospitality and warm welcome.

Comrades:

Yemen has known a thousand years of injustice and oppression under the reactionary regime. Numerous revolutions broke out, but were soon crushed. Today, our revolution is a total, strong, sweeping revolution; it is a revolution that extends to all spheres, to the structure, the spirit, the regime, and the various aspects of life—a revolution against injustice, tyranny, reaction, and the collaborators of imperialism. We are still in the midst of the battle. Thousands upon thousands of combatants have died as martyrs for the cause of freedom and dignity. We will not stop fighting until Yemen achieves the freedom, justice, and peace to which it aspires, and reaction and its imperialist collaborators are defeated.

Since the revolution broke out on September 26, 1962, announcing the end of the odious reactionary government and the fall of the corrupt monarchy that had deprived the Yemeni people of their freedoms and rights and prevented numerous generations from keeping pace with the development of civilization, the Yemeni people have been and continue to be exposed to a series of attacks by imperialism and reaction.

The Yemeni revolution was not only a revolution aimed at seizing power, but also a social, cultural, and economic revolution. All peoples have the right to freely choose the form of government that suits them best. The reaction backed by the hateful Anglo American imperialism and in order to defend its strategic interests in the region, it continues to attack the Yemeni people, a people who believe in their right to life and who have broken the chains of slavery and humiliation, who have overcome the barriers of class and privilege and have achieved, thanks to their sacrifices and their continuous struggle, their independence and freedom.

For three years, the revolutionary people of Yemen have been fighting with all their might against reaction, imperialism, and its agents. Thousands of their children have died, and some continue to die as martyrs.

We fight in the motherland using all means and with all the strength inspired by our faith in law and justice, and by your support and that of our many friends. In this regard, we will not forget to thank, in the presence of representatives of the peoples of the three continents, our elder sister, the United Arab Republic, for the support it has given us in our struggle, providing us with weapons, money, and men.

We support the struggle of occupied South Yemen, led by the National Liberation Front, against Britain. We call for the independence of the region, the liquidation of military bases, and the freedom of the people. The people of occupied South Yemen are firmly confronting the imperialists' savage terrorist operations and will achieve victory sooner or later.

The Yemeni people wholeheartedly support the causes of liberation. They particularly support the right of the Palestinian people to regain their rights, to return to their homeland, and to abolish Israel, which is nothing more than an agent of imperialism and a form of neocolonialism that serves imperialist interests.

We support Oman's struggle to expel the colonizers. We denounce the war unleashed by US imperialism in South Vietnam and the aggression perpetrated against North Vietnam. However, a people who have inflicted one of imperialist France's greatest defeats will know how to defeat vacillating US imperialism. We support the struggle of the Dominican people, as well as that of all the peoples of Southeast Asia and Latin America. We support the causes of the peoples who still suffer the yoke of imperialism in Angola, Mozambique, Portuguese Guinea, Southern and Northern Rhodesia, South Africa, and other parts of the African and Latin American homeland.

We affirm the need to work toward a ban on the use and stockpiling of nuclear weapons, as well as China's accession to the United Nations, because there can be no peace without China.

Your causes are ours and ours is yours, your struggle is ours and ours is yours. We are one body that strives for right and justice, and God helps those who help each other.

Comrades:

I was eagerly awaiting this red light (indicating the red light appearing in the stands) because the color red is the symbol of life, struggle, and victory.

Down with Imperialism and Long Live the Solidarity of the Peoples of the Three Continents!

Long Live Peace and Friendship of the Peoples!

Salvador Allende (Chile)

Senator and a Leader of the Socialist Party

The insolence and restlessness of imperialism have reached such heights, in the face of the sudden growth of the popular movement, that it has brazenly put forward the so-called Johnson Doctrine. This doctrine asserts that the United States reserves the right to intervene unilaterally, by force of arms, anywhere in Latin America where it deems the social order—that is, its economic and political interests—to be threatened.

The Johnson Doctrine represents the absolute negation of the principle of self-determination of peoples, nonintervention, and the sovereignty of our nations. Moreover, in place of geographical borders, it proposes so-called "ideological borders," which implies the restriction of free thought and the shameless defense of its illegitimate interests. Ultimately, it serves as both a warning and a declaration that the US will violently suppress the triumph of national liberation movements in our lands. For the Chilean people, as for all Latin American nations, the Johnson Doctrine is an explicit declaration that imperialists will respond with violence to any popular movement on our continent capable of seizing power.

This reality compels the Chilean popular movement—which has achieved significant victories in expanding and deepening democracy in our country—to now clearly recognize that the United States will forcibly block its democratic and legal path to power. Consequently, it also obligates us to intensify our struggle: to mobilize the masses, to link anti-imperialist action to the daily demands of the people—through strikes, land occupations, collective mobilization, and the awareness that revolutionary violence must and will counter reactionary violence.

It will be the Chilean people themselves and the conditions of our nation that determine which methods we use to defeat the imperialist enemy and its allies. We are not blind to the fact that this struggle is exceedingly harsh and difficult for a single country, and to ease this burden, we must rely on international backing, support, and solidarity.

Imperialism is strong and powerful, but collectively, the oppressed peoples are far stronger and fully capable of defeating it. This is why we hold in the highest regard the anti-imperialist struggles of all peoples worldwide and embrace them as our own.

The Second Declaration of Havana, ratified by the General Assembly of the People of Cuba, stated: "What is the history of Latin America if not the history of Africa, Asia, and Oceania? And what is the history of these peoples if not the most ruthless and cruel history of imperialism across the entire world?" We stand with the peoples of Asia, Africa, and the Arab world who are fighting with arms in the Congo, the Portuguese colonies, Yemen, Laos, and especially Vietnam, against our common enemy.

We regard their struggles as invaluable support for the Latin American peoples who, in their own ways and on their own fronts, resist imperialism. We stand with the combatants of Guatemala, Colombia, Venezuela, Peru, and above all the courageous Dominican people, whose heroic battle to secure their freedom and expel the Yankee invaders we wholeheartedly endorse. We are also with all those striving to defeat imperialism. We have stood, stand now, and will always stand with Cuba, which courageously builds socialism. Let us not forget that this nation faces relentless imperialist aggression daily, exemplified by the merciless economic blockade. This island, less than a hundred miles from US shores, raises the banner of dignity—not only for its people but for all of Latin America and the oppressed peoples of the world.

Comrades and Delegates:

Representatives of the Chilean popular movement have come to this historic conference to emphasize that its utmost importance lies in the possibility of forging, on the basis of uncompromising anti-imperialist struggle, a militant unity for the liberation of Asia, Africa, and Latin America. The unity of peoples in their emancipatory struggle is the essential foundation for ultimate victory.

We hope this conference will give rise to a coordinated and enduring action by the mass organizations represented here, to resolutely combat imperialism. This requires creating appropriate structures and mechanisms—without undermining existing or future regional bodies—to more tightly intertwine their struggles with those of Latin American nations.

We further assert that this conference must produce an initiative to permanently link and coordinate the anti-imperialist actions of Latin American peoples. The 1961 Mexico Conference for National Sovereignty, Economic Emancipation, and Peace and the 1962 Havana Congress of Peoples for Self-Determination and Non-Intervention are landmark steps in the process of unifying our continent's anti-imperialist popular movements.

Comrades:

The Chilean delegation will strive to ensure that this conference equips the solidarity of the peoples of the three continents with the strongest tools for action, prioritizing their commitment to global anti-imperialist unity. Unity grounded in intransigent struggle to defeat the forces obstructing the advance of Asia, Africa, and Latin America toward democracy, socialism, and peace. Unity to decisively launch an offensive and secure the economic independence and political sovereignty of our peoples. Unity to restore the dignity denied to humanity today. Unity to eradicate hunger, disease, and moral and physiological misery. Unity to build a new society free of exploiters and exploited. Unity to construct socialism.

Raúl Roa García

Foreign Minister of the Republic of Cuba

First of all, I would like to express my gratitude once again for the honor bestowed upon my country by appointing me president of this conference. The conference's specific activities have now concluded. This is certainly not the time to make a detailed assessment of its outcome.

That will surely be done, but it can be categorically stated that the First Tricontinental Conference constitutes the highest expression of the solidarity movement achieved to date in Asia, Africa, and Latin America.

The continents are now one and will march as one. The three continents now have a fighting body, which is the Tricontinental Organization, whose headquarters have been conferred on Cuba, a very high honor that Cuba will know how to reciprocate.

I can assure my fellow delegates that the commitments Cuba undertakes as the headquarters of the provisional executive secretariat and the Committee to Aid Liberation Movements will be fully fulfilled. The people of Cuba, the revolutionary government of Cuba, and the Communist Party of Cuba do not preach with words, they preach with actions like fists.

Cuba, let the delegates from Asia, Africa, and Latin America know, will not fail in this task either.

I would also like to thank, because it is obligatory, and I also believe it is extremely gratifying, all those who have worked on this conference, many anonymous comrades, unknown to you, who have been the pillars of the development of our activity, who are participants in the triumph that this conference represents. I want to thank them for the effort they have made, on behalf of all of us, because they truly deserve it.

Now, new perspectives are opening up for us. The Tricontinental Organization has now been established; the conference has represented a blow to the backbone of imperialism, colonialism, and neocolonialism. Zoological fear is already beginning to shake our enemies, as can be seen from Harriman's declarations. They are already terrified, even though the conference has barely concluded its activities.

When this impetuous torrent that constitutes and represents this conference sets out like an unstoppable avalanche, the imperialists will have only one way out in history: the grave we are going to dig for them.

Asia, Africa, and Latin America have risen together in the struggle for total and definitive liberation. The course of history never goes backward. It marches inexorably forward, and the course of history is with the liberation movements, with progressive and revolutionary humanity.

The future is ours.

I don't want to bother you any longer. We have already talked a lot throughout this conference, we have discussed tirelessly, we have exchanged all our points of view. The effort that has been made has been extraordinary.

I believe that not only has solidarity emerged as a political expression, it has been invigorated and enriched at this conference, but solidarity among ourselves has also been strengthened throughout the daily contacts we have had. The truth is that the conference has concluded as we wanted it to, as a reaffirmation of the spirit of revolutionary and anti-imperialist solidarity that unites the peoples of Asia, Africa, and Latin America.

We can joyfully throw this in the faces of our enemies. The conference has been an act of reaffirmation, an inexorable pronouncement against colonial, neo-colonial, and imperialist domination, led by Yankee imperialism.

Yankee imperialism, like every form of colonial or neocolonial expression, has its days numbered, and consequently, this conference has an inexorable duty: to contribute with all its strength to accelerate the total and definitive overthrow of imperialism.

For us, there is only one path: struggle, and there is only one slogan for all continents.

Homeland or Death for Asia, Africa, and Latin America!

Fidel Castro

Prime Minister of the Republic of Cuba and
First Secretary of the Communist Party of Cuba

Dear Delegates and Cuban Comrades:

The significance of this event, which culminates tonight, is not lost on us. In the face of all the omens of imperialism, in the face of all its predictions, which revealed the great hope that this conference would end in nothing, that this conference, revolving around the problems of the international communist movement, was destined to split and was destined for a resounding failure, what has happened has perhaps occurred least of all, perhaps never expected: that the conference has been a success, that this conference has created a tricontinental organization, that agreements have been reached that reflect the most heartfelt aspirations of the peoples fighting for their liberation, that a committee to assist liberation movements has been created. And not only that: something that unquestionably pains the imperialists greatly is that Cuba has been chosen as the headquarters of the executive secretariat of the organization until the next Tricontinental Conference is held.

It's not that we're expressing a sense of national pride here. Given the unique circumstances surrounding our country, its geographical location, the imperialists' efforts to isolate it from the world, the measures adopted to ensure that virtually no one can visit us, the fact that this conference has been held so successfully in our homeland, and that, despite all obstacles and difficulties, it has been deemed a suitable location for the temporary headquarters here, is undoubtedly something that pains the Yankee imperialists immensely.

This has been a great victory for the revolutionary movement. Never before has a meeting of such breadth and magnitude taken place, in which the revolutionary representatives of eighty-two peoples gathered to discuss problems of common interest. Never before has such a broad meeting, because the peoples of three continents were represented here, the revolutionary movements of the peoples of three continents, who share a common anti-imperialist position, who represent the struggle of their peoples, from different ideas or philosophical positions, or from different religious beliefs, often representing different ideologies, but who have something in common: the most common thing that unites the peoples of these three continents and the entire world today, which is the struggle against imperialism, the struggle against colonialism and neocolonialism, the struggle against racism, and, ultimately, all those phenomena that are the contemporary expression of what we should call imperialism, whose center, whose axis, whose main support is Yankee imperialism.

And what the peoples have in common in this era was what made the meeting, the agreements, and the conclusions of this conference possible. It was not, of course, an easy task; it may seem easy, but it was not, and could not be, an easy task, because it is natural that where representatives meet of such diverse peoples, of such diverse movements, with peculiar problems that practically express all the current problems of the world, it was not easy; it could not be achieved without hard work developing criteria and agreements acceptable to all.

We recalled in recent days, when various problems were being discussed, when the final declaration was being discussed, how Karl Marx and Friedrich Engels had spent many months developing and drafting the *Communist Manifesto*, and how, after revising it many times, retouching it, and perfecting it, they had published it. Naturally, our conference, having only two weeks—less than two weeks, just a few days—found it necessary to prepare a document that would reflect the various criteria and be drafted in a way that would satisfy all the delegations as broadly as possible. And despite these circumstances, we produced a document that is undoubtedly the most profound, the broadest, and the most radical ever prepared and agreed upon at a conference of this kind.

For the first time, representatives from the peoples of Latin America participated alongside the peoples of Africa and Asia. Naturally, in the case of Latin America, the majority, almost all, of the representatives were from the movements and peoples fighting or will fight for liberation. And only our people represented, in this case, the only people totally liberated from the domination of Yankee imperialism and established as a revolutionary power.

We understand that this conference will unquestionably occupy a place in the history of the peoples' struggle for their liberation, in the history of the revolutionary movement. We also understand that the established connections, the ties that have been created between all the movements fighting against imperialism around the world and the organizations that have been created, will play an unquestionable role in supporting, solidarizing, and expanding the revolutionary struggle.

We have had the opportunity to gain a deeper and more detailed understanding of the thinking and specific situation of each of the movements currently fighting for their liberation. We have had the opportunity to learn about the specific situation of each of the peoples struggling, and above all, we have had the opportunity to see how the solidarity of peoples among themselves is growing, how the strength of the revolutionary movement is growing on a global scale, and how the aid of some peoples to each of the peoples struggling is growing and will continue to grow in the times to come, the aid of all peoples to each of the peoples struggling, the aid, on a scale and at a level humanity has never before known, of peoples to one another. And how, despite the military and technical might of the imperialists, the united strength of the revolutionary peoples will unquestionably be much more powerful.

Imperialism will inevitably be defeated. Who has taught us that lesson? The people have taught it to us. Who among the people has taught us the most extraordinary lesson in these times? The people of Vietnam. Vietnam is a small country; the imperialists have divided it into two parts: North Vietnam and South Vietnam. For us, the revolutionaries, it is a single Vietnam.

The Yankee imperialists have unleashed against the people of South Vietnam a large part of their power in: hundreds of thousands of regular soldiers of the imperialist armed forces, hundreds of thousands of soldiers recruited by the puppet government, hundreds of airplanes, thousands of helicopters, and yet the Yankee imperialists have not been able to crush that part of the Vietnamese people.

Trying to intimidate their brothers from the other side of Vietnam, they began bombing daily with hundreds of planes, to demand surrender, to try to bring the Vietnamese to their knees, and yet, as the imperialists themselves confess, instead of gaining ground, they have lost ground. And in the face of the increasingly tenacious and heroic resistance, more and more planes, more and more bombs; and to the astonishment of the world, the people of Vietnam, giving the most extraordinary example of heroism that the history of any liberation movement has ever known, because no liberation movement has ever had to confront more powerful forces, is nullifying and defeating the power of the Yankee imperialists.

But they don't just bomb Vietnam. They also incessantly bomb the patriots of Laos, and threaten to bomb and attack the people of Cambodia. These attitudes, these threats from the Yankee imperialists reveal their impotence, they reveal their desperation. It is the consequence of a situation that is becoming increasingly critical in that part of the world, the consequence of the defeats they have been suffering in that area of Asia where, without a doubt, a decisive battle is being fought between the peoples and imperialism, not only Yankee imperialism, but Yankee imperialism and its allies, Yankee imperialism and its partners in adventure in Asia, expressed through the mobilization of South Korean soldiers, Australian soldiers, Thai soldiers, and the attempts to enlist the complicity, whether in military or auxiliary forces, of the greatest possible number of governments in the world.

That battle against the people of Vietnam and against the people of Laos demonstrates, together with the threats against Cambodia, the need to maximize aid and solidarity to these peoples.

The Yankee imperialists have the support of a state there, which is Thailand, where they have numerous bases, numerous troops, from which they threaten Laos, Vietnam, and Cambodia. This does not mean that this situation will continue indefinitely; we are sure that, like the people of Vietnam, Laos, and Cambodia, the time will also come for the Thai people to hold the Yankee imperialists accountable; the time will come when this people, also oppressed and exploited, inspired by the example of their neighboring sister nations, will also join the struggle against the imperialists.

But in the meantime, the imperialists have not only taken the war to Vietnam, all of Vietnam and Laos, but they are also threatening Cambodia. And Cambodia is a small country, not yet attacked, but seriously threatened by the Yankee imperialists. Therefore, there is an unquestionable need for us revolutionary states to help strengthen the defenses of the small people of Cambodia.

Speaking with the representative of that country during his participation in the Tricontinental Conference, upon hearing from him about the situation in his country and the dangers that threaten it, we expressed this view. We also told him that we Cubans, although we are a small state and are a great distance from Cambodia, were willing to contribute to the extent of our ability to strengthen its defenses and that we only needed them to express this to us, we only needed them to ask us in any circumstance they deemed pertinent, that we were willing to make our contribution.

And that is also our disposition toward Laos and toward North and South Vietnam!

We are a small state, quite close to the coasts of the imperialist metropolis. Our weapons are eminently defensive, but our men, wholeheartedly, our revolutionary militants, our fighters are ready to fight the imperialists anywhere in the world!

Our country is a small country; our territory may even be partially occupied by the enemy, but that would never mean the cessation of our resistance; but the world is large, and the imperialists are everywhere, and for Cuban revolutionaries, the battlefield against imperialism encompasses the entire world!

Without boasting, without showing off, without immodesty of any kind, this is how we Cuban revolutionaries understand our internationalist duty; this is how our people understand their duties, because they understand that the enemy is one, the same one that attacks us on our shores and in our lands, is the same one that attacks others. And that is why we say and proclaim that the revolutionary movement can count on Cuban combatants in any corner of the Earth!

Thousands and thousands of Cubans have expressed their desire and willingness to march anywhere in the world, wherever they are needed, to help the revolutionary movement and this is logical.

If the Yankee imperialists take the liberty of bombing wherever they please and sending their mercenary troops to suppress the revolutionary movement anywhere in the world, the revolutionary peoples feel the right to help, even with their physical presence, the peoples fighting against the Yankee imperialists, and thus, if everyone helps to the extent of their ability, if everyone helps to the extent of their possibilities, the Yankee imperialists will be defeated. And if anywhere they are destined to suffer a crushing defeat, that place is Southeast Asia. Because there it is possible to establish a balance of forces incomparably superior to that of the Yankee imperialists.

Therefore, we have no doubt that they will be defeated, that they will be crushed by the peoples of that region themselves, and if they increase their forces and those of their reactionary allies, they will be crushed not only by the forces of those peoples, but also by the forces of the socialist camp and other peoples.

That's why the Yankee imperialists launch their hypocritical peace offensives to try to confuse, to try to deceive. And that's why the people of Vietnam have said, and they have said very well, that the only peace, that true peace will only be achieved when the Yankee imperialists stop attacking, and when the Yankee imperialists stop occupying the territory or part of the territory of Vietnam, and when the Yankee imperialists remove their mercenary troops and military bases from the territory of Vietnam.

That is to say, the imperialists have been told the only thing that can be told to them under the circumstances, that true peace, since they are the only disturbers of the peace, will be achieved when they withdraw from Vietnam.

And it's clear that the imperialists are fighting a hopeless battle there, that the imperialists are fighting a struggle there in which they are inevitably destined to face defeat. And consequently, they want to exchange defeat for a false peace.

And it is logical that the people of Vietnam refuse, it is logical that the people of Vietnam are not willing to trade their victory for that kind of false peace.

And if we were in a similar situation, I'm absolutely sure we would say exactly the same thing, and that we would refuse to negotiate under bombs, and that we would refuse to negotiate under aggression, and that we would refuse to negotiate under occupation.

And for that reason, our people and the conference unanimously supported the positions and points of the government of the Democratic Republic of Vietnam and the liberation movement of South Vietnam.

On this issue, the most pressing topic today, there was practically unanimous agreement. And it's very good that the Yankee imperialists know the degree of solidarity that exists among all the peoples of the world with Vietnam. It's good that the Yankee imperialists understand the degree of support that the people of Vietnam have all over the world.

And for this reason, we consider that this conference of solidarity of the peoples of the three continents has expressed and acted in such a way that the support and the feeling of solidarity toward Vietnam has become evident, and it will also grow. And the same for Vietnam, toward Laos and toward Cambodia, which are the peoples there under attack or at risk of aggression.

On all the problems of Asia, Africa, and Latin America, the conference's position was similar. The peoples and liberation movements of Africa, and so as not to forget anything, I want to mention also a small country there in that part of Asia, fighting for its liberation, which is, although not well known, a people fighting bravely: the people of North Kalimantan received the warm support of the conference, as did the people of Yemen and the people of Palestine.

Those from Africa—as I was saying—the liberation movements that were represented with so much dignity at this conference: the people of Guinea, occupied by Portugal, and the Cape Verde islands, represented here by one of the most serious revolutionary movements in Africa, and by one of Africa's most lucid and brilliant leaders, Comrade Amílcar Cabral, who has given us enormous confidence in the future and the success of their struggle for liberation; the liberation movements of Angola and Mozambique, two other Portuguese colonies, who are fighting with weapons for their liberation; the people of Zimbabwe, oppressed by the racist minority of Southern Rhodesia; the people of the Congo (Léopoldville); the oppressed people of South Africa; the protectorates of Swaziland, Bechuanaland, and Basutoland, whose grammatical roots are revealing to us the imperial profile of the country that colonized them.

And finally, all the African liberation movements were worthily represented at this conference and enjoyed the warm support and solidarity of all the delegates.

In Africa, the imperialist attempt to penetrate, divide, and subjugate is becoming increasingly apparent. And coups d'état have become fashionable in recent weeks. Coups d'état in the Congo; coups d'état in Africa, in the Central African Republic; coups d'état in Nigeria according to cable reports, demonstrate imperialism's desperate efforts to strengthen its hold on that part of the world.

A decisive battle is also playing out in Africa, and the role of revolutionary movements, and the role of new states that have not been infected by the evil of neocolonialism, will be of extraordinary importance in resisting this push and penetration of the imperialists. Because there, aid to the revolutionary movement, decisive aid to liberation movements, decisive aid to the majorities oppressed by racists, will be a decisive factor. Equally decisive will be the sense of responsibility, seriousness, and unity of African revolutionary leaders.

Some movements have suffered blows and setbacks. But these setbacks should not serve to discourage them; these setbacks should serve as lessons, so that they can adopt the measures and take the necessary steps to overcome the current difficulties and thus overcome the flaws and weaknesses of the revolutionary movement.

The solidarity movement, which began in Africa and Asia and has now spread to the third continent of the world, oppressed and exploited by imperialism, will have its next event—by agreement of the conference in the city of Cairo, thus fulfilling the invitation of President Nasser, who offered the capital of the United Arab Republic as the site of the next Tricontinental Conference in 1968, and we are certain and we must therefore make every effort that by that date, among the peoples who have freed themselves from imperialism and colonialism, we will be able to greet several more brother peoples of Africa.

The problems of Latin America, beginning with the most burning and critical problem, which is the problem of the military occupation of Santo Domingo by the regular soldiers of Yankee imperialism, deserved the attention of this conference and the full support of the delegates representing their peoples.

In the coming years, Latin America will face, on the Dominican stage, one of its most serious struggles. Santo Domingo, a small country occupied by tens of thousands of Yankee soldiers, faces a long and hard struggle. Santo Domingo, the Dominican people, will not have to face the Yankee imperialists alone.

In many other nations of the Americas, the conditions for revolutionary armed struggle are ripe. This struggle has also been underway for some time in Venezuela, Peru, Colombia, and Guatemala.

In Latin America, not one, not two, not three peoples should be left fighting alone against imperialism. The balance of power of the imperialists on this continent, the proximity of their metropolitan territory, the zeal with which they will seek to defend their dominions in this part of the world, demands on this continent, more than anywhere else, a common strategy, a common and simultaneous struggle.

If the imperialists do not have to confront only the Dominican people, or only the people of Guatemala, or only the people of Venezuela, or only the people of Colombia, or only the people of Peru, if they also have to fight, at the same time as in each of these peoples, against the other oppressed peoples, such as Brazil, Bolivia, Paraguay, Ecuador, Argentina, and other peoples of Central America; if the struggle is waged on a broad scale; if each one of these revolutionaries of this continent fulfills their duty and the duty of every revolutionary, which as the Havana Declaration says, is to make revolution, to make revolution in deeds and not in words, not to be revolutionary only in theory, but revolutionary in practice; if revolutionaries invest less energy and less time in theorizing, and dedicate more energy and more time to practical work; and if they do not make so many agreements and so many alternatives and so many dilemmas and they finally understand that sooner or later all the peoples, or almost all, will have to take up arms to liberate themselves, then the time for the liberation of this continent will advance. And between those who theorize and those who criticize those who theorize and at the same time begin to theorize, unfortunately a lot of energy and a lot of time are wasted.

We believe that on this continent, among all or almost all peoples, the struggle will take the most violent forms. And when you know that the only right thing to do is to prepare for when that struggle comes, to prepare!

Naturally, this struggle will first erupt where, as the Havana Declaration states, the conditions of imperialist oppression are most stark, where all avenues are absolutely closed, as is the case in most countries of this continent. And even where the bourgeoisie and imperialism still exercise their class rule through constitutionalist means, as is the case in Uruguay, the strength of the mass movement and the revolutionary spirit of the people are manifested ever more clearly.

And we must express our country's deep sympathy for Uruguay, because it is a tiny, tiny country, without mountains, surrounded by two reactionary giants, and where it has always, invariably, without exception, in every circumstance, stood side by side with the people of Venezuela in solidarity and support for the Cuban Revolution.

And we still remember how, following the severance of diplomatic relations with Cuba, by agreement of the OAS, imposed by the United States as a sanction against Cuba, the people of Uruguay, led by their revolutionary organizations, took to the streets and protested with incomparable energy against that servile and traitorous act against the people of this continent.

Well then: on this issue of Latin America, you, honorable delegates, will allow me to expand on some considerations, since we are located on this continent.

And the Yankee imperialists have not only used the economic blockade against us, not only armed aggression, not only mortal threats in certain circumstances, not only perpetrated all kinds of sabotage, spy leaks, and pirate attacks against this country, but Yankee imperialism has resorted to more subtle weapons against our country, such as propaganda and slander. And not only that, but Yankee imperialism and its agents have tried to destroy the prestige of the Cuban Revolution, they have tried to present the Cuban Revolution as marginalized from the revolutionary struggles of this continent, and they have tried, in the most vile and slanderous manner, to discredit the revolution. And they have used every means, every action, every weapon.

Of course, the imperialists would be interested in a concrete discussion of these issues; any irresponsible person, any charlatan, any puppet, would be happy to assert any irresponsibility, any slander.

It is well known that only the enemy would be interested in how this word called "solidarity" is put into practice, not only with the revolutionary peoples of this continent, but throughout the world.

But what happened?

There's a fact I'm going to use as an example to demonstrate how imperialism and its agents work, and it's an extraordinarily interesting fact. I'm referring to the campaign waged by Yankee imperialism and its agents regarding the departure of our comrade Ernesto Guevara. I believe this is an issue that must be taken by the horns to clarify some things.

Comrade Ernesto Guevara—a few revolutionaries in this country and a few revolutionaries outside this country know when he left, what he has been doing during this time and, of course, the imperialists would be very interested in knowing, with all the details, where he is, what he has done, how he does it and, of course, it seems they don't know and if they know, they hide it very well.

But, of course, these are things that time, when circumstances permit, will allow for clarification. But we revolutionaries don't need such clarifications; it's the enemy who uses these circumstances to try to intrigue, confuse, and slander.

Comrade Guevara joined us when we were in exile in Mexico, and from the very first day, he clearly expressed the idea that when the struggle ended in Cuba, he had other duties to fulfill elsewhere. We always gave him our word that no state interest, no national interest, no circumstance would make us ask him to stay in our country, or hinder the fulfillment of that desire, or that vocation. And we fully and faithfully fulfilled that promise we made to comrade Guevara.

Naturally, if Comrade Guevara was going to leave the country, it was logical that he would do so clandestinely. It was logical that he would move clandestinely. It's logical that he hasn't been calling journalists, it's logical that he hasn't been holding press conferences. It's logical that, given the tasks he set for himself, he should have done so in the manner he did. And yet, how much the imperialists have tried to take advantage of this circumstance, and how they have done it.

That's why I brought some papers. Don't be scared thinking I'm going to read you all the papers here. I'm just going to read you a few things, because here is what all the imperialist and bourgeois newspapers have written regarding the case of Comandante Guevara, what the United States newspapers, their magazines, their wire agencies, the bourgeois newspapers of Latin America and around the world have written. And let's see who precisely the main spokespeople for the imperialist campaign of intrigue and slander against Cuba in relation to the case of comrade Guevara have been. First, certain elements that have been constantly used against the revolutionary movement in recent decades.

And so, if you give me a little time, among so much data I'm going to look for a very interesting one.

Ah, I found it! It's a UPI [United Press International] cable from December 6, 1965, which says: "Ernesto Guevara was assassinated by Cuban Prime Minister Fidel Castro on the orders of the USSR," declared Felipe Albaguante, leader of the Mexican Trotskyists, in statements to *El Universal*. He added that Che was killed for insisting on putting Cuba on the Chinese side.

This, naturally, was in line with a campaign that Trotskyist elements began to unleash everywhere simultaneously.

And so, on October 22, an article was published in the weekly magazine *Marcha* in which a well-known Trotskyist theorist, Adolfo Gilly, stated that "Che left Cuba due to disagreements with Fidel over the Sino-Soviet conflict, and that Che was unable to impose his opinion on the leadership." He said that "Che, in a confused manner, advocated extending the revolution to the rest of Latin America, in opposition to the Soviet line." He said that "the Cuban leadership is divided between a conservative wing, which includes old leaders of the PSP [Popular Socialist Party], Che's supporters, and Fidel and his team, who are in a position of conciliatory centrist oscillation." He said that "Che left Cuba because he lacked the means to express himself and that Fidel was afraid to confront the masses to explain the Che case."

This same Trotskyist theorist, on October 31, 1965, as a reporter for the Italian newspaper *Nuevo Mundo*, wrote an article describing the Cuban leadership as "Philo-Soviet" and accusing Fidel of "not having politically explained to the people what had happened to Che." He said that "Commander Guevara was defeated by the PSP and the Castro team." He criticized Che for "not having taken the struggle to impose his thesis to the masses" and concluded that "the Cuban state, paralyzed by its own policy, did not openly support the Dominican revolution." I will address this in more detail later.

In the October 1965 issue, the Spanish Trotskyist newspaper *Batalla* declared that "the mystery surrounding the Che Guevara case must be cleared up." It said that "friends of Che Guevara suspect that the letter read by Castro is a forgery and wonder if the Cuban leadership is moving toward submission to the Kremlin bureaucracy."

Around the same time, Argentina's official Trotskyist organ published an article claiming that Che Guevara was dead or imprisoned in Cuba. It states that "he came into conflict with Fidel Castro over the functioning of the unions and the organization of the militias." It adds that "Che Guevara opposed the integration of the Central Committee with Castro's favorites, especially army officers, followers of Moscow's right wing."

But one of the dirtiest, most vulgar, and most indecent writings is the one written by the leader of the Latin American Political Bureau of the Fourth International in the Italian newspaper *Classe Operaria*. Regarding this admittedly long article, I'll only read three paragraphs. It begins by saying:

> One aspect of the worsening global crisis of the bureaucracy is the expulsion of Guevara. Guevara has been expelled now, not eight months ago. The argument with Guevara lasted eight months, and it wasn't eight months spent drinking coffee; they fought hard, and perhaps there were deaths, perhaps there were gun battles. We can't say whether Guevara was killed or not, but there's a right to assume that he was. Why hasn't Guevara appeared? They haven't presented him in Havana for fear of the consequences, of the reaction of the population, but ultimately, by hiding him, they produce the same effect. The population says: Why doesn't Guevara come out, why doesn't he appear? There are no political accusations, there is political praise for him. Why haven't they presented Guevara? Why hasn't

he spoken? How is it possible that one of the founders of the Cuban workers' state, who until recently traveled the world in the name of the workers' state, suddenly says: "I'm bored with the Cuban Revolution, I'm going to make the revolution somewhere else?" On the other hand, they don't say where they've gone, and they don't show up. If there's no disagreement, why don't they show up? The entire Cuban people understand that there's an enormous struggle and that this struggle isn't over.

Guevara wasn't alone, nor is he alone. If they're taking these measures against Guevara, it's because there's a large, very large, faction on his side. And in addition to this very large faction, there's enormous concern among the people.

Recently, the Cuban government issued a rather severe decree: "It is necessary to return all weapons to the State." At the time, the issue was somewhat confusing; now it's clear what the purpose of this resolution was; it was to combat the Guevara faction. They are afraid of an uprising.

Another paragraph:

Why have they silenced Guevara? The Fourth International must carry out a public campaign in this regard, demanding Guevara's appearance, Guevara's right to defend himself and discuss, to appeal to the masses, and to distrust the measures taken by the Cuban government, because they are bureaucratic and perhaps murderous measures. They have eliminated Guevara by silencing his struggle; they have silenced Guevara. Even though his position was not consistent from a revolutionary point of view, because it tended toward harmonizing his positions within the revolutionary trend.

And later he says:

This demonstrates not the power of Guevara or of a Guevarist group in Cuba, but the ripeness of conditions in the rest of the workers' states for these positions to bear fruit in a short time. The bureaucracy is not fooled by maneuvers and measures of this kind. For the bureaucracy, the elimination of Guevara represents an attempt to liquidate a base for the possible regroupment of revolutionary tendencies that continue the development of the world revolution. This

> is the basis for the liquidation of Guevara, not only because of the danger he represents to Cuba, but because it includes the rest of the Latin American revolution.
>
> Guatemala stands next to Cuba, Guatemala stands next to Cuba, with its program of socialist revolution, and yet its strength and the speeches of its supreme leader, Fidel Castro, have not been able to prevent the November 13 Movement from transforming into a revolutionary socialist movement and fighting directly for socialism.

It is not at all by chance that this gentleman, the leader of the Fourth International, proudly mentions here the case of Guatemala and the November 13 Movement, because it is precisely in relation to this movement that Yankee imperialism has used one of the most subtle tactics to liquidate a revolutionary movement, which was to have the agents of the Fourth International leak to it, who—through ignorance, through the political ignorance of the principal leader of that movement—made it adopt nothing less than that discredited thing, that antihistorical thing, that fraudulent thing that emanates from elements so demonstrably in the service of Yankee imperialism, such as the program of the Fourth International.

How did this happen? Yon Sosa was, without a doubt, a patriotic officer. Yon Sosa led a group of army officers, in whose crushing, by the way, the mercenaries who later invaded the Bay of Pigs participated, and through a merchant who was in charge of the political side of the movement, the Fourth International arranged for that leader, ignorant of the profound problems of politics and the history of revolutionary thought, to allow that agent of Trotskyism—about whom we have no doubt that he is an agent of imperialism—to be in charge of editing a newspaper in which the program of the Fourth International was copied cover to cover.

What the Fourth International committed with this was a true crime against the revolutionary movement, to isolate it from the rest of the people, to isolate it from the masses, by infecting it with the nonsense, the discredit, and the repugnant and nauseating thing that Trotskyism is today in the field of politics. Because if at one time Trotskyism represented an erroneous position, but a position within the field of political ideas, Trotskyism became, in subsequent years, a vulgar instrument of imperialism and reaction.

These gentlemen think so much that, for example, in relation to South Vietnam, where a broad revolutionary front has united the vast majority of the population and various sectors of the population, has united them closely around the liberation movement in the struggle against imperialism, for the Trotskyists this is absurd, this is counterrevolutionary. And these gentlemen go so far as to dare, to do something unusual in the face of the facts and realities of history and the revolutionary movement, to express themselves in this way.

Fortunately, in Guatemala, the revolutionary movement is saved. And it is saved thanks to the clear vision of one of the officers who, along with Sosa, had initiated the revolutionary movement and who, understanding that folly, that stupidity, separated from the November 13 Movement and, with other progressive and revolutionary sectors, organized the Rebel Armed Forces of Guatemala. And that young officer, who had such a clear vision of the situation, is the one who has represented the Guatemalan revolutionary movement at this conference: Comandante Turcios.

Comandante Turcios has the merit of not only having been one of the standard-bearers of the armed struggle for the liberation of his oppressed people, but also the merit of having saved the Guatemalan revolutionary movement from one of the most subtle and most perfidious stratagems of Yankee imperialism, and of raising the revolutionary banners of Guatemala and its anti-imperialist movement, rescuing them from the filthy hands of these mercenaries in the service of Yankee imperialism.

We hope that Yon Sosa, whose patriotic intentions at the beginning of the struggle no one doubts, and whose status as an honorable man no one doubts, at the same time that we do have very serious reasons to doubt his attitude as a revolutionary leader—will not take long to distance himself from these elements and rejoin the revolutionary movement in Guatemala, but this time under another direction, under another guide who did demonstrate, in moments like these, clarity of vision and the attitude of a revolutionary leader.

This position of the Trotskyists is the same one adopted by all the newspapers and advertising agencies of Yankee imperialism, the same one in relation to the case of comrade Ernesto Guevara, the entire imperialist press of the United States, its wire agencies, the press of the Cuban counterrevolutionaries, the bourgeois press throughout the continent and the rest of the world. This campaign of slander and intrigue against revolutionary Cuba in relation to the case of Comrade Guevara, brought all the reactionary imperialist and bourgeois sectors, all the slanderers and schemers against the Cuban Revolution, into perfect agreement.

Because it is unquestionable that only reactionaries and only imperialism can be interested in discrediting the Cuban Revolution, destroying the confidence of revolutionary movements in the Cuban Revolution, destroying the confidence of the peoples of Latin America in the Cuban Revolution, destroying their faith.

And that is why they have not hesitated to use the dirtiest and most indecent weapons.

This same Mr. Gilly, who from time to time poses among other North American intellectuals in the magazine *Monthly Review* of the United States, had the gall to write the following paragraph, which is worth analyzing, regarding the Santo Domingo crisis. He said:

> A high point of this crisis must have been the Dominican Revolution, where the Cuban workers' state was paralyzed by its own policies, failing to openly support the revolution, while in Cuba there was tremendous internal pressure for a policy of active support. If the crisis long predated Santo Domingo, Santo Domingo undoubtedly precipitated the revolution.

This gentleman has the audacity to accuse the Cuban Revolution of not having actively supported the Dominican Revolution. And while the imperialists were accusing Cuba, while the imperialists were trying to justify their intervention by saying that leftist and communist elements, trained in Cuba, were there at the forefront of the uprising, while imperialism was accusing Cuba and presenting the Dominican Revolution not as an internal problem but as an external one, this gentleman accuses the Revolution of not having actively supported it.

And what is meant by active support? Was it intended that Cuba, whose weapons and resources are known, could and should prevent the landing of US troops in Santo Domingo? Cuba has the weapons to defend itself, and, in a far inferior proportion to the imperialists, defensive weapons.

And these gentlemen are so miserable, so shameless, that they try to blame Cuba for not having prevented . . . Because what else does active support mean? Because everything Cuba could have done under those circumstances, everything Cuba could have done and should have done, it did. And asking Cuba to prevent the landing is like asking Cambodia in Southeast Asia to prevent the bombing of North Vietnam and prevent the occupation by the Yankee marines of South Vietnam.

Unfortunately, Cuba's forces are limited. But to the extent of those forces, and in the most optimal way possible, and in the most decisive manner, as well as most appropriate to the circumstances, it lends and will lend its fullest support to the revolution.

For those who believe that this country fears the imperialists, for those who believe, in a spirit of superiority or with an insolent delusion of superiority over no one, that this country fears the imperialists, it would be well for them to have lived a few hours here in this country, during the October Crisis, and when for the first time a small people like this one saw itself threatened with a massive barrage of nuclear missiles on its territory, the attitude that this people had and the attitude that the revolutionary government had.

Much nonsense, much nonsense, and much foolishness are written, and above all, it is written by the irresponsible, when certain documents cannot be made public; but one day humanity will know, and one day humanity will acknowl-edge all the facts. That will be the day when the wretches see that no comrade Guevara was murdered, when every step of his steps will be known in minute detail, when Cuba's position in those difficult days and the serenity of this people will be known; when this is understood, no one, no matter how insolent, no matter how provocative, will dare to question the sense of solidarity of this people and the courage of this people. This courage is demonstrated by the very fact of their conduct. Despite this being a country ninety miles from the imperi-alist metropolis, enormous dangers will hang over its head in the coming years, to the extent that the revolutionary movement grows, a revolutionary movement that grows above all from the example of the Cuban Revolution, a revolutionary movement that grows, that becomes gigantic, because of the example of Cuba, because of Cuba's victories, because of Cuba's position against the enemy.

And we must bear in mind that when this country defies that danger, this is not a country with millions of men under arms, this is not a country with thermonuclear weapons, because here our rockets are moral; and the number of millions is not infinite, the number of men is not infinite, but [rather] the dignity and decorum of this people.

And it will be the coming years that will speak for us, and it will be the coming years that will be responsible for crushing the slanderers: not these, who are known agents of the imperialists, but the confused ones, the schemers, those who allow themselves to be schemed and serve as instruments of lies against our revolution.

Highly rewarding is what this conference demonstrated, because this con-ference demonstrated many things. It demonstrated, first, how discussions can revolve, above all, around what truly matters, especially around what matters to the peoples who are struggling: how people, regardless of their strength, their resources, their size, have a voice and opinion, and how people can have their own criteria and independent voices.

That was demonstrated at this conference.

But, in addition, we Cubans can take satisfaction in the fact that Cubans and revolutionary movements have always stood together, in the same positions, regardless of continent; and how united strength, how revolutionary criteria, how the most honorable positions have prevailed; and how at this conference, as a counterbalance to the schemers and slanderers, the peoples, the revolutionary liberation movements, have always, at all times, demonstrated great, immense confidence in Cuba and its revolutionary party, and how for this reason this country was honored by granting it the general secretariat and temporary head-quarters of the organization.

And considering the work carried out by the Cuban delegation, by the Cuban Solidarity Committee, working in favor of the conference, fighting tirelessly to overcome all obstacles, maintaining at all times a principled, objective, and fair position, which has even jeopardized Cuba's relations with some countries, such as Indonesia, because, having left it to the Cuban delegation to decide, the Cuban delegation rejected the official Indonesian delegation, jeopardizing its relations with an important state in that part of the world.

And although for us all states are of equal importance, and all peoples have equal rights, this fact nevertheless serves to demonstrate to what extent the Cuban delegation was, or tried to be fair, and tried to be objective, and tried to maintain a principled position.

We know how hard all the delegations worked, because according to those who have attended several international conferences, this is one of the conferences where the work was most serious and tireless. Therefore, having been assigned to Cuba as the host, and with it the general secretariat of the organization, our party's political bureau agreed to appoint comrade Osmany Cienfuegos as the organization's secretary general.

All delegations have had the opportunity to learn about the effort and honesty with which comrade Osmany exerted this effort, both in the preparatory work and in the development of the conference. It must be said that everyone cooperated, everyone contributed, in one way or another, to unifying criteria and to the success of this conference. Because, as I said before, not all these criteria always coincided, but everyone, in the end, with a truly selfless effort, contributed to its success.

I don't want to end without referring to two issues: one, the deep concern that overwhelms us all in the face of the events in Indonesia, in the face of the news coming out of Indonesia that more than one hundred thousand revolutionary militants have been savagely murdered; in the face of the news that [D. N.] Aidit and other leaders of the Indonesian Communist Party have been murdered. I want to express our condemnation, our protest, and our solidarity with the Indonesian revolutionaries, persecuted today by the militarist reaction fueled by Yankee imperialism. And, at the same time, as a tribute to someone who had much to do with the success of this conference, I recognize that Ben Barka was a decisive factor with his perseverance, with his personal work, in organizing this First Tricontinental Conference, and his effort and his work were the cause of the problem that occurred. It is widely believed that Ben Barka was cruelly and cowardly murdered. And if this solidarity conference is duty-bound to take a step precisely out of loyalty and as a basic obligation to the one who worked so devotedly for its success, it must demand that Ben Barka's murder be clarified and that Ben Barka's killers be punished.

All the evidence points directly to the Moroccan minister of the interior, General [Mohamed] Oufkir, on whom all the suspicions and all the evidence fall.

This conference must not rest until the facts are completely clear, including the perpetrators and masterminds of Ben Barka's assassination, the assassination of the president of the preparatory committee for this Tricontinental. And this repugnant, monstrous event demonstrated from the outset imperialism's interest in obstructing the conference, in making it fail. However, the results of this conference demonstrate that Ben Barka's blood was not shed in vain, and that Ben Barka's crime, his assassination—like the assassination of Lumumba, like the assassination of Aidit, like the assassination of Sandino—that with none of its horrible crimes, with none of its barbaric acts, imperialism will be able to stop the victorious march, the final liberation of the peoples.

It is right that we dedicate our memory to those who have sacrificed themselves for the victory of their peoples, to those who have fallen victim to imperialism on every continent; and that we resolve to always be faithful to that cause, always be faithful, in Asia, Africa, and Latin America, to the cause of those who have given their lives and blood for the liberation of peoples.

Our country, a people who, as you have been able to see, are a people of diverse ethnic integration, the result of the mixture of peoples from different continents, deeply united with Latin America, deeply united with Africa, deeply united with all the peoples of all continents, has done its utmost to make the stay of the delegations here pleasant, it has overflowed with all the enthusiasm, and all the hospitality, and all the warmth of which it is capable.

Thousands of Cubans, tirelessly, without regard for rest or vacations, have worked for the success of this conference, have worked to serve the representatives of our sister nations. Our entire people have experienced the great celebration of international solidarity in these days.

Our people have felt each and every one of the problems of other peoples as their own. Our people, as I told you on January 2, welcomed you with open arms, and bid you farewell with closed arms, as a symbol of a bond that will never be broken and as a symbol of their fraternal and supportive feelings toward other peoples who struggle, for whom they are also willing to give their blood.

¡Patria o Muerte!

¡Venceremos!

Structure of the Conference

Structure of the Conference

Chair of the Conference

President	Raúl Roa García	Cuba
Vice President	John Tettegah	Ghana
Vice President	Nguyen Van Tien	South Vietnam
Vice President	Pedro Medina Silva	Venezuela
Secretary	Youssef El Sebai	UAR

Commissions and Sub-Commissions

Economic Commission

President	Adda Benguettat	Algeria
Vice President	Aluízio Palhano Pedreira	Brazil
Secretary	Moudaf Haffar	Syria

Organization Commission

President	Abdoulaye Diallo	Guinea
Vice President	Wal Lyong Kim	Korea
Secretary	José A. Naranjo	Cuba

Political Commission

President	Khaled Mohieddin	UAR
Vice President	Tuyen Tran Danh	North Vietnam
Secretary	Rodney Arismendi	Uruguay

Sub-Commission for Burning Issues

President	Euclides Gutiérrez Félix	Dominican Republic
Vice President	Shizuma Kai	Japan
Secretary	Edward Ndlovu	Zimbabwe

Sub-Commission for Vietnam

President	Turcios Lima	Guatemala
Vice President	Edouard-Marcel Sumbu	Congo (L)
Secretary	Tran Van Tu	South Vietnam

Sub-Commission for Colonialism and Neocolonialism

President	Julien Boukambou	Congo (B)
Vice President	Roberto García Urrutia	Peru
Secretary	Ibrahim Abu Sitta	Palestine

Social-Cultural Commission

President	Huat Sambath	Cambodia
Vice President	Luiz Andrade de Azevedo	Angola
Secretary	Inés Pinto Escobar	Colombia

Selected
Photographs

Closing event at Charlie Chaplin Theater. *Archive of* Granma *newspaper*.

General view of delegates. *Archive of* Bohemia *magazine*.

Fidel Castro gives closing speech. *Archive of* Granma *newspaper.*

Billboard that reads: "We Salute the First Tricontinental Conference."
Archive of Granma *newspaper.*

Co-chairs of the Conference: Raúl Roa García (Cuba), Pedro Medina Silva
(Venezuela), Nguyen Van Thien (Vietnam). *Archive of* Bohemia *magazine.*

Conference graphic. *Archive of* Bohemia *magazine.*

Amílcar Cabral & Fidel Castro at the Augusto Cesar Sandino Stadium in Santa Clara. *Archive of* Granma *newspaper.*

Henriette Yimbou Malanda and Dominique Etamba [Congo (Brazzaville)]. *Archive of* Bohemia *magazine.*

Conference delegates. *Archive of* Granma *newspaper.*

Mark Shope (South Africa) speaks on behalf of the World Federation of Trade Unions. *Photographed by Alberto Korda. Archive of* Bohemia *magazine.*

Carnival in Cienfuegos in honor of the Tricontinental. *Photographed by Carlos Nuñez. Archive of* Bohemia *magazine.*

From left to right: Reinaldo Peñalver (Prensa Latina, Cuba); Manuel Marqué Pardiñas, director of *Politica* (Mexico); Santiago Alvarez, director of ICAIC Newsreel (Cuba); Dan Thi Than (North Vietnam); Melba Hernandez (Cuba); Hilda Gadea Acosta (Peru). *Photographed by Mariano Ferré. Archive of* Bohemia *magazine.*

Members of the General Secretariat of OSPAAAL at the founding of the organization under the portraits of César Augusto Sandino, Patrice Lumumba, and Nguyen Van Troi, martyrs of liberation from Latin America, Africa, and Asia. *Archive of* Bohemia *magazine.*

Fidel Castro with delegates. *Archive of* Granma *newspaper.*

Delegates watching the news in the lobby of the Habana Libre Hotel.
Photographed by Alberto Korda. Archive of Granma *newspaper.*

Members of the Cuban delegation (includes Haydee Santamaría, Manuel Piñeiro, Carlos Rafael Rodríguez). *Photographed by Mariano Ferré. Archive of* Bohemia *magazine.*

Josephine Baker, artist and civil rights activist (United States), in the lobby. *Photographed by Mariano Ferré. Archive of* Bohemia *magazine.*

Luis Andrade de Azevedo, head of delegation of Angola, gifts flag of the Liberation Movement to Cuban delegates.

Brazilian delegation hands flag to Guido Gil, head of the delegation of the Dominican Republic, in sign of reparation of the presence of Brazilian troops in that country. *Archive of* Granma *newspaper.*

US delegate Robert Williams speaks with Comandante Victor Dreke (Cuba), *Photographed by Mariano Ferré. Archive of* Bohemia *magazine.*

Vilma Espín (Cuba) and Florence Mophosho (South Africa). *Photographed by Mariano Ferré. Archive of* Bohemia *magazine.*

Exchange among delegates from Latin America: Comandante Turcios Lima (Guatemala), Luis Torres (Colombia), Antonio Tenorio Adama (Mexico), Jorge Enrique Turner Morales & Floyd Britton (Panama), Roberto Garcia Urritia (Peru), John W. Cooke & Abel Alexis Latendorf (Argentina), Norman Pietri (Puerto Rico).
Photographed by Mariano Ferré. Archive of Bohemia *magazine.*

Young Vietnamese fighter Dan Thi Thanh and her comrades greet Fausto Diaz, veteran of the Bay of Pigs. *Photographed by Carlos Nuñez. Archive of* Bohemia *magazine.*

Delegation of the National Liberation Front of South Vietnam.
Archive of Bohemia *magazine.*

Pelegrín Torras de la Luz, Vice Minister of Foreign Relations (Cuba) speaks to delegation from Kenya. *Archive of* Bohemia *magazine.*

Vilma Espín (Cuba) and Aruna Asaf Ali (India) at a lunch hosted by the Federation of Cuban Women. *Photographed by Carlos Nuñez. Archive of* Bohemia *magazine.*

Meeting of delegates from Latin America. *Archive of* Bohemia *magazine.*

Fidel Castro gives closing speech. *Archive of* Granma *newspaper.*

Delegation of the African Party for the Independence of Guinea Bissau and Cape Verde: Pedro Pires, Amílcar Cabral, Domingo Ramos, Vasco Cabral.
Archive of Granma *newspaper.*

The delegates of Zimbabwe (Rhodesia) denouncing the brutalities of racism. *Photographed by Mariano Ferré. Archive of* Bohemia *magazine.*

General view of delegates. *Photographed by Mariano Ferré. Archive of* Bohemia *magazine.*

A representation of the Armed Forces of Tanzania led by Liuetenant Coronel Ali Mahfudh, General Chief of Staff. Also seen Comandante Victor Dreke (Cuba). *Archive of* Bohemia *magazine.*

Maria Amalia Lopes Fonseca, delegate from the Portuguese colonies of Africa to the Executive Secretariat of the OSPAAAL, is received at Jose Marti International Airport by secretary general of the organization Captain Osmany Cienfuegos and Joaquín Mas Martínez, Miguel Brugueras, and Hugo Ruiz. *Photographed by Constantino Arias. Archive of* Bohemia *magazine.*

FROM LEFT TO RIGHT: Nguyen Van Thien (South Vietnam), Paul Lantimo (Haiti), Chieh Shuu Chang (China), Florence Mophosho (South Africa), Bijamal Ramazanova (USSR), Luisa Gonzalez (Costa Rica), Amad Jamaluddin Abdulla (Arab Peninsula), Lee Siew Shoh (Malasyia), Kim Riong Gu (DPRK), Pauline Miranda Clerk (Ghana), Abdul Hamid Khan Bashani (Pakistan), Aruna Asaf Ali (India)

Resolutions

GENERAL RESOLUTION APPROVED BY THE ECONOMIC COMMISSION ON JANUARY 11, 1966

The Economic Commission of the Tricontinental Conference, met in Havana from January 3 to 15, 1966;

After having studied the draft resolutions submitted by the Cuban Delegation, as well as the documents of the Economic Seminar held in Algiers, in February, 1965,

Considering that one of the tasks of the national liberation movements is the elimination of imperialism, colonialism, and neocolonialism, headed by the United States, and the consequences of their domination in the economic sphere;

Considering that in order to attain such a goal it is necessary to adopt principles of common struggle against imperialism, colonialism, and neocolonialism, headed by the United States, for the achievement and consolidation of economic emancipation for the countries of the three continents;

Considering that the economic relations between the movements which lead liberated zones and revolutionary states must be based on solidarity and fraternal aid;

Considering that one of the worst consequences of imperialist, colonialist, and neocolonialist exploitation is that technical progress has not developed in a great number of countries, many of them remaining in a patent state of educational backwardness;

Considering that the economic blockades imposed by imperialist, colonialist, and neocolonialist states against the peoples of Africa, Asia, and Latin America constitute a serious threat to the national independence and economic development of these peoples, and a standing menace to the countries of these continents;

Considering that a high percentage of the population of the countries striving for their economic emancipation are still working with a low productivity in agriculture and other fields of primary production, on account of their technical backwardness, resulting from long years of imperialist domination, the income in most of these countries being extremely low;

Considering that in order to obtain adequate economic growth in these countries, a greater supply of skilled labor force is required;

Considering that it is necessary to develop a just economic policy between the countries of the three continents and the rest of the world;

Considering that the development of the economic, commercial, and financial relations between the countries of the three continents and the developed capitalist countries should be carried out upon bases which ensure their economic growth and national independence;

Considering that exploitation by imperialism, colonialism, and neocolonialism has imposed upon the lesser-developed countries an economy of monoproduction of non-manufactured goods;

Considering that in the development of their international rule, the imperialist, colonialist, and neocolonialist countries have made use of loans as tools for the economic penetration and political subordination of the lesser-developed countries;

Considering that this type of foreign indebtedness helps to perpetuate underdevelopment, because—through amortization and usurious interests—it withdraws resources essential to the developing countries, it being evident that many colonial countries, upon gaining national independence, have found such foreign debts, incurred by colonialist governments or rulers who are puppets of imperialist powers, a heavy burden on their economies;

Considering that the permanent fluctuation in the prices of primary products in international trade, acts to the detriment of developing countries and should be avoided;

Considering that these measures adopted by the imperialist countries bring about the depression of the prices of these products and fluctuation of international trade of primary products, and consequently a constant reduction of the share of lesser-developed countries in international trade, and check the expansion of agricultural output in these countries;

Considering that the destruction of the old feudal and semifeudal structures which check the development of agriculture is not only a historic need, but also an act of justice towards those who till the land, and a decisive step in favor of national liberation;

Considering that the carrying out of a true agrarian reform brings in its wake the promotion of agricultural development, the expansion of the domestic market, the rise of the standards of living and nutrition of the peoples, and the increase of the export capacity;

Considering that the imperialists are now demagogically upholding in the lesser-developed countries the banner of agrarian reform, with a view to appease the demand of it by the peoples;

Considering that a true agrarian reform strikes at and eliminates the big landowners, who are allies of imperialism and the support of the most reactionary oligarchies;

Considering that the economic development of countries liberated from imperialism, colonialism, and neocolonialism implies the full development of their natural resources and their industrialization;

Considering that the struggle of the peoples of Africa, Asia, and Latin America against the domination of imperialism, colonialism, and neocolonialism is closely related to the struggle of the workers of capitalist countries against the monopolies, and that close cooperation between these forces is of great importance for the total defeat of imperialism;

Proclaims:

1. Its adherence to the principle of the elimination of the exploitation of man by man through non-capitalist development and its culmination in socialism, according to the concrete conditions in each country;

2. That the common struggle of the peoples of Africa, Asia, and Latin America to liquidate imperialism, colonialism, and neocolonialism, headed by the United States, and to obtain and consolidate their economic emancipation, constitutes an absolute necessity;

3. That the economic relationships between revolutionary states and movements which lead liberated zones must be based on active solidarity, fraternal aid, and common interest of the peoples of the three continents;

4. That
   a) national control of the basic natural resources,
   b) nationalization of the banks and enterprises vital to the national economy,
   c) state control of foreign trade and foreign exchange,
   d) the growth of the public sector, are vital instruments in the anti-imperialist struggle and important factors in accelerating economic development with the aim of building an independent national economy;

5. That the aim of the lesser-developed countries is to achieve their economic emancipation through the full development of their natural resources and industrialization, in accordance with the conditions prevailing in each country;

6. That the countries liberated from imperialism, colonialism, and neocolonialism must develop their national economies based on self-reliance, that is: the maximum and rational utilization of their own economic, physical, and human resources, complemented with the efficient and rational utilization of the assistance from the socialist camp and the more developed anti-imperialist countries;

7. That only planning can offer a coherent system to promote and efficiently develop economic relations, to facilitate the mobilization and channeling of the peoples' energies, depending in the first place on their own resources and making rational use of their material and human potential, as well as of foreign cooperation, in particular the aid of the socialist countries, to accelerate development and consolidate economic liberation, the real control of its natural resources by each country in order to overcome the sad consequences of imperialist exploitation and promote economic and technical transformation for the benefit of our popular masses, and, finally achieve a considerable economic growth;

8. The need of putting an end to the permanent fluctuations of the prices of primary products and the fixing in an equitable way of these prices, in a rational relation to the level of prices of industrial products;

9. Its determination to defeat the economic blockade imposed by imperialism, colonialism, and neocolonialism, and to struggle in every way, joining its forces and coordinating a genuine economic action, to protect and consolidate their economic independence and free the masses of the people from all oppression;

Favors:

Establishing forms of economic cooperation among the liberated countries with revolutionary governments, and between these countries and the socialist countries, which allow the former a maximum development of their natural resources by means of trade based on fair prices and long-term agreements;

Notes that:

The imperialist countries have utilized loans as an instrument of economic penetration and political subordination of the lesser-developed countries, and that this type of foreign indebtedness contributes to perpetuate underdevelopment, because, through the amortizations and exorbitant interest rates, it extracts essential resources from the developing countries which, having achieved national independence, find a heritage of foreign debt contracted with the ruling powers by governments on the payroll of imperialism.

The measures adopted by the imperialist countries in flagrant violation of the recommendations and principles agreed upon in international conferences, and which tend to consolidate agricultural protectionism, maintain artificial prices for agricultural products and subsidize directly or indirectly, agricultural production, result in the fall of prices and fluctuation in the international market for primary products, therefore producing a constant diminishing of the share of the lesser developed countries in international trade.

Consequently, the Conference

Declares:

That the economic, commercial, and financial relations between the countries of the three continents and the developed capitalist countries, should be carried out on a basis that will guarantee their development and national independence, based on the principle of self-determination, non-interference, and the establishment of generalized, non-reciprocal, preferential measures in favor of the lesser-developed countries, without exception;

The right of the lesser-developed countries to reconsider and repudiate the spurious and antinational debts that may have been imposed on their economies through the complicity of colonial or neocolonial governments;

Condemns:

The so-called "assistance" and "technical aid," "Alliance for Progress," "Food for Peace Program," etc., which the imperialist countries subordinate to political and military considerations;

Denounces:

1. The activities of international credit and monetary organizations which act as instruments for the control of the economy of the countries of Africa, Asia, and Latin America;

2. The activities in the colonial countries of the foreign monopolies, which deplete their natural resources and collaborate actively with the colonialist oppressive forces to impede the liberation of those territories;

3. The investments of international monopoly capital, which compromise the independence of the countries in which they are made and absorb natural resources and foreign exchange, causing inflation in their economies;

4. Monopoly control by imperialism of international means of transportation, which allows it to obtain high profits to the detriment of the lesser-developed countries;

5. The violation of human rights by the racist minority governments of South Africa and Southern Rhodesia against the African peoples of those territories, and of Portugal against the peoples of its African colonies, and by Israel against the Arabs of Palestine, and invites the countries of the three continents to impose economic embargoes against those racist governments, which are instruments of international imperialism;

6. The reduction by the United Nations of the amount of the fund for the assistance of the Arab refugees of Palestine, and supports their demand for the increase of that fund for the assistance of the Arab refugees of Palestine, so that they may live under less inhuman conditions;

Demands:

From all revolutionary forces represented in the Tricontinental Conference, the intensification of their efforts so that the authentic representatives of the countries that are fighting, weapons in hand, may receive economic, financial, and material aid of all types, including weapons and ammunition; to liberate their countries and consolidate world peace;

Affirms:

1. That the destruction of the old feudal and semifeudal structure that hinders the development of agriculture is not only a historic necessity, but an act of justice for the peasants and a decisive step in favor of effective liberation of the countries of the three continents as well;

2. That the carrying out of a genuine agrarian reform giving the land to those who till it, either in the form of cooperatives or individual property for the small peasant, of state control or self-management, promotes agricultural livestock development, the expansion of the domestic market, raising the standard of living and increasing exports;

3. That a genuine agrarian reform is that which strikes at and liquidates feudal and semifeudal property, the owners of which are the natural allies of imperialism and the support of the most reactionary oligarchies;

Appeals:

To the peoples of the three continents to continue and accelerate by all possible means the process of agrarian reform and the building of an independent national economy in their countries, as a means of developing the revolution in the world, and of restoring dignity to Man in Africa, Asia, and Latin America;

Salutes:

The revolutionary workers of the different countries, who have undertaken militant action in support of the peoples of Africa, Asia, and Latin America, including direct action, boycotting the loading and unloading of ships transporting weapons, in protest against the repression of liberation movements, and invites them to increase their vigilance and efforts to jointly defeat imperialism and its lackeys.

ECONOMIC COMMISSION

RESOLUTION CONDEMNING THE ECONOMIC BLOCKADE OF THE UNITED STATES UPON CUBA

The Conference condemns the imperialist economic blockade imposed by the United States upon militant Cuba, and urges the United States to lift this imperialist blockade immediately.

The Conference also stresses the need of socialist states and countries of the Third World to expand and promote their economic relations with Cuba in view to breaking this aggressive blockade and help Cuba to overcome this obstacle and carry on its socialist build-up.

The Conference takes into consideration that putting an end to this imperialist blockade and the success of the Cuban Revolution is the concern not only of militant Cuba but also of the progress of all Afro-Asian-Latin American countries and the future of World Peace.

ORGANIZATION COMMISSION

RESOLUTION OF THE ORGANIZATION COMMISSION

The First Solidarity Conference of the Peoples of Africa, Asia, and Latin America;

Considering the broadness assumed by the Revolutionary Movement in the continents of Asia, Africa, and Latin America;

Aware of the urgent need to coordinate and intensify solidarity with the purpose of reenforcing the struggle that has been carried on by the revolutionary movements of Asia, Africa, and Latin America against imperialism, colonialism, and neocolonialism;

Decides as an immediate measure on the establishment of the following objectives and structures:

Name

Afro-Asian-Latin American Peoples' Solidarity Organization.

Objectives

To unite, coordinate, and encourage the struggle of the peoples of Asia, Africa, and Latin America against imperialism, colonialism, and neocolonialism, headed by US imperialism;

To give effective support to the national liberation movements in the three continents, using all the means within its reach;

To support the revolutionary struggle, as an inalienable and imprescriptible right of the peoples before imperialism, colonialism, and neocolonialism;

To give firm and solidary support to the liberated countries of the three continents, which, as a consequence of the revolutionary process carried out by their peoples, are the victims of all forms of imperialist aggression;

To defend the right of the peoples to give themselves the government and the law of their choice as well as the socioeconomic system that their sovereign will determines, without any foreign interference;

To cooperate with those of our peoples who are liberated in our continents, to secure their independent development and halt the attempts of the imperialist powers directed towards the destruction of their political, economic, and cultural development;

To organize the solidarity of the peoples of the three continents and serve as permanent link among the different movements which are members of the organization;

To give the firmest and broadest support to the battle against racialism and all forms of racial discrimination in the three continents;

To take charge of the implementation of the measures adopted at the First Tricontinental Conference.

Executive secretariat

1. It will be composed of a secretary general and twelve secretaries, four for each continent. All will be elected from among the members of this First Solidarity Conference of the Peoples of Africa, Asia, and Latin America.
2. It will have its temporary seat in the city of Havana, Cuba.
3. The functions are the following:
   e) To implement the decisions of the Conference.
   f) To prepare the Second Solidarity Conference of the Peoples of Africa, Asia, and Latin America which will be held in 1968 in the city of Cairo, United Arab Republic. This Second Tricontinental will decide the seat of the Organization.
   g) To present before the Second Solidarity Conference of the Peoples of Africa, Asia, and Latin America the draft for the final structure of the Tricontinental Organization.
   h) To supervise the functioning of the Committee of Assistance and Aid to the National Liberation Movements and of Struggle Against Neocolonialism.

4. It is responsible before the Conference and shall submit to it a report on the tasks which have been accomplished.

THE COMMITTEE OF ASSISTANCE AND AID TO THE NATIONAL LIBERATION MOVEMENTS AND OF STRUGGLE AGAINST NEOCOLONIALISM

1. It is constituted by twelve members, elected by this Conference.
2. It chooses from among its members one chairman, one vice chairman, and one secretary.
3. Its objectives are:
   i) To promote, increase, and coordinate the effective solidarity with the national liberation movements;
   j) To apply the measures and to use the necessary means in order to give a real existence and practical efficiency to the fundamental objectives of the Organization, especially those which encourage armed struggle as lawful defense against imperialist violence;
   k) To provide all the necessary moral, political, and material aid to the national liberation movements, particularly to those that wage armed struggle against imperialism, colonialism, and neocolonialism;
   l) To organize a constant campaign, with all the means within its reach, against the growing policy of imperialist aggression throughout the world and their propaganda directed to conceal, with myths and falsehoods, their vandalic actions in the three continents.

POLITICAL COMMISSION

GENERAL POLITICAL RESOLUTION

The First Solidarity Conference of the Peoples of Africa, Asia, and Latin America, assembled in the capital of Cuba, marks the first occasion on which the representatives of the peoples of the three continents gather in an international conference to acquaint themselves with common problems and goals, and exchange experiences that will make possible the necessary solidarity, in order to put an end to colonialism and neocolonialism and to assert the right to self-determination of the peoples.

This Tricontinental solidarity is necessary to face the increasingly aggressive policy of imperialism, especially North American imperialism. This confers great relevance to this Conference, the convening of which has been made possible by the successes achieved by the struggle for national liberation in the three continents.

The First Solidarity Conference of the Peoples of Africa, Asia, and Latin America meets precisely at a time when the imperialists can no longer contain the emancipating wave of the peoples.

As a result of their struggle for liberation, a vast and powerful group of countries has emerged that opposes imperialist exploitation and its aggressive policy, and endeavors to consolidate their independence and defend their sovereignty.

The successful battles waged by the peoples against imperialist domination are gradually weakening its foundations; in South Vietnam imperialist troops are daily being defeated; in Algeria a powerful colonial army, backed by NATO, was unable to resist the vigorous thrust of the Algerian people; the imperialists have made unsuccessful efforts to crush the revolution in Africa. The Cuban Revolution is stronger every day and advances in the construction of socialism, defeating the aggressive policy of the United States.

The Cairo Afro-Asian Conference, held in 1958, was the natural result of the historic 1955 Bandung Conference and the principles it upheld. The Bandung principles acquired a popular and broadly revolutionary meaning in this Cairo Conference, when the peoples of the Afro-Asian continents gathered for the first time under the flag of solidarity in their common fight against imperialism and colonialism.

Before the Cairo Conference of 1958, the solidarity of Afro-Asian peoples had already acquired a concrete and positive form, which effectively contributed to defeat the tripartite aggression of Israel, Great Britain, and France to Egypt in 1956. During the eight years following the first meeting of the popular forces of Asia and Africa, the militant struggle and the close cooperation and solidarity have favored the achievement of many victories against imperialism and colonialism.

The Great October Socialist Revolution, the victory of the Chinese Revolution, the creation of the World Socialist System, the tremendous victories of the peoples against colonial domination in Africa and Asia, and the triumph of the Cuban Revolution in the American continent, have created new and more favorable conditions than ever for the liberation struggle of the peoples.

The strengthening of the world socialist system and the overwhelming development of National Liberation Movements in Asia, Africa, and Latin America hastened the disintegration of the colonial system. This has been the great triumph of the peoples in their struggle for national liberation. A new stage of the fight has arrived when the countries who have attained political independence are faced with new tasks, which are the obtaining of economic autonomy on the basis of the development of national resources, raising the standard of living, and multilateral development of culture and education. The completion of these tasks is inseparably joined to the fight against imperialism, which hinders social and economic progress.

If the peoples of the three continents fight unswervingly against imperialism, colonialism, and neocolonialism, headed by North American imperialism, they will be able to defeat any enemy, no matter how powerful.

The Conference has stressed the fact that imperialists have stepped up their aggressive activities, unleashing wars against the peoples and desperately trying to save themselves. For imperialism, because of its very nature, opposes the national emancipation of the peoples; its system has been and is based on plundering and the unlimited exploitation of the riches of the countries they have subjected.

The statements of the delegates at the Conference have confirmed that North American imperialism leads the aggressive policy of the imperialists. The most desperate actions against the peoples, as in Vietnam and the Dominican Republic, are carried out by Yankee imperialists. North American military bases surround the world. The aggressive pacts in which the United States is the leading power, cover all continents and oceans. The United States is behind each aggressive action carried out by the other imperialists, such as that against the Congo by the Belgian imperialists; against the Zimbabwe people by the racist minority led by Ian Smith with the obvious complicity of the British, French, and Portuguese imperialists and the Nazi government of South Africa; by the fascist government of Portugal against the patriots who struggle in Angola and Mozambique and in the so-called Portuguese Guinea. And it also intervenes in China's territory of Taiwan, maintaining the corrupt Chiang Kai-shek clique; in South Korea, preventing the unification of the country; and in Latin America, attacking Cuba and promoting reactionary military coups, as in Brazil and other countries.

On the other hand, we know that the Federal Republic of Germany is one of the principal bases of the colonialist policy of the Portuguese Government and of the war being carried on against the people of Angola, Guinea, and Mozambique. The criminal complicity of the Federal Republic of Germany is particularly through financial aid, the providing of arms to the Portuguese Government, as well as through the treatment given to Portuguese soldiers wounded in Africa. The trend of international events in recent years shows that Yankee imperialism is the main stronghold of reaction, that imperialism is the international gendarme and the first enemy of the peoples of Asia, Africa, and Latin America, as well as that of all peoples of the world.

Having built up West Germany as an imperialist bastion, with many former Nazi war criminals in high positions, West German imperialism is not only a big threat to world peace but is most active in supporting Yankee imperialism as the gendarme of world reaction. In Asia, Africa, and Latin America, West German imperialism is sending money, armaments, and mercenaries to suppress the national liberation movements as for example in Vietnam, Southern Rhodesia, South Africa, Israel, Venezuela, and other countries.

This Conference denounces and condemns West German imperialism as the most important ally of Yankee imperialism.

The rebellion of the peoples who suffer the oppression of imperialism grows with each passing day. Their struggle weakens imperialism, tearing from it every position it has snatched.

But the defeat of imperialism will not be brought about spontaneously. The experience of history confirms this.

Each victory achieved towards ending oppression and exploitation has required the revolutionary struggle of the people.

When an imperialist power has withdrawn, pretending to be magnanimous in the concession of political independence to colonies which it held by force of arms, it has always been because that open and harsh possession had become incompatible with the level of the struggle and the maturity of the national consciousness of the oppressed people. And in most cases the withdrawal has been more formal than real, inasmuch as they have preserved their hold on the main sources of wealth in the former colony, the monopoly control of its foreign trade and financial resources, with which they hope to substitute the old colonial dependence by neocolonialism. This demands from the newly liberated countries the continuation of the struggle against imperialism, colonialism, and neocolonialism, to achieve full political independence, self-reliance in economy, and national identity in culture, to fulfill their political independence by achieving economic independence, without which the former is to a great extent fictitious. This is well known by the peoples of Africa and Asia who, on breaking their colonial chains, have had to face the vital task of recovering their sources of wealth as an indispensable basis for the development of their economies and the consolidation of their independence.

There are today in the three continents objective conditions for the development of the revolutionary struggle for full national liberation. The dramatic gap between the wealthy imperialist nations and the poverty-stricken nations of the three continents, subjected to colonial and neocolonial rapacious exploitation had never before been made more evident. Nor have the peoples of Africa, Asia, and Latin America been more conscious of the fact that the fundamental cause for that growing gap, is the plunder and systematic exploitation to which they have been subjected by imperialist monopolies, with the complicity of native traitors and oligarchies.

Not all peoples have reached the same stage of their struggle for full liberation, but to a greater or lesser extent, there are objective conditions for the anti-imperialist revolutionary struggle in the three continents, as evidenced by its growing power. Such conditions emerge from the very existence led by the masses of Asians, Africans, and Latin Americans, from the dramatic contrast between their standard of living and the wealth of the exploiting classes, and the fighting spirit grows with the example of people such as that of Vietnam, who with unsurpassed heroism, is defeating the soldiers of the most powerful imperialist power, and the army of its puppet.

The existence of these objective conditions determines the maturity of the liberation process. This Conference is convinced that, in the face of the imperialist violence, the peoples of the three continents must strike back with revolutionary violence, both to safeguard national independence once it has been won, and to achieve the liberation of peoples who are struggling to throw off the yoke of imperialist exploitation. History proves that when the imperialists and their allies seek, through repression, to prevent the changes demanded by the exploited peoples, they must resort to the most energetic forms of struggle, of which armed struggle is one of the higher stages, to achieve final victory.

In order to reach victory it is necessary to open the appropriate channels for the heroism of the people. Revolutionary anti-imperialist vanguards have upon their shoulders the historical responsibility of leading the revolution when the people are already on the march. Not only prestige, but the very reason for the existence of these vanguards is committed in this implacable struggle against the forces which want to stop the progress of mankind.

The Conference clearly establishes that in the face of imperialist limited warfare tactics, where conditions are already mature, the effective answer is the promotion of liberation wars, in every region where the conditions are ripe, of which the supreme example is Vietnam, where the United States, upon increasing their intervention, create the conditions for a later and more overwhelming defeat. But the struggle should not be limited to Vietnam. Imperialism should be struck wherever it intervenes, and also those who may imitate its aggressions against the peoples. The battle against oppressive imperialism must be total. Imperialists continue to ignore the right of all peoples to self-determination. With incredible cynicism, imperialists pretend that the increasing struggle of the peoples for their national liberation is the result of external factors. They have used this argument in an attempt to justify their criminal intervention in Vietnam and the Dominican Republic, Congo, Cyprus, and in other places. The US House of Representatives recently proclaimed the alleged right of the United States to intervene with armed forces in any Latin American country in order to crush the people's rebellion.

The Conference solemnly proclaims that all progressive countries, as well as all revolutionary movements, will extend a consistent and unconditional aid to all peoples engaged in a struggle for national liberation or subjected to an imperialist aggression in any part of the world.

With this obscure policy and its conspiracies, imperialism, headed by the United States, has created a climate of violence that affects world peace and security. Thousands of military bases have been established in all cases against the people's will and are used to suppress the struggle for liberation and self-determination of the countries in the regions in which they are located. We denounce the inter-American forces of intervention and also the mobile units of intervention stationed in France, as well as the military bases that this power, and other imperialist states, maintain in certain African States. Peoples are fighting against these bases, among them the peoples of Thailand, Aden, Puerto

Rico, and French Guiana. The active mobilizations carried out in Japan should be especially noted. The Organization for African Unity (OAU) reaffirms in its resolutions the liquidation of all NATO military bases. Pressures and threats, political and economic aggression of every sort, pirate attacks and blockades, and even armed aggression are part of the aggressive arsenal, gradually used by imperialists in a distinct manner, according to the thesis of escalation.

The peoples of Asia, Africa, and Latin America, struggling for their national liberation and defending their sovereignty, are making a historic contribution to the strengthening of world peace, threatened by the warmongering policy of imperialism.

The vandalic actions carried out against the people of Vietnam are the most outstanding manifestation of the aggressive world strategy of Yankee imperialism.

The invading Yankee forces in Vietnam and their puppet troops have competed with—if not surpassed—the barbaric actions of Hitler's hordes. Mutilations, savage tortures, mass assassinations, destruction of defenseless villages and of crops by fire and napalm, use of poisonous chemical products against men and forests, continuous bombings by all sorts of airplanes, all imaginable atrocities have been tried out by North American aggressors, and the victims have been men and women, old people and children.

The Conference condemns that the United Nations is being frequently used by Yankee imperialism as an instrument of its aggressive policies against the movements for national liberation, as well as the aggression against other countries as Congo, Korea and the Dominican Republic. At the same time, it denounces the UNO [United Nations of Organization], which, manipulated by the United States, has deprived the People's Republic of China of its legitimate seat in the midst of that organization.

Opposing that challenge of moral principles, universally accepted, in the face of that brutal violation of international law, the heroic reply of the Vietnamese is making the aggressors pay dear for their barbaric actions. It is necessary to multiply the solidarity of the people of the whole world with the Vietnamese people to support its heroic struggle in all ways—including armed volunteers, if necessary.

In their eagerness to avoid the defeat that awaits them, the imperialists have been spreading their war in South-East Asia.

US imperialism uses Thailand as its military base to bomb the regions of Laos liberated by the patriotic forces, and the threats, pressures, plots and aggressions against the Government of the Kingdom of Cambodia, are evidence of this policy of expansion of their colonial war.

In recent weeks, North American imperialists have been hypocritically talking about unconditional peace negotiations, and they have talked too much about the fourteen points. This is a smoke screen to disguise their new plans for aggression and extension of the war in Vietnam.

While this shameless maneuver takes place, imperialists continue their criminal aggressions against the Vietnamese people. The Conference supports the four points set forth by the Government of the Democratic Republic of Vietnam and the five points of the National Liberation Front of South Vietnam, and appeals to all peoples to fight for their implementation as the only acceptable solution to the situation in Vietnam.

The defense of the rightful cause of the Vietnamese people has become a fundamental task for the revolutionary strategy of the people of Africa, Asia, and Latin America, but at the same time, that defense today is totally identified with the interests of all men and women, defenders of national sovereignty, democracy, and peace, and is in accordance with the ideals of mankind.

The Far East has been a favorite place for imperialist depredations. Their aggressive maneuvers against the People's Republic of China, the use of Japan as a gigantic aggressive and nuclear base, the occupation by force of South Korea by Yankee imperialism and the constant hostility against the People's Democratic Republic of Korea, are evidence of imperialist action. Above all, Yankee imperialism has been lately trying to maneuver the "aggressive military alliance of North-East Asia" (North-East Asia Treaty Organization-NEATO), joining the puppet clique of South Korea and the militarist forces of Japan through the "South Korea–Japanese Treaty" and illegally manipulating this Treaty in order to use Japanese militarist forces as "storm troops" in their aggressions to Asia, and in this manner create a serious situation in Korea and Asia in general.

On the other hand, British imperialists have created the neocolonialist product of the so-called "Malayasia" and the fake "independence" of Singapore, through which they hope to perpetuate colonial domination in Southeast Asia. The huge military bases in Malaya (including Singapore) are part of the aggressive North-East Asia Treaty Organization (NEATO).

At the same time, oppression continues with increasing intensity against the people of North Kalimantan, who have been in revolt since December 8, 1962, demanding complete independence.

The Conference strongly supports the struggle of the people of Korea for the sovereign unification of their country and the expulsion of Yankee troops from South Korea, and declares its complete solidarity with the struggle of the people of Korea and Japan in rejection of the "South Korea–Japanese Treaty," and against the maneuver to set up the "Military Alliance of North-East Asia." The Conference also supports the struggle of the peoples of Laos, Cambodia, and Thailand for the preservation of their independence and sovereignty.

The Conference also supports the democratic progressive forces of Indonesia in their struggle to consolidate their achieved independence against the Indonesian rightists who, with the reactionary elements within the army as their backbone, cooperate with and are instigated by the US imperialists, through the CIA.

At the present time, the case of Southern Rhodesia provokes the outrage of Africa and of all the progressive people throughout the world. Therefore, the Conference calls upon the progressive countries and organizations of Africa, Asia, and Latin America to render immediate, unlimited material, and effective aid to the people of Zimbabwe struggling for the liberation of their country.

In the overall fights against colonialism, neocolonialism, and imperialism in Africa, the contradictions of imperialism in general have sharpened in South Africa, and it seems like a joint political, economic, and military strategy of the imperialist exploiters and oppressors to impose their racist tyrannies on the overwhelming African majority, constituted by indigenous people. The existence of a joint colonialism in South Africa facilitates the joint repression of the fighting masses by British and North American imperialism supported by their NATO allies, especially Portugal and West Germany. South Africa was turned into an imperialist force, into a stronghold of colonial and fascist repression, which threatens the security and independence of the African states and of world peace. In this joint colonialist strategy, the fascist Republic of South Africa occupies a foremost role, due to its military and economical power and its fascist ideology of racial hatred and supremacy of the white man. A combined action of all progressive peoples and countries is called for, especially of all African peoples, to halt the continuation in power of this odious regime. We condemn the fascist government of the Republic of South Africa and call for the solidarity of all progressive and revolutionary governments in moral and material support to the struggle of the peoples of South Africa and South West Africa who are victims of the Verwoerd fascism and racism.

We unconditionally declare our militant support to the heroic patriots who are fighting in the so-called Portuguese Guinea, Angola, Mozambique, and to the peoples of the islands of Cape Verde, the islands of São Tomé, Príncipe, in the so-called French Somaliland and the Island of Réunion under French rule, and all the other struggling people on the African continent.

We express our most active and concrete support to the armed revolution of the Congolese people, and denounce the armed aggression by the Anglo-American and Belgian coalition. We denounce the logistic support by the United States and its puppets, Israel, Belgium, and the German Federal Republic, to the de facto rulers in Léopoldville.

In all these cases we denounce the support by the Federal Republic of Germany, France, and Japan to the colonialist powers and the racist governments. We likewise denounce the refusal of the French government to expose these regimes in the international organizations, because the French government, in this way, maintains the possibility of taking from these organizations the right to condemn the colonialist policy it still practices in the Antilles, French Guiana, and Réunion.

The Conference denounces the Afro-Malagasy Common Organization (AMCO), the African version of the Organization of American States (OAS), raised by French imperialism in complete accord with US imperialism. The recent turbulent events in the member countries of this Organization, expose their countries and all of the countries of Africa to clearly evident dangers of the instauration of dictatorial regimes similar to those which North American imperialism imposes on Latin America.

Imperialists and colonialists cling to their positions in the Middle East, and it is necessary to aid the peoples of this region in their struggle to eliminate foreign exploitation and consolidate their independence.

To this end, we demand the immediate independence of occupied South Yemen, denounce the fake Federation, and also the dismantling of the British military bases located in Aden and Cyprus and North American bases established in the territory of Saudi Arabia, which constitute a serious threat to the peoples in this area. We also call for solidarity of all peoples with the Arab population of Palestine in their just cause against colonialism and Zionist racism.

The right of the Palestinian people to recover their land is a just right. We express our firm solidarity with the right of the people of Cyprus to attain full and unrestricted independence and for them as a whole, without interference or pressure from imperialist or any other foreign power, to exercise the right to determine their own future.

The development of fighting solidarity with Latin American peoples which struggle with arms in hand against the native oligarchies, servants of the United States, such as those of Venezuela, Colombia, Peru, and Guatemala, or who suffer the brutal repression of military tyrants as Brazil, Ecuador, Bolivia, and other countries, is of particular importance, because Latin America constitutes the rear guard of the most powerful and brutal imperialism, the principal supporter of colonialism and neocolonialism throughout the world.

Each blow given by the struggle of Latin American peoples against their Yankee and native oppressors, doubly weakens North American imperialism. For this reason, the Conference calls for the development of maximum militant solidarity with Latin American peoples. It especially calls for solidarity with the Dominican Republic, whose territory was violated and bloodied by Yankee marines, who continue to occupy the country under the befouled and bloody label of the OAS, the Ministry of Colonies of the United States. There is scarcely a day on which a patriot does not fall assassinated in the Dominican Republic. Its people, who have given such a heroic example by resisting for weeks on end and with very few weapons the thousands of Yankee marines and airborne troops, need the most energetic support from all the anti-imperialist and progressive forces.

Puerto Rico remains under the colonial domination of North American imperialism, that not only denies it its rights to independence, but has also turned it into a huge military base equipped with atomic weapons and from which the government of the United States organizes interventionist actions in Latin American countries. We express our solidarity with the struggle of the Puerto Rican people, and demand the abolition of colonialism in that and other American territories, such as the Guianas, Martinique, and Guadeloupe. We recognize the transfer of full powers to the puppet coalition government of British Guiana as merely nominal independence, which is meant as a screen for the establishment of an Anglo-American and neocolonialist state.

Special mention should be made of the solidarity with Cuba, whose people defend and carry on their revolution, building socialism only ninety miles away from the United States. Its selection as site of the First Solidarity Conference of the People of Africa, Asia, and Latin America is the highest acknowledgement of its Revolution and of its significance for the peoples of the three continents. Cuba, a small country, located geographically near the United States and surrounded by puppet governments submissive to Yankee imperialists and therefore hostile to her, thousands of miles away from the socialist countries, from whom she receives solid support, has proved, with the victory of its Revolution, despite all the aggressions carried out or encouraged by the United States, that when a people is determined to fight until death for its freedom and independence, with a firm and unyielding leadership, the revolution is both possible and invincible. That is why it is a source of encouragement and stimulus for all the peoples of the three continents who fight for their full national liberation. That is also why the imperialists have tried to check the militant support of the Cuban Revolution, by reverting to the most brutal forms of intervention.

But nothing can stop the development of the revolutionary struggle in Latin America. Venezuela proves this. The support of North American imperialists to the Venezuelan oligarchy has been unable to choke the struggle for liberation, just as the high budgets fed by the oil boom, which is a source of fabulous riches for the Yankee monopolies, or the terror unleashed against the heroic brother country, have failed.

The guerrilla fight is consolidating itself and growing, and to the war cry "Free our country or die for Venezuela!", their liberation forces are forging future victory with heroic blows.

The Panama Canal Zone is being used as a springboard for the invasion of the countries fighting for their liberation, and with the military base at Guantanamo and the bases at Puerto Rico, it forms the Caribbean triangle. This is done against the will of the Panamanian people, who have suffered the aggression of Yankee troops for demanding the return of the Zone and the Canal, and the respect of their sovereign rights in all of their territory.

Throughout all Latin America the fight for liberation, justly called second war of independence, extends together with the countries already taking part in armed action. Other Latin American peoples are fighting at various levels and with very different methods. The very powerful working class strikes, the activities in solidarity with Cuba and the Dominican Republic, the public demonstrations for the defense of liberty, the self-sacrificing underground struggle against tyrannies, and the revolutionary actions of the masses, announce that in all Latin America the hour of liberation has come.

In the United States, principal bastion of imperialism and reaction, the struggle of the Negro people against the hateful discrimination which it is subjected to, is intensifying every day, as also is the opposition of the North American people to the foul war that the Johnson administration is carrying on against Vietnam. The Conference greets these just struggles and calls upon all progressive and democratic forces of the three continents and of the world to give them their warm support.

The Conference further proclaims the necessity for establishing closer relations of cooperation with socialist countries, the working class, and other revolutionary and progressive organizations of the peoples of Europe and of North America.

Faced with the criminal alliance of the reactionary forces, the peoples of the three continents respond with active, dynamic, and militant solidarity and with the will to meet every imperialist aggression with revolutionary action, pledging themselves to this fight until they totally liquidate every form of oppression by imperialism, colonialism, and neocolonialism.

RESOLUTION IN SUPPORT OF THE CUBAN REVOLUTION

The First Solidarity Conference of the Peoples of Africa, Asia, and Latin America:
Considering: The historic significance of the Cuban Revolution for the developments for national liberation in these three continents;
Considering: That since the revolutionary victory of the Cuban people an essential turn has taken place in the process of anti-imperialist struggle in Latin America, and that thus the national liberation of this continent has reached a higher stage;
Verifying: That the imperialist government of the United States has not eased in its purposes of crushing the Cuban Revolution by resorting to every means, such as the brutal economic blockade; implacable political hostility; continuous infiltration of spies, saboteurs, and subversive agents; mercenary invasion; provocation from the Yankee military base arbitrarily located in its territory; acts of vandalism; and by maintaining a real permanent threat of direct armed attack;
Verifying: That the heroic Cuban people have firmly answered imperial aggression and have maintained themselves on the alert to face and defeat any attack, as they did in Playa Girón, when in just seventy-two hours they inflicted on North American imperialism its first military defeat in America, and at the same time that they make efforts and succeed on all fronts, have obtained great victories in the field of education; in the extraordinary campaign against illiteracy, in the

culture of the people, in public health, and in the field of economy, whose most important achievement was the 1965 sugar harvest;

Resolves:

To express its full support to the Cuban Revolution, as a significant far-reaching event for the national liberation movement of the peoples of Latin America and all oppressed peoples of the world;

To strongly condemn the unceasing aggressions that the government of the United States has been carrying on in its vain intentions to destroy the achievements that the Cuban people have won through armed struggle and impelled with their work and efforts;

To make theirs the demands contained in different aspects expressed by Major Fidel Castro, Prime Minister of the Cuban Revolution:

1. The ceasing of the economic blockade and all commercial and economic pressures exerted by the United States in all parts of the world against our country.
2. The ceasing of all subversive activities, launchings, and landings of arms and explosives by land or air, organization of mercenary invasions, infiltration of spies and saboteurs, actions that are carried out from the territory of the United States and other accomplice countries.
3. The ceasing of all piratical attacks carried out from bases in the United States and Puerto Rico.
4. The ceasing of all the violations of our naval and air space by US planes and warships.
5. Dismantlement of the naval base of Guantanamo and restitution of the Cuban territory occupied by the United States;

To develop to a larger extent among the peoples of Africa, Asia, and Latin America, demonstrations of solidarity and support towards the heroic struggle of the Cuban people, which on the very threshold of the North American empire carry on the first socialist revolution of America, destroying the dogma of geographic fatalism and showing the possibilities of revolutionary struggle and victory to the people of this continent;

Declares: That any aggression of North American imperialists against the revolutionary people of Cuba will meet the retaliation of the sister countries of the three continents.

RESOLUTION CONDEMNING THE SO-CALLED INTER-AMERICAN PEACE FORCE AND THE GOVERNMENTS THAT SUPPORT IT

The First Solidarity Conference of the Peoples of Africa, Asia, and Latin America:
Considering: That Yankee imperialism landed forty-two thousand men in the Dominican Republic to check the revolutionary advance of the people of that country, at the time it was carrying on an armed struggle for democratic liberties;

Considering: That the imperialist forces murdered more than four thousand Dominican men, women, children, and elder persons who aspired to make true the rights of the people, and who struggled to achieve a patriotic and revolutionary government that would raise the banner of the Constitution of 1963;

Considering: That with the aim of disguising and masking the hated and brutal Yankee intervention in the Dominican Republic, the Organization of American States (OAS) transformed North American troops and troops of the puppet governments of Brazil, Paraguay, Nicaragua, Honduras, and Costa Rica, into their instrument, the so-called Inter-American Peace Force;

Considering: That the so-called Inter-American Peace Force is but a Yankee military force trampling on Dominican sovereignty, which has cost so much blood to these heroic people in the course of their historic process, while the OAS tries to conceal all the crimes perpetrated by Yankee imperialism with the participation of the Latin-American puppet troops, by labeling as peace its aggression and counterrevolutionary war;

Considering: That the Inter-American Peace Force represents the armed counterrevolution of Yankee imperialism in Latin America, and that it is necessary to impose imperialist violence in the strongest and most resolute way, so as to encourage our peoples against the leader and main force of the world imperialist system;

Considering: That the abject governments of Brazil, Paraguay, Nicaragua, Honduras, and Costa Rica, that submissively have lent themselves to the savage occupation of the Dominican Republic, have humiliated their own peoples with their antinational and treacherous behavior, contrary to the great patriotic and revolutionary tradition of Latin America;

Resolves:

1. To condemn the so-called Inter-American Peace Force, actually a Yankee repressive army disguised as Latin American and that forcibly occupies today the territory of the brother people of the Dominican Republic, tearing their sovereignty apart;

2. To demand the immediate withdrawal of the Yankee occupation forces, as well as Latin American puppet troops from Brazil, Paraguay, Nicaragua, Honduras, and Costa Rica;

3. To condemn the governments of Brazil, Paraguay, Nicaragua, Honduras, and Costa Rica that have landed their troops on Dominican soil, against the will of their own peoples, carrying out the command of Yankee imperialism.

RESOLUTION ON THE INTER-AMERICAN PEACE FORCE

The Inter-American Peace Force, recently created by North American imperialism through the Organization of American States (OAS), constitutes an instrument of terror and aggression used by the United States.

Its purpose fundamentally consists of intervening in all countries where, according to the opinion of North American government officials, the national liberation movement has made fundamental advances in the struggle towards the conquest of power.

It began to operate in the Dominican Republic in April, as a consequence of the heroic action of the Dominican people, who decided to find a revolutionary solution to the existing social and political situation of the country. From that moment on, the Inter-American Peace Force has been increasing its military strength under the actual command of North American army officers and under the fictitious or simulated direction of Latin American army officers.

The Inter-American Peace Force was not legally created as a permanent body by the Organization of American States, but the OAS is ready to give it the legal existence which facts have already evidenced.

This body constitutes the organized union of the reactionary military officers of Latin America and its creation is in itself, a flagrant violation of the sovereignty of all Latin American states and of the rights of the peoples to self-determination.

The action of this military unit is an expression of the intentions of imperialism towards the movements for national liberation, which should prepare themselves to face this new element added to the complex of circumstances surrounding the actions of liberation.

The Solidarity Conference of the Peoples of Africa, Asia, and Latin America condemns the action of the Inter-American Peace Force and agrees to offer militant solidarity to the peoples who are facing and will face it as a necessary corollary of their aspirations of liberty, sovereignty, and self-determination.

RESOLUTION ON THE O.A.S.

The Solidarity Conference of the Peoples of Africa, Asia, and Latin America declares:

1. That since its proclamation, in the past century, the doctrine of the so-called Pan-Americanism came forth to prevent the regional unity of Latin America and to infuse new life to the Monroe Doctrine, which is the base of the imperial hegemony policy of the United States in Latin America.

2. That the Organization of American States, within the Inter-American System, is the instrument created in post-war years and fitted to the new conditions begotten by it, to carry out the traditional policy of plunder and loot of the United States in the Western Hemisphere.

3. That the Inter-American Treaty of Reciprocal Assistance of Rio de Janeiro, signed in 1947, is the first institutional manifestation of the "cold war" in America, and through it the United States has bound the Latin American countries to its strategy of military aggression.

4. That the provisions of the constitution of the OAS, that is, the Charter of Bogotá, establish close links between the Organization and the Treaty of

Rio de Janeiro, thus binding the Organization of American States to the political and military obligations of the said Treaty.

5. That since its shameful complicity with the military aggression of the United States against the people of Korea in 1950, the Organization of American States has followed the same imperialist line of "anticommunism" and "cold war," becoming a mere appendix of the aggressive North American foreign policy.

6. That in 1954 the Organization of American States impudently violated its own Charter, brutally trampling on the principles of non-intervention, a cornerstone of the Inter-American system, when in connivance with the exploiting monopolist interests of the United Fruit Company plotted the invasion of Guatemala and the overthrow of its popular and democratic regime.

7. That since the victory of the Cuban Revolution in January, 1959 the Organization of American States, despite the rightful and numerous denunciations of the Revolutionary Government of Cuba—systematically ignored by that organization—has concealed the cowardly, criminal, and illegal activities of the United States when the latter, with the complicity of the governments of Guatemala, Nicaragua, Costa Rica, and others, and using the territories of these countries, promoted the subversion and the launching of the mercenary invasion against Cuba that ended in ominous defeat in Playa Girón.

8. That with the complicity of the Organization of American States, dozens of piratical attacks were launched from military bases located in the United States and in countries of the Caribbean, scores of provocations and armed aggressions have been carried out from the Guantanamo Naval Base—a piece of Cuban territory occupied by the military forces of the United States Government—and countless violations of the sovereign air space of Cuba have been committed by military North American planes.

9. That once more, at the beginning of 1964, the OAS beheld in guilty silence the massacre of hundreds of young Panamanians by the United States military forces stationed in the Canal Zone, ignoring the just Panamanian denunciations.

10. That the Organization of American States, with unprecedented cynicism, and letting the aggressors play the role of prosecutors of their own victims, illegally and arbitrarily decided the expulsion of Cuba from the Organization, and imposed all kinds of sanctions against the people and the Revolutionary Government of Cuba, in open contradiction of the very principles of the Charter of Bogotá.

11. That with the creation of the so-called "Inter-American Peace Force" at the time of the armed invasion of the Dominican Republic by military forces of the United States, the Organization of American States has

become the gendarme of the fraternal peoples of the continent and a threat to the peace and security of the world.

12. That in open contradiction with all principles of international law, including that of non-intervention, formulated in the Charter of Bogota, the Organization of American States has established a trusteeship in the Dominican Republic, maintaining at the same time the military occupation of that country.

13. That the isolated positions adopted in recent years by several Latin American governments in regard to certain aspects of the pro-imperialist policy of the Organization of American States (OAS), have not and could not frustrate or even diminish the antidemocratic nature of this Organization.

Consequently, the peoples of Africa, Asia, and Latin America, in condemning the abject actions of the OAS, servile instrument of the policy of economic, political, and military domination of Yankee imperialism in Latin America,

Proclaim:

That neither the peoples of Latin America nor the governments that may come into power as a result of the victory of the national liberation movements in this continent are bound to any agreements or treaties of the Organization of American States, particularly the Inter-American Treaty of Reciprocal Assistance, and those that deny in practice the principles of nonintervention, self-determination, sovereignty, equality, and independence;

That the Organization of American States has no juridical or moral authority whatsoever to represent the Latin American continent;

That the only organization able to represent Latin America, will be the one created by the democratic and anti-imperialist governments born from the free will of the peoples of Latin America.

RESOLUTION CONDEMNING THE RESOLUTION ADOPTED BY THE HOUSE OF REPRESENTATIVES OF THE UNITED STATES

The First Solidarity Conference of the Peoples of Africa, Asia, and Latin America, held in Havana, from January 3 to 15, 1966,

Aware: That the House of Representatives of the United States of America has adopted Resolution 560, dated September 20, 1965, ratifying the continuation of the policy of intervention of the Government of the United States, as previously stated in the cynical Monroe Doctrine, and by which they arrogate the right to intervene in the internal affairs of any country in the continent, with total contempt for the peoples, and ignoring the elementary rules of international relations, in violation of the treaties that express the right of self-determination;

Considering: That North American imperialists impute to external forces the increasing fight of the Latin American peoples for the liquidation of foreign domination which they themselves exert;

Considering: That the recent armed interventions of the imperialist Government of the United States in the Dominican Republic, Panama, and other countries, add up to the long list of aggressions suffered by Latin American countries for almost one century;

Considering: That with resolutions of this kind the imperialists pretend to legalize their piratical actions;

Proclaims:

The right of all peoples to oppose imperialist violence with revolutionary violence and calls upon all the peoples to offer their moral and material support to those who fight for the liberation of Latin America.

The participants in this Conference express their solidarity to the Latin American peoples whose sovereignty is threatened by the above-mentioned Resolution and they:

1. Reject the pretensions of the House of Representatives of the United States that arbitrarily intends to arrogate the right of intervening in the internal affairs of Latin American countries.

2. Proclaim the right of the peoples of Latin America and of the whole world to carry out the social, economic, and political changes they deem necessary.

3. Ratify their support to the principle of total respect for the sovereignty of all states.

4. Proclaim the right of the peoples and governments of Latin America to request the assistance of any other state in the world in case the imperialists intervene in their internal affairs, and the right and duty of all countries to offer moral and material support to the peoples of our continent.

GENERAL RESOLUTION ON WEST GERMAN IMPERIALISM

The First Solidarity Conference of the Peoples of Africa, Asia, and Latin America, held in Havana, Cuba, from January 3 to 15, 1966,

Considering: The trustworthy antecedents on the militarism of West Germany, and its policy directed to make West Germany a North American military base, equipped with atomic weapons, making it the principal focus of war in Europe as well as for its colonialist ambitions,

Agrees:

To denounce the close relationship between Yankee imperialism and the imperialism of West Germany in the development of an aggressive policy which endangers world peace.

The imperialism of West Germany, principal ally of North American imperialism, attempts against the peace, liberty, and independence of the peoples.

The Conference condemns the imperialism of West Germany and considers that its defeat is an important objective in the struggle of the peoples.

RESOLUTION ON THE USE OF GURKHAS BY BRITISH IMPERIALISM AND OTHER COUNTRIES

The First Solidarity Conference of the Peoples of Africa, Asia, and Latin America, considering the use of mercenaries, especially Gurkhas from Nepal, to check the liberation movements of the peoples of Asia, Africa, and all parts of the world, unanimously condemns such practices and demands that the Nepalese Government immediately revoke any treaty with British imperialism which allows the use of Gurkhas by British imperialism and other countries as tools of intimidation and aggression in North Kalimantan or elsewhere and under whatever other circumstances.

RESOLUTION ON MILITARY PACTS AND FOREIGN MILITARY BASES

This Conference takes note of the struggle of the people all over the world against aggressive military pacts, military bases on foreign soil, the stationing of foreign troops on the territories of other nations as aggravating cold war tensions and undermining the independence and sovereignty of nations.

The US Government is taking military assistance of NATO powers to escalate the war in Vietnam. The Seventh Fleet is being used in a vain attempt to crush the liberation struggle of the brave people of South Vietnam. It is using the bases and troops of the military pact members against the people of Vietnam.

The hundreds of military bases set up by the US and other imperialist powers in Asia, Africa, and Latin America are being used for espionage, sabotage, and provocations and for blackmailing the free countries, and against those peoples who are fighting for national independence.

This Conference, in the interests of independence and sovereignty of nations and in the interest of world peace demands:

1. That all aggressive military pacts and alliances be abrogated;
2. That all foreign military bases be dismantled;
3. That all foreign troops be withdrawn.

RESOLUTION ON MILITARY BASES IN FOREIGN COUNTRIES

The First Solidarity Conference of the Peoples of Africa, Asia, and Latin America, held in Havana, from January 3 to 15, 1966:

Considering: That the imperialists have created a vast system of military bases, which are in fact police detachments in charge of protecting their economic interests in every part of the world, and that are, at the same time, the instruments for hindering and curbing the advance of the struggle of the peoples for their liberation and self-determination in the countries where they are located;

Persuaded: That these military bases are generally established in those territories without the consent of the peoples, who on various occasions have expressed their disapproval of the existence of those installations, so that in many of those countries great mass movements fight for the suppression of the said bases;

Conscious: That North American imperialism has established thousands of bases and military installations and has placed tens of thousands of its troops in foreign countries where the people have expressed their opposition, and where great mass movements in favor of the liquidation of those bases and against imperialism headed by the United States, have taken place;

Conscious: That this system of aggressive bases against the interests of our peoples is also a fundamental part of the warlike, violent and tense policy of the imperialists, designed to fulfill their purposes of exploitation, and being a constant danger to the sovereignty of the states;

Taking notice: That the presence of troops in several countries of the three continents is another of the three elements of domination at the service of the colonialists and neocolonialists, and that it also represents a flagrant violation of the sovereignty of the states, a means of exerting pressure against the nations and a hindrance to their emancipation and development, and a permanent threat to international peace;

Condemns: The existence of military bases and the presence of troops in foreign countries;

Demands: The immediate withdrawal of all troops, the dismantling of the military bases and the restitution of the territories encroached;

Recognizes: The right of the peoples and governments to refuse to accept the maintenance in their territories of such means of pressure, which attempt against their sovereignty and supports the struggle for their definitive liquidation;

Calls: On all the peoples to fight with decision against the establishment of any kind of foreign military installations and the quartering of foreign troops in other countries;

Denounces: With the greatest energy the schemes of the imperialist powers, that have forcibly imposed upon the recently emancipated countries such treaties that legalize the maintenance of bases and the presence of troops for the purpose of perpetuating their domination and of threatening the security of other peoples;

Supports: The just claim of the Revolutionary Government of Cuba for the withdrawal of the military base that the Government of the United States of America has installed in the Bay of Guantanamo, against the will of the Cuban people, and from which it has launched, and still launches, provocative and subversive actions.

RESOLUTION ON MILITARY BASES
IN THE INDIAN OCEAN

The Tricontinental Conference takes note of the preparation for the establishment of new military bases by British and American imperialism in some of the islands in the Indian Ocean.

This is part of Anglo-American strategic plans of strengthening military positions east of Suez and Britain is to provide the island sites while the USA is to meet the cost of installation and equipment.

This Conference condemns the moves as a serious threat to the sovereignty and security of all countries which are in the Indian Ocean area, such as those of East Africa, Pakistan, India, Burma, Indonesia, and Ceylon and calls upon the peoples of the three continents to launch a huge campaign against the establishment of such military bases in coordination with the solidarity movements in the countries of the Indian Ocean area.

This Conference further notes that these Anglo-American bases in the Indian Ocean are intended as an instrument to suppress the growing national liberation forces in the Seychelles, Chaglos, Mauritius, Réunion, the Cocos, the Comoro, and other islands, as well as to convert them into neocolonialist enclaves of the French, British, and US imperialists.

PARTIAL RESOLUTION ON MILITARY BASES

All foreign military bases are tools in the hands of the imperialists to maintain colonialism and neocolonialism, to perpetuate the imperialist way of life as is shown adequately by the formation of the Federation of Malaysia, the case of Cyprus and the Federation of South Arabia, and others, to contain and obstruct the national growth of the developing countries, in the pursuit of their respective national identities.

RESOLUTION CONCERNING
PEACEFUL COEXISTENCE

Peaceful coexistence refers exclusively to the relations among states of different social and political regimes.

It cannot refer to coexistence among the exploited social classes and their exploiters within a country; it can neither refer to the struggle of the peoples victimized by imperialism against their oppressors.

Consequently, the arguments of peaceful coexistence cannot be wielded the way imperialism and its followers have pretended, to limit the rights of the peoples to make their social revolution.

Peaceful coexistence assumes the unrestricted respect for the principle of self-determination of the nations and sovereignty of all states, big and small.

The defense of the principle of peaceful coexistence conveys the repulse of imperialistic aggression, of the criminal use of force against the people, and of the decisive repulse of foreign intervention in the internal affairs of other states, all of which represents the violation of the principle of peaceful coexistence. It entitles the progressive and democratic states of the world to repel the aggressor and help the victims with all their means. When all the democratic and progressive states offer their most decisive help to the victimized peoples, they are keeping alive the principle of peaceful coexistence.

RESOLUTION ON THE INTERNATIONAL WEEK OF SOLIDARITY

On the annual celebration of the week of solidarity of the peoples of Africa, Asia, and Latin America in their struggle against colonialism, neocolonialism, and imperialism;

Considering: The international situation, characterized by the expansion of imperialist aggressions, headed by United States imperialism and directed against the independence, freedom and national rights of the peoples of Asia, Africa, and Latin America; understanding the extraordinary importance of the efforts of the peoples of all continents to resist imperialist aggression and the strengthening of the solidarity of all anti-imperialist forces with the peoples of Asia, Africa, and Latin America, who are carrying out struggle for independence and economic liberation;

Considering: The historical importance of the First Solidarity Conference of the Peoples of Africa, Asia, and Latin America which began a new stage in the struggle of the peoples against the forces of colonialism, neocolonialism, and imperialism, headed by North American imperialism;

The conference resolves:

To celebrate annually, from January 3 to 10, the International Week of Solidarity of the peoples of Africa, Asia, and Latin America, who struggle against colonialism, neocolonialism, and imperialism, in honor of the First Solidarity Conference of the People of Asia, Africa, and Latin America.

The Conference calls upon all anti-imperialist forces, progressive and democratic organizations to participate actively in the celebration of an international week of solidarity of the peoples of Asia, Africa, and Latin America, organizing rallies and meetings intended to unite the peoples of the three continents against imperialism and colonialism.

May the imperialists feel in the days of the international week of solidarity all the strength and power of the fraternal ties uniting fighters against colonialism, neocolonialism, and imperialism, their strong determination to continue their fight until the complete extermination of all those oppressive and reactionary forces throughout our beautiful planet.

GENERAL RESOLUTION ON MEHDI BEN BARKA

Considering: That Comrade Mehdi Ben Barka, leader of the National Union of People's Forces of Morocco and Chairman of the Preparatory Committee of the Tricontinental Conference, was kidnapped in Paris on October 29, 1965;

Considering: That nearly three months have elapsed since the disappearance of brother Ben Barka with no news about his fate, and that the most alarming possibilities cannot be ruled out;

Considering: That the results of the investigations made public establish without the slightest doubt the total, direct, and indirect responsibility of General Oufkir, Minister of Interior of the Moroccan Government, as well as the complicity of certain French official services;

Considering: That the French Head of State has given his own personal formal assurances that investigations will be conducted to the end with diligence and firmness;

The First Solidarity Conference of the Peoples of Africa, Asia, and Latin America:

Denounces: The hideous crime against our comrade Ben Barka, which can only serve the interests of imperialism and reaction;

Pays: A vibrant and fraternal homage to Mehdi Ben Barka, who has done so much for the progress of his people and for the cause of the revolutionary movement in the three continents;

Demands: That this tragic affair be elucidated and that any guilty parties, whether they be in Morocco, France, or anywhere else be mercilessly punished;

Notes: The solemn commitment of President [Charles] De Gaulle that the investigation be pursued regardless of its implications and consequences;

Declares: That all the organizations taking part in the Conference and the "Committees of Solidarity" with Ben Barka strive untiringly in order to obtain a full clarification of his disappearance.

RESOLUTION ON THE CONSTITUTION
OF A COMMITTEE OF SOLIDARITY WITH
MEHDI BEN BARKA

In view of the fact that the kidnapping of Mehdi Ben Barka, leader of the National Union of Popular Forces of Morocco and president of the Organizing Committee of the Tricontinental Conference, is an offense to all revolutionary movements of the Third World;

In view of the fact that the fate of our comrade is still unknown and that there is alarming news which make us fear the worst, since three months have already elapsed since his disappearance;

In view of the fact that the search for him may take longer than is expected;

The Conference decides to create a Committee of Solidarity with Ben Barka, presided by the National Union of Popular Forces with the purpose of trying all means in order to establish the true facts of this affair.

The executive organization which will be created by this Conference will undertake the implementation of the necessary measures for the establishment of that Committee, in cooperation with the National Union of Popular Forces of Morocco.

MESSAGE TO THE WORKING CLASS AND TO THE POPULAR MOVEMENTS OF EUROPE AND NORTH AMERICA

The delegates of the popular movements, gathered at the First Solidarity Conference of the Peoples of Africa, Asia, and Latin America, representing the nations of three continents that have suffered the secular exploitation of colonialism, neocolonialism, and imperialism, practiced by the ruling classes of the United States and the principal capitalist powers of Europe; conscious of the fact that in order to defeat imperialism, headed by the United States, the peoples of Asia, Africa, and Latin America and the peoples of Western Europe and of North America must strengthen their solidarity in the anti-imperialist revolutionary struggle, take this opportunity to address ourselves to the workers, intellectuals, students, and the progressive sectors of those countries.

We salute the struggle waged by the working class of the capitalist countries of Europe and North America against the policy of war and aggression of the imperialists and for the liquidation of the exploitation to which they are subjected. The Conference especially acknowledges and welcomes the increasing popular movements in the United States against the interventionist and aggressive war launched by the North American Government in Vietnam, and urges the peoples of the United States to carry on this struggle.

The Conference calls upon the working class and the popular movements in Europe and North America to increase and tighten the bonds of solidarity and cooperation with the peoples and liberation movements of Africa, Asia, and Latin America. Our struggle is the same, and we have a common enemy. The liberation of Africa, Asia, and Latin America will accelerate the emancipation of the oppressed classes in capitalist countries. The new world for which we fight today opens great perspectives to all mankind, and we all have a place of honor in the fight to conquer it.

MESSAGE OF SALUTATION AND STIMULUS TO THE PEOPLE OF THE UNITED STATES

The First Solidarity Conference of the Peoples of Africa, Asia, and Latin America, sends the following message to the people of the United States:

We, the representatives of the peoples of the three continents, which constitute the immense majority of mankind, meeting in Havana, a few miles from the coast of the United States, wish to send our message of solidarity and stimulus to the North American people for the struggle they carry on against the war and aggressive policy of the government of President Johnson in various parts of the world.

We greet with emotion the great movement of protest and condemnation that is extending throughout the country against the war of aggression waged against the people of Vietnam by the Johnson administration.

We fraternally greet the position taken by the working people, the most distinguished professors and intellectuals of that nation, whose civic and courageous protests are contributing to enlighten public opinion on the despicable conduct of their government.

We congratulate the youth of your country who, risking unjust prosecution and punishment, refuse to become accomplices of the crime of genocide perpetrated by Johnson's Government against the Vietnamese people, and who destroy their draft cards in order not to participate in the slaughter.

We strongly wish that the spirit of victory and unity in the struggle against the forces of reaction should reach, as a stimulus, the brave fighters for civil rights of the Negro people of the United States, who for centuries have been submitted to a double form of discrimination and exploitation because of their social condition and the color of their skin.

The participants in this Conference, when expressing their solidarity, unite their voices with those of all the honest citizens of that country, to protest against the barbarous crimes committed on both Black and white citizens by the savage fanatics grouped in the Ku Klux Klan and in other racist organizations, and in demand of an absolute respect for the lives of the Negro people of the United States.

There is no doubt that the war in Vietnam is contributing to awaken consciences, for it has shown the greed of the North American monopolies, that do not hesitate to commit the most atrocious crimes in order to obtain the maximum profit from war.

At times using the pretext of defending democracy or liberty, and at others the argument of protecting the lives and properties of North Americans living in Latin America, Johnson's government attacks and continues to attack sovereignty; it attacks the democracy that it claims to represent and defend; it attacks the national liberation movements; it attacks international law and the lives of the peoples.

Nevertheless, it is not only against Johnson or Goldwater that the citizens of the United States fight; they also fight against the mono-lithic and inflexible imperialist policy, based on the power of the dollar, whose spokesmen talk of liberty and democracy, but at the same time use, against the people of Vietnam, the hideous napalm and white phosphorous toxic gas, cynically called "benevolent incapacitator," and commit every crime in their fruitless efforts to crush an indomitable people who will not stop their heroic fight until they have achieved victory.

The participants in the Conference view with satisfaction how the different actions taken by the North American people against war and towards the strengthening of peace, in favor of civil rights and against the policy of aggression carried on by the agents of the monopolies, converge in a stream each day more powerful.

We rejoice in the active presence of the working people, of the progressive intellectuals and professors, of students and young people who, significantly, march in the front ranks of the courageous actions against the criminal policy of Johnson's government.

Each action taken by the people of the United States in these difficult and adverse circumstances, has the support of our peoples who also, in the three continents, are facing the same cruel enemy.

The moment has arrived for going beyond the stage of simple declarations and entering into total action. It is necessary that Johnson and his warmongering clique understand that none of their vandalic acts will remain unpunished. It is necessary that North American mothers prevent their sons from being sent to our countries as cannon fodder to defend the selfish interests of a few score of privileged men. It is necessary that the youth of your country refuse to die in order to keep alive those who take advantage of and speculate with the suffering and the blood shed by the great exploited masses; that the North American people cooperate with our peoples through their struggles, in the untiring fight to defeat the common enemy of the peoples of the world, namely North American imperialism.

RESOLUTION ON THE RIGHTS OF AFRO-AMERICANS IN THE UNITED STATES

The First Solidarity Conference of the Peoples of Africa, Asia, and Latin America, held in Havana, Cuba, from January 3 to 15, 1966;

Considering:

1. That racial violence and brutal discrimination unleashed in the United States against Afro-American men, women, and children and the white humanitarians who sympathize with them, is another manifestation of the exploitation of man by man;

2. That the Afro-Americans have the universal and inalienable right to legitimate defense, just as all other oppressed people who struggle under the most brutal repression and tyranny, for human rights and full liberation;

3. That the struggle of Afro-Americans against racial oppression in the United States has never been so widespread or so violent, and that the people in the Negro ghettos are increasingly identifying their struggle for liberation with that of the oppressed and exploited peoples of Africa, Asia, and Latin America;

4. That during the riots in Watts (Los Angeles) and Chicago, Afro-Americans openly proclaimed they were fighting a common cause with their Vietnamese brothers against racism and North American imperialism;

5. That, although, geographically, Afro-Americans do not form part of Latin America, Africa, or Asia, the special circumstances of the oppression which they suffer, to which they are subject, and the struggle they are waging, merits special consideration and demands that the Tricontinental Organization create the necessary mechanisms so that these brothers in the struggle will in the future, be able to participate in the great battle being fought by the peoples of the three continents;

Resolves:

1. To strongly support the Afro-Americans in their struggle for human rights and survival, in common with the progressive forces which defend this struggle;

2. To condemn the murder of Malcolm X, the arbitrary imprisonment of William Epton, and likewise of the victims of the violence unleashed by imperialism against the leaders and militants who face it.

GENERAL RESOLUTION OF THE POLITICAL COMMISSION ON COLONIALISM AND NEOCOLONIALISM

The First Solidarity Conference of the Peoples of Africa, Asia, and Latin America, convened in the capital of Cuba, verifies that notwithstanding the undeniable struggle of the oppressed peoples for their liberation, there still remain millions who are victims of colonialism and of neocolonialism. Our time is characterized by great revolutionary progresses. The process of creation of a new world, more perfect, more harmonious, and more just is taking place in front of us. We are living in the times of the collapse of the colonial system of imperialism, in the times of the awakening and of the renaissance of the countries of Asia, Africa, and Latin America. Imperialism, at the breakdown of its colonial system, resorts to new methods in order to maintain, under its control, countries close to independence and to reduce to a mere formal political independence those nations that have already obtained independence by breaking their colonial chains. Thus neocolonialism has been added to the old colonialist policy, already in agony.

Imperialism is the result of the domination in developed capitalist countries of cartels, trusts, and financial corporations, that have as a main and final purpose the obtention of maximum profit, one of its most important sources being the looting and exploitation of colonies and of neocolonial countries, principally by using the exportation of capital which permits the owner of that capital to lord it over their economies. In the colonies, imperialism adapts traditional societies to the purposes of its exploitation, turning them into simple dependencies of the metropolis, suppliers of cheap raw materials and buyers of manufactured goods of the powers that own them. In the case of the countries that have won their political independence, imperialism does its best to maintain them in similar economic dependence through the possession of their main sources of wealth and by monopolist control of their foreign trade and of their financial resources that together with the investments of capitals on the part of imperialist monopolies, form the principal support of neocolonialism. The first victims of this neocolonialist policy were the Latin American countries, the majority of which, having achieved their political independence in the last century, were submitted to the economic penetration of the rising British imperialism, in the first place, and, on a smaller scale, French imperialism; then, later on, in a predominant way, North American imperialism.

In Africa and Asia, using similar methods, British and French imperialists, when the recognition of national independence became unavoidable for them in numerous countries of those two continents, because of the development of national conscience and the revolutionary struggle of their peoples, made great efforts to deprive this independence of its real contents, to reduce it to a formal independence in a great measure, which has forced the peoples of the already independent countries of Africa and Asia to fight to redeem their sources of wealth, consolidating in this way their political independence.

To guarantee its domination, imperialism tries to destroy the national, cultural, and spiritual values of each country, and forms an apparatus of domination which includes national armed forces docile to their policy, the establishment of military bases, the creation of organs of repression, with technical advisers from imperialist countries, the signing of secret military pacts, the formation of regional and international warmongering alliances; it encourages and carries out "coups d'etat" and political assassinations to assure puppet governments; at the same time that it resorts, in the economic field, to deceptive formulas, such as the so-called Alliance for Progress, Food for Peace, and others similar, while using international institutions such as the International Monetary Fund and the International Bank for Reconstruction and Development to reenforce its economic domination.

Imperialism uses the old ruling classes for its domination, the so-called bourgeois compradors, certain sectors of the national bourgeoisie which it controls through financial instruments, and it even deceives and subdues sectors of the exploited classes and resorts to various forms of corruption through venal leaders of the so-called "free" trade unions and organizations that are tools of imperialism. Other means used by imperialism are the policy, carefully stimulated, of divide-and-rule, using for this the religious, cultural, racial, and political ideology of the oppressed masses, as well as the suppression and prohibition of informative literature from the socialist countries and of the anti-imperialist organizations in other countries, and a calculated policy to control and distort any news about the national liberation struggle, with the purpose of keeping these oppressed peoples in ignorance of these facts.

In its useless efforts to maintain the colonies and perpetuate colonial domination, imperialist countries use the most brutal methods of repression and armed aggression in its most savage forms, just as Portugal does in its African colonies. North American imperialism, hiding behind the flag of the United Nations, after the proclamation of independence in the Congo, brutally intervened and overthrew the legitimate government of Lumumba. Furthermore, the United States and Belgium, with the help of the United Kingdom, have carried out an open repression in the Congo, using mercenaries. Imperialism also uses other more subtle forms, just as French colonialism does in the Antilles.

For the countries that have recently attained their independence, their greatest threat is the subtle methods of neocolonialism, that even under the excuse of giving economic "aid" to those countries, makes sure of new ways of penetration in their economies for the monopolies. It is very important to denounce vigorously the neocolonialist policy of imperialism, not only in its political aspects but in its economic, military, and cultural aspects as well.

A first important characteristic is joint colonialism. Formerly, each imperialist power resolved by itself the problems of its colonies, opposing the interference of other powers in what was considered its "sphere of influence." This was the case of the European colonial powers in Africa and in Asia. And, in America, the expression of this policy was the "Monroe Doctrine." The only base for the division of the colonies and of the spheres of influence was the correlation of forces of the imperialist powers.

Today this situation has changed. The rising of the socialist world, the growing drive of the national liberation movement, the uncontrollable crumbling of the world of colonial slavery have determined the impotence of the colonialist powers, when acting separately, to suppress the national liberation movements. If in 1888, Great Britain, France, Germany, and Italy were able to suppress by the most bestial force and terror the popular struggles of East Africa in order to subdue them, these times have gone, as proved by the cases of Suez and Algeria.

At the time of the nationalization of the Suez Canal, British and French imperialists, with the support of Israel, even resorted to armed aggression, and suffered a defeat.

In Algeria, French imperialists engaged all their military resources, but the National Liberation Movement triumphed. This impotence determined the imperialists to resort to collective colonialism, that is to say, to joint participation against the liberation movements of the oppressed peoples, as in the Congo and prior to that, in Algeria; joint exploitation by North American, British, French, West German, and Japanese monopolies of the natural resources of the Asian and African countries; use of military alliances in the struggle against the national liberation movements, such as the NATO, in the case of Algeria and now of the Portuguese colonies, the SEATO in Laos and against Vietnam, and the proposed NEATO, by the signing of the Japanese-South Korean Treaty. Yankee imperialists have been able to use the United Nations Organization to cloak their neocolonialist plans, as in the well-known cases of the Congo and Korea, and they try to use it for the same ends in other countries.

Never before had imperialists displayed so great a concern for the defense of their common class interests. The collapse of colonialism threatens to liquidate their sources of strategic raw materials, their fulcrums for domination in all the continents to deal a mortal blow to their "hinterlands" on which they depend for their existence. Because of this, the traditional colonialist countries are forced to give up their positions to the United States and to the Federal Republic of Germany, at present the strongest imperialist powers. Six years ago, a Belgian newspaper, *La Nation Beige*, clearly explained the situation:

> Only four colonial powers remain in Continental Europe: Belgium, France, Spain, and Portugal, which all together have a population of eighty million. To imagine that they can offer resistance alone, or even together . . . is an unrealizable dream. Under these circumstances, and with the present development of events, all Europeans run the risk of being expelled from Africa . . . The action required is evident: the supreme rights of a few and feeble countries should be replaced by the powerful sovereignty of all Europe . . .

To this could be added: "and of the United States."

Joint colonialism is not an expression of the strength of the colonialist powers, but just the opposite, of their increasing weakness. And it does not eliminate the inter-imperialist contradictions, nor the fierce struggle of the monopolies of each imperialist country to displace their rivals from other countries, because these contradictions are inseparable from imperialism.

An outstanding example of joint colonialism is that of the European Common Market in its relations with the African countries, of which French imperialism is the main beneficiary. By means of the concession of preferences, and even the duty-free entry of goods into African countries associated with the ECM, the imperialist countries which form it secure tariff advantages for their manufactured goods exported to those African countries, as well as advantages for the investment of their capitals.

Thus, the old European colonial powers apply in their former colonies in Africa and Asia the same policy which the United States applied in the independent countries of Latin America where, under the disguise of a policy of trade reciprocity, it secured a privileged, and sometimes even a monopolist position in the foreign trade of these countries, achieving at the same time exceptional advantages for its investments, with which it has controlled the main sources of riches of most of the Latin American countries. The principal beneficiaries of this typical neocolonialist policy of the ECM are the French and West German imperialists.

Another important feature of neocolonialism is the increasing participation of imperialist states, as such, in investments in underdeveloped areas, mainly under the form of the so-called "aid." The imperialist "aid" is, above all, an instrument of oppression of the underdeveloped countries. It is a new form of export of capitals, destined to create the precise conditions for the development of the bellicose plans of the imperialists, particularly those of North America, and also for the exploitation of the natural resources of the above-mentioned underdeveloped countries by imperialist monopolies. This so-called "aid" is generally granted in the form of loans, getting the underdeveloped countries into ever-increasing debts, to the extent that presently it takes many of them over one fourth of their net income in foreign exchange to pay the amortizations and interests of their debts, as is the case of all underdeveloped countries.

These loans of capitalist countries are always conditioned. For example, the country that receives the loan pledges itself to use that loan for buying goods, at exorbitant prices, from the lending country; in this way the imperialists not only receive interest on the loan at a high rate, but also obtain large profits from the sale of their goods.

Another outstanding feature of neocolonialism is the use of international financial institutions, such as the International Monetary Fund, the International Bank for Reconstruction and Development, the Inter-American Development Bank, and others at the service of the expansion policy of imperialism, and in particular North American imperialism, because the United States controls these institutions. As a matter of fact, the United States alone has 25 percent of the votes in the IMF, 34 percent in the IBRD, and 41 percent in the IDB. Having this control, the United States uses these institutions for its imperialist ends, with this double advantage: it has at its disposal, in addition to its own funds, those of the underdeveloped countries who are members of those institutions, and it does not appear as directly imposing burdensome political and economic conditions on these nations.

An example of this utilization are the loans granted by the World Bank since its foundation in 1946 to 1959 to eleven African countries, for a total of 627,500,000 dollars. How was this apparently impressive total allocated?

One third of the loans went to the Union of South Africa for the construction and modernizing of communications, so as to facilitate the export to the United States of uranium and other strategic materials; for payment of the electric power installations, turbogenerators and other equipment for the uranium mines and other mines in that country. And it so happens that North American monopolies have special "interest" in South African mines, not to mention that these loans were a means of strengthening the fascist and bestially racist government which has been imposed on the Black people, which form an overwhelming majority of the population.

The Congo also received, while it was still a Belgian colony, IBRD loans to construct the communications and to develop the transportation necessary for facilitating the exploitation of uranium and other mineral deposits, the uranium mines of the Union Minière du Haut-Katanga in particular, which undertaking forms part of the international financial group headed by Nelson Rockefeller.

Numerous similar examples can be cited throughout Africa. In contrast, not a single loan has been granted for a project signifying a basic construction for the industrial development of the African countries, such as that of the Aswan Dam, or, if granted, have been subject to burdensome terms.

As to the International Monetary Fund, the examples of Latin America are well known. The peoples of the Argentine, Bolivia, Peru, and others know very well the results of the "plans of stabilization" imposed by the IMF as a condition for "aid": hunger and poverty for the people, a paradise for the imperialist monopolies.

This colonial and neocolonial exploitation to which underdeveloped countries are submitted has terrible consequences for the peoples. A dramatic example of these consequences is that the annual rate of per capita income in Asia, Africa, and Latin America, excepting the socialist countries of Asia, is less than 140 dollars a year. On the other hand, that of the imperialist powers fed by the plundering and exploitation of the natural resources of the underdeveloped countries is much higher, and in the case of the United States, the main imperialist usufructuary, the rate is 2,506 dollars per year.

North American imperialists, through their Central Intelligence Agency, are trying to divide the National Liberation Movements with racial, sectarian, and religious lines and they use vacillating and opportunist elements inside the national liberation movements in an effort to deviate the revolutionary people, efforts in which they use bribery, blackmail, and corruption.

This has been proved, among other cases, in those of Guatemala, Iran, and the so-called British Guiana. Recent events in Indonesia, which led to the anti-democratic and anti-progressive disturbances, were also instigated by the CIA.

After having analyzed the different manifestations of neocolonialism, the Conference points out that this is a new form of colonial domination and exploitation used by the imperialists, especially by North American imperialism, main exploiter and oppressor of the contemporary world.

Colonialism and neocolonialism are the biggest cancer of contemporary mankind. It is the duty of every country and people to eliminate them from the face of the globe.

With this end in view, the First Solidarity Conference of the Peoples of Africa, Asia, and Latin America resolves:

1. To appeal for the militant support for the just struggle of the peoples who fight to achieve their liberation from colonial oppression and to salute the peoples of Angola, Mozambique and the so-called Portuguese Guinea, São Tomé, Príncipe, the Spanish colonies, Aden and Oman, included in the artificially created Federation of South Arabia, Kalimantan and Malaya (including Singapore), Puerto Rico and British Guiana, of Guadeloupe, and all other colonial countries and territories struggling for their national independence; To condemn the policy of massive expatriation practiced by French imperialism in respect to the population of Guadeloupe, Martinique, and Réunion;

2. The active and dynamic solidarity with the countries suffering the aggression of imperialists and particularly North American imperialism; in the first place, this solidarity must express itself in relation to Vietnam, the center of the present struggle against North American imperialism, and whose people is heroically facing and inflicting continuous defeats on the Yankee invading troops and their puppets and is bringing down United States planes that devastate its country. This solidarity must be extended to Laos and to Cambodia, victims of constant United States aggressions; It must also be actively expressed to Cuba, which suffers the economic blockade of the United States and other various forms of aggression; and to the Democratic Republic of Korea, and to all countries suffering from the hostility of imperialism, as in the cases of Congo (Brazzaville), Ghana, Guinea, Mali, and Tanzania in Africa; To condemn the reactionary governments in their conspiracy against the people as in the case of Nigeria. This is equally valid in some African States such as Senegal, Upper Volta, Cameroon, Niger, Ivory Coast, Madagascar, Morocco, [Libya,] and Tunisia, whose governments are instruments of neocolonialism;

3. To support by all means the national liberation struggles in countries which although formally independent, have long suffered the exploitation and oppression of imperialism in many forms, in Asia, Africa, and Latin America. Armed liberation struggle is turning into a fundamental manner of struggle in Venezuela, Colombia, Guatemala, Peru, Oman, and Congo

(Léopoldville), whose peoples and fighters should be effectively supported;
To support and encourage the peoples of the former British colonies in the
Caribbean, such as Jamaica, Trinidad and Tobago, and the former African
colonies, such as Niger, Senegal, Rwanda, Uganda, Nigeria, Cameroon,
Dahomey, and others that are now under neocolonial domination, in their
struggle for real national liberation;

4. To proclaim that, confronted with the armed violence that imperialism,
headed by North American imperialism, uses to smother the increasing
liberation struggle, it is a right and a duty of the peoples who are attacked,
to employ revolutionary violence. To uphold with solidarity this struggle
in the case of each country and urge all countries of the three Continents
to give all their moral support as well as their material, political, and diplomatic aid to the revolutionary movements in armed or political struggle,
which is necessary for guaranteeing victory over imperialism, colonialism,
and neocolonialism in the three continents, is also a right and a duty of all
the peoples;

5. To reaffirm solemnly the ten principles approved in Bandung
in 1955, to govern relations between states. To condemn, consequently, aggression, intervention, subversion, and imperialist control in the States of Asia, Africa, and Latin America, and
also the use of arms or any other method employed by imperialists;
To denounce the North American occupation of Okinawa and Ogasawara
that were robbed from Japan and turned into dangerous North American
military bases to launch aggressions against other countries of Asia, and
in particular Vietnam;

6. To demand the withdrawal of all foreign interventionist forces now in the
territory of Congo (Léopoldville) and the cessation of Yankee and Belgian
imperialist aggressions as well as the withdrawal of the mercenaries at
their service;

7. To condemn the invasion of the Dominican Republic by Yankee marines
and the interventionist troops of the Organization of American States and
to demand their immediate withdrawal;

8. To denounce the strengthening of the North American and European
imperialist policy, that favors reactionary "coups d'état" in Latin America,
Africa, and Asia to impose governments subdued by Washington, as in
the cases of Ecuador, Honduras, and Guatemala, or any other imperialist powers as in the case of some countries in Africa, and to proclaim
solidarity with the peoples that are victims of this aggressive policy;
In all these "coups d'état" that are the expression of neocolonialist policy
of the United States and the European powers in Latin America, the Organization of American States or the Self-Malagasy Common Organization

(political and military bloc at the service of North American and European imperialism) have acted as accomplices. The conference energetically condemns this policy. It particularly condemns the recent reactionary "coup" perpetrated in the Dominican Republic;

9. To demand the most rigorous international sanctions, including measures of force against the colonialist powers which deny independence to the colonial countries and peoples;

10. To call on all peoples to support the struggle for the independence of Puerto Rico, military bastion of Yankee imperialism in Latin America, used for aggression against Cuba and the movements of liberation. This solidarity is of particular importance since in the Caribbean area, where imperialist aggression and anti-imperialist struggle are especially accentuated, the existence of a Yankee colony provided with nuclear weapons, threatens, not only the liberation of Latin America, but also world peace;

11. To condemn all states allied to Portugal in the North Atlantic Treaty Organization (NATO) that continue to give economic and military aid to the Portuguese government, and to demand the immediate suspension of these activities;

12. To call upon all the revolutionary governments and all the peoples to give their most active support to the struggle being carried on in South Africa against the inhuman policy of apartheid practiced by the fascist government of Verwoerd, as well as to lend militant solidarity to the people of Zimbabwe fighting against the terror imposed by the racist government of Ian Smith. This solidarity is important because the imperialists are trying to set up a colonial group with South Africa, Southern Rhodesia, and the Portuguese colonies of Mozambique and Angola, to oppose the independent countries of the National Liberation Movement of Africa;
To call upon all the anti-imperialist forces of the three continents to give their firm support to the campaign of international solidarity, for political and economic sanctions and for the imposition of an embargo on oil and arms against the fascist government supporting white supremacy in South Africa;
Condemns British imperialism for its direct responsibility in creating the conflicting situation in Zimbabwe, submitting the Africans to systematic robbery of their lands, and sharing with the racist minority the product of the exploitation of this people. British and United States imperialists declare they are opposed to the racist government, in an effort to mislead public opinion, as is revealed by the British government's declaration of "replacing" Smith's regime by another, equally racist, which would allow them to continue the exploitation and plundering of Southern Rhodesia. In fact, the British government sold three submarines to South Africa at the beginning of 1965, and it keeps on training South African parachut-

ists in England; the United States maintains deals with South Africa to furnish it with "ground to air" missiles, in spite of a supposed prohibition; Appeals to progressive governments and peoples throughout the world to support firmly the peoples of Basutoland, Bechuanaland, and Swaziland, in their struggle against the treacherous plans of British imperialists and of the fascist regime of South Africa, to establish and maintain puppet governments in those countries. This support is essential, because the imperialists are in the process of establishing neocolonialist regimes in these countries, thus creating "buffer states" to protect their financial interests in South Africa and in South West Africa;

13. To develop the most firm solidarity with the Black population of the United States struggling against the inhuman practice of racial discrimination imposed by imperialists in the United States.

The Conference also resolves to greet and support the growing struggle that the North American people carry on against the colonial war the United States is waging against Vietnam;

To reaffirm solemnly the inalienable right of all peoples to achieve complete sovereignty and to carry on an internal and external independent policy. The Conference condemns decidedly any violation of the boundaries by imperialist states, and the criminal practices of economic and military blockades directed against the movement of national liberation. The Conference declares its support of all measures directed against the neocolonialist policy, and especially declares itself to be:

—in favor of the revision and modification of all bilateral and multilateral agreements imposed by imperialist powers, that conflict, directly or indirectly, with the sovereignty or with the economic interests of the countries that have economic liberty;

—in favor of the eradication of the military bases in the liberated countries, as well as the withdrawal of all troops and foreign military personnel from these countries;

—for the cessation of the undercover carry on, organizing anti-government activities that the imperialist powers plots and terrorist activities in the liberated countries.

The Conference calls upon all anti-imperialist and anticolonialist forces to close ranks in the struggle against imperialism, especially against North American imperialism, chief enemy of the peoples, and to achieve complete victory of the national liberty and independence of Asia, Africa, and Latin America.

RESOLUTION ON SOUTH WEST AFRICA

The Tricontinental Conference held in Havana, Cuba, reaffirms the unshakeable solidarity of the peoples of the three continents with and total support for the people of South West Africa in their just struggle against the Verwoerd fascist and racist administration, and for complete national liberation and independence.

RESOLUTION ON SOUTH AFRICA

This Conference condemns the fascist regime of apartheid as the most brutal and barbaric system of racist and national oppression existing in the world today.

The African people are subjected to the worst form of colonial exploitation and slavery conditions under a special type of colonialism exercised by the white minority in South Africa.

Verwoerd's apartheid regime maintains its fascist dominion over the African and non-white peoples in South Africa, through the terror and violence exercised by the police and with unrestricted militarism.

The Verwoerd regime, in complicity with the white racist government of Southern Rhodesia, the fascist Portuguese colonialists of Mozambique and Angola, with the support of international imperialism, is a serious threat to world peace and security.

This Conference considers the bitter and hard militant revolutionary struggle carried on by the people of South Africa for the ousting of the Verwoerd regime and for liberty and human dignity, an important part of the world's struggle against imperialism, colonialism, and neocolonialism.

This Conference urges all the anti-imperialist forces of the three continents to occupy their places in the campaign for international solidarity, in order to impose economic, political, and cultural sanctions and place an embargo on petroleum and arms, against the white minority government of South Africa.

Furthermore, it urges all anti-imperialist forces to compel the business partners of South Africa, i.e., Great Britain, USA, France, West Germany, Belgium, Italy, and Japan to impose these sanctions.

This Conference vigorously and urgently exhorts all anti-imperialist and democratic organizations of the world to give their full material support to the fighters for the liberty of South Africa, thus contributing to the most effective accomplishment of their armed revolutionary struggle.

RESOLUTION ON ANGOLA

The First Tricontinental Conference greets the armed struggle carried on by the people of Angola for their national liberation under the leadership of the Popular Movement for the Liberation of Angola (PMLA);
Considering: the difficult situation created in Southern Africa by the unilateral proclamation of independence of the white minority headed by Ian Smith in Southern Rhodesia;
Considering: that the existence in this part of Africa of a military bloc formed by Portugal, South Africa, and Southern Rhodesia, is a permanent threat for

Africa and world peace and that it tends to suppress the just aspirations of the African peoples oppressed by the Portuguese colonial rule, by the racists of Southern Rhodesia, to the strengthen-norities [sic] of Southern Rhodesia;

Considering: that the development of the armed struggle in the Portuguese colonies under the leadership of the Nationalist Organizations united in the CNOPC is a most valuable contribution for the solution of the problem of South Africa, and by the white mining of African Unity and of all anti-imperialist forces;

Considering: that the development of the armed struggle is closely related to the possibilities of transit of arms and troops in the African countries, especially those bordering Angola, the First Tricontinental Conference recommends those countries to comply with and implement the decisions taken at the Fourth Conference of the Organization of Solidarity of the Afro-Asian Peoples, as well as those adopted by the heads of states and governments in Accra, requesting all neighboring states of the Portuguese colonies to allow the transit of men and supplies necessary for the early success of the liberation movement struggle;

Appeals to the solidarity committees of the peoples of the three continents to strengthen their support to the Popular Movement for the Liberation of Angola (PMLA), which is the organization that leads the armed struggle of the people of Angola, by all possible means, including the supply of arms.

The Tricontinental Conference recommends that the 4th of February of each year, anniversary of the beginning of the armed struggle, be observed as a day of international solidarity with the people of Angola.

RESOLUTION ON THE ARAB PENINSULA

The First Solidarity Conference of the Peoples of Africa, Asia, and Latin America, held in Havana from January 3 to 15, 1966:

Supports the struggle of the people of the Arab Peninsula, under the leadership of the Arab Socialist Front, for the realization of the following aims:

1. Liberation of the Arab Peninsula from the imperialist Saudi Arabian regime.
2. Establishment of a democratic socialist regime liberating the people from all types of misery [and] servitude, and providing them with a decent free life;

Denounces the existence of American or British military bases in the Arab Peninsula, the so-called Saudi Arabia, and demands their immediate liquidation;

Vehemently condemns the absolute dictatorship, the atrocities committed by the Saudi Arabian government to suppress the liberties of the people and deprive them of a democratic system of government; and the prevalence of disease, poverty, ignorance and demands the immediate release of political prisoners and those now under arrest;

Considers the appellation "Saudi Arabia," of the Arab Peninsula an act that violates the peoples' rights, and demands its immediate change;

Demands the establishment of a democratic rule where the peoples exercise full rights;

Considers the arms deals concluded between the United States and Britain and the Saudi Arabian government an act of aggression against all democratic and freedom-loving forces and a violation of world peace.

RESOLUTION ON BASUTOLAND, BECHUANALAND, AND SWAZILAND

This Conference, noting with deep concern the general developments in Southern Africa, wherein the British government actively promotes the interests of three-and-a-half million whites at the expense of the twenty-one million African people in that part of the African continent,

And aware of the interference of the fascist regime of South Africa in the affairs of all the neighboring countries,

Vehemently condemns the British government for conniving with the Verwoerd government to place in power puppet governments in Bechuanaland, Swaziland, and Basutoland;

Wholly associates itself with resolution No. AHS/36 of the African Heads of State and Government meeting in Accra in October 1965, declaring continued support to the liberation movements in these countries;

Calls on the British government to accede to the demands of the peoples of these countries for free and democratic elections before independence, and

Further demands the immediate withdrawal of the British forces presently stationed in Swaziland, and

Calls for the dismantling of the Anglo-South African military base on the borders of Bechuanaland, South West Africa, and Zambia.

RESOLUTION ON BRAZIL

The question of neocolonialism takes on new characteristics with the April 1, 1964, military coup in Brazil.

This coup, inspired, financed, and prepared by North American imperialism, is clearly aimed at preventing the economic liberation of the country from the neocolonialist forms of exploitation, and seeks the complete economic and political submission of Brazil by means of an economic and financial policy which will paralyze and set back the industrial development of Brazil, in order to maintain the country as a supplier of raw materials with an agricultural economic base.

We propose to include in the draft resolution the condemnation of this new blow of North American imperialism that not only maintains but aggravates neocolonialist exploitation in Latin America.

RESOLUTION ON BURUNDI

The First Solidarity Conference of the Peoples of Africa, Asia, and Latin America, gathered in Havana, (Cuba) from January 3 to 15, 1966, greets the workers and youth of Burundi, organized in the Workers' Federation of Burundi, (WFB) and the Rwagasore National-ist Youth (RNY) who after a year are still deprived of their syndical and democratic rights.

It has noted with indignation the arbitrary arrest and the imprisonment without trial of labor leader Agustin Ntamagara and youth leaders Francois Bangemu and Prime Niyongabo, despite the many protests of different international organizations.

The Delegates to the First Tricontinental Conference, on behalf of the peoples of the three continents that they represent:

Demand the immediate rehabilitation of the Workers' Federation of Burundi and of the Rwagasore Nationalist Youth;

Demand from the Burundi government the respect for liberties, established in the conventions of the International Labour Organization, which Burundi has subscribed, and the respect for the democratic liberties established by the constitution;

Demand the freedom of Agustin Ntamagara, Secretary General of the Workers' Federation of Burundi, Francois Bangemu and Prime Niyongabo, President and Secretary General, respectively, of the Rwagasore Nationalist Youth.

RESOLUTION ON CAMEROON

The First Solidarity Conference of the Peoples of Africa, Asia, and Latin America convened in Havana from January 3 to 15, 1966,

Considering the war of genocide that the repressive troops of French neocolonialism are waging against the people of Cameroon;

Considering the diabolic efforts of the reactionary government of Cameroon to increase the imperialist troops, maintain French military bases in the country, enroll mercenaries from the OAS, as well as former Nazis, aimed to repress the people of Cameroon, and to increase every year the number of imperialist technicians who control the state, the administration, and the national economy;

Considering the fascist policy of the puppet regime of Yaounde, characterized by the lack of freedom of opinion, of association, of press, syndical freedom, or other elementary forms of democratic liberties;

Considering the arbitrary arrests and imprisonments of the patriots that take place daily in Cameroon, as well as the illegal confinement of more than forty thousand patriots in governmental forced labor camps and prisons of Cameroon;

Considering the systematic and joint recolonization of the country organized by the imperialist powers belonging to the European Common Market, especially France, West Germany, Great Britain, and the United States of America, particularly characterized by the submission of the government of Ahmadou Ahidjo, the penetration of the monopolies of the imperialist powers in the basic sectors of the national economy;

Considering the acute impoverishment of the popular masses, increased unemployment, growing illiteracy, disease, and other social disasters:

Denounces the aggression carried out by French imperialist forces against the people of Cameroon through the puppet government of Yaounde;

Condemns the fascist actions of the reactionary government of Ahidjo that deprives the people of Cameroon of their fundamental liberties and surrenders to imperialism the essence of national sovereignty;

Demands the withdrawal of the imperialist troops, the dismantling of the foreign military bases, the immediate freedom of the political prisoners, the suspension of arbitrary arrests and of judicial processes, as well as the unconditional amnesty of the patriots who are victims of arbitrary treatments;

Demands from the organizations participating in this Tricontinental Conference that they join the campaign for the deliberation of the political prisoners of Cameroon, according to the appeal made by the International Association of Democratic Jurists;

Makes a vibrant appeal to all the anti-imperialist forces of the world to grant effective aid to the patriots of Cameroon who are engaged in the struggle against the aggressive imperialist forces and against the fascist dictatorship of Cameroon.

RESOLUTION ON THE FIGHT FOR THE LIBERATION OF THE CONGO (L)

The First Solidarity Conference of the Peoples of Africa, Asia, and Latin America, held in Havana, Cuba from January 3 to 15, 1966:

Warns that mercenary troops of native traitors, incessantly supported by North American imperialism with its Belgian allies, intervene in the internal affairs of the Congolese people and support the de facto Léopoldville government hindering the liberation struggle of that fraternal people and favoring activities which impede the liberation process undertaken by the Congolese patriots, who have vowed not to make any kind of compromise with North American imperialism, the sworn enemy of the peoples;

Considering the necessity that progressive governments of Africa, Asia, and Latin America effectively support the liberation struggles of the Congolese people, and oppose the permanent aggressions of North American imperialism and its Belgian allies,

Condemns the permanent intervention of North American imperialism and its Belgian allies against the revolutionary liberation struggle of the Congo;

Calls on the governments of progressive states of the three continents to support and offer aid to the liberation struggle that the Congolese patriots maintain against North American imperialism, its Belgian allies, mercenary traitors, and the de facto Léopoldville government.

RESOLUTION CONCERNING POLITICAL PRISONERS IN BRITISH GUIANA

This Tricontinental Conference condemns the emergency government of British Guiana and the acts of imprisonment without previous trial; and urges Great Britain and the Government of British Guiana to put an end to the state of emergency, and to uphold the democratic rights and liberties established in the Constitution of British Guiana.

RESOLUTION ON GUADELOUPE

The First Solidarity Conference of the Peoples of Africa, Asia, and Latin America, held in Havana, from January 3 to 15, 1966:

Considering: that Guadeloupe is kept in a state of dependency by French imperialism;

Considering: the existence of a colonial situation characterized by violence and economic, political, social, and cultural oppression;

Considering: the existence of a machinery of oppression and repression, as well as the spoliation suffered by the people of Guadeloupe;

Considering: the denial of fundamental liberties and the threats constantly imposed on personalities and the principal revolutionaries of Guadeloupe;

Considering: that the Guadeloupe issue is not an internal affair of France;

Considering: the process of second colonization resulting from the French "Law of Departmentalization" of March 19, 1946;

Considering: the risks that the existence of colonialist and neocolonialist bases in the area means to the countries in the Caribbean and Latin America;

Condemns: the colonialist policy of the French government in Guadeloupe, particularly the expatriation of the youth;

Affirms: the right of Guadeloupe to national independence;

Pledges: its unconditional support to the organizations that struggle for the total liberation of the country in accordance with the objectives of the Conference;

Strongly recommends: to all brother countries to state before international organizations the problem of Guadeloupe. Pledges itself to give all necessary aid to the revolutionaries of Guadeloupe for the complete and definitive decolonization of their country.

RESOLUTION ON HAITI

The Tricontinental Conference of the Peoples of Africa, Asia, and Latin America emphatically condemns the acts of terrorism perpetrated by the government of M. Duvalier against Haitian workers and patriots.

The Conference has heard with horror the revelation of the odious crimes committed by the Duvalier Government against the patriots in Haiti.

It expresses its desire that that practice of detentions, tortures and the massacre of entire families because of the political ideas of any member of a Haitian family cease.

The Conference demands that, from now on, justice be met to Haitian prisoners and denounces the assassinations regularly perpetrated against political prisoners in Haiti.

It demands that the International Commission of Human Rights take into account the constant violations of civil liberties in Haiti, the absolute rejection of the basic human rights of the Haitian people by the present government of that country, and that the whole world be informed of the results of the investigation.

The Conference shall do everything possible to inform international public opinion of the desperate situation in which the Haitian people find themselves, and promises to denounce, on each occasion, the atrocities committed by the dictatorship of Duvalier, a faithful lackey of Yankee imperialism.

The Conference gives its firm support to the revolutionary anti-dictatorial and anti-imperialist struggle of the Haitian patriots fighting to reconquer democracy and economic independence.

RESOLUTION PROTESTING THE PERSECUTION OF DEMOCRATS IN INDONESIA

The historical First Afro-Asian-Latin American Conference taking place in Havana from January 3 to 15, 1966, attended by delegates from many countries and observers of international organizations and countries, with profound concern has been following the recent developments in Indonesia.

The developments are such that the rightists and the reactionary elements within the Indonesian military forces as the backbone, in cooperation with and instigated by the US imperialists through the CIA have attacked the Indonesian people and nation, violating democratic liberties and have split the anti-imperialist national united front which has given important contributions to the struggle of the peoples for the defense and achievement of national independence as well as for the consolidation of Afro-Asian-Latin American peoples' solidarity. They are now stepping up and intensifying an anti-popular and anticommunist campaign.

While splitting and dividing the revolutionary unity of the Indonesian people and paying lip service by claiming to stand behind President Sukarno, they are actually continuing with their crime of persecuting all progressive forces, in particular the communists.

So far, tens of thousands of people within the progressive movements in Indonesia have been cruelly murdered or tortured, exposing the fascist nature of the present reactionary forces in power. More than one hundred thousand people have been arrested. Among them are outstanding leaders in the workers', peasants', women, youth, and student movements, and also prominent scientists, writers, and journalists. More than fifteen universities, academies, and hundreds of schools have been arbitrarily closed, their professors and students expelled or arrested. More than thirty newspapers have been banned and more than three hundred journalists arrested and persecuted.

In the name of "revolutionary actions," the Indonesian rightists and the reactionary elements in the Indonesian army as the backbone, are launching every type of counter-revolutionary actions. In the name of "left" they are turning the situation to the right. In the name of suppressing the "September 30 Movement" they are carrying out a step-by-step coup by most traitorous methods. In the name of suppressing the "September 30 Movement" they are suppressing communists, and under the anticommunist banners they suppress every democrat, no matter whether he is a nationalist, a religious person, or a communist.

In facing the barbarous action of the Indonesian reactionaries, the Indonesian people, especially the workers and peasants who were subjected to very long suffering from the ruling antipeople groups and were steeled in long years of struggle, have come out in a more determined resistance through various forms of struggle. Together with the rank and file of the four Armed Forces of the Indonesian Republic, they are now marching forward to defend and safeguard the achievements of the Indonesian revolution and the revolutionary thinking of president Sukarno.

Fully relying on the Indonesian progressive forces and the solid unity and solidarity of the Afro-Asian-Latin American peoples in their common and persistent struggle against imperialism, the First Afro-Asian-Latin American Conference strongly protests the antidemocratic action of the Indonesian reactionaries in power and demands the restoration of democratic liberties in Indonesia, as well as the release of all democrats under arrest.

In the interests of our common struggle against imperialism, colonialism, and neocolonialism and the subversion practiced by the imperialists and their lackeys, and in accordance with our sacred duty to step up solidarity actions in the spirit of Afro-Asian-Latin American solidarity, let us express our support to the progressive and patriotic forces in Indonesia.

RESOLUTION ON JAMAICA

Aware of the struggles of the Jamaican people for over three hundred years against the oppressive and exploitative domination under British colonial rule, and
Realizing that the political independence gained by Jamaica in 1962 has merely meant the transfer of power from direct colonial rule to the hands of a small reactionary property-owning class in Jamaica, which continues to serve the interests of British and American imperialism at the expense of the Jamaican people, and
Conscious of the fact that the so-called "independence" has meant no change or improvement in the lives and material conditions of the poor and exploited

masses of the Jamaican people, and that the Jamaican people are dissatisfied and fed up with the present unequal and unjust system of class exploitation, and
Aware that under the present system, and with the complicity of the ruling clique in Jamaica, the wealth produced by the Jamaican workers is owned by the British and American imperialists through their monopolies in Jamaica whose profits are shipped abroad, with no benefit for the Jamaican workers;
Be it resolved that the Solidarity Conference of the Peoples of Africa, Asia, and Latin America condemns the neocolonial exploitation and oppression of the Jamaican people by British and American imperialists and upholds the right of the Jamaican people to take whatever steps may be necessary, to swiftly terminate this exploitation and oppression and obtain the ownership and control of the wealth of their country which is produced by their own labor.

The Conference encourages and supports all actions of the Young Socialist League and Unemployed Workers Council in heightening the consciousness of the Jamaican people for the swift and effective overthrow of the present unjust system and neocolonialist yoke.

RESOLUTION IN SUPPORT OF THE STRUGGLE OF THE JAPANESE PEOPLE

The First Solidarity Conference of the Peoples of Africa, Asia, and Latin America:
Considering the importance of the struggle of the Japanese people, who are courageously fighting against US imperialism and the Japanese reactionary forces and for the realization of independence, peace, and democracy;
Fully supports the Japanese people in their struggle against the US imperialist aggression in Vietnam and the Japan–South Korea Treaty, for the withdrawal of US military bases and troops in Japan and the return of US occupied Okinawa and Ogasawara to Japan, against the call of US nuclear submarines at Japanese ports, nuclear armament of the country and the turning of Japan into a base for nuclear attacks, against the revival of Japanese militarism, and for the abrogation of the Japan–US Security Treaty.

The Conference,
Expressing solidarity with the Japanese people in their struggle for the prevention of nuclear war, the complete prohibition of nuclear weapons and the relief of atomic bomb victims,
Supports the convocation of the Twelfth World Conference against A and H Bombs which will be held in Japan, in August of this year.

RESOLUTION ON 'MALAYSIA'

"Malaysia" is a US-British neocolonialist product. Huge military naval and air bases in "Malaysia" form the backbone of the US-British global strategy "East of

Suez" and aim at suppression of the liberation struggles of the peoples of Malaya (including Singapore) and Kalimantan Utara, at intimidation and subversion of the people of Indonesia, and at aggression of other countries in the whole region.

This Conference firmly supports the people of Malaya (including Singapore) and Kalimantan Utara in their just struggle for national liberation.

The recent proclamation of the phony "independence" of Singapore following its separation from "Malaysia" was only an imperialist plot to save "Malaysia" from total collapse and an attempt to stabilize the US-British imperialist "rear" in SE Asia for expansion and escalation of the US war of aggression in Vietnam to the rest of Indochina and to China itself.

RESOLUTION ON MOROCCO

The First Solidarity Conference of the Peoples of Africa, Asia, and Latin America, held in Havana from January 3 to 15, 1966:

Denounces the trend of the rulers of Morocco towards the establishment of an open military and repressive dictatorship. This trend was evidenced by the "conspiracy of July, 1963," confirmed by the repression of the demonstrations of March 1964 and recently crowned by the kidnapping of Mehdi Ben Barka;

Verifies the deterioration of the economic and social situation which has made more acute the impoverishment of the masses and underdevelopment, and has strengthened the control of the imperialist monopolies over the economy of the country;

Notes with satisfaction the development of the consciousness of the popular masses, that have expressed, through demonstrations of workers and students and by the current of discontent in the rural sections, their condemnations of the policy of impoverishment and their rejection of its neocolonialist domination;

Proclaims its full support to the struggle of the popular forces against the feudal and neocolonialist empire and for the establishment of a true democracy in Morocco;

RESOLUTION ON MARTINIQUE
AND FRENCH GUIANA

The Tricontinental Conference of the Peoples of Africa, Asia, and Latin America firmly condemns the colonial regime imposed by the French Government in territories of its ancient empires such as Martinique, Guiana and Réunion, as well as the political repression carried out in those countries.

The Conference denounces the trickery of the French Government which tends to make world public opinion and particularly that of Africa, Asia, and Latin America, believe that it has completely finished the decolonization of the countries that were under its rule, and that Martinique, Guiana, and Réunion are French overseas departments.

The Conference affirms that the existing problem today in those so-called overseas departments is essentially a political one, namely that of the colonization of those countries.

The Conference unconditionally supports the united struggle of the anticolonialist forces of Martinique, Guiana, and Réunion that ask for the substitution of the present status by one of autonomy that recognizes the right of the peoples of those countries to conduct their own affairs.

The Tricontinental Conference denounces the grave threat which the installation of a missile base signifies not only for Guiana, but also for the whole Latin American continent.

RESOLUTION ON NICARAGUA

The participants in the First Solidarity Conference of the Peoples of Africa, Asia, and Latin America, gathered in the city of Havana:

Denounce the Bryan-Chamorro Treaty, imposed by the United States on Nicaragua in 1914, in order to construct a canal in its territory, thus lessening its sovereignty and deserving the strong repulse of the progressive forces of Nicaragua.

RESOLUTION ON NIGER

Considering: That after more than six years the people of Niger still live under the terror which characterizes the present regime imposed by the French forces of repression;

Considering: That on March 8, 1960, Niger only nominally became an independent republic, such independence having been granted by France after securing for herself the wealth of the country through illegal agreements;

Considering: That a savage oppression daily afflicts the masses who express their hostility towards the unpopular regime of the Diori and Boubou Hama clique;

Considering: That there has been an almost total lack of freedom of expression or assembly, of trade union, political, or social organizations for more than six years;

Whereas the fascist Diori regime has committed mass murders since 1962, and particularly in 1964, when the people of Niger, under the leadership of the Sawaba Party rose in arms in order to make the neocolonialists of Niger respect the Declaration of Human Rights, which the puppet regime of Niger signed at the United Nations;

Considering: That for more than four years several leaders of the Sawaba Party, as Adamon Sekou, former Minister of Public Works and member of the Political Bureau, Hima Dembele, former Deputy, Assana Mayaki, Aboubacar Kao, former Minister, Zhodi, former Minister, Mounkaila Issifi, former Deputy, Alhadji Amadou Gabriel, former Mayor, all members of the Political Bureau, and many other well-known militants loved by the people, have been held in the neocolonialist goals of Niger;

Considering: That the present regime's clique, panic-stricken by the actions of the Niger militants, employs all the old methods of fascist repression, public executions, hangings, night murders, rapes, etc.;

Considering: That the USA have supplied a significant quantity of modern arms and munition to the Government and have asked Israel to send military and civil instructors in order to train the puppet army and the civil reactionary clique in the use of arms;

Considering: That in spite of the imperialist coalition of the USA, Israel, France, Federal Germany, the people of Niger, under the leadership of the Sawaba Party, is more determined than ever to wage its just struggle until the final victory;

The Delegation of Niger (Sawaba) to the First Tricontinental Conference
Demands:

The reestablishment in Niger of freedom of expression, and political and labor organizations;

The immediate and unconditional liberation of thousands of political prisoners who have been held in prison for many years;

The immediate ending of mass and individual murders and a total amnesty for all political prisoners.

The Delegation of the Sawaba Party requests the active solidarity of the peoples of Asia, Africa, and Latin America, in their just struggle against neocolonialism, imperialism, and for the true independence of their country.

RESOLUTION CONDEMNING THE GOVERNMENTS OF THE FEDERATION OF NIGERIA

This Solidarity Conference of the Peoples of Africa, Asia, and Latin America notes with deep concern the recent and continuous events in the Federal Republic of Nigeria, which resulted in the loss of many properties and lives.

We condemn unequivocally the rigged elections and the consequent imposition of the regime on the people which has been directly responsible for these events.

We further condemn the role of the Federal Government under the leadership of Tafawa Balewa and particularly the use of the army and police to terrorize the common people by the display of naked brutality against the resentment of the people which is mounting.

We condemn their inability to face the ballot box and to contest a fair and free election.

In view of the fact that Nigeria today is passing through a period of acute both political and economic crisis, in order to replace the present reactionary regime, we support the popular front of all the progressive forces of Nigeria called "the peoples' front."

In view of the reactionary nature of the Nigerian government, they handed over our patriotic comrades from the Niger Republic, Cameroon, and Senegal to be imprisoned and murdered.

We condemn the neocolonialists headed by the US war mongering imperialists in their intensifying efforts to turn Nigeria into the main stronghold of neocolonialism in Africa.

We condemn the Governments of the Federation of Nigeria as the headquarters of all forces of reaction and subversion against Africa.

We condemn the same for the intensification of British, West German, and US economic stronghold on Nigeria.

We call on this Conference, in view of the strategic position of Nigeria, to take note of the great threat imperialism possesses against African, Asian, and Latin American peoples.

RESOLUTION ON OMAN

The First Solidarity Conference of the Peoples of Africa, Asia, and Latin America condemns the barbarous action of the British Government against the people of Oman;

Calls for the immediate removal of British troops and the return of democratic rights to the people of Oman;

Recognizes the inalienable right of the people of Oman to self-determination and independence in accordance with their freely expressed wishes.

RESOLUTION ON PALESTINE

As a military base, Israel was used in 1948 to expel the rightful Arab owners of Palestine. It was used in 1956 against the great revolution of Egypt to protect the interests of the imperialists in the Suez Canal. In 1963, Israel was used to crush the revolutionary force in Congo and to help Moise Tshombe, the imperialist stooge and agent par excellence in Africa. Israel was called upon by its imperialist masters to send regiments of paratroopers to fight against the revolutionary forces. Israel also trained the mercenary armies in Congo, has a military mission there and built a military school for training paratroopers of the Congolese reactionary government. Moreover, General Joseph Mobutu, the Chief of Staff of the Congolese army, has been recently trained in Israel. In 1964, Israel sent continuous shipments of arms to the reactionary government in Portugal to be used against the liberation movements in Angola and Mozambique. In 1965, imperialists called upon Israel to send shipments of arms to the remnants of the reactionary forces in Yemen. Actually Israel is sending medical gifts to US imperialist forces in South Vietnam and Israel has chartered all of its freighters to the US Government for transport of military equipment to South Vietnam.

In addition to all this, Israel has become an arsenal of arms in the Middle East. These arms, which within two years will include atomic weapons, are to be used by the imperialists against liberation movements in Africa and Asia.

Israel is not only a military base, it is also an economic base for imperialists. As such, the Israeli economy has become a pool for world monopolies. After having been discredited as instruments of capitalism, imperialism, and exploitation, these monopolies no longer function directly in the continents of Africa and Asia but rather through affiliated companies in Israel. Almost all financial institutions, business firms, and industrial establishments are affiliated with American firms.

In order to protect the interests of these monopolies the US Government shows great concern in strengthening Israel and safeguarding its economy. Up till 1962 US governmental loans and grants in aid to Israel have amounted to about $1.5 billion. In addition, Israel is allowed to sell bonds in the US and until 1962 Israel sold of these bonds an amount equal to $500 million. Israel, through the United Jewish Appeal, has also collected over one billion dollars from the US till 1952. In order to help this drive, the US Government exempts these donations from taxation.

1. The Conference warns against what is called Israel technical and financial aid and considers it a new disguised method of US imperialism and neocolonialism.

2. The Conference requests from all progressive parties and committees to multiply their efforts to combat the Zionist infiltration and penetration in their countries and to abrogate the various agreements concluded with Israel.

RESOLUTION ON PARAGUAY

Whereas:

1. A tyrannical military-civil and antinational regime has been imposed upon the Paraguayan people for the benefit of North American imperialism,

2. This tyranny represses by all means of violence the longing for freedom of the Paraguayan people,

3. Murders motivated by politics, tortures inflicted by the police, violations, jailing, subjection to forced labor in concentration camps, maintain all the people of Paraguay in permanent terror,

4. Thousands of patriots have been and continue to be victims of these outrages and crimes of Stroessner's tyranny,

5. The Paraguayan people maintain a firm resistance and struggle to overcome the tyranny, to vanquish Yankee imperialism, and to recuperate in full their sovereignty and self-determination,

The First Solidarity Conference of the Peoples of Africa, Asia, and Latin America,

Appealing to the solidarity of the peoples and the righteous will of more than one thousand million people, represented by the popular and national delegations of this Tricontinental Conference, condemns the imposed tyranny in Paraguay, and demands the immediate liberty of hundreds of Paraguayan patriots, imprisoned for political and trade union activities. In the name of the following prisoners of the tyranny we send fraternal and solidarity greetings to the combatants of the country of Paraguay:

Gilberta Verdun de Talavera
Antonio Maidana
Jose Tomas Nuñez
Vicente Maidana Arias
Derliz Villagra
Julio Rojas
Salustiano Cabrera
Aurelio Paul Centurion
Napoleon Ortigoza
Emilio Barreto
Ramon Chamorro Riveros
Graciela Galeano
Alfredo Alcorta
Dr. Livieres Banks Acosta
Teresita Asilvera de Patiño

RESOLUTION ON THE POLITICAL SITUATION OF PARAGUAY

Whereas:

The people of Paraguay are subjected by a tyranny which has suppressed by violence and terror all democratic liberties and the most elemental human rights;

That regime is the utmost expression of the interests of the large landholders, the oligarchy and North American imperialism which impede the progressive development of Paraguay;

The peasants, workers, students, and sectors of the middle class, of the national industry and commerce are victims of political persecution and economic and social exploitation of the most degrading form;

The intervention of Yankee imperialism in the financial, economic, social, cultural, and military policy of Paraguay, and in its internal and international policies, alienates the popular and national sovereignty of the people of Paraguay;

Paraguay has been occupied by Yankee imperialism, not only to exploit and oppress the people, but also to make use of its territory as a strategic base for counter-revolutionary action on continental dimensions, taking into account its exceptional geographic situation, its great petroleum reserves, and its potential sources of hydroelectric energy;

The dictatorship and Yankee imperialism have converted Paraguay into a great prison of persecuted, tortured, or assassinated patriots;

In the prisons, police stations, and concentration camps of Paraguay there are to be found hundreds of political and trade union prisoners of all sectors under inhuman conditions;

The Paraguayan people struggle not only to recuperate their political and economic rights, but also to overthrow imperialism and the dictatorship which oppress them, in order to establish a democratic regime with full sovereignty and independence;

The First Solidarity Conference of the Peoples of Africa, Asia, and Latin America, **Resolves:**

1. To forcefully condemn the antinational military regime which exists today in Paraguay;
2. To denounce and condemn the aggressive, interventionist, and counterrevolutionary plans of North American imperialism in Paraguay;

To express the fullest solidarity of the First Tricontinental Conference with the struggles of the Paraguayan people for their liberty, sovereignty, and independence and to extend this solidarity to the hundreds of political and trade union prisoners of all sectors, whose immediate liberty it demands.

RESOLUTION ON PUERTO RICO

The First Solidarity Conference of the Peoples of Africa, Asia, and Latin America, held in Havana, Cuba, from January 3 to 15, 1966:

Considering that Puerto Rico is the only direct colony of North America in Latin America, and as such, the country most intervened by imperialism on the American continent;

Considering that the territory of Puerto Rico has been turned into a gigantic base for direct military aggression against the Latin American liberation movements, a fact giving the independence of Puerto Rico particular urgency among the emancipation struggles of Latin American peoples;

Considering that imperialism forces the young people of Puerto Rico to take part in the foul war of aggression against the people of Vietnam, thus exacting a barbarous legalized tribute in blood because of Puerto Rico's colonial situation;

Considering that the people of Puerto Rico are fighting an unequal, long, and difficult struggle against the most brutal, hypocritical, and reckless imperialist power of all time: the United States of America;

Considering that Puerto Rico suffers pitiless economic exploitation by North American monopolies, which have forced a million of its people (a third of its population) to emigrate to the United States, in the greatest exodus known in the history of the American continent, to become victims of social, national, and racial discrimination;

Considering that numerous Puerto Rican patriots are suffering lengthy terms of prison in the United States and Puerto Rico for their struggle in favor of the independence of Puerto Rico, and that militants of the liberation movement are the object of continued and systematic persecution by the repressive organs of imperialism;

The Conference:

Denounces that the title "associated free state" with which North American imperialism has tried to disguise the nature of their direct colonial regime in Puerto Rico, does not in any way correspond to reality, characterized as it is by the direct control that imperialism exercises over the economic life of Puerto Rico, its national territory, the life of its young people, its foreign relations, its banking, its commerce, its press, its means of communication, its educational system, etc.;

Denounces the preponderant role that North American imperialism has assigned to its military bases in Puerto Rico, and the fact that Puerto Rico is the imperialist center in the Caribbean from which it exports neocolonialism and counterrevolution;

Greets the campaign undertaken by the Pro-Independence Movement of Puerto Rico calling on all Puerto Rican young people to resist imperialist intentions to use them as cannon fodder in the foul war being waged by the United States against the heroic people of Vietnam;

Supports the struggle of the Puerto Rican people for their national independence and recognizes the paramount importance of that struggle within the general framework of the anti-imperialist movement in Latin America;

Resolves to condemn North American imperialism for keeping numerous Puerto Rican patriots imprisoned, and supports the campaign of the Puerto Rican Pro-Independence Movement in favor of the immediate release of these fighters;

Agrees to proclaim the 23rd of September of each year the **Day of Solidarity of the peoples of Africa, Asia, and Latin America with the struggle of the Puerto Rican people for their independence**;

Recommends that the necessary steps should be taken, so that a delegation of the Puerto Rican Pro-Independence Movement may tour the countries of Africa, Asia, and Latin America, to inform as many people as possible in those countries, about the case of Puerto Rico, and to call for their moral and material support to the extent that the cause of the people of Puerto Rico deserves.

RESOLUTION ON RWANDA

The First Solidarity Conference of the Peoples of Africa, Asia, and Latin America, gathered in Havana from January 3 to 15, after having analyzed the political situation in Rwanda before and after its independence and aware of the recent events which took place in the political, economic, social, and cultural fields in that country,

Considering that despite the proclamation of its independence in 1962, Rwanda continues to be ruled by American-Belgian neocolonialism; that domination is manifested by:

1. The strengthening of imperialist positions and Belgian and American neocolonialist monopolies in the political, economic, military, and cultural fields;
2. The illegal suppression of the most elementary democratic liberties;

Considering that the government of Kayibanda, backed by imperialism and by Belgian neocolonialism in its antinational, anti-democratic, anti-social policy, carries out a bloody repression manifested by:

1. The suppression of freedom of opinion, freedom of association, freedom of the press;
2. The establishment of special courts of puppets of the government helped by Belgian military personnel who are to judge the alleged political offences and crimes;
3. The employment of Belgian troops based in Rwanda for the suppression of the popular meeting as in the massacres of November 1959, May 1960, July 1961, and December 1963 to January 1964;

Considering the distressing problem of half a million Rwanda patriots who have been expelled from their country by the Belgian imperialists and their present lackeys in power in Rwanda, which is one of the anguishing problems of this kind in Africa;

Considering the resulting struggle carried on by the people of Rwanda in its patriotic organizations (the National Union of Rwanda and the General Union of the Workers of Rwanda) for the true independence of Rwanda, for democracy and social progress;

The Tricontinental Conference greets the courageous struggle of the people of Rwanda for independence and national liberation of their country;

Demands:

—the immediate withdrawal of Belgian troops, the dismantling of foreign military bases in Rwanda's soil,

—the reinstatement of all democratic organizations,

—the liberation of all the patriots arrested in the prisons of Rwanda and the respect of democratic liberties,

—the return of half a million refugees expelled from their territory by the occupation forces;

Calls for:

all democratic forces of the world to express their solidarity and their active support to the people of Rwanda;

Asks:

all states members of the Tricontinental Conference to refrain from having relations of any kind with the neocolonialist regime installed in the heart of Africa.

RESOLUTION ON SENEGAL

Considering the serious situation created in Senegal by the neocolonial regime of Senghor, characterized by:
  a) the unconditional submission to the imperialist financial groups, especially the French;
  b) the systematic suppression of all democratic organizations, political parties, trade unions, youth, women, and student organizations, of all other associations' that refuse to support the antinational and antipopular policy;
  c) the arrest, neutralization, or expulsion from the country of the leaders of the patriotic or religious national opposition;

Considering on the other hand, that this extremely pro-imperialist policy reveals itself in international affairs by the systematic alignment of the policy of the government of Senghor, to Western diplomacy, which at present is characterized by:
  a) the total support of Senghor to the puppet and pro-American government of Léopoldville;
  b) the refusal of the Senghor government, closely related to the puppet governments of the AMCO [Afro-Malagasy Common Organization], to render political and diplomatic support, demanded by the people of Senegal to the fraternal people of Zimbabwe;
  c) the refusal to condemn the American aggression and to denounce the imperialist crimes in Vietnam, as well as the equivocal policy followed with the People's Republic of China, the only representative of the Chinese people;

The Solidarity Conference of the Peoples of Africa, Asia, and Latin America strongly condemns the present dictatorial regime of bureaucratic and parliamentarian bourgeoisie, headed by Senghor, upheld by French imperialism in Senegal;

Condemns most firmly the pro-Western policy of the Senghor government and the open complicity of the Senegalese official circles with the hateful campaign carried out by the puppets of AMCO against the policy of independence and of African rehabilitation of the patriotic and progressive African states;

Proclaims its militant solidarity with the Senegalese patriotic forces, which in the spirit of the anti-imperialist struggle of the peoples of Asia, Africa, and Latin America unceasingly struggle against the neocolonial government of Senegal for the attainment of true independence;

Calls upon all nationalist and patriotic forces to unite in order to frustrate any solution of a neocolonialist type so as to ensure popular solution to the deep crisis in which Senghor and his regime have plunged Senegal.

RESOLUTION ON FRENCH SOMALILAND

The First Solidarity Conference of the Peoples of Africa, Asia, and Latin America, condemns the presence of French colonialism in [Djibouti], a part of the Somali homeland, and demands the liquidation of French colonialism and freedom and independence for the Somali people in [Djibouti], so that they may be able to reunify their homeland.

The Conference denounces the collusion between Ethiopian and United States neocolonialism to transform [Djibouti] into a US military base, as well as the French military base there.

The Conference affirms the necessity of total unification of the Somali people.

RESOLUTION ON SUDAN

The First Tricontinental Conference denounces the conspiracies of the imperialists and their agents to separate the southern provinces and stands against the actions of the reactionary regimes in Sudan in expelling the opposition from the parliament and prohibiting the democratic organizations.

We, the representatives of the peoples of Asia, Africa, and Latin America support the just struggle of the Sudanese people for democracy and for maintaining the unity of their country.

RESOLUTION ON SUDAN

The First Conference of the Peoples of Africa, Asia, and Latin America taking place in Havana, fully aware of the political situation in the Sudan, adopts the following:

1. Condemns imperialists' and Zionists' intrigues directed towards the separation of the southern provinces of the Sudan from the northern part as an act of aggression against the liberation movement in the Congo (L) and other fighting peoples in Africa and the Arab East and against the independence and sovereignty and unity of the Sudan;
2. Fully supports the Sudanese people in their struggle against anti-democratic measures taken by the reactionary government of the Sudan and the expulsion of opposition from parliament.

We consider these measures directed not only against democratic liberties of the Sudanese people, but also against liberation movements in Africa, especially in the Congo (L) and elsewhere.

RESOLUTION ON THAILAND

The First Solidarity Conference of the Peoples of Africa, Asia, and Latin America, convened in Havana from January 3 to 15, 1966:

1. Strongly condemns US imperialism, which occupies Thailand and turns Thailand into its neocolony and that, in coordination with the Thanom

[Kittikachorn]–Praphas [Charusathien] traitorous clique arrests, suppresses, and persecutes Thai patriots and democrats by using police and military armed forces;

2. Strongly condemns Thanom–Praphas' clique which has established a fascist dictatorship in Thailand, and strongly condemns its barbarous violation of human rights;

3. Demands from the Thanom–Prapas government the release of patriots and democrats, as well as political prisoners who are unjustly arrested and imprisoned;

4. Strongly condemns US imperialism for using Thailand as its military base for launching aggressive war against Vietnam, Laos, threatening Cambodia, as well as other countries in South-East Asia;

5. Demands that US imperialism withdraw all its military bases, all its aggressive troops and aggressive headquarters of SEATO from Thailand;

6. Supports the just and right armed struggle and other various forms of struggle of the Thai people.

RESOLUTION OF UGANDA

Since the development of the international situation is such that even the reactionary regimes would like to maintain contact with socialist countries in order to conceal their reactionary domestic policies we propose:

1. That facilities should be extended to the freedom fighters in those neocolonialist countries.

2. That when giving help to countries with reactionary regimes, this help should not constitute an obstacle to the revolutionary movements.

RESOLUTION ON VENEZUELA

In the main address of the Venezuelan Delegation to the General Assembly of the Solidarity Conference of the Peoples of Africa, Asia, and Latin America, we affirmed that after the practical application of the "Johnson Doctrine," the peoples of Latin America should carry out national liberation struggle on the basis of other realities and with a spirit which permits the solution of all continental problems.

The United States of North America have created a global tactic to counter the liberation struggles of our peoples with armed violence. Today Yankee imperialism will not allow any of the traditional demonstrations of dignity and sovereignty (as timid as they may be) unless they are completely identified with the interests of finance capital and the oligarchic accomplices that serve them. Bourgeois legality, as the representative democracies of Latin America understand it, is not enough to perpetuate the regime of exploitation and misery, of the "Free Associated State and of Neocolonialism" as the governments that best respond to maintenance of the typical structures of underdevelopment. Yankee imperialism has definitely proclaimed that it understands no other way than that of force. Our own experience is recent, and even more recent is the genocide perpetrated by North American imperialism against the fraternal people of the Dominican Republic. Latin America must turn its eyes on the Dominican Republic, not to be frightened but to discover the global strategy of our enemy, to learn this lesson and plan a strategy that will allow us to defeat it once and for all. This strategy can be none other than a simultaneous war. By simultaneous war we understand, not the application of a general outline, because the Latin American reality is not unique and indivisible. On the contrary, even in areas of one country, realities change and vary. It is necessary that each of the peoples of Latin America face the problem of political power and create the conditions for armed struggle.

Venezuela has chosen the armed struggle as the best means of struggle against imperialism. The enemy has taught us that political power cannot be won without overthrowing the state organization created by imperialism, without annihilating the repressive army, without annihilating the colonial or semi-colonial ruling superstructure. Without the above we cannot think of annihilating imperialism and its lackeys. The reactionary army must be substituted by a revolutionary army to guarantee the implementation of plans that satisfy the people's aspirations.

That is why we Venezuelans have chosen armed struggle, without discarding other means of struggle. We combined armed and unarmed methods, legal and illegal, mass and commando methods. We consider that what is important is not the struggle itself, but the annihilation of imperialism and the taking of political power in order to put into practice a revolutionary and mass program.

We ask for militant solidarity which we also give. Today the Venezuelan struggle has reached a point of development which permits us to respond to our revolutionary duties, which have always been defined by the principles of proletarian internationalism.

Venezuela today needs the support of the peoples of the world in order to develop its liberation struggle. Imperialism unblushingly aids its lackeys. We consider that the peoples who struggle for their liberation also must unblushingly aid revolutionary movements, such as ours, which guarantee the defeat of imperialism. We ask:

1. That all countries recognize the Venezuelan National Liberation Front as the organization that leads the armed struggle against North American imperialism and the national oligarchies in our country;

2. To form an Organization to coordinate the Latin American struggle;

3. Solidarity of all the peoples of the world with the struggle that the Latin American peoples are waging to obtain political power; Within the framework of the Tricontinental Organization to create a special fund to aid the peoples who are carrying out revolutionary struggle in Latin America, especially Venezuela;

4. That all possible means to liquidate the Yankee blockade against Cuba be used.

RESOLUTION ON AID TO THE REVOLUTIONARY STRUGGLE OF THE PEOPLES OF COLOMBIA, VENEZUELA, AND PERU

The First Solidarity Conference of the Peoples of Africa, Asia, and Latin America, held in Havana, Cuba, from January 3 to 15, 1966,

Whereas:

1. The military forces of the governments of Colombia, Venezuela, Ecuador, Panama, and other countries of the Caribbean and the Southern part of the Continent periodically carry out joint military maneuvers under the direction of the US Army, with the obvious purpose of blackmailing and threatening the national liberation movements and the armed struggle in those countries;

2. The "Gorilla" International, under US command, also intervenes in the training of anti-guerrilla troops, which shows the existence of the complete military strategy of US imperialism in these areas of Latin America;

3. The US military missions, with specialized branches of all kinds (land, sea, and air detachments, and police) direct and plan operations intended to repress the armed struggle in Colombia, Venezuela, and Peru;

4. The resources of the Alliance for Progress are destined to finance the above-mentioned military operations; US bombers and fighter planes, piloted by Yankees, attack guerrilla zones, and US helicopters transport troops to combat sites;

Be it resolved:

1. To lend the most determined assistance to the revolutionary movements in Colombia, Venezuela, Peru, Panama, Ecuador, and other Caribbean and South American countries, to counteract with the most effective measures the effects of US imperialism's all-out aggressive policy;

2. To denounce before all countries of the three continents, Yankee intervention in the armed struggles of Colombia, Venezuela and Peru, and to promote the militant solidarity of the combatants in those countries

among themselves and with the peoples of the three continents, in the great struggle for national liberation.

SUB-COMMISSION OF BURNING ISSUES

RESOLUTION ON CAMBODIA

Aware of the Declaration of December 21, 1965 of a spokesman of the Government of the United States of America, renewing accusations against Cambodia and confirming the authorization given to the high North American military officers of the region to attack the Cambodian territory by land or by air wherever they deem it necessary;

Noting that this open and official threat from the US Government, after numerous violations and attacks to the land, air, and maritime borders of Cambodia by the US and South Vietnam armed forces is a prelude to the large-scale extension of the aggression war against Vietnam;

Considering: First, that these intentions of the United States Government are contrary to international law, to the Charter of the United Nations and to the Geneva Agreements of 1954,

Second, the danger of a general conflagration resulting from this declaration of intention from the United States Government, as well as from numerous attacks against the Khmer borders and territory by the United States–South Vietnamese armed forces is real and extremely serious,

Third, the duty of justice and peace-loving powers demands the urgent adoption of measures to stop the criminal maneuvers of North American imperialism and its lackeys in South-East Asia against world peace;

Aware of the declaration of the Royal Cambodian Government and the notes addressed to the Co-Chairmen of the Geneva Conference on Indochina of December 26, 1965, as well as the resolution of the Twentieth National Congress of Cambodia of December 28, 1965;

The Tricontinental Conference held at Havana condemns the policy of aggression adopted by the Government of the United States of America and its Asian lackeys and others, against peaceful and neutral Cambodia;

Requests from all governments of truly anti-imperialist countries to take urgent and concrete measures to put an end to the belligerent policy of the USA against Cambodia and to the criminal aggression of the United States and their mercenary forces against the peoples of Indochina;

Requests that following the example of the OAU countries towards the Rhodesian racists, all justice and peace-loving countries refuse every political, diplomatic, economic, and cultural cooperation with the United States Government and all Governments which lend their active support to its policy of aggression in Indochina.

RESOLUTION ON THE CONGO (L)

The First Solidarity Conference of the Peoples of Africa, Asia, and Latin America, convened in Havana from January 3 to 15, 1966,

By giving its valuable and effective support to the sacred cause of the Congolese people, the Conference has found in the armed struggle of the people of the Congo an exalting example in their noble task of giving impulse and developing the common struggle of the peoples of the three continents against imperialism, colonialism, and neocolonialism, the only way in which peace and quiet can exist in the three continents, in particular, and in the whole world in general;

Considering: that the Congolese people has been the object of permanent aggression from the imperialist powers since 1960;

Considering: that the intervention of North American imperialism in all sectors of national life, and its infiltration of financial oligarchies constitute the most notorious sign of neocolonialist penetration, of domination and exploitation;

Considering: that the presence of the imperialist armed forces in the military bases of Kitona and Kamina constitutes a very serious threat against the sovereignty of the Congolese State, in particular, and against the security of Africa in general;

Considering: that this situation, evidenced in the past by the disastrous role played in the Congo by the United Nations Organization controlled by the United States of America, and more recently by the growth of a racist regime, marks a series of declarations raised in Africa against the United States of America, as was the case in Latin America and Asia, on the Vietnamese question;

Confirming: that for more than five years, American imperialism has been trampling on the constitutional rights of the Congolese State, namely: national independence, sovereignty, unity, and territorial integrity, in order to enslave it;

Considering: that the armed struggle of the Congolese people constitutes an evident contribution to the struggle for the liberation of the peoples of Africa, Asia, and Latin America against imperialism, colonialism, and neocolonialism, and that in this respect it deserves the support of the militant solidarity of the peoples of our three continents;

The First Solidarity Conference of the Peoples of Africa, Asia, and Latin America, convened at Havana from January 3 to 15, 1966:

3. Affirms its total support to the armed struggle for the liberation of the Congolese people, who have always received the demonstrations of solidarity of the revolutionary peoples;

4. Decides to create a Tricontinental committee of solidarity for the just struggle of the Congolese people against the cruel and relentless aggression of imperialism;

5. Vigorously denounces and condemns the military fascist regime installed in the Congo by Yankee imperialists and their accomplices;

6. Demands the immediate and unconditional withdrawal of the mercenaries now in the Congo, and the dismantling of the military bases at Kamina and Kitona;
7. Invites all the Governments of the countries of Asia, Africa, and Latin America to deny recognition to the puppet regime of traitor Mobutu;
8. Invites all the progressive governments and organizations of the three continents to support and concretely aid the armed struggle of the Congolese People and to recognize the National Council of Liberation ("CNL") of Congo, as the sole genuine representative of the Congolese people by offering it unreserved moral, political, diplomatic, and material support.

RESOLUTION ON KOREA

The First Solidarity Conference of the Peoples of Africa, Asia, and Latin America held in Havana, capital of Cuba, from January 3 to 15, 1966, strongly condemns the occupation of South Korea by US imperialism.

Due to the occupation of South Korea by US imperialists, Korea has been divided into two parts for the past twenty years; Korea's unification has not been achieved; and the Korean people are undergoing unmeasurable national misfortunes and sufferings.

US imperialists are brutally oppressing and massacring the people in South Korea; they badly destroyed and ruined the national economy and the people live in extreme distress.

In flagrant violation of the Korean Armistice Agreement, the US imperialists brought into South Korea various kinds of new types of weapons, turned it into a nuclear and rocket base, perpetrating incessant war provocations, thus aggravating tensions in Korea.

The Conference demands the immediate withdrawal from South Korea of the US imperialists' aggressive troops which are the fundamental cause of all the misfortunes of the South Korean people and the main obstacle to Korea's unification, and actively supports the Korean people in their struggle for the unification of the country by themselves, without any foreign interference.

Despite the strong opposition of the Korean and Japanese peoples and the denunciation of world public opinion, US imperialists, instigating the Japanese reactionary government and the puppet clique of Pak Jung Hi in South Korea, have of late fabricated the criminal "South Korea–Japan Treaty," by all means of fraudulence and intrigue, creating thereby a new dangerous phase in the overall situation in Korea and Asia.

The "South Korea–Japan Treaty" is an aggressive treaty, devised by US imperialists as an integral force to maintain the system of their imperialist rule in order to revive Japanese militarism as "shock brigade" in their aggressions in Asia.

US imperialists, hastening the rearmament of the Japanese militarists, are quickly opening to them the way to reinvade other countries.

The Conference resolutely condemns the aggressive "South Korea–Japan Treaty," which opens the road of reinvasion and expansion to the Japanese militarists and the vicious scheme of the US imperialists for setting up the "North-East Military Alliance" to oppose the socialist countries and the national independent states in Asia, to suppress the national liberation struggles in this area, and to make "Asians fight against Asians."

Today, the Japanese militarist forces, availing themselves of the US aggression on Asia, are scheming to reinvade South Korea, and to make their old dream of ruling over Asia come true.

Once the "South Korea–Japan Treaty" is fully put into force, South Korea will become a dual colony of the US and Japan; a new obstacle will be created on the road to Korea's unification; and the peace and security of Korea and Asia will be under serious menace.

Today, the Japanese militarists, under the cover of the "South Korea–Japan Treaty," are infiltrating into South Korea on a large scale and intensifying military collaboration with the South Korean puppet clique.

As evidenced by the plans of "Operation Three Arrows" and "Operation Flying Dragon," recently disclosed, the Japanese militarist forces are already preparing their attack against the Democratic People's Republic of Korea, the People's Republic of China, and the Soviet Union in cooperation with the United States.

Considering that it is an urgent task for peace in Asia and in the world to disrupt the scheme of the Japanese militarists who, backed by the US imperialists, are taking the path leading to invasion of Asia, the Conference entirely supports the Korean people in their struggle to reject the "South Korea–Japan Treaty" and to smash the schemes for setting up the "North-East Military Alliance."

The Conference calls on the Asian, African, and Latin American peoples to set a "Month of Solidarity with the Korean People" from June 25, the day when the US imperialists launched their aggressive war against Korea, to July 27, the day of the signing of the Armistice agreement, and to organize and display during this period large movements and actions in support of the just struggle of the Korean people.

RESOLUTION ON CYPRUS

The First Solidarity Conference of the Peoples of Africa, Asia, and Latin America greets and supports in every aspect the heroic struggle of the people of Cyprus for the total freedom, unrestricted independence, and territorial integrity of Cyprus; **Strongly condemns** any intervention from any foreign power in the internal affairs of Cyprus;

Strongly condemns any aggression or threat of aggressions by any foreign power against Cyprus;

Strongly condemns all imperialist pressures exercised on the Government of Cyprus to abandon its non-aligned policy and be subjugated directly or indirectly by NATO;

Strongly believes that the Cyprus problem is an internal affair of the people of Cyprus and that its solution should be exclusively in the hands of the people, who as a whole should decide their own future;

Supports unreservedly the right of the people of Cyprus as a whole to exercise the right of self-determination;

Condemns the existence of foreign military bases on the territory of Cyprus and considers these bases as a menace to peace in the Middle East and a threat to the neighboring Arab countries, and strongly supports the demand for their elimination;

Expresses its firm determination to render every assistance to the people of Cyprus for the achievement of their rights.

RESOLUTION ON THE DOMINICAN REPUBLIC

Considering: That the North American military intervention in the Dominican Republic on April 28, 1965, took place precisely when the Dominican people were in the midst of a successful insurrection against the pro-imperialist military forces—controlled from the North American Embassy by Tapley Bennet and the military attachés—which were fighting the popular movement to enforce the 1963 Constitution and restore Juan Bosch—who had been elected by majority—in the presidency. All this clearly showed the reactionary aggressiveness of imperialism, which was already an enemy even of the so-called representative democracy form of government;

Considering: That the military intervention in the Dominican Republic opens a new cycle of counter-revolutionary interventions in Latin America and threatens the only Latin American country freed from the domination and exploitation of imperialism: Cuba;

Considering: That the North American military intervention has dragged into complicity the governing oligarchies of Brazil, Paraguay, Nicaragua, Costa Rica, which have sent troops to coerce the heroic Dominican people who struggle for freedom and independence;

Considering: That each day the invading troops of imperialism remain on Dominican soil, more patriots are killed—the total already exceeds three thousand—and the poverty and suffering of the Dominican people increase;

Considering: That the military occupation of the Dominican Republic implies immediate and direct control of the Dominican State by imperialism, that this seriously changes the political status of the Dominican Republic, degrading it from a dependent semi-colonial country to a government by mandate, violating all principles and rules established in the constitutional charters of all international organizations;

Considering: That in order to perpetrate this violation to the national sovereignty of the Dominican Republic, imperialism has organized the counterrevolutionary regional army for Latin America cynically called Inter-American Peace Force (IPF);

Considering: That in this crime against the Dominican people and against its desires for independence and freedom, the Organization of American States has acted the same way as it did in its foul condemnation of the revolutionary people of Cuba, serving as an assistant to the executioner of the peoples of the world: North American imperialism;

Considering: That the United Nations Organization (UNO) witnessed the crimes committed by Yankee troops against the civil population not only on disembarking, but also on the 15th and 16th of June, 1965; witnessed the genocides committed by the puppet government of Antonio Imbert [Barrera]; those of the trusteeship established by imperialism through the Organization of American States (OAS), all of which actions are contrary to its declarations of principles, the Charter of the United Nations. And that the latter limited itself to the simple and deplorable role of informing the events and mediating. It did not condemn this brutal aggression, least of all the chief entity responsible, the imperialist Government of the United States;

Considering: That at present the military chiefs guilty of genocide, are the principal support imperialism counts on for its plans of unlimited occupation and perpetuation of its neocolonial domination of the Dominican Republic;

Considering: That the Dominican people have heroically resisted aggression, fighting the invaders, arms in hand, that they have not lost courage in the unequal struggle, but on the contrary, day by day have intensified their combativeness, taking advantage of every possible means of winning their national war, to free their country from invaders and fully recover sovereignty and national independence;

Considering: That in the struggle of the Dominican people against the imperialist invading troops, men of different nationalities, have died: Jack Vieu (Haitian), Andre Rivier (French), Illio Capossi (Italian), fighting shoulder-to-shoulder with the Dominican patriots;

Considering: That international solidarity contributes to the struggle of the Dominican people against imperialist domination;

Resolves:

To recognize the signs of fascism and war, as a means of domination typical of the imperialist system in decadence, in the ferocious military occupation of the Dominican Republic, which violates all principles of self-determination and non-intervention;

To condemn the imperialist government of the United States as aggressors and violators of the sovereignty of the Dominican people;

To alert the Latin American peoples, and especially Cuba, about possible imperialist aggressions to prevent their independent development;

To condemn the oligarchic governments of Brazil, Paraguay, Nicaragua, Honduras, and Costa Rica as accomplices in the brutal aggression that drenches Dominican soil in blood;

To condemn the Organization of American States as the perfect political instrument of North American imperialism for the neocolonial domination of Latin America;

To **condemn** the UNO for its incapability and hesitation in defending the rights of self-determination and sovereignty of the peoples of the world, especially in Africa, Asia, and Latin America, and particularly of the Dominican people in the face of US military aggression against said country;

To condemn the integration of the Inter-American Peace Force, as detrimental to the sovereignty of the peoples and the incarnation of international counter-revolution in Latin America;

To demand the immediate withdrawal from Dominican soil, of all foreign troops: North American, Brazilian, Paraguayan, Nicaraguan, Honduran, and Costa Rican troops;

To condemn the Dominican military officers who sided with those who trample on Dominican soil, contributing to foreign domination and to the threat against all Latin American peoples; to call for militant solidarity with the Dominican people, realizing that, besides solidarity and material aid, the greatest contribution to the Dominican cause and to that of all peoples who struggle against colonialism and neocolonialism is to widen and deepen the struggle against imperialism in every country;

That April 24 to 30 of this year be proclaimed the "Week of Solidarity with the Dominican People."

RESOLUTION ON GUATEMALA

The First Solidarity Conference of the Peoples of Africa, Asia, and Latin America, after reviewing the prevailing situation in the Republic of Guatemala, confirming the determination of the people of Guatemala to achieve the total liberation of their country from Yankee imperialist domination, and recognizing the revolutionary war fought by the Guatemalans under the flags of the rebel armed forces;

Expresses its full solidarity with the people of Guatemala and their armed fight and supports their conviction that they can only accomplish their genuine and true aspirations of freedom and independence, when Yankee imperialism and the puppets from the native oligarchies that serve them have been defeated and definitely expelled from the country;

Condemns the repression unleashed by the ruling clique against all sectors of the Guatemalan peoples, especially the crimes perpetrated against the peasants, in its useless efforts to curb the revolutionary drive;

Demands the freedom of all political prisoners, who are deprived of liberty for no other reason than having fought for the freedom and independence of their country; and also, the ending of the tortures and abuses applied by the military dictatorship;

Denounces the connivance of Yankee imperialism and the ruling oligarchies of the neighboring Central American countries, that under the so-called Central American Defense Council maintain a joint army, meant to oppress the peoples throughout the entire isthmus, and especially to repress, as it has already done, the people's guerrilla forces which are forming in Guatemala;

Denounces the electoral maneuvers plotted by the ruling clique led, at the moment, by the tyrant Peralta Azurdia, directed at giving a spurious constitutional backing to this unpopular repressive regime, with which it seeks to confuse certain sectors and denaturalize the popular efforts to support the revolutionary war;

Expresses the will of the peoples of Asia, Africa, and Latin America to support the Guatemalan people in their struggle, and calls for the granting of all possible aid which will permit them to accelerate the development of the revolutionary war until the achievement of total victory; defeating the lackeys of imperialism, freeing themselves from oppression, and thus contributing to the liberation of Latin America.

RESOLUTION ON LAOS

The First Solidarity Conference of the Peoples of Africa, Asia, and Latin America;

1. Notes with anxiety that the present tension in Laos becomes more serious each day because of the interventions and aggressions of North American imperialists and their satellites, which constitute a flagrant violation of the Geneva Agreements of 1962 on Laos of which they are signatories, thus impeding the reestablishment of peace, of neutrality, and of national harmony in Laos;

2. **Condemns** formally North American imperialism for having outrageously violated the Geneva Agreements of 1962 on Laos, and continuing its policy of intervention and aggression against Laos and particularly, its methods of war by destruction and massacre, by means of air raids against the Laotian people, and its plans for sending North American troops and those of their satellites to occupy Middle and Lower Laos, in order to extend their war of aggression from South Vietnam to Laos;

3. **Demands** from North American imperialists the correct implementation of the Geneva Agreements of 1962 on Laos; the total withdrawal from the Laotian territory of all their military personnel, of their arms and war material, as well as those of their satellites, that have been illegally introduced and, above all, the immediate suspension of North American air raids over the territory controlled by the patriotic forces of Laos;

4. **Supports** actively the people of Laos in their struggle against North American imperialist aggressors and their puppets, for the defense of the Geneva Agreements of 1962 on Laos, the safeguarding of the Tripartite Government of National Union and the neutrality of Laos. Firmly supports the position of the four points and the measures stated in the five points proclaimed for the solution of the question of Laos as expressed in the Manifest of October 13, 1965, of the National Political Conference of Alliance between the Neo Lao Haksat and the patriotic neutralist forces of Laos;

5. Calls upon the peoples and upon the governments of the countries of Asia, Africa, and Latin America as well as upon the peace-loving peoples and governments, of the world, to unite in a collective manifestation of solidarity with the people and the patriotic armed forces of Laos and to agree to give them effective aid, both material and moral, an indispensable increase in strength that should make them capable of defeating the intervention and aggression of North American imperialists and attaining their legitimate aspirations, which consist of promoting a peaceful, neutral, independent, democratic, unified, and prosperous Laos.

RESOLUTION ON MOZAMBIQUE

The First Solidarity Conference of the Peoples of Africa, Asia, and Latin America:
Greets the armed struggle that the heroic people of Mozambique carry on, under the leadership of FRELIMO (Liberation Front of Mozambique);
Assures the people of Mozambique and its organization, the FRELIMO, of its total support to the struggle they are leading against Portuguese colonialism and for their total national independence;
Denounces and condemns the coalition of the governments of South Africa, Southern Rhodesia, and Portugal, whose aim is to impose white supremacy in the South of Africa;
Denounces and condemns the cooperation between the Portuguese and the British police in Swaziland and in Rhodesia, which has already resulted in the kidnapping of several Mozambique nationalists in these two countries;
Calls upon world public opinion to demand liberty for all Mozambique nationalists arbitrarily imprisoned by Portuguese colonial authorities;
Expresses its gratitude to the peoples, governments, and organizations which support the people of Mozambique in their struggle for a real national liberation and, particularly, to the people and the government of Tanzania;
Supports the decision of the IV Conference of the Organization of the Solidarity of the Peoples of Africa and Asia, and declares the 25th of September as the Day of Solidarity with the people of Mozambique.

RESOLUTION ON PALESTINE

The First Solidarity Conference of the Peoples of Africa, Asia, and Latin America, held in Havana, Cuba, from January 3 to 15, 1966;

—Having heard the report of the representatives of the Palestine Liberation Organization and the reports of some of the delegates of the three Continents regarding colonialist and Zionist usurpation of Palestine and aggression on its people;

—Having reviewed the resolutions of the Afro-Asian Solidarity Council Sessions, and Conferences held in Cairo, Conakry, Bandung, Cyprus, Algiers, Moshi, and Winneba on this issue;

—Having studied the conditions in which Israel was imposed on Palestine, and analyzing the role of the former at the service of colonialism and neocolonialism in their fight against the liberation forces, and against progress and peace in the region;

—Believing in the right of peoples to freedom, independence, and self-determination and, faithful to the revolutionary principles of the Tricontinental Conference; mainly, the unity of aim and the unity of destiny of the peoples in their common anti-imperialist struggle;

Considers Zionism as an imperialist movement by its very nature, aggressive and expansionist in its aims, racialist in its structure, and fascist in its means and methods;

Considers the Zionist settler-state as an imperialist base and as a subservient instrument and obedient tool of imperialism to be used for aggression and imperialist economic, political, and cultural penetration and infiltration in the three continents. As such, Israel constitutes a threat to world security and peace and an impediment to the development and progress in the area;

Considers the right of the Palestinians to liberate their country as an extension to their inherent and inalienable right of self-defense;

Condemns the Zionist Movement and the existence of Israel in the occupied part of Palestine;

Asks for the severance of all political relations with Israel, its economic and cultural boycott, and its expulsion from international organizations; and in particular, requests from all progressive parties and committees to double their efforts to combat the Zionist infiltration and penetration in their countries and to abrogate the various agreements concluded with Israel;

Condemns the imperialist conspiracy of the US, West Germany, and Britain to protect Israel, to support it, and supply it with destructive armaments;

Condemns severely the mass immigration to occupied Palestine organized by imperialism and Zionism in order to consolidate Zionist occupation of Palestine and promote their aggressive designs;

Warns against the so-called Israeli technical and financial aid and considers it a new disguised method of US imperialism and neocolonialism. Calls upon all national committees and organizations to give material and financial aid to Palestine in its struggle against the Zionists;

Fully supports the Palestine Liberation Organization in its struggle to liberate Palestine;

Vigorously condemns and denounces the strategic aid given by the Zionist State of Israel to some African puppet governments in order to dominate and repress liberation movements in their countries, above all in the Congo (Léopoldville).

RESOLUTION ON THE SITUATION OF PANAMA

The First Solidarity Conference of the Peoples of Africa, Asia, and Latin America,
Considering:

1. That Yankee imperialism, by imposing the Treaty of 1903 has arrogated a series of rights contrary to the interests of the Republic of Panama;

2. That, based on said Treaty, the United States have declared perpetual ownership of the monopoly over the present Canal, which monopoly they have extended to the construction of any inter-oceanic route in the Republic of Panama;

3. That North American imperialism has under its control, with commanding and jurisdictional functions, part of the Panamanian territory, in which territory there are troops, military bases, courts and repressive bodies, postal stamps, trade, education, and population, beyond the control of the Republic of Panama and ruled by the laws of a foreign state;

4. That this state of things injures the territorial integrity of Panama, minimizes its sovereignty and threatens the Republic through armed pressure;

5. That the aforementioned military bases are training centers of imperialist and local reactionary armed forces fighting against national liberation movements in Latin America and throughout the world, and are repressive instruments against their respective peoples;

6. That said bases are also centers of attack to the peoples of the world with missile launching sites and nuclear platforms used by North American imperialism for nuclear blackmail, which are a menace to world peace;

7. That from said bases, troops have been sent in the past to occupy the Republic of Panama, and more recently attack a patriotic demonstration of the Panamanian people during the anti-imperialist gesture of January 9 10, 11, and 12, 1964, and on the other hand, air raids have been launched against Guatemala, Cuba, and other peoples. They are also the meeting place for Latin American militarist conspiracies, where the overthrow of various Latin American governments has been decided;

8. That Panamanian laws are ignored, and foreign culture and education, contrary to the interests of Panama, are fostered in the Canal Zone;

9. That discrimination in the Panama Canal Zone is exercised against the Panamanian workers and those of other nationalities regarding salaries social benefits, working conditions, and the different means of entertainment and education;

10. That during January 9, 10, 11, and 12, 1964, the Panamanian people suffered a brutal attack from North American troops stationed in the so-called Canal Zone, with the result of twenty-one dead and more than five hundred wounded in an obvious demonstration of the criminal nature of North American imperialism.

11. That immediately after the events mentioned above, and as the conclusion to more than sixty years of anti-imperialist struggles the Panamanian people demanded, and are still demanding the following:

Substitution of the 1903 Treaty on the basis mentioned below:

1. Abrogation of the Clause of perpetuity and of Clause V of the Treaty, referring to the monopoly of the United States for the construction of any inter-oceanic route in the Isthmus of Panama.

2. Restitution to the Republic of Panama of the territory which comprises the so-called Canal Zone, in order to secure the territorial integrity of the Panamanian state, and eliminate the presence in Panamanian soil of the obstacles to the full exercise of its true and effective sovereignty, and in consequence, secure the dismantling of the military bases, and the withdrawal of the Yankee troops.

3. Establishment of a joint Panamanian–North American commission for the administration of the Canal, with the understanding that the Canal will be returned to Panama in a short term;

4. That the special case of Panama, invaded and occupied by foreign troops, deserves special attention because these troops are quartered in military bases that not only violate Panamanian sovereignty, and are a means of oppression of the people of Panama, but also serve as training centers for action against the national liberation movements in Africa, Asia, and Latin America, and as an instrument of the Yankee policy of nuclear blackmail which threatens world peace;

5. That taking into consideration the occupation of part of its territory by foreign military bases, the situation of Panama is similar to the occupation of Guantanamo, Cuba, by Yankee imperialism, and that of Puerto Rico, subjected by force to a classical colonial status;

6. That it constitutes a basic condition for Panama, from the point of view of the exercise of its sovereignty and its right to self-determination, the

withdrawal of the imperialist troops from its territory and the dismantling of the bases in which they are quartered;

7. That, without regard for the aspirations expressed by the Panamanian people, and further pursuing its policy of aggression against the people Yankee imperialism is plotting to increase its rule in Panama and intensify its use as a conspiracy center against the overwhelming growth of the liberation struggles of the peoples of Africa, Asia, and Latin America, by means of the construction of another canal through Panama, and the establishment, in an even larger scale, of military bases throughout the Panamanian territory;

8. That this intention is evident in the so-called Robles–Johnson Declaration and in the threats of violence and repression from the pro-imperialist lackeys of the reactionary and fraudulent regime of Panama, constituting a historical challenge that the people of Panama will be able to face with the solidarity of the peoples of Africa, Asia, and Latin America;

Decides:

1. To condemn the use of the territory or the utilization of the land of a brother country for the aggression of other peoples;

2. To express solidarity with the Panamanian people in their aspiration to attain full sovereignty and self-determination by the restitution of the Panamanian territory of the Canal Zone, with the consequent abrogation of Yankee jurisdiction in the Zone; the dismantling of the military bases and the withdrawal of occupation troops, extending this solidarity to the Panamanian aspiration to liquidate the imperialist monopoly of the inter-oceanic route and the return of the Canal to the people of Panama within a short period of time;

3. To declare that this solidarity extends to all the forms of struggle which the Panamanian people may decide to use in order to attain the above mentioned aspirations, and to confront the schemes of the imperialists and the local oligarchy, tending to impose on Panama the construction of another Yankee Canal and the installation of new military bases for the strengthening of its strategy of aggression against the national liberation movements, and nuclear blackmail against the peace-loving peoples of the world.

RESOLUTION ON PERU

The Solidarity Conference of the Peoples of Africa, Asia, and Latin America:
Considering: that as a response to the start of the armed struggle in Peru which aims at total liberation of the people in this country, the government of Fernando Belaunde Terry has launched a brutal repression against the popular forces, especially the peasants, including mass executions of peasants in the rural zones where the guerrillas operate, indiscriminatingly bombing with napalm

the inhabitants of the villages in these regions; jailing the leaders and militants of the left-wing political organizations of students and workers, most of whom have been submitted to incredible tortures in the best tradition of the dark ages of nazi-fascism and jailing the wives of the leaders of the guerrillas;

Considering: that in order to frighten people so that they will not give support to the guerrillas, the puppet and pro-Yankee government of Belaunde has passed the Death Penalty Law for those who fight in the guerrillas or give their direct or indirect support to them;

Considering: that the Peruvian Parliament, integrated by the representatives of the most backward and darkest reactionary forces, has created investigating committees for the "subversive activities," unleashing a most hysterical "MacCarthist" persecution against all progressive organizations and personalities of the country;

Decides:

To demand from the dictatorial and pro-Yankee government of Belaunde Terry to put an end to the executions of peasants and guerrilla fighters, the cessation of napalm air raids, and of the cruel methods of torturing prisoners, the immediate release of political, labor, and student prisoners and of the wives of the leaders of the guerrillas;

To demand the abrogation of the Death Penalty Law and the dissolution of the "MacCarthist" committees created by the Peruvian Parliament;

To denounce before world public opinion the brutal trampling of human rights carried out by the unpopular government of Belaunde Terry.

RESOLUTION ON PERU

The Solidarity Conference of the Peoples of Africa, Asia, and Latin America:

Considering: that Peru is an economically backward country, as a result of the existing semifeudal relations of production and the deforming action of its economic structure carried out by Yankee imperialism, which has taken over the main natural resources of the country and controls its foreign trade, and that all this, as it is logical to infer, obstructs the independent economic development of the country;

Considering: that the above mentioned semifeudal conditions and the dependency upon Yankee imperialism which Peru is suffering and which maintain the country as merely a raw material producer, and keep the Peruvian people, especially the peasants, in the worst possible conditions of poverty, hunger, unemployment, illiteracy, and indescribable super-exploitation;

Considering: that the poverty and hunger in which the Peruvian people find themselves could only disappear with the change of the unfair economic structures of the country and the ousting of imperialism,

Considering: that for decades attempts have been made to bring about this change by peaceful means without any results, due to the strong opposition of the exploiting and imperialist sectors who have always replied with violence to the just aspirations of the Peruvian people;

Considering: that the present government of Fernando Belaunde Terry, because of the class interests it represents, has been unable to solve the fundamental problems of the country, despite his commitment to do so with demagogic electoral promises;

Considering: that in view of the violence that the Belaunde government has unleashed to crush the struggle of the different exploited sectors of the country for their legitimate revindications, the people have come to the conclusion that there is no other way out but to respond in the same form, i.e., with organized revolutionary violence;

Considering: that the Peruvian people has begun the guerrilla armed struggle to achieve its total liberation,

Decides:

To support resolutely and in all forms the armed struggle undertaken in Peru, the way bravely chosen by the Peruvian people to achieve its definite and total economic and political independence.

RESOLUTION ON THE SO-CALLED PORTUGUESE GUINEA AND CAPE VERDE ISLANDS

The Tricontinental Conference of the Peoples of Africa, Asia, and Latin America:

Greets the successful development of the armed struggle carried on by the people of the so-called Portuguese Guinea and the Revolutionary Armed Forces of the People, under the leadership of the African Independence Party of the so-called Portuguese Guinea and of Cape Verde Islands. (PAIGC);

Encourages the people of Cape Verde Islands and its national organization, the PAIGC (African Independence Party) to continue their efforts in order to extend the armed struggle to Cape Verde Islands;

Gives assurances to the people of the so-called Portuguese Guinea and of Cape Verde Islands of its total support to their heroic struggle against Portuguese colonialism and for total and complete independence;

Proclaims its unconditional support to all the measures that the PAIGC considers necessary to take on the political level, to consolidate the achievements of the struggle in Guinea and in order to harmonize the international juridical situation of the people of Guinea with the specific situation of that country;

Expresses its recognition to all African peoples and in particular to the people of the Republic of Guinea, to its government and to the Democratic Party of Guinea, for the support that they have never ceased to give to the people of the so-called Portuguese Guinea and of Cape Verde Islands and to its National Party.

RESOLUTION ON THE COUNTRIES UNDER PORTUGUESE DOMINATION

The First Tricontinental Conference, held in Havana from January 3 to 15, 1966, after having analyzed the situation in the Portuguese colonies:

Denounces and condemns the backward and criminal policy of the colonial-fascist government of Portugal;

Denounces and condemns the allies of the Portuguese government, and in particular the member countries of NATO, who give it aid and assistance in its criminal policy against Angola, the so-called Portuguese Guinea, the Islands of Cape Verde, Mozambique, and São Tomé and Príncipe;

Greets the heroic struggle of the peoples of the Portuguese colonies for their national independence;

Recognizes that armed struggle is the effective way for the liquidation of Portuguese colonialism and the achievement of the just aspirations of the people of the Portuguese colonies for freedom and national independence;

Calls upon the people of the countries of Africa, Asia, and Latin America and all the organizations of solidarity of the three continents to give to the struggling organizations of the Portuguese colonies the necessary aid for the development of their struggle of liberation and particularly:

a) Aid in arms and military equipment, necessary for the development of the armed struggle;
b) Facilities for transit of military material;
c) Financial aid;
d) Aid in sanitary, school, and education material and consumer goods for the supply of the fighters and the population in the liberated areas;
e) Facilities for documentation, entry, sojourn, and circulation in the countries of Africa, Asia, and Latin America to the fighters for freedom of the Portuguese colonies.

RESOLUTION ON THE ISLANDS OF SÃO TOMÉ AND PRÍNCIPE

The First Solidarity Conference of the Peoples of Africa, Asia, and Latin America:

Considering: the policy of obscurantism and of exploitation followed by the government of Portugal in São Tomé and Príncipe, which expresses itself in particular by the maintenance of forced labor in those countries;

Considering: the policy of repression of the Portuguese government for suppressing the just aspirations of the people of São Tomé and Príncipe for self-determination and for independence, as well as the growing intensification of the means employed by the PIDE [Portuguese International and State Defense Police] and the colonial army;

Considering: the tradition of struggle of the people of São Tomé and Príncipe and their effective contribution to the liquidation of the Portuguese colonial system;

Decides to greet and support, by all possible means, the struggle of the people of São Tomé and Príncipe for their liberation and independence.

RESOLUTION ON SOUTH AFRICA

The Conference notes that South Africa is:

1. The stronghold of colonialism in Southern Africa and is actively supported by the imperialist powers of Britain, USA, West Germany, France, Japan, Italy, and Belgium;
2. Fast being transformed into a major industrial and military center, and a springboard for imperialist domination throughout the African continent, and in particular in Southern Africa;
3. Part of a vicious Fascist Axis comprising Southern Rhodesia, the so-called Portuguese Territories of Angola and Mozambique, and itself;
4. Continuing, despite international public opinion, to practice the most diabolical form of racism in the twentieth century. This brutal and barbaric system notoriously known throughout the world as apartheid, is responsible for the increasing oppression of four-fifths of the South African population merely on the basis of color.

The Conference further notes that:

1. Over eight thousand leaders, cadres, and revolutionary activists including Nelson Mandela, Walter Sisulu, and Bram Fischer of the National Liberation and Trade Union Organizations are languishing in the dreaded South African prison of Robben Island and other prisons;
2. Over fifty political prisoners in South Africa have been sentenced to death, among them, the heroic ANC and Trade Union Leader Vuyisile Mini, who went to the gallows shouting the battle cry of *"Umkhonto we Sizwe"* (Freedom for the Nation) and *"Amandla Ngawethu"* (Power to the People);
3. Resistance to white domination in South Africa has now entered the stage of armed struggle.

The Conference, in condemnation of imperialist domination in South Africa, therefore calls upon all members represented here to work for:

1. The complete economic, diplomatic, cultural, and exporting boycott of South Africa, as well as for an oil and arms embargo on South Africa;
2. The strengthening of the National Liberation Organization in South Africa, and its armed units by giving it all possible material and moral support;
3. The unconditional release of all South African political prisoners;

4. The defeat of the Ian Smith regime in Rhodesia, the fascist Salazar regimes in Angola and Mozambique, and for the achievement of full national independence by the oppressed African people in these countries.

RESOLUTION ON OCCUPIED SOUTH YEMEN

The First Solidarity Conference of the Peoples of Africa, Asia, and Latin America held in Havana from January 3 to 15, 1966:

Having assessed the actual situation in Occupied South Yemen, and well aware of the intentions and conspiracies of British colonialism against the future of the people in the region;

Having taken note of the victories scored by the all-out armed revolution under the leadership of the National Front for the Liberation of the Occupied South Yemen, and in confirmation of the principles that inspired this meeting;

Hails the heroic struggle waged by the people of the Occupied South Yemen to liberate themselves from British colonialism and the puppet reactionary regime;

1. **Considers** the armed struggle in the Occupied South Yemen the sole effective means to liquidate British colonialism and its aggressive military bases, to put an end to the rule of the sultans, feudalists, and other agents of colonialism propped up in the region against the wish and interests of the people of the region;

2. **Considers** the National Front for the Liberation of Occupied South Yemen which leads the armed Revolution against colonialism and neocolonialism in the Occupied South Yemen as the sole representative of the people of the region;

3. **Condemns** British colonialist criminal acts, the brutal war of extermination waged against the people of the region, strafing of the villages, burning of the crops and farms, contaminating of the water wells, and rendering homeless tens of thousands of men, women, children, and the aged, not stopping short of killing hundreds;

4. **Condemns** all the terrorist barbarous measures perpetrated by the British colonial authorities against the people and demands the immediate release of the political detainees and cessation of the inhuman tortures they are subjected to;

5. **Denounces** all the colonialist conspiracies and designs Britain hatches against the interests of the people and considers the faked Federation of South Arabia it set up in Occupied South Yemen as nothing short of a tool in the hands of the colonialists and a preliminary step to neocolonialism;

6. **Denounces** all British attempts to establish a regime that does not represent the people in the region, with the intent of granting a nominal independence in 1968; calls on all states not to recognize such an independence;

7. **Call** on all revolutionary organizations in the world to back and support the peoples of the Occupied South Yemen in their just struggle against British colonialism;

8. **Urges** the anticolonialist and anti-imperialist liberated States to provide the National Front for the Liberation of Occupied South Yemen with funds and arms to enable it to continue the armed struggle till the final realization of the aims of the people;

9. **Calls** on International Relief Organizations to supply foodstuffs, medicine, and clothes to the destitute refugees, the victims of the British aggressive military operations.

RESOLUTION ON ZIMBABWE (SOUTHERN RHODESIA)

The First Solidarity Conference of the Peoples of Africa, Asia, and Latin America, convened in Havana, Cuba, from January 3 to 15, 1966:

1. **Notes** that the Unilateral Declaration of Independence by the British settlers in Zimbabwe (Southern Rhodesia) on November 11, 1965, is an aggressive conspiracy devised by Britain itself as a means to:
   a) Entrench white race supremacy and white minority colonial rule in Zimbabwe;
   b) Establish a permanent white-versus-Black iron curtain in Africa along the river Zambezi with white minority-ruled states in the South and African majority-ruled states in the North;
   c) Consolidate fascist states in Southern Africa to act as bastions for imperialist aggression, subversion, and recolonization of Africa;
   d) Enslave the African people of Zimbabwe as source of cheap labor for exploitation and maintenance of British capitalist monopoly;
   e) Perpetrate a race and color war in Zimbabwe for the sole purpose of providing a pretext for sabotaging and frustrating the independence of African States and the right of self-determination and national independence of the African people of Zimbabwe;

2. **Considers** that the Unilateral Declaration of Independence constitutes a declaration of war against the African people of Zimbabwe and an imperialist threat to peace in Africa and the world. Therefore, this Conference strongly condemns Britain for:
   a) Conspiring against the African people of Zimbabwe by granting minority independence to its fascist kith and kin under the guise of a Unilateral Declaration of Independence;
   b) Arming and training its kith and kin as a strong military force, long before the seizure of the illegal independence with a view to use this

military force against the African people of Zimbabwe in maintaining its minority and the illegal independence.

3. In view of this naked aggression and conspiracy by the British against the African people of Zimbabwe, this Conference:

a) **Supports** the firm stand of the people of Zimbabwe as clearly expressed by ZAPU to keep on struggling relentlessly until the British aggression and colonial rule are ended in Zimbabwe;

b) **Recognizes** the Zimbabwe African People's Union (ZAPU) as the only Liberation Movement and the only authentic representative of the African people of Zimbabwe;

c) **Proclaims** its firm solidarity with the people of Zimbabwe, which confront a life-or-death struggle, expressing its moral support to their struggle;

d) **Urges** the socialist and independent countries and all progressive organizations of Asia, Africa, and Latin America to offer their determined and unconditional support, material, and economic, to Zimbabwe African People's Union, giving all facilities to the intensification of their struggle, in order to obtain the victory on the colonial government and British imperialism;

e) **Establishes** a Special Committee for Zimbabwe, consisting of four countries.

This Committee of four countries shall consist of Zimbabwe and one country from each of the three continents to implement this Resolution. The Special Committee will be composed by the United Arab Republic, in representation of Africa; Cuba, representing Latin America; and the Democratic Republic of Vietnam, representing Asia;

f) **Demands** the immediate freedom of all political prisoners and detainees, as well as the abolition of the existing ghettos.

SUB-COMMISSION OF VIETNAM
GENERAL RESOLUTION ON VIETNAM

The First Solidarity Conference of the Peoples of Africa, Asia, and Latin America, held at Havana, the capital of the Republic of Cuba from January 3 to 15, 1966, with the participation of 512 representatives of 82 national liberation movements of countries of the three continents, as well as numerous observers of international and regional organizations, and guests from all the parts of the world, has given particular attention to the Vietnam problem, the most important question in this Conference.

The Conference has listened to the reports of the delegations of the NLFSV [National Liberation Front of South Vietnam] and the DRV [Democratic Republic of Vietnam] and wholly approves them. All delegates that have taken the floor during the Conference have unanimously expressed, on behalf of their respective peoples, their feelings of deep sympathy and admiration and their total and unreserved support to the people of Vietnam who heroically wage a just struggle in defense of their sacred homeland with unswerving determination and growing victories against the criminal war of aggression of North American imperialism, head of world imperialism. By extending its valuable and efficient support to the sacred cause of the Vietnamese people, the Conference has found such a popular war an exalting example in its noble task of promoting and developing the common struggle of the peoples of the three continents against imperialism, colonialism, and neocolonialism, headed by US imperialism, for the liberation of the peoples, social progress, and world peace. The Conference verifies that for more than eleven years, North American imperialism has been trampling on the sacred national rights of the Vietnamese people: independence, sovereignty, unity, and territorial integrity that were solemnly recognized by the Geneva Agreements of 1954 and that the United States were pledged to respect. The United States impudently pursues a neocolonialist policy of systematic intervention and military aggression against the heroic people of Vietnam.

Lately, faced with the repeated victories won by the people of South Vietnam in the legitimate defensive struggle to safeguard national independence and peace and in order to avoid defeat, the United States of America daily intensifies the war of aggression against South Vietnam, with the increasingly massive participation of its own armed forces and those of its satellite countries, of its strategic air force and the Seventh Fleet, and "escalates" the war with ever increasing air raids and attacks against the DRV, a sovereign and independent country.

Faced with their continued defeats, North American imperialists are feverishly preparing new aggressive plans to increase United States forces to 250,000 by the middle of the year, and later to 300,000 more; to further increase weapons and war material, multiplying their military operations and air raids with B-52 bombers at a growing rhythm in South Vietnam, and spreading them to Laos and Cambodia. To serve their criminal designs, North American aggressors deliberately use scientific discoveries and technical achievements, napalm and white phosphorous bombs, chemical products and toxic gases, and a strategic air force, aiming at the systematic and total destruction and extermination of the population of Vietnam: massacring the defenseless civil population, destroying whole villages; bombing hospitals, schools, cultural institutions, markets, hydroelectric dams, heavily populated industrial and economic centers. The repeated attacks of the US air and naval forces are intensified day and night, in an effort to hinder all activities, peaceful work, causing systematic destruction and extermination on Vietnamese territory.

Expressing the common feelings of millions of people in the three continents, the Conference denounces in the strongest possible way the North American imperialists as war criminals condemned by all the peoples of the world, by all mankind, for their brazen and rapacious war against Vietnam. The Conference particularly denounces their present maneuvers to intensify, widen, and make more dangerous than ever the war in Vietnam, Laos, and Cambodia. The Conference condemns their crimes of aggression against Vietnam as a blatant violation of the rights of the peoples to self-determination, of the 1954 Geneva Agreements on Vietnam and of international law. Human conscience is deeply disgusted and indignant at the barbaric genocide of the North American aggressor who shows total contempt for the most elementary human rights.

The Conference strongly condemns the brutal and deliberate aggression against the DRV, a sovereign and independent country, as a clear act of international piracy that constitutes a very dangerous precedent and a threat to the sovereignty of independent states in the three continents.

The Conference considers that no reason whatever could be invoked to justify such unspeakable crimes against the Vietnamese people who are separated from the USA by an ocean and who love independence and peace. The Conference denounces and strongly condemns the piratical policy of the United States of America that tends to enslave the people of South Vietnam, transforming South Vietnam into a new type of colony and an American military base to test their strategy, tactics, weapons, and war material in order to stop the national movements of liberation and subjects the peoples of the three continents, to prepare for war against socialist countries and to undermine the peace in South-East Asia and in the world.

The Conference ascertains that every time President Johnson intensifies and extends the war of aggression, he comes forth with his fallacious maneuvers of the so-called "will of peace" and "unconditional negotiations."

Recently, together with the intensification, to the highest degree ever, of military operations in South Vietnam, their extension to Laos and Cambodia and the accelerated preparation of new plans of aggression with massive introduction of new troops, arms and war equipment in South Vietnam, the Johnson Administration has undertaken a new peace "offensive," presenting fourteen points which advanced the questions of provisional cessation of bombardments against North Vietnam, and of taking the Geneva Agreements of 1954 as a "basis for peace" and "unconditional negotiations."

The Conference strongly denounces and condemns the new maneuvers of intensification and extension of the war carried out by North American aggressors. It also fully condemns and rejects the new misleading propositions of "unconditional negotiations" of the Johnson Administration, as well as the treacherous maneuvers leading to disguise the recent ever-increasing measures of intensification and extension of the war of aggression, to appease and deceive the North American and world public opinion, to force the Vietnamese people to accept the conditions of North American aggressors, in order to enslave South

Vietnam with impunity, to divide Vietnam definitively, and to sabotage the Geneva Agreements of 1954.

It denounces and strongly condemns the new "offensive of peace" of President Johnson as a maneuver leading to extremely dangerous new steps of military recklessness in Vietnam, in Indochina and in South-East Asia. It gives its total support to the declaration of the spokesman of the Ministry of Foreign Affairs of the Government of the Democratic Republic of Vietnam of January 5, 1966, and to that of January 6, 1966, of the Central Committee of the National Front of Liberation of South Vietnam on this question.

The Conference strongly condemns the extension of the war of aggression against Laos and Cambodia and supports the just struggle of the people of Laos for independence, neutrality, and peace. It also supports the people and the Government of the Kingdom of Cambodia in their struggle against North American aggressors to defend the territorial integrity, independence, and neutrality of Cambodia. The Conference warmly acclaims the solidarity of the struggle that closely unites the peoples of Indochina, in their common struggle against North American imperialists.

The aggressive war against Vietnam as well as that of the Dominican Republic and other peoples in Asia, Africa, and Latin America, the crimes committed by the North American aggressors clearly reveal that they are the number one enemy of the peoples of the three Continents and of all mankind.

The Conference reaffirms the inalienable and imprescriptible right of the people of Vietnam as well as of all the peoples of the three continents, to use all available means, especially just war, to defend the homeland from foreign aggression.

The Conference warmly greets the resounding victories of the Vietnamese people in their determined struggle against the ferocious aggressive war of North American imperialists. The Conference expresses the deep appreciation of the peoples of the three continents for the great sacrifices made by the Vietnamese people whose heroism is universally respected.

Nowadays, when the peoples of Asia, Africa, and Latin America rise up with an irresistible impulse against imperialism, colonialism, and neocolonialism, the struggle of the people of Vietnam against North American imperialism is an integral part of the struggle of the peoples all over the world for the achievement of their fundamental objectives at the present stage of history, that is to say, national liberation, socialism, and the safeguarding of world peace.

The Conference considers that the struggle of the people of Vietnam is in itself a direct support, and a powerful contribution especially through the rich experiences accumulated, to the national liberation movements of the peoples of the three continents, above all to the peoples who are at present carrying on a struggle, such as the peoples of the Dominican Republic, of the Congo (Léopoldville), of Laos, etc., and at the same time, it constitutes a brilliant and encouraging example and a stimulus to all the progressive peoples of the world. The peoples of the three continents and of the whole world have the duty to support and help the just struggle of the Vietnamese people and to provide them with profound and fraternal solidarity in their struggle against the common enemy, imperialism, colonialism, and neocolonialism, headed by North American imperialism. This is why the struggle of the Vietnamese people is justly considered the most important problem of today's struggles of the peoples in the world and has the unanimous support of all peoples of the world. Actively backed and with the aid of the socialist camp, the countries of Asia, Africa, and Latin America, the international working class, and the progressive and peace-loving forces of the world, the Vietnamese people score more and more victories each day. The United States aggressors are weaker and more isolated than ever. Nothing can save them from the inevitable defeat.

The Vietnamese people will win.

The Vietnamese people love peace, but genuine peace cannot be separated from independence. The Conference declares its full support to the five-point declaration of March 22, 1965, of the NLF of South Vietnam and to the four-point stand of April 8, 1965, of the government of the Democratic Republic of Vietnam. The Conference considers that these are the only just bases for the solution of the Vietnam problem, respect for the sacred fundamental rights of the people of Vietnam to independence, sovereignty, unity, and territorial integrity which have been solemnly recognized by the Geneva Agreements. It is on this basis that a stable and lasting peace could be reestablished in Vietnam, thus contributing to the sovereignty of peace in South-East Asia and in the world.

The Tricontinental Conference, joining its voice to that of the Vietnamese people and of all the peoples of the world demands:

Immediate ceasing of the American aggression against South Vietnam, immediate withdrawal of all American troops and those of the satellite countries from South Vietnam, dismantling of North American military bases in South Vietnam;

Immediate, final, and unconditional ceasing of air raids and other acts of aggression against the territory of the Democratic Republic of Vietnam;

Compliance with and implementation of the 1954 Geneva Agreements by the Government of the United States of America;

Recognition of the National Front of Liberation of South Vietnam, as the only true and legal representative of the people of Vietnam, and the right of the Vietnamese people to decide its own affairs, without foreign intervention and on the basis of the political program of the National Front of Liberation of South Vietnam.

Peaceful reunification of Vietnam should be achieved without foreign intervention; it is an internal affair of the people of the two zones.

The United States Government must solemnly express its recognition of the four points of the Government of the Democratic Republic of Vietnam of April 8,

1965, and prove this by concrete actions. It is only thus that a political solution to the Vietnam problem could be envisaged.

The Conference denounces and rejects all maneuvers leading to United Nations intervention, any attempt of intervention of foreign armed forces in the Vietnamese question and any solution contrary to the declaration of the government of the Democratic Republic of Vietnam dated April 8, 1965.

The Conference expresses its admiration for the firm determination of the Vietnamese people—deeply grateful for the support and the aid of the peoples of the three continents and of the world—to continue the struggle until the liberation of the country from all US aggressors, and the final achievement of its fundamental objectives: national independence, unity, and peace.

The Conference warmly welcomes the support of the peoples of the three continents and of the world to the people of Vietnam, and makes an urgent appeal to the peoples of the three continents, to progressive forces, to all democratic organizations and personalities in all the world for the unceasing intensification of mass movements at all social levels to:

Unite all efforts in order to defeat the new adventurous steps of US militarists, the new plans of war intensification and expansion including the bombings of Hanoi and Haifong in North Vietnam; to denounce the present peace maneuvers of the North American authorities; to demand the immediate cessation of the war of aggression in South Vietnam, the immediate, final, and unconditional cessation of air raids against North Vietnam, the withdrawal of all North American troops as well as the troops of satellite countries from South Vietnam, dismantling of North American military bases in South Vietnam, observance of the 1954 Geneva Agreements, to let the Vietnamese people decide their own affairs;

To develop in every way and in every aspect an active solidarity with the people of Vietnam; demonstrations, rallies of protest, boycotts against the loading and transportation of arms and war material and of North American troops, collection of funds, medicines, food; shipment of weapons and war equipment, celebration of days and weeks of solidarity, as well as commitments such as the enlistment of volunteers to fight side by side with the Vietnamese people, whenever they call for help; all this in accordance with the specific conditions existing in each country, to intensify the struggle against imperialism, colonialism, and neocolonialism in the countries of the three continents and in the world, constitutes a direct support to combine that struggle closely with the struggle of the Vietnamese people.

The Conference calls on the governments of all peace-loving countries to recognize de facto and de jure the National Front for Liberation of South Vietnam as the sole genuine and legal representative of the South Vietnamese people.

The Conference appeals to the peoples of the three continents and the peoples of the world to organize from March 12 to 19, 1966, a week of solidarity with the Vietnamese people.

In order to coordinate and unceasingly intensify the solidarity movement towards the Vietnamese people, multiply the forms and increase the efficiency of that movement, the Conference decides to establish a tricontinental committee of solidarity with the just struggle of the Vietnamese people against the aggression of the North American imperialists.

The Conference warmly greets the ever-increasing movement of struggle of the people of the United States, comprising a great number of justice-loving people, thousands of young people, women, students, professors, scientists, writers, artists, and religious personalities, who protest, in many different and increasingly energetic ways, against the war of aggression and who support the just struggle of the people of Vietnam.

The Conference makes an urgent appeal to the people of the United States to develop further and more intensively the mass movement with a view of denouncing the deceiving maneuvers of peace of the North American officials, especially to respond to the December 16, 1965, appeal of the Vietnam Day Committee in the US to demand the immediate, definite, and unconditional cessation of the bombings and of the war of aggression against Vietnam, which are contrary to the essential principles proclaimed by the Constitution of the United States and harmful to the national interests of the North American people themselves, and to support the just cause of the people of Vietnam.

Aware of the serious threat that endangers the common destinies of the peoples of Asia, Africa, and Latin America as a result of the war waged by North American imperialists against the Vietnamese people, the First Solidarity Conference of the Peoples of Africa, Asia, and Latin America expresses its deep conviction that the struggle of the Vietnamese people, supported by the countries of the socialist camp, by the peoples of the three continents, by the working class and the working people of the capitalist countries, including the people of the United States, by all the progressive forces of the world, will finally succeed, South Vietnam will be free, Vietnam will be peacefully reunified, and the independent Vietnamese people will be able to work for the happiness and progress of mankind peacefully and in close cooperation with the great family of fraternal peoples of the three continents and of the peoples of the world.

RESOLUTION ON THE CREATION OF 'THE TRICONTINENTAL COMMITTEE FOR THE SUPPORT OF THE VIETNAMESE PEOPLE' IN ITS STRUGGLE AGAINST THE AGGRESSION OF YANKEE IMPERIALISM

The First Solidarity Conference of the Peoples of Africa, Asia, and Latin America, held in Havana from January 3 to 15, 1966:

Whereas: The aggression of North American imperialism against the Vietnamese people is part of a worldwide plan of war and aggression on the part of imperialism all over the world. The war of aggression carried out by North American imperialism against the people of South Vietnam is a "war of experimentation" waged by imperialism to enslave the South Vietnamese people, both to test its strategical and tactical weapons, and train officers and soldiers with a view to using them to repress the liberation movements of the peoples of Africa, Asia, and Latin America. The US Air Force and Navy bombings and attacks against the Democratic Republic of Vietnam, an independent and sovereign country, constitute an insolent challenge to world public opinion, in order to set a precedent so that Yankee imperialists may intervene and attack our countries and the peoples of Africa, Asia, and Latin America at will;

Whereas: The heroic and victorious struggle of the South Vietnamese people under the leadership of the National Liberation Front of South Vietnam and the heroic resistance of the North Vietnamese people under the leadership of the Government of the Democratic Republic of Vietnam, are an integral part of the struggle of the peoples of Asia, Africa, and Latin America against the common enemy, imperialism, colonialism, and neocolonialism, headed by North American imperialism to achieve freedom, independence, peace, and social progress. The outstanding victories of the people of Vietnam constitute common victories for our peoples on the three continents and an endless source of inspiration and encouragement to the movement of national liberation;

Whereas: Now, more than ever, it is the main task of all peoples of the world, particularly the peoples of our three continents, to defend and energetically support the just and patriotic struggle of the people of Vietnam against Yankee aggression, until final victory;

Whereas: It is the duty of our Conference to especially emphasize its militant support to the heroic people of Vietnam,

Agrees

First: To establish the Tricontinental Committee of support to the people of Vietnam, fighting against the aggression of North American imperialism, with the following basic purposes:

To inform our peoples in a more extensive and profound way about the criminal war of aggression of North American imperialism against the people of Vietnam, in order to intensify the struggle against this unjust war of aggression. To inform in a more extensive and profound way and fully support the just and heroic patriotic struggle of the people of Vietnam against Yankee aggression, as well as the just and legitimate position of the National Liberation Front of South Vietnam and the Government of the Democratic Republic of Vietnam, on the solution of the Vietnamese problem;

To mobilize, organize, coordinate, and intensify the movements of solidarity, support, and aid to the Vietnamese people, in every aspect, moral, political, material, and economic, including the aid of volunteers and arms, within the framework of each country, each continent and tricontinental;

Second: The Committee will meet at least twice a year or more if necessary and will report its activities to all countries participating in the First Tricontinental Conference;

Third: The composition of the Tricontinental Committee for support to the people of Vietnam in its struggle against the aggression of Yankee imperialism is as follows:

—President: National Liberation Front of Venezuela;

—Three delegates representing three continents:

Asia: People's Democratic Republic of Korea;

Africa: National Liberation Front of the Congo (Léopoldville);

Latin America: Republic of Cuba,

—Two delegates representing the two zones of Vietnam:

Democratic Republic of Vietnam, National Liberation Front of South Vietnam.

The site of the Committee is Havana.

RESOLUTION ON THE INTERNATIONAL AID FUND FOR VIETNAM

The Political Commission of the Conference decides to transfer the proposal of the delegation of the Soviet Union concerning the creation of an "International Fund of Aid to Vietnam" to the Tricontinental Committee of Solidarity with the Peoples of Vietnam, for its study.

COUNTRIES THAT FORM THE TRICONTINENTAL COMMITTEE FOR THE SUPPORT OF THE VIETNAMESE PEOPLE

AFRICA	ASIA	LATIN AMERICA
Congo (L)	Korea	Cuba
	North Vietnam	Venezuela
	South Vietnam	

GENERAL RESOLUTION

Introduction

One of the gravest consequences of the colonization of Africa, Asia, and Latin America has been the systematic destruction of the cultures and historical value systems of each people.

The colonial system did not stop at the dismembering of the social structures, the displacement of entire populations, the imposition of artificial territorial and linguistic boundaries, the wiping out of large number of our peoples due to forced labor in mines and plantations, but has attacked with equal violence the cultural heritage of our countries.

Before colonization, great civilizations had developed on our three continents. The natural conditions of our tropical and subtropical regions were no obstacle for the blossoming of brilliant cultures.

Pre-Columbian America had known the flourishing civilizations of the Aztecs, Mayas, and Incas. This was also true of Black Africa, with its civilizations of Zimbabwe, Benin, and the Congo, and the high intellectual level attained by the Mali and Ghana Empires. In North Africa, within the historical framework of Islam, the Arab world not only gathered the cultural heritage of ancient Egypt, India, China, and Greece, but itself made great advances in the arts and sciences of the time. In Asia, the peoples of India, China, Japan, Vietnam, Cambodia, and Indonesia were able to develop high civilizations. The mercantile brutality of colonialism deprived these cultures of all possibility of upsurge and renaissance. Imperialism, for its part, uses its powerful technical media to introduce into all countries of our three continents a great body of literature based on an ethnocentric view of the world and on hatred and prejudice against non-white peoples.

At best, those cultures which escaped total destruction were consistently persecuted, denigrated, and denied. Each people's cultural dynamism rapidly degenerated into a body of fragmented folkloric traditions, of dress and culinary habits, and of local arts and crafts which could not replace the historical continuity of the creative originality and achievement of our peoples.

Ferocious exploitation, misery, famine, racial discrimination, inferiority complexes, and the loss of personality and self-respect are so many aspects of colonialism which induced a deep inhibition of culture and knowledge. For decades, hundreds of peoples were condemned to an endless repetition of the same legends, stories, popular songs, and oral literature, so as not to die spiritually frozen.

Only the national liberation struggles can put an end to this state of cultural stagnation, of general alienation, and restore to our cultures in Africa, Asia, and Latin America, their rightful place in history, their dynamism, their capacity for rejuvenation and perpetual creation. Only the national liberation struggles can restore our sense of adequacy and competence and the will and purpose to forge our own destiny in total freedom. This is why, now, in our three continents, culture is the medium through which our peoples can, within the very framework of their own national liberation process, become aware of their capacity to transform the life of society, write their own history, gather the best of their cultural heritage, and unify these factors which intervene in the historical formation of the nation, on a democratic and popular basis.

The national liberation struggle not only sets culture free, wresting it from its century-long stagnation, but gives it new fields for expression and creation. This struggle provides culture with new elements for its own authenticity, vigor, inner rhythm, and growth. There exist, then, close and inseparable links between the liberation struggle and the shaping of national culture. The armed struggle itself is a cultural fact which mobilizes, through a heroic process, the psychological resources, the emotional strength, the impatience, and the aspirations of each people of Africa, Asia, and Latin America and gives them wide access to their lost cultural fecundity.

The liberation struggle, which is at present the highest form of self-awareness, unifies those factors which define a nation and elevates to universal dimensions the special vocation of each one of our peoples. National culture, in the present stage, can only recover its legitimacy through the anti-colonialist and anti-imperialist struggle.

In this era, this struggle demands that the revolutionary forces of the three continents oppose the policy of the imperialist aggression, directed by the United States, which may be seen equally in the domain of the cultural activity of the peoples of Africa, Asia, as well as of Latin America.

The Social and Cultural Commission took up, in the course of its work, different topics of interest to the Revolution in the sphere of culture.

The Commission adopted detailed resolutions, of whose contents we offer the following resume:

1. **On imperialist cultural and ideological penetration**

   Imperialist cultural and ideological penetration is carried out in nations still subject to colonial and imperialist domination, as well as in those countries which have achieved state sovereignty. This penetration is a permanent threat to countries which are carrying out social revolutions.

   Imperialism tries to paralyze the national consciousness of the peoples by introducing its own decadent culture through mass communications media such as the cinema, magazines, newspapers, and the establishment of so-called "cultural centers." Under the pretext of "cultural exchange and cooperation," United States imperialism tries to bribe many intellectuals through the so-called foundations, for example, the Ford, Kellog,

Rockefeller, and Kennedy foundations; just as it tries to place universities of Africa, Asia, and Latin America under the control of United States universities. It also carries out seditious campaigns through the so-called "Peace Corps."

The Commission recommends to this Conference that:

It is necessary to wage an immediate active struggle to stop and to oust once and for all, from the cultural lives of the peoples, the manifestations for the colonialist, neocolonialist, and imperialist influence led by the United States.

2. **On the cultural revolution in those countries freed from the imperialist yoke**

   The cultural revolution is an inseparable part of the social revolution.

   The countries of Africa, Asia, and Latin America that have been freed from colonial and imperialist domination present a picture of acute educational and cultural backwardness. Without a deep cultural revolution it is impossible to overcome underdevelopment and eliminate the colonialist and imperialist legacy.

The Commission recommends to this Conference that:

The fundamental aspects of the cultural revolution be studied using the following points as a basis:

   a) The elimination of illiteracy and the elevation of the general educational level of the population.
   b) The fostering of technical and scientific education on the secondary and higher levels.
   c) The encouraging of literature and the arts.
   d) The stimulation of curricular and extracurricular sports and physical education activities.
   e) The organization of the revolutionary political education of the peoples of the new free society and especially of the workers and peasants.

3. **On the technical and scientific revolution**

   The countries who free themselves from colonialism and imperialism find themselves in a situation of economic deformation and underdevelopment and in an obvious technical and scientific underdevelopment.

   Each liberated country must undertake a technical and scientific revolution which is a very important part of the cultural revolution.

   The social revolution cannot consolidate itself unless the technical revolution is carried out, and a higher stage of economic development is achieved.

   The educational aspect of this revolution, i.e., the formation of technical cadres, should be carried out following the policy of the economic planning of the state.

The Commission recommends to this Conference:

The careful study of the principles of the scientific and technical revolution and the greatest exchange of experiences regarding this between countries, as well as the mutual exchange of fraternal aid.

4. On the cultural and scientific heritage

The scientific and technological wealth of the countries whose monopolies have filched out the natural resources of three continents and have exploited their peoples, has fed on the misery, sweat, and blood of millions of human beings.

The peoples of Africa, Asia, and Latin America have contributed far more than their share to the scientific and technological achievements of the imperialist countries. They claim their right to the free use of these advances in thought and in science as a necessity for development.

The Commission recommends to the Conference:

The abolition of all copyrights providing profits to monopolistic commercial entities, as well as the copyrights of authors who refuse, for political reasons, to have their work reprinted in developing countries. This recommendation does not mean ignoring the legitimate rights of authors who are willing to offer their scientific contributions to the entire human race.

5. On the formation of national cadres

The formation of national cadres is a most urgent task. It should be undertaken with priority in the recently liberated countries.

The spheres of this formation take in cadres of the following types: scientific and technical for agriculture and industry; high-level scientific researchers, teaching personnel, cultural and political.

The formation of national cadres must be carried out with the best of the revolutionary youth of each country. This formation must be done in the spirit of the nation and in the best internationalist tradition.

The Commission recommends to this Conference that:

In the countries of the three continents, great attention should be given to this gigantic task. All revolutionary countries are urged to provide high-level professors and technicians to the developing countries so that the latter may form their own technicians and scientists.

6. On Social Security

Hundreds of millions of men throughout the world exist in sub-human living conditions because of colonialist and neocolonialist exploitation imposed by imperialism, especially by United States imperialism.

Through revolution, the peoples must win the right to a better life.

The Commission recommends to this Conference that:

The following basic principles of a program of social security and assistance be adopted:

a) Protection for all urban and rural workers and their families.

b) No discrimination in this protection because of race, nationality, sex, age, religion, or ideology.

c) Organization of the social security system on the basis of the degree of economic, social, cultural, and administrative development of each country.

7. On Public Health

The greatest achievements in public health can only be attained in the countries that make their social revolution.

Malnutrition, tuberculosis, endemic diseases, and all such ills, consequences of rapacious imperialist exploitation, persist in many countries.

The Commission recommends to the Conference that:

To establish the basic principles of a serious public health structure:

a) Public health must be the responsibility of the state.

b) Public health must answer to the interest of the people emphasizing not only the medical care aspect but also that of preventive medicine.

c) Public health must be planned and directed by a single organism.

d) Public health should focus its greatest attention on the problems that affect the great masses, such as vaccination, general sanitary attention, the prevention of epidemics, hospital attention, etc.

e) Public health should rest on the massive participation of the people in the health tasks.

8. On Physical Education, Sports, and Recreation

Physical education, sports, and recreation play an important part in the integral formation of man; in preventive medicine; in bettering the productive forces of the country; in the struggle for national liberation and national defense; in the better understanding among peoples.

To attain these goals it is necessary to make use of the resources of the peoples who make the revolution; to have a sole and centralized orientation; to eliminate commercialism in sports; to form technical cadres in this field; to have the massive participation of the people.

The Commission recommends to the Conference:

a) The establishment in each liberated country of organs that will direct and carry out plans on the aforementioned and unify the orientation and resources of the state.

b) The establishment of a coordination that will facilitate bilateral and multilateral exchange between the countries of Africa, Asia, and Latin America.

On the Tricontinental Cultural Cooperation

The Commission recommends:

1. To promote and organize the translation, printing, and distribution of classical and modern literary and scientific works that by virtue of their quality and content may break the cultural monopoly of the so-called "Western and Christian civilization."

2. To promote and organize the exchange of pictorial, photographic, folkloric, and scientific exhibitions to facilitate a better knowledge of the traditional and contemporary culture of our peoples.

3. To promote and organize the exchange of theatrical, ballet, circus, puppet, and other types of shows.

4. To increase the exchange of teachers and students on the secondary and university levels.

5. To promote a campaign of repudiation of the press, radio, television, and the writers and artists who have been bribed by imperialism and who try to move against the course of history and the full intellectual development of the peoples.

6. To create on a tricontinental scale a cadres training school for the struggle against imperialism, colonialism, and neocolonialism, in the political, economic, and cultural fields.

7. For the partial or complete realization of this program in each of the countries participating in the First Tricontinental Conference, to institute a campaign to create a common fund for the defense and expansion of the national cultures of the peoples of Africa, Asia, and Latin America. In order to build up this fund, writers could make contributions of their books; painters could contribute their paintings; sculptors, ceramists, decorators, etc., their works. Simultaneous campaigns could be carried out for the collection of funds in work centers by women's organizations, colleges, and universities.

8. To organize a Cultural Affairs Commission within the body created to maintain tricontinental solidarity and the common struggle against imperialism.

9. In order that the Cultural Affairs Committee of the Tricontinental Organization may have a permanent organ of information, contact and exchange, the publication of a monthly or a bimonthly magazine with special editions for the peoples of Africa, Asia, and Latin America should be promoted.

10. To organize a Social Research Bureau. This bureau should work to coordinate such activities, in close cooperation with pertinent research activities being carried out by socialist countries; should collect, analyze, and make available social and economic information to the liberation movements and, whenever necessary, carry out specific studies at the request of the liberation movements.

11. To establish a cinematographic section which would deal mainly with the collection of documentation on liberation struggles. Such a cinematographic section should have documentary film archives, groups of cinema experts and cameramen at the service of the organ, with laboratories and mobile filming equipment; it should use all possible channels established by the solidarity of the peoples of the three continents for the effective distribution of full length and documentary films that may be produced in the spirit of this resolution. The receipts obtained from the distribution of these films would be used to increase diffusion and to improve technical and artistic quality.

Regarding National Liberation Movements and Tricontinental Cultural Cooperation

Recommends:

12. Those who fight against social and racial discrimination to involve themselves in the anti-imperialist struggle and help the Negroes of the United States and the people of the Union of South Africa and Zimbabwe, in particular, in the preservation and development of their cultures.
13. A total cultural boycott of South Africa and to work unceasingly for the total isolation of the fascist white regime of South Africa by [banning] all cooperation in academic, cultural, and sporting activities.
14. **Considering** that the Indian population of various Latin American countries lives in a situation of discrimination similar to that under which the Afro-American population of the USA, suffers; that the situation of extreme exploitation and oppression under which millions of Latin American Indians live, is the immediate result of the colonial heritage and feudal remnants existing in countries like Guatemala, Peru, Ecuador, Bolivia, and Paraguay maintained by imperialism; the Tricontinental Conference denounces the discriminatory treatment of the Indian population and reaffirms that only national liberation struggles can eliminate these ills.
15. **Recognizing** the special situation in Panama, where imperialism develops a profound cultural penetration which affects cultural values and traditions;
16. **Resolves** to unite the efforts of all participating organizations in support of the Panamanian peoples;
17. **Considering** that the countries waging an armed struggle of national liberation carry on at the same time duties of reconstruction in the social and cultural domain; confirming that in the vast regions of Angola, Guinea, and Mozambique that have been liberated from colonial domination, the political and mass movements of the Portuguese colonies carry out a cultural and social task in benefit of the population; considering the necessity

that the independent countries of Africa, Asia, and Latin America express their active solidarity to this struggle by encouraging all measures already taken in the liberated zones by FRELIMO, the PMLA, and the PAIGC in the fields of literacy and sanitation;

18. **Recommends** that revolutionary cadres of the three continents assist in the accomplishment of social and cultural development in the countries which are fighting for their national liberation.

On Coordination of the Activities of the Social Organizations of the Three Continents

The peoples' forces of Africa, Asia, and Latin America are great and their enthusiasm in the struggle to find the appropriate ways and means to solve their common problems is extraordinary. Since the imperialists have tried to keep us divided so as to perpetuate their domination over our peoples, it is the duty of all revolutionaries to carry out the correct revolutionary strategy: to unite all truly anti-imperialist forces to oppose imperialism, colonialism, and neocolonialism, led by the US.

This is why we are bound by the necessity of strengthening the ties of cooperation among the different mass social organizations of the three continents.

On the Role of Youth

The Conference underlines the great revolutionary role played by youth in the struggle for liberation from imperialism, colonialism, and neocolonialism. In many countries, the youth, especially the students, have played an important role in the struggle for liberation;

Considers that the youth of today are the hope of tomorrow and will play an important role in the cultural, economic, and social development of the respective countries. If the revolutionary movement ignores these young people, the reactionary forces led by world imperialism will organize them to use them for counter-revolutionary and fascist activities;

Recommends to all of its participants that they work together in order to:

1. Increase their participation in the national liberation movement.
2. Increase the number of solidarity festivals, to encourage meetings and cultural exchanges among the young people of the three continents.
3. Encourage youth organizations, to establish contacts with all of the organizations working on a worldwide scale for solidarity with the anti-imperialist movement, for world peace and friendship.
4. Grant support to the ninth World Festival of Youth and Students for Solidarity, Peace, and Friendship. And work for its celebration in a country of Africa, Asia, or Latin America.

On the Role of Women

Considering that the women of Africa, Asia, and Latin America are an indispensable force in the struggle against imperialism, colonialism, neocolonialism; and for national reconstruction;
Considering the great contribution given by the women of the three continents in the liberation struggles of their respective countries;
Considering that women must free themselves from the social bondage imposed on them by feudal and bourgeois tradition;

The improving of the social status of women, their increasing role in society and their political education will exert a great influence on the stability of the family, the ideological and moral level of all of society and will make substantial contributions to the revolutionary upsurge and the national construction of developing nations;

Recommends that the countries of Africa, Asia, and Latin America:

—help women to foster their movements;

—encourage women's organizations to establish contacts and to consider the means of cooperating with the International Democratic Women Federation so as to unify their efforts in the struggle against imperialism and old and new colonialism.

On the Role of Workers

The First Tricontinental Conference notes with great satisfaction that the workers in Africa, Asia, and Latin America are making significant contributions to the struggle against imperialism and for national reconstruction. In many countries the workers have played a leading part in the liberation struggles.

Considering that the future of all the developing countries will depend largely upon the extent to which the working class is organized, united, and educated to shoulder the tasks of national resurgence and industrial reconstruction, the Conference recommends to all its participants:

1. To promote trade union rights and liberties through progressive legislation and to develop appropriate struggles to get them implemented.
2. To organize, on official and unofficial levels, the workers' education programs in correspondence with the social and cultural economic needs of the nations.
3. To link the trade union struggles with all the liberation and anti-imperialist struggles going on in the three continents.
4. In view of the redoubled efforts by world imperialism through ICFTU [International Confederation of Free Trade Unions] to disrupt, demoralize, and divide the trade unions, it has become imperative to intensify efforts for trade union unity and to establish and increase contacts with the World Federation of Trade Unions which has been consistently fight-

ing for support and solidarity with national liberation struggles and trade union struggles in developing countries.

5. To combat the global strategy and tactics of imperialism and ICFTU, it is necessary to educate the workers in the spirit of internationalism and encourage trade unions to cooperate with such international organizations as are fighting against imperialism, colonialism, and neocolonialism.

6. Neocolonialists and feudal forces go on generating reactionary ideas among the workers through their organizations and through discriminatory labor practices so as to foment racial, communal, and cast prejudices and differences. Trade unions must relentlessly fight against such tactics of these exploiting classes and cement class and national unity on the basis of revolutionary ideas and struggles.

7. The Tricontinental solidarity movement must organize exchange of visits between the cadres and leaders of trade union Organizations of Afro-Asian and Latin American countries so as to develop mutual solidarity and understanding on the role of trade unions in these struggles against imperialism, colonialism, and neocolonialism, headed by the US

8. Recognizes February 7 as a Day of Solidarity with the exploited and oppressed workers of South Africa who live under the iron heel of fascist domination.

9. Urges all organizations represented in this First Tricontinental Solidarity Conference to:

   a) Condemn the crimes of the fascist and illegal government of Verwoerd and demand the release of political prisoners, i.e., workers, students, youth and revolutionaries;

   b) Organize annually meetings and demonstrations on June 26 as an act of solidarity with the imprisoned patriots languishing in the dungeons and concentration camps of the Verwoerd fascist regime, and

   c) Demand the suppression of concentration camps.

RESOLUTION ON THE CULTURAL AND IDEOLOGICAL PENETRATION OF IMPERIALISM

Considering that cultural and ideological penetration of imperialism takes place among nations still subjected to colonial and imperialist domination, as well as among those that have achieved national sovereignty, constituting a permanent threat to those countries carrying out their social revolution;

Considering that cultural and ideological penetration of imperialism is one of the fundamental weapons of neocolonialism;

Considering that in the face of the ideological and cultural invasion of imperialism, it is necessary to defend the peoples' national culture and vigorously promote their growth and development;

Considering that it is essential to strengthen the peoples' national pride in their traditions of struggle and culture, and thus stimulate the strengthening of national feelings. This task must be carried out in a spirit of respect for the cultures of other peoples so that it may serve to deepen the feelings of genuine international solidarity;

Considering that the culture and ideology of imperialism must be opposed by revolutionary ideas;

Considering that it is necessary for many peoples to defend their national languages, their literature, and cultural development. The official use of foreign languages cannot but weaken national feelings. The languages inherited from imperialist powers should be considered within a rational framework of relations among peoples and can be useful for cultural exchange, but should never substitute national language. To some peoples, the defense of their national language against deformations and debasement is their specific task. For others, the task is one of linguistic development or reconstruction, to enable an integral expression for nations speaking these languages for centuries;

Considering that in order to achieve their objective of economic, political, and military domination, the imperialists, especially those of the United States supported by the reactionary forces of the three continents in the role of subordinate allies, take steps to wipe out the peoples' culture and traditions; attempt to paralyze the peoples' national consciousness by the introduction of their own decadent culture and by using the means of mass communication such as the cinema, magazines and newspapers designed for children, youth, and the general public, establish so-called cultural centers in the principal cities, and, in addition, try to "yankee-ize" the intellectuals;

Considering that the imperialists, especially those of the United States, try to strengthen their influence in the fields of education, the arts, and the working-class movement, and that their attempts are progressively more aggressive in that they are directed not only at the reactionary elements but are also designed to influence the workers, by the employment of enormous financial and technical resources, and likewise through the use of sinecure posts;

Considering that the United States imperialists, after concluding military pacts with the reactionary governments of Africa, Asia, and Latin America on the pretext of "cultural exchange and cooperation," created a committee for relations between intellectuals, subsidized by large sums of money via the so-called Ford, Kellogg, Rockefeller, and Kennedy "foundations." Thus the imperialists permit many intellectual workers and research scientists to take part, to a certain extent, in the military programs of war and aggression, and since these intellectuals benefit themselves in an opportunistic manner and use as a pretext the difficult conditions they find themselves in to carry out research work, these research and cultural workers are used directly or indirectly to serve the aims of the imperialists, and are set to work against their respective nations;

Considering that the United States imperialists are carrying out an extensive undermining operation by means of the so-called "Peace Corps" which functions in the cities and the countryside;

Considering that the United States imperialists are trying to subordinate the university teaching of each country to the universities of the metropolis; and that they are availing themselves of invidious sociological research projects in order to carry out political, economic, and intellectual espionage;

Considering that a veritable invasion of pornographic publications, distorting and defaming the peoples' struggle for their liberation, is pouring over many countries of the three continents;

The Tricontinental Conference believes that it is urgent to wage an active struggle to rid all manifestations of colonialism, imperialism, and neocolonialism led by the US and assimilate in the same manner the best of the world's culture and create and develop national culture based on its own people.

RESOLUTION ON SOCIAL SECURITY

Considering that hundreds of millions of men all over the world live under subhuman conditions imposed by imperialist, colonialist, and neocolonialist exploitation. Its policy of domination destroys the sovereignty and free determination of the subjugated peoples and at the same time employs the riches extracted from them, not for their development and well-being, but for distribution, on the one hand, as benefits for the minorities that monopolize capital, and on the other, for nourishing the high budgets for armaments which guarantee precisely the continuity of the regime of exploitation;

Considering that it is urgent to immediately obtain better standards of living for all peoples of the world who now suffer from ignorance, starvation, disease, and the defects caused by malnutrition, overcrowding, unemployment, premature mortality, and poverty, to which they are reduced by imperialist exploitation as a system of maintaining its hegemony;

Considering that it is imperative that the peoples submitted to the imperialist yoke should intensify their struggle for liberation, relying also on their ardent desires for a better social and economic security to strengthen their positions and, at the same time, to conquer at all costs the right to a better life, organizing the reiterated and systematic demand for those benefits to be derived from a program of social security and welfare;

The Conference formulates as basic principles of a Social Security and Welfare Program the following:

    a) Protection for all workers both urban and rural and their families. Preservation of the indispensable means of life in cases of sickness or accidents, either general or occupational, maternity, temporal or permanent disability for work, old age, loss of income caused by the death of the head of the family, excess number of dependents, and work stoppage.

b) So as to facilitate and increase the services established to render such protection, there will be no discrimination because of race, nationality, sex, age, religion, ideology, or nature of the occupation, except some cases of work of women and work in dangerous or noxious conditions.

c) Organization of the regime of social security on a basis that facilitates the assignment of rights, taking into account the degree of economic, social, cultural, and administrative development of the country in such a way as to insure the complete enjoyment of the allocations.

The Conference recommends:

The elaboration of structures and plans of social security corresponding to the situation created by the colonialist regime and the necessity to solve and eliminate its consequences.

RESOLUTION ON PUBLIC HEALTH

Considering that Public health has as its objective the attainment for the masses of a healthy life in a physical, mental, and social environment in accord with the principles of medical sciences. Public health so defined, cannot be only an end of the liberated peoples, but also a means of social transformation intrinsically linked to the historic development of the peoples;

Considering that the greatest accomplishments in public health can only be obtained in a social system firmly established on a scientific basis, with a deep preoccupation for its historic transformation, with an active and conscious participation of its components, and having as final orientation the well-being of man;

Considering that in our three continents, as a legacy from the imperialist domination, the situation of public health presents alarming characteristics. Malnutrition, tuberculosis, endemic illnesses, and all diseases persist in many countries, as a conscience of the rapacious, ravenous, and bloody exploitation imposed on our peoples by imperialism;

The Conference considers as principles on which a serious public health structure must rest, the following:

a) Public health must be a responsibility of the state and it must be the state which assumes the concrete forms of its realization.

b) Public health has to be total in its structure and organization, and in accord with the interests of the people. It must be integral in character, emphasizing not only the assistant aspect but also the preventive.

c) Public health must be planned and directed by a central organization, capable of assuming all functions.

d) Public health must take a preferential interest in those problems affecting the great masses, such as vaccination and general health services; especially in the prevention of epidemies; problems of infancy; guarantee of sufficient beds for hospitals; rapid increase in the number of professional and technical personnel trained with the full understanding that their activities will have the highest social and common goal, far distant from any commercial or lucrative interest. Public health plans for rural areas should be stressed.

e) Public health must be based on a correct and massive participation of the people in all campaigns for health.

RESOLUTION ON THE CULTURAL AND SCIENTIFIC HERITAGE OF MANKIND

Considering that the oppressed nations and those in process of development are in a state of great scientific and technical backwardness, due to centuries of foreign oppression; and that the technical and scientific wealth of the countries whose monopolies have plundered the natural resources and men and women of the economically underdeveloped world has fed throughout the years on the poverty, sweat, and blood of millions of human beings from these three continents;

Considering that the impoverished people of Africa, Asia, and Latin America, together with the working class and all exploited peoples of these same metropolies have provided the capital and the conditions for the enormous growth of monopolies, and, with it, the flourishing of huge scientific and technical cultures that have in turn served to increase colonial and imperialist exploitation;

Considering that peoples from the three continents have more than paid their contribution to the technical and scientific progress of the imperialist countries, and as a necessity for this development, claim the right to the free use of these achievements of thought and science;

Considering that in a world which is becoming free both on a national and a social level, culture, in all its manifestations, is to an ever-greater extent the heritage of all humanity, it is the duty of all revolutionaries to contribute to its liberation from the commercial bonds imposed by the old order;

The Tricontinental Conference therefore, stands for the abolition of all copyrights which benefit commercial monopoly organizations and of those authors who refuse, for political reasons, to allow the reproduction of their works, which could contribute to the benefit of mankind, in the developing countries. This statement does not entail any disregard of the genuine rights of authors favorably disposed to the circulation of their contributions to science to all mankind.

The Conference hopes that the revolutionary countries will find the ways to satisfy this legitimate desire, in such degree as their economies permit. In order to promote this policy, the Conference appeals to authors and research scientists to generously support this resolution.

RESOLUTION ON THE CULTURAL REVOLUTION IN COUNTRIES LIBERATED FROM THE IMPERIALIST YOKE

Considering that the cultural revolution in the countries liberated from the imperialist yoke is an integral part of the social revolution, and that it is necessary to defeat the colonialist and imperialist inheritance by maintaining a vigorous vigilance against the ulterior ideological penetration of imperialism;

Considering that the countries of Africa, Asia, and Latin America, liberated from colonial and imperialist rule, are in a state of acute educational and cultural backwardness;

Considering that the liberation of these countries is but the first step on the road to national reconstruction and the creation of truly free states;

Considering that the popular forces assume leadership in public affairs;

Considering that the education of the people must go hand in hand with measures for the transformation of the agrarian situation and the economy as a whole;

Considering that the cultural revolution in the liberated nations must be carried out according to the stage of national development, and that the emphasis of the revolution must be placed on various aspects of this level;

The Tricontinental Conference states that without a profound cultural revolution, it is impossible to overcome underdevelopment and eliminate the colonialist and imperialist heritage.

The Tricontinental Conference points out these essential aspects of the cultural revolution:

1. Increase the standard of general instruction of the population:
   a) Carry out a general campaign against adult illiteracy in the first stage of the revolution.
   b) Create institutions to educate the workers and farmers, and organize courses following the illiteracy campaign courses to raise the education level to that of elementary school.
   c) Create primary schools so that every child may have a school and teacher.
   d) Develop secondary schools of a general character.
2. Increase secondary and higher technical-scientific education. It is necessary to create technical schools and technological institutes related to the perspectives of national economic development, and tied closely to the country's production sphere.

On the other hand, special attention should be given to university education. Universities should be transformed into centers for the development of national cadres of all kinds and should respond mainly to the urgent need of training high-level technical and scientific personnel, in order to face the country's economic and technical underdevelopment.

The priority given to the natural sciences and technological education in the universities should not lead to the neglect of the social sciences.

The universities and higher education centers should contribute to scientific research related to the great schemes of national development.

3. The development of the arts and literature is a question that deeply affects the most valuable traditions of the people. Special institutions should be created for these matters and support be given to artists and writers, in the firm conviction that their work will contribute to the strengthening of the peoples' national and social consciousness.

4. Educational and non-educational activities related to physical education are formative elements, especially of children and young people. The spirit of friendly competition and healthy exercise in sports should be increased, working towards the elimination of the professional spirit in sporting events, giving back to them their original content as a cultural expression and as friendly relationship between the peoples.

5. Organize political revolutionary instruction among the citizens of a newly liberated society, especially of the working class and the peasants. This political revolutionary instruction should be based entirely on revolutionary ideas. Ideas inspired by respect for the workers, by love for free labor, by revolutionary traditions of the people, by universal brotherhood of all the workers and peoples, by hatred of colonialist and imperialist oppression, by revolutionary democracy and love of the country, should form part, among other scientific appreciations of social development, of the contents of political instruction.

RESOLUTION ON THE SCIENTIFIC AND TECHNICAL REVOLUTION

Considering that the countries liberated from colonialism and imperialism are in a status of economic deformation and underdevelopment, as well as in evident technical and scientific backwardness;

Considering that the present needs of production, on the other hand, demand the use of complex means, whose application and functioning require a degree of skill based upon the knowledge of scientific principles and technical experience;

Considering that without modern means of production and without skilled scientific and technical personnel it is impossible to raise productivity in industry and agriculture and therefore increase production in such a way as to satisfy the growing needs of the population, and thus make highly profitable the different branches of production which should guarantee the essential material and financial accumulation, to carry out the economic and social development programs;

Considering that the scientific and technical revolution is a process which comprises the introduction of modern means of production and the training of skilled personnel. It is necessary to take it into serious consideration among social and cultural matters;

Considering that in those countries with a high economic development, new technical means are built up as a result of the needs of the economy and the subsequent scientific progress;

Considering that each liberated country has to make its own scientific and technical revolution, has therefore to train its own middle and high-level technical cadres, a very important part of the cultural revolution;

Considering that no revolution can achieve social success if there is no scientific and technical revolution, and if a higher level of economic development is not reached that will provide the means for progress of the new free society;

Considering that in the educational field, the scientific and technical revolution should contemplate the state's policy of economic planning, emphasizing the training of technicians;

The Conference recommends:

That countries liberated from the yoke of imperialist, colonialist, and neocolonialist exploitation, should pay special attention to the implementation of the principles of the scientific and technical revolution and to the rigorous study and exchange of experience on the subject, in order to provide extensive and fraternal mutual aid to achieve these far-reaching objectives.

RESOLUTION ON PHYSICAL EDUCATION, ATHLETICS, AND RECREATION

Considering that various forms of colonialist, neocolonialist, or imperialist exploitation, have hindered the mass participation of the peoples of the three continents in athletic activities, and have detracted from the true nature and object of athletics, physical education and recreation;

Considering that physical education, athletics, and recreation have great importance:

    a) In the integral formation of man; that is, in its physical and spiritual development.

    b) For the better knowledge and understanding of peoples.

    c) In preventive medicine and the corresponding individual health.

    d) As a means of improving the productive force of the country.

    e) In maintaining the people in perfect physical condition for fighting for liberation and for the defense of the country.

    f) As a powerful factor for the integration of all components of society;

Considering that to bring physical education, athletics, and recreation to the whole population it is necessary:

a) to use the resources of peoples who make their revolution; popular organizations; public enthusiasm; the multiple facilities for using installations and means to those ends.

b) to adopt the measures tending to eliminate anything that may be harmful in some sports.

c) to propitiate, with the support of popular organization, a sole and centralized orientation, that will be at the same time the driving force of the physical education activity.

d) to eliminate commercialism in athletics.

e) to propagate intensely, with ideological content, the high principles that must guide physical and athletic education.

f) that physical and athletic education should progressively develop fully qualified technical cadres.

g) that in the general formation of teachers and professors, and in their constant betterment, the integral development of the teaching profession should be considered as a fundamental factor in order to bring to the school, actively and by example, physical and athletic education.

h) that the quality of athletics should be the result of the mass participation of the people.

i) to promote a high organization, discipline, systematization, and scientific development with a view to participating in international events.

j) that athletics should be made available to all sectors of the population, which implies the implementation of special plans in remote regions wherever they exist, especially in rural areas.

Considering that for the implementation of the aforementioned principles, and for a better use of indispensable resources, each country requires the creation of a suitable body for directing, orienting, channeling, and controlling the entire program for athletics, physical education, and recreation, in accordance with the needs of the masses; and in order to unite the efforts of all peoples, and develop exchanges among them, it is necessary to establish those bonds that facilitate the implementation and execution of the program adopted, taking into consideration the characteristics and conditions of each country;

The Conference recommends:

a) The establishment in each country of an organization for directing and carrying out plans for physical education, athletics, and recreation that will unite the guidance, the resources and their application.

b) The establishment of coordination to facilitate bilateral and multilateral exchanges among the African, Asian, and Latin American countries, which at the same time would permit the strengthening of a line of action capable of unifying opinions, evaluating experiences, and determining the forms of aid and struggle for the aforementioned revolutionary principles.

c) The organization of sporting institutions in the independent countries or the proper use of those already existing, to give assistance to the peoples who are still under imperialist domination, ensuring in this manner the development of sportsmen in these countries.

RESOLUTION ON THE FORMATION OF NATIONAL CADRES

Considering that the formation of national cadres is a most urgent task which should be given high priority in newly-liberated countries: This vast effort in the field of education should be considered, within the planning of the revolutionary state;

Considering that the creative fields of national cadres include the formation of economic and administrative cadres; technical and scientific cadres in agriculture and industry; high-level scientific cadres; research, teaching, cultural, and political cadres;

Considering that the planned promotion of national cadres is a consequence of the development of the cultural revolution;

Considering that this purpose requires the creation of institutions of specialized learning aimed at the achievement of these social objectives. In a parallel manner, this purpose requires the reorganization of institutions existing before the Revolution, in such a way that they should be redirected in accordance with the new goals;

Considering that the formation of national cadres should be based on the best elements of the revolutionary youth of each country. In this sense, a wide system of scholarships should be established, in order to ensure the access of youths from the working class, sons of workers and peasants, to the new institutions, created or reorganized. This system of scholarships may cover studies abroad, especially of technical and scientific matters;

Considering that the young scholarship students must be made aware that it is only through the effort and sacrifices of the working class of their country that they can be adequately educated and can gain access to higher education. Therefore, they should, in their field of specialization, fulfill the duties that the Revolution may determine, in accordance with its needs, and be loyal to the political ideals and achievement of the Revolution;

Considering that national cadres should, as far as possible, be formed within their own countries. They should be educated in the national spirit and in the best internationalist traditions;

The Conference declares that: it is the unavoidable duty of all revolutionary countries to provide on a free basis high-level professors and technicians to developing countries, to foster the formation of their scientists and technicians.

GENERAL DECLARATION OF THE FIRST SOLIDARITY CONFERENCE OF THE PEOPLES OF AFRICA, ASIA, AND LATIN AMERICA

The First Solidarity Conference of the Peoples of Africa, Asia, and Latin America was held in Havana, capital of the Republic of Cuba, from January 3 to 15, 1966. A highly significant task has been carried out. For the first time in history, a very broad representation of the revolutionary forces in eighty-two countries of the three continents has exchanged experiences and initiatives, strengthened the ties of revolutionary and anti-imperialist solidarity, and adopted basic agreements in the fight against the system of imperialist, colonialist, and neocolonialist exploitation, against which they have declared a war to death. The deliberations of the Conference have evidenced the fact that imperialism, colonialism, and neocolonialism, led by Yankee imperialism, are following a policy of systematic intervention and military aggression against the countries of the three continents.

The Conference was held at a time in which the peoples of Asia, Africa, and Latin America, as well as in other parts of the world, wage a violent struggle against all forms of imperialist, colonialist, and neocolonialist domination led by Yankee imperialism. The world situation favors the development of the revolutionary and anti-imperialist struggle of the oppressed peoples. The increasing wave of the national liberation movement in Africa, Asia, and Latin America is an outstanding event of enormous significance.

Imperialism will never renounce voluntarily to its policy of exploitation, oppression, plunder, aggression, and intervention. The peoples of Asia, Africa, and Latin America know by their own experience that the main bulwark of colonial oppression and international reaction is Yankee imperialism, implacable enemy of all the peoples of the world. To destroy the domination of Yankee imperialism is an imperative issue for the complete and definitive victory of the anti-imperialist struggle in the three continents and all efforts of the peoples should converge towards that aim.

The true nature of imperialism, colonialism, and neocolonialism has been dramatically revealed in the debates of the Conference. On comparing the benefits, profits, and riches drawn out by imperialist monopolies from the miserable living conditions of the peoples of the three continents, the acute character of one of the major contradictions of our days is observed: the contradiction between imperialism and oppressed nations and peoples. Yankee imperialism is the main pillar of oppression; it leads, provides, and supports the world system of exploitation.

The monopolies from imperialist powers draw out for their benefit enormous riches from the peoples of Asia, Africa, and Latin America. This spoliation has been secularly carried out under different forms. They seize the natural resources of the soil, subsoil, and maritime platform, control through investments the most important sectors of industry and services, as well as foreign trade, and impose their harmful conditions on the relations of international exchange, fully controlling banks and national finances.

This situation as a whole determines that the imperialist, colonialist, and neocolonialist powers exercise economic domination over the subject countries and carry out systematic plunder which our peoples suffer, being compelled to pay tributes to fill the coffers of the monopolies.

The rate of annual per capita income of exploited nations of the three continents is incredibly lower than that of the exploiting powers. The astronomical figures which reveal the profits obtained by the monopolies are in sharp contrast with the extremely high index of infant mortality, the percentage of illiteracy, the almost total lack of schools, of medical and hospital assistance services, and in short, the conditions of hardship, unemployment, hunger, and poverty in which our peoples live.

This injustice is more starkly revealed considering the tremendous contrast between the promising future that the present development of science, technology, and culture offers to mankind, and the shocking fact that the exploited masses of Asia, Africa, and Latin America are deprived of every possibility of access to the enormous material and intellectual wealth that knowledge and human work have accumulated for centuries. Our peoples cannot profit from the achievements of science and technology because the system of exploitation allows them no opportunity, and, consequently, they find themselves in a disadvantageous position which increasingly widens the gap between victims and henchmen as far as standards of living are concerned. The impossibility for the peoples of Asia, Africa, and Latin America to reach this higher level of material and intellectual living standard under the present social and economic structures to which they are subjected today, is quite evident. The desperate conditions of poverty, hunger, and ignorance in which the exploited masses of the three continents live are also obvious. These are reasons enough to definitely condemn the imperialist, colonialist, and neocolonialist oppression and exploitation.

In its eagerness to prop up this system led by Yankee imperialism, in order to face the powerful drive of the peoples, it fosters and maintains international tensions, threatening peace and security; encircles the globe with aggressive military bases; concludes military pacts in open violation of the principles of national sovereignty; proclaims, with incredible cynicism, the alleged right to interfere in the internal affairs of other countries and to occupy by force all or part of their territories, arrogating the shameful role of international gendarme; finances and supplies arms to decadent colonial nations so that they may keep their preys and to share profits with them; insolently and arrogantly insists on imposing its ideology, using for this end a worldwide propaganda network; tries to influence all peoples with the decadent expressions of its culture; distorts history, twists facts, and uses slander as a fighting weapon; imposes economic blockade in the vain attempt to wield the people through a siege of hunger and being impotent to do so, insists in extending that turbid and criminal conduct to the commercial policy of its allies; schemes the promotion and support, on a world scale, of antipopular and antinational regimes which sustain the system of exploitation; covers the map with its capital, annually drawing out millions of dollars for its monopolies; it commits all sorts of abominable crimes against the peoples, and busily prepares the attack against the socialist countries and against world peace.

By the very nature of their system of exploitation, imperialism, colonialism, and neocolonialism strongly resist independence, sovereignty, and national and social liberation of the peoples. Opposing them, the oppressed peoples of the world fight for the principles of self-determination, sovereignty, and independence of the nations. The movement of liberation of the peoples of the three continents has developed into one of the most important forces of the world struggle against imperialism, colonialism, and neocolonialism, and together with the peoples of the socialist countries and international proletariat, plays a decisive role in the history of mankind. The imperialists isolate themselves and become weaker. The crisis in their system is more acute every day.

The interests of national liberation are closely bound to the needs of the social revolution. The movement for national liberation, the demands of the peasants for land, the struggle of the working class for its great social and political gains, the determined action of the youth and students, the demands of intellectual workers and other sectors of the population for their trampled and scorned rights, the fight against oligarchies and military dictatorships at the service of the ruling classes, the battles against racial discrimination and other social inequalities are a powerful current and form part of a movement destined to play a transcendent role in the progress of mankind.

The peoples that have succeeded in abolishing the exploitation of man by man by the establishment of socialism, give with their example and aid a valuable impulse to the struggle of the peoples oppressed by imperialism.

To the extent in which the movement of liberation of the peoples of Asia, Africa, and Latin America advances, the working class and the progressive sectors of capitalist nations will be able to help this movement in a more direct and effective manner. The increasing movement of civic protest of the North American people because of the war waged by the government of the United States against the Vietnamese people, is an unequivocable evidence.

The effective revolutionary actions of the National Liberation Front of South Vietnam and the heroic resistance of the Democratic Republic of Vietnam, are contributing to raise the fighting spirit and the political awareness of the people of the United States, who with ever-growing vigor, express their opposition to war. This is evidence that the liberation of Asia, Africa, and Latin America will hasten the struggle of the working class and other oppressed sectors of the population in the United States and the developed capitalist countries in Europe against the rule of monopolist capital, and against exploitation and for social progress. In its turn, the development of this proletarian class struggle and that of all workers in capitalist countries, will contribute to the advance of the struggle for national liberation of Asia, Africa, and Latin America and, thus, the common efforts will defeat the common enemy of all peoples: imperialism and, particularly, Yankee imperialism, the most ferocious and oppressing of them all.

A group of countries in the three continents has achieved political independence; many others are fighting to attain it. Those who have attained their independence and those who are struggling for it, close today their ranks in the Solidarity Conference of the Peoples of Asia, Africa, and Latin America and study the means to face their international duties with regard to the common cause of all peoples: the liquidation of the colonialist, neocolonialist, and imperialist system of oppression and exploitation.

There are still territories which suffer under the most backward forms of the colonial system. The representatives of those peoples are present in this Conference. In order to face the serious problems involved in economic and social development and the complete liberation of the countries of Asia, Africa, and Latin America, it is imperative to uphold the principles of self-determination of states, national sovereignty, and political independence.

The Conference PROCLAIMS the inalienable right of all peoples to full political independence and to resort to all forms of struggle that may be necessary, including armed struggle, to conquer that right. There is no more important task for the subjugated peoples of Asia, Africa, and Latin America.

The nations of Asia, Africa, and Latin America which have achieved their political independence are becoming aware that the juridical status of a formal sovereignty does not suffice to insure full liberation. In order to achieve total liberation it is necessary to eliminate all means of imperial exploitation, to carry out deep changes in the social and economic structures, and to set the material and technological foundation on which a society of free men can be built. Political emancipation must be followed by economic liberation. Only thus can social equality of all men and true independence of all states be insured.

The peoples of the independent countries in Asia, Africa, and Latin America must oppose every type of infiltration, subversion, oppression, exploitation, and plunder by imperialism and develop to the utmost their initiatives and resources, strengthen reciprocal aid and cooperation with friendly countries, destroy imperialist and colonialist forces, oppose neocolonialist aggression and infiltration, and build and advance their national economy and culture.

The Conference PROCLAIMS, as common principles of the struggle of the peoples that in Asia, Africa, and Latin America are determined to eradicate every remnant of imperialist economic domination and to build their own economies, and as a program for those who are still striving to attain their liberation, the right to national control of the basic resources, to the nationalization of the banks and vital enterprises, to the state control of foreign trade and exchange, to the increase of the public sector, to the reconsideration and rejection of the spurious and antinational debts which were imposed upon their economy, to the achievement of a true agrarian reform, which would eliminate the feudal and semifeudal ownership, advance the agricultural development, raise the standard of living of the farmers and other agricultural workers, and contribute to the increment of national economy and export.

The implementation of these principles will permit the full development of their natural resources and its industrialization according to the prevailing conditions in each country, thus achieving their economic emancipation.

The imperialists make every effort to strangle the countries who have conquered their independence by imposing obstacles on their trade, using the monopolist control of transportation, resorting to criminal blockade, ruining their economies through the forced lowering of prices of primary products and the constant fluctuation of those prices.

The Conference PROCLAIMS the right of all liberated peoples to trade with all other countries of the world on an equal basis, the need to put an end to the constant fluctuation of prices of the basic products and to fix these prices on a fair basis so that they be rationally related to those of the industrial products and the urgency of breaking the imperialist blockade of trade and transportation of the liberated countries through the common struggle of the peoples of the three continents, with the cooperation of the progressive forces of the rest of the world.

The imperialist, colonialist, and neocolonialist rule leaves a dramatic balance of technological backwardness to the peoples of Asia, Africa, and Latin America, which prevents the city and country workers, whose effort is the foundation of national development, from increasing their productivity through the application of more advanced techniques in agriculture and in industry.

The Conference PROCLAIMS the right of the peoples to have access to technique and the need of the liberated countries for the massive formation of technical cadres selected from amongst the people, which implies an educational revolution starting from the eradication of illiteracy, and leading to technical revolution.

The countries which free themselves of imperialism inherit the most terrifying lack of public health services; no hospital nor auxiliary centers of medical services, and no professionals to increase them.

The Conference PROCLAIMS the right of the peoples of the three continents to enjoy a healthy life and to adequate medical assistance and preventive medical services, and the need of the liberated countries to receive all possible aid from the more developed countries of Asia, Africa, and Latin America to establish a system of medical and hospital services, with special emphasis on the training of medical and auxiliary cadres that must carry out this massive task under the planned direction of the state and with the broadest popular participation.

Racial discrimination is practiced by the imperialists, colonialists, and neocolonialists in important areas of the world, and reveals itself in its most repulsive, brutal, and diabolic form in the policy of apartheid, which oppresses and offends the people of South Africa and threatens the people of Zimbabwe, subjecting them to a permanent state of servitude. It is an instrument of exploitation and is one of the most unfair and barbaric forms of inequality.

The Conference PROCLAIMS the full equality of all men and the duty of the peoples to fight against all expressions of racism and discrimination, and therefore, its full support to the struggle of the people of Zimbabwe against the racist government of Ian Smith and to the international movement of solidarity against the South African regime, and calls on all countries represented at the Conference to impose a political and commercial blockade on South Africa, as well as a boycott on the shipment of arms and petroleum.

Military pacts, the existence of military bases and the presence of imperialist or mercenary troops in foreign territories are a violation of national sovereignty and a danger to peaceful relations among States. Imperialism maintains this situation to strangle national liberation movements, intimidating their neighbor countries and committing aggressions against the newly-liberated countries.

The Conference PROCLAIMS the right of the peoples to free themselves of foreign military bases and makes an appeal to step up the fight for the achievement of this aim and against military pacts and the presence of imperialist or mercenary troops.

The peoples of Asia, Africa, and Latin America struggle to defeat the local reactionary classes, which, servile to foreign interests, help to maintain the system of neocolonial exploitation. In this struggle the reactionary classes offer a fierce resistance and it will not be an easy task to take away from them the power with which they exploit and oppress the peoples. The revolutionary and patriotic struggle of each people is a contribution to the liberation of the other countries.

The Conference PROCLAIMS the right of the peoples to their political, economic, and social liberation by the means they deem necessary, including armed struggle, so as to achieve this goal.

Imperialism and the reactionary classes in every country face the liberation movement of the peoples by using all the military, political, and pseudo-juridical resources within their reach. They ignore their international commitments. They try to mask their crimes inventing all kinds of fallacious arguments to violate the principle of self-determination and national sovereignty and the right of the peoples to bring about revolutionary changes in their economic and social structures. They do not hesitate to resort to all kinds of crimes and abuses; subversion, infiltration of spies, saboteurs, and criminal agents; direct aggression to thwart the legitimate aspirations of our peoples; they resort to violence and the use of their armed forces to carry out their objectives.

The Conference PROCLAIMS the right of the peoples to meet imperialist violence with revolutionary violence, to safeguard in those circumstances the national sovereignty and independence.

The struggle that the peoples of Asia, Africa, and Latin America wage to this effect, is a decisive contribution to the anti-imperialist fight in the three continents, as well as an effective one for the liberation of their own peoples and the insurance of world peace. Each popular victory inspires new victories.

The Conference PROCLAIMS the right and the duty of the peoples of Asia, Africa, and Latin America and of the progressive states and governments of the world, to give material and moral support to the peoples who are fighting for their liberation or suffering direct or indirect aggression from the imperialist powers.

North American armed forces now occupy the territory of the Dominican Republic. Imperialism, against the will of the Dominican people, intervened in the popular revolution to uphold its puppets, violated national sovereignty, trampled on the principle of non-intervention, and murdered not only those involved in the fighting, but also their women and children.

The Conference PROCLAIMS, therefore, the right of the Dominican people to fight the North American occupation forces by all the means within their reach, mainly through popular revolutionary war, and the right to request the support of all the peoples and governments of the world.

The heroic resistance of the Vietnamese people against the imperialist aggressors, not only conforms with the righteous defense of the independence of that country, but also safeguards the right to self-determination and sovereignty of all the people of the world.

The Conference strongly CONDEMNS the war of aggression of Yankee imperialists in South Vietnam, and their bombings of the Democratic Republic of Vietnam, and condemns them as war criminals for their barbaric actions against the Vietnamese people. The Conference DENOUNCES the deceiving peace statements of Johnson's government and totally SUPPORTS the points set forth by the government of the Democratic Republic of Vietnam and by the National Liberation Front of South Vietnam for the solution of the Vietnamese problem. The Conference PROCLAIMS that the National Liberation Front of South Vietnam is the only and true representative of the people of South Vietnam and EXPRESSES its firm conviction that under its leadership, the Vietnamese people will undoubtedly achieve its final victory.

The Conference PROCLAIMS its solidarity with the armed struggle of the peoples of Venezuela, Guatemala, Peru, Colombia, the so-called Portuguese Guinea, Mozambique, Angola, Congo (Léopoldville), and with the decision of the peoples of the Cape Verde Islands, São Tomé and Príncipe, to put an end to colonial domination; SUPPORTS the peoples of French Somaliland, of the Spanish possessions of Africa and the people of Zimbabwe, Basutoland, Bechuanaland, and Swaziland in their right to self-determination and independence, the colonial peoples of Latin America, Puerto Rico, the Guianas, Martinique, Guadeloupe, and others in their struggle for national independence and self-determination, the right of the people of Cyprus to an unrestricted independence and complete self-determination, supports the peoples of Malaya (including Singapore) and North Kalimantan in their struggle for national liberation and for the dismantling of foreign military bases and the withdrawal of foreign troops, and also the demand for immediate independence for South Yemen (occupied) and the dismantling of the British military base in Aden and the North American bases established in Saudi Arabian territory; CALLS UPON the solidarity of all peoples with the Arab people of Palestine in their just struggle for the liberation of their homeland from imperialism and Zionist aggression; CONDEMNS the policy of aggression of the government of the United States against peaceful and neutral Cambodia, and advocates the rejection of any political, economic, diplomatic, and cultural cooperation with Yankee imperialists and with all the puppet governments that help the North American government in its policy of aggression against the Indo-Chinese peoples; SUPPORTS the heroic struggle of the people of Laos against North American imperialists and their puppets; DENOUNCES the aggressive maneuver of Yankee imperialists, who in alliance with the Japanese militarists and in connivance with their puppets of South Korea, intend to establish the North-East Asia Military Alliance as storm troops against the Korean people and the peoples of Asia, in order to provoke a grave situation in that part of the world; and also SUPPORTS the struggle of the Korean people for the reunification of their homeland and the expulsion of Yankee troops from South Korea, and expresses its solidarity with the fight of the Korean and Japanese peoples for the abrogation of the South Korean–Japanese Treaty; and CONDEMNS as an act of aggression against the Cuban people, the blockade of Cuba by North American imperialists, who have prohibited the sale of foodstuffs and medicines, and calls upon the peoples of the three continents to increase their trade with this aggrieved fraternal country, so as to definitely break the blockade that the imperialists have tried to impose.

In the face of the attacks of the reactionary forces directed by Yankee imperialists, the Conference CALLS FOR the militant, active, and dynamic solidarity of the peoples of Asia, Africa, and Latin America, and exhorts them to intensify under the anti-imperialist banners, the national liberation movement, to develop it even more and unite all progressive mankind in that struggle.

Imperialism tries to dull the national consciousness of the peoples through the penetration of its decadent culture, employing means of mass communication for these purposes, destroying the scientific, technical, and cultural heritages of the countries it exploits.

The Conference PROCLAIMS the right of all peoples to maintain and develop their cultural heritage, nourishing it with the contributions which arise from the exchange of genuine cultures of other peoples and the need that the peoples of the three continents wage an active fight to expel from their cultural life the expressions of imperialist influence, thus enriching the lives of their peoples with their true art and culture.

The Conference extends a warm greeting to the working class and progressive movements of the capitalist countries in Western Europe and the United States, and invites them to strengthen even more the fraternal ties of solidarity with the peoples of the three continents to jointly fight against the imperialist monopolies and the policy of intervention and aggression, since they also are victims of the exploitation and oppression system.

The First Solidarity Conference of the Peoples of Africa, Asia, and Latin America and the organization that has emerged from it proclaim themselves genuine representatives of the anti-imperialist, anticolonialist, and anti-neocolonialist, patriotic and nationalist will and fighting spirit of the peoples of the three continents.

The Conference PROCLAIMS that the main task of the peoples of Asia, Africa, and Latin America is to intensify the struggle against imperialism, colonialism, and neocolonialism so as to conquer and consolidate national independence, democracy, social progress, and peace.

The peoples of the three continents, determined to sweep all obstacles in their way and to struggle unyieldingly for a new Asia, a new Africa, and a new Latin America, definitely emancipated from imperialism, colonialism, and neocolonialism, will be united in a tight sheaf until final and total victory is achieved. They have full confidence in their future.

The coordination of the efforts of the of Asia, Africa, and Latin America accomplished at this Conference, and the future tasks and fundamental perspectives that have been established, will turn the active solidarity of our continents into a historic instrument of tremendous drive that will destroy the strongholds of imperialism, colonialism, neocolonialism, the foundations of which have already been shaken by the victorious liberation movements in recent years, and by the inexorable course of history.

THIS GREAT HUMANITY HAS SAID, *"ENOUGH"* AND HAS STARTED TO MOVE FORWARD, AND ITS GIGANTIC MARCH WILL NEVER STOP UNTIL IT CONQUERS FINAL LIBERATION.

LIST OF DELEGATES, OBSERVERS, GUESTS, AND PRESS AT THE TRICONTINENTAL CONFERENCE

The Official Cuban Credentials List
Presiding Chairs:
- Raúl Roa García (Cuba), President
- Yousef El Sabai (UAR), Secretary General
- John K. Tettegah (Ghana), Vice President
- Pedro Medina Silva (Venezuela), Vice President
- Nguyen Van Tien (South Vietnam), Vice President

Delegates by Country/Organization:
1. Algeria – Algerian Committee of Afro-Asian Solidarity (FLN)
   - Lakhdar Brahimi, Algerian Ambassador to the UAR (President)
   - Hamid Bencherchali, Secretary (Chargé, a.i.), Embassy, Havana
   - M. Adda Benguetat, Secretary General of AAPSO
   - Mohamed Heneche (or Herieche), FLN Foreign Relations Committee member
   - Ahmed Zemirline, National Assembly Deputy representing FLN
   - Mohamed Maghraoui, National Assembly Deputy representing FLN
   - Abdel Krim Gheraieb
2. Angola – Peoples' Movement for the Liberation of Angola (MPLA)
   - Luis Andrade de Acevedo, MPLA (President)
   - Miguel Baya Antonio
   - Luis de Almeida, MPLA

- Paulo Teixera Jorge, permanent military representative of MPLA in Cairo
- Nicolau Spencer, MPLA
- José Cesár Augusto, MPLA
- Daniel de Costa García, MPLA
- Mario de Andrade, MPLA

3. Arabian Peninsula – Socialist Front for the Liberation of the Arabian Peninsula
   - Ahmad Jamalludin Abdulla (President)
4. Argentina – National Committee for the Conference of Solidarity of the Peoples of Africa, Asia, and Latin America
   - John William Cooke, Peronist representative (President)
   - Alcira de la Peña, Argentine Communist Party
   - Carlos Alberto Lafforgue, Youth Movement Coordinating Commission
   - Jorge Ruben Queijo, Unified Movement for Labor Coordination
   - Juan Antonio Sander, Argentine University Federation
   - Abel Alexis Latendorf, Peoples' Vanguard Party (PVP)
   - José Gabriel Vazeilles Ullma
5. Basutoland – Congress Party
   - Gerard Ramoreboli, Congress Party (President)
   - Koenyama Chakela, Congress Party
   - Ramangeleo Saloman Tsinyane, Congress Party
6. Bechuanaland – Peoples' Party of Bechuanaland
   - Peter Dick Marupins, Peoples' Party (President)
   - Bobby Mack, Peoples' Party
7. Bolivia – National Committee for the Conference of Solidarity of the Peoples of Africa, Asia, and Latin America
   - Mario Miranda Pacheco, executive secretary of the National Liberation Front of Bolivia (FLIN) (President)
   - Gabriel Porcel Salazar, representative of Bolivian Miners Confederation (FSTMB) and PRIN
   - Mario Monje Molina, Communist Party of Bolivia
8. Brazil – National Committee for the Conference of Solidarity of the Peoples of Africa, Asia, and Latin America
   - Alusio Palhano Pedreira Ferreira (President)
   - Max de Costa Santos, Popular Action Group
   - Carlos Tavares
   - Celso Ridan Barcelos, Popular Liberation Front
   - Iván Ramos Ribeiro, Communist Party of Brazil

- Francisco Santilli
- Alexina Lima Crespo de Paula, wife of peasant leader, Francisco Juliao Arruda de Paula

9. Burundi – Worker's Federation of Burundi
- Nicomede Bigirimona, labor leader (President)

10. Cambodia – Cambodian Afro-Asian Solidarity
- Huot Sambath, Cambodian Ambassador to the UN (President)
- Um Samuth, director of Cambodian University's Plastic Arts School, technician to set up cultural exposition
- Toutch Vutthi, Counselor of Embassy stationed at UN
- Moeng Kiv, technician to set up cultural exposition
- Sunchong Sunther, helped set up cultural exposition

11. Colombia – National Committee for the Conference of Solidarity of the Peoples of Africa, Asia, and Latin America
- Diego Montaña Cuellar, member of the central committee of the Colombian Communist Party (PCC) (President)
- María Inés Pinto Escobar, student in Paris
- Santiago Solarte, member of PCC, writer
- Camilo Losada Campos, Southern Colombian guerrilla bloc
- Baltasar Fernández Alvarez, representative of Southern Colombian guerrilla bloc
- Theodosio Varela Acosta

12. Congo (Brazzaville) – National Revolutionary Committee of the Congo (NRC)
- Julien Boucambou, Vice President of the National Assembly (President)
- Gustavo Aba Gandion, editor of Dipanda, NRC
- Henriette Yimbou Malanda, NRC
- Dominique Ntamba, NRC central committee member

13. Congo (Léopoldville) – National Liberation Council of the Congo
- M. Gabriel Yumbu, secretary general of Supreme Council of Congolese Revolution (Cairo) (President)
- Empira Nkumu (or Comila Nkumu), member of Executive Council and National Liberation Council
- Madam Bernadette Kaputula, Nationalist Women's Federation leader
- Placido Kitungive, National Liberation Council representative in Cairo
- Sebastian Ramazani, National Liberation Council
- Nenriette Malada

- Michel Mongali
- Eduard Marcel Sambu, National Liberation Council
- Buka Masaku, National Liberation Council
- Martin Broboy, National Liberation Council
- Ali John, Congolese Supreme Revolutionary Council

14. Costa Rica – National Committee for the Conference of Solidarity of the Peoples of Africa, Asia, and Latin America
    - Arnoldo Ferreto Segura, People's Vanguard Party (PVP) (President)
    - Hernan Monterrosa Lopez, member of PVP
    - Luisa Gonzalez Gutierrez de Gonzalez, PVP & Alliance of Costa Rican Women

15. Cuba – Communist Party of Cuba (PCC)
    - Osmany Cienfuegos Gorriarán, Minister of Public Works (President)
    - Raúl Roa García, Minister of Foreign Affairs
    - Manuel Piñeiro Losada, Vice Minister of Interior
    - Carlos Rafael Rodríguez, Central Committee, PCC
    - Miguel Martín Pérez, Secretary General of Young Communist League (UJC)
    - José Alberto Naranjo Morales, President of Havana JUCEI
    - Lionel Soto Prieto, National Director of Schools of Revolutionary Instruction (EIR)
    - Haydee Santamaría Cuadrado, Director of Casa de Las Americas
    - Jesús Montané Oropesa, Minister of Communications
    - Lázaro Peña González, President of Revolutionary Cuban Workers Central (CTC-R)
    - José Matar Frangie, Director of the Committees in Defense of the Revolution
    - José Ramírez Cruz, Director of National Association of Small Peasants (ANAP)
    - Carlos Lechuga Hevia, President of the National Council of Culture
    - Pelegrin Torras de la Luz, Vice Minister of Foreign Affairs
    - Arnol Rodríguez Camps, Vice Minister of Foreign Affairs
    - Juan Mier Febles, Vice Minister of Education
    - Melba Hernández Rodríguez, President of Cuban Committee for Solidarity with Vietnam
    - Giraldo Mazola Collaco, Director of Cuban Institute for Peoples' Friendship (ICAP)

- Eugenio R. Balari, Director of youth weekly Mella, UJC
- Joaquín Mas Martínez, member of UJC and WFDY
- Lázaro Mora, Vice President of FEU
- Eduardo Delgado Bermúdez, Director of Political Region for Southeast Asia and Oceana, Ministry of Foreign Affairs
- Ramón Sánchez Parodi
- Carlos Alfaras Varela, Director of Political Region for Africa and Middle East, Ministry of Foreign Affairs
- Ricardo Alarcón de Quesada, Director of Political Region for Latin America, Ministry of Foreign Affairs
- Fernando Álvarez Tabío, Director of Institute of International Policy, Ministry of Foreign Affairs
- Marío García Incháustegui, Director of International Organization of the Ministry of Foreign Affairs
- Raúl Valdés Vivó, PCC
- Antonio Carrillo Carreras, Ambassador to France
- Jorge Serguera Riveri, Ambassador to Algeria and Congo (Brazzaville)
- Armando Entralgo González, Ambassador to Ghana and Dahomey
- Luis García Guitar, Ambassador to the UAR
- Oscar Oramas Oliva, Chargé d'Affaires to Algeria
- José Venegas Valdespino, member of FEU and vice president of IUS
- Rafael Fernández Moya, member of UJC
- Luis Garcia Peraza, member of UJC
- Francisco Valdés, member of UJC
- Arquimides Colombié, member of UES
- Silvio Rivera, member of Cuban Institute for Peoples' Friendship (ICAP)
- Roberto Valdés
- Alfredo Guevara Valdés, Director of Cuban Institute of Art and Cinematographic Industry (ICAIC)

16. Chile – Popular Action Front (FRAP)
- Salvador Allende Gossens, Socialist Senator (President)
- Waldo Atías Martín, FRAP
- Clodomiro Almeyda Medina, FRAP
- Elean Pedraza Casanova, Communist Party of Chile (PCCh)
- Luis Figueroa Mazuela, president of Chilean Labor Central (CUTCH)
- Manuel Rojas Sepulveda, Communist writer, FRAP

- Walterio Fierro, FRAP
- Jorge Montes Moraga, National Deputy, PCCh
- Oscar Núñez Bravo

17. China – Chinese Committee for Afro-Asian Solidarity
- Wu Xueqian, representative of Chinese AASC (President)
- Tien Min Kuo, interpreter
- Su Tien Yang, interpreter
- Ming Sin Tang, interpreter
- Chang An You, interpreter
- Yao Yao Ching Chung, interpreter
- Yang So, Vice President of AAPSO and writer
- Liang Keng, permanent secretary of CPR AAPSC
- Ta Wei Tsien, deputy secretary general, All-China Youth Federation
- Rui Chau Hsu, representative of Chinese AASC
- Wu Hasu Shang, representative of Chinese AASC
- Yi Chen Chung, representative of Chinese AASC
- Ming Chuan Tung, representative of Chinese AASC
- Tien Hui Chen, interpreter (female)
- Yuan Nung Tao, alternate secretary, China Committee for World Peace
- Yang Pai Ping
- Tsien Li Chen, representative of Chinese AASC
- Wuan Chen Chong, representative of Chinese AASC
- Chen Tzo Yin, representative of Chinese AASC
- Chang Chieh Hsun (Zhang Jiéxun), representative of Chinese AASC
- Chen Yu, representative of Chinese AASC, newsman on Sinjua
- Liao Chen Chih, member of AASO and newsman on Sinjua
- Chu Tzu-Chi, representative of Chinese AASC
- Run Ho Hein, interpreter
- Chang Lin Yu, representative of Chinese AASC
- Tuang Hai Yeh, interpreter
- Yu Ying Lin, interpreter
- Fei Yi Li, interpreter
- Wang Chi-fan, member of AAPSO, secretariat of AAPSC
- Shen Yi, assistant secretary, Chinese Peoples' Committee for Defense of World Peace
- Chen Shong Huang, representative of the National Association of Chinese Journalists

- Li Shou-pao, secretary general of YMCA
- Yun Chun Li, Sinjua, interpreter
- Chen Lo Min, Sinjua, interpreter

18. Cyprus – Cyprus Committee of Solidarity
- Christos Christofides, Member of Parliament (President)
- Joseph Yamakis, AASO member, Member of Parliament
- Georgios Savyides, AASO member

19. Dominican Republic – National Committee for the Conference of Solidarity of the Peoples of Africa, Asia, and Latin America
- Guido Rafael Esteban Gil Díaz, June 14th Revolutionary Movement (President)
- Asdrubal Domínguez Guerrero, Dominican Communist Party (PCD)
- Euclides Gutiérrez Félix, June 14th Revolutionary Movement (MR-1J4)
- Cayetano Rodríguez del Prado, Dominican Popular Movement (MPD)
- Carlos Miguel Amiama Martínez, June 14th Revolutionary Movement

20. Ecuador – National Committee for the Conference of Solidarity of the Peoples of Africa, Asia, and Latin America
- Carlos Ramírez Ortiz (President)
- Teodulo Aray

21. El Salvador – National Committee for the Conference of Solidarity of the Peoples of Africa, Asia, and Latin America
- Sergio Pérez, Communist Party of El Salvador (PCES) (President)
- Pedro Martínez, University Students Action (AEU) (may have been the pseudonym of Victor Manuel del Valle Monterosa)

22. French Guiana – The Guiana Committee of Solidarity to the First Tricontinental Conference
- Regino Lucie Prevot (President)
- Jean Marie Robe
- Georges Giffard, president of Guiana Students Union and member of Guianan People's Union

23. Ghana – Convention Peoples Party
- John Kofi Barku Tettegah, secretary general of All-African Trade Union Federation (President)
- Nathanial Welbeck Azarco, Ministry of State, Convention Peoples Party
- Winifred Asare Brown, Convention Peoples Party

- Yaw Manu, University of Ghana, Convention Peoples Party
- Kow Bondzie Brown, Convention Peoples Party
- Pauline Miranda Clerk, Office of the President
- George Kofi Awonoor-Williams, managing director of State Film Corporation
- Emmanuel Ofori Baah, Director of the Bureau of African Affairs
- Patrick Ofei Henaku, Ambassador to Cuba
- Kofi Batsa, editor of *Spark*
- Charles L. Patterson, head of Presidential Office
- Dr. Ekow Daniels, Justice Minister, Convention Peoples Party
- Kwamina Arku-Nelson
- Miss Cecile Elise McHardy, author
- Anthony Korsah-Dick, First Secretary, Ghanian Embassy, Havana

24. Guadeloupe – National Committee for the Conference of Solidarity of the Peoples of Africa, Asia, and Latin America
- Olivier Gerard (President)
- Guy Daninthe, AAPSO
- Rene Aude, President of General Association of Guadeloupe Students
- Dr. Michel Numa, Guadeloupan Front for Autonomy

25. Guatemala – Rebel Armed Forces (FAR)
- Luis Agusto Turcios Lima, leader of the FAR (President)
- Gustavo Solares Ortiz
- René Condon
- Orlando Fernández Ruiz
- Francisco Marroquin

26. Guyana – People's Progressive Party (PPP)
- Cheddi Jagan, leader of the PPP (President)
- Lall Bahadur (or Lall Baeder Labacka)
- Joseph Rodríguez

27. Guinea – Democratic Party of Guinea
- Abdoulaye Diallo, Secretary General of the Foreign Ministry (President)
- Cissé Fodé, secretary of AASO and Guinean Ambassador to the UAR
- Mamady Mohamed Sakho, JRDA National Council
- Mami Kouyate, Chargé d'Affaires at Guinean Embassy, Havana
- Ibrahim Kourouma, reporter for Prensa Nacional

- Fanta Conde
- Jean Baptiste Dee, President of Pan-African Union of Journalists and head of Presidential Information Office in Guinea

28. Guinea (Bissau) – African Party for Independence
- Amilcar Cabral, Secretary General of the African Party for Independence (President)
- Vasco Cabral
- Pedro Pires
- Domingo Ramos
- Joaquín Pedro da Silva

29. Haiti – Unified Democratic Front of National Liberation (FDULN)
- Paul Lantimo, Chair of (FDULN) and Central Committee of the Haitian National Liberation Peoples' Party (President)
- Jacques Lacour
- Pigeon Velage
- Leslie Jean
- Edmond Pierre

30. Honduras – National Committee for the Conference of Solidarity of the Peoples of Africa, Asia, and Latin America
- Ricardo Moncada Zavala (President)
- Raul Parra
- Longino Vidal Beccera

31. India – Indian Association for Afro-Asian Solidarity
- Aruna Asaf Ali, AASC member (President)
- Rao Nallan Narasinha, businessman
- Homi F. Daji, member of AASO, Communist MP
- E. Prabhaker Menon, pacifist
- Jagannath Sharma from Kanpur
- Sara Simba Ladli, lawyer
- Dr. Tondon Sat, Punjab professor
- Harman Singh from Kanpur, district secretary of the CP
- Mehita Balvaj, editor of newspaper Patriot
- Chatur N. Malviya, Indian representative to AASO permanent secretariat, Cairo
- Avior Shiriniwas R. Chari, lawyer
- Mohamed Kalimullah, IAAASO General Secretary
- Mohammed Noor, member of Kashmir Legislature and AASO
- Chandra Sekhar, MP, member of AASO, PSP member from Uttar Pradesh

32. Indonesia – Association of Solidarity of Afro-Asian Peoples
    - Ibrahim Isa, representative of AAPSO in Cairo (President)
    - Francisca Fanggidej
    - Willy Hariandja, PKI member in China, labor union leader
    - Umar Said, editor of Djarkarta Daily Ekonomi Nasional, who resides in China, member of AASO
    - fnu [first name unknown] Suhardto, member of AAPSO in Cairo
    - fnu Soodhartono
    - Edy Soonardji
    - fnu Sugiri, living in Prague
    - fnu Margono, member of Pemuda Rakjat, recently living in Budapest
33. Iran – Iranian Committee for Afro-Asian Solidarity
    - Dr. Amir H. Dibadj (President)
    - Rahman Nader Zehtab
34. Iraq – Iraqi Committee for Afro-Asian Solidarity
    - Salum Abd Al Wahab (President)
35. Jamaica – National Committee of Solidarity for the Conference of the Peoples of Africa, Asia, and Latin America
    - Dennis Vernon F. Daly, attorney, Vice President of Young Socialist League (YSL) and AASC (President)
    - Adolphus Roy Jeffrey, member of Socialist Party (SPJ) and active in Unemployed Workers' Council (UWC) and AASC
36. Japan – Japanese Committee of Afro-Asian Solidarity
    - Kai Shizuma, JAASC (President)
    - Ide Hiroshi, newsman and AASO representative
    - Toshio Tanaka, member of JAASC and Japanese CP
    - Kaneko Mitsuhiro, member of AASO, Japanese CP
    - Kitazawa Masao, AAPSO, Cairo
    - Osaki Susumu, progressive lawyer
    - Itai Shosaku, Secretary General of JAASC
    - Ono Yoro, JAASC, from Hokkaido UN
    - Nishina Akira (or Nishida Tetsu), progressive lawyer
    - Kitazawa Yoko
37. Jordan – Jordanian Committee of Afro-Asian Solidarity
    - Sadik Sadik Rishaydar (President)
38. Kenya – Kenya African National Union Party (KANUP)
    - John Nbirfo Njonjo, MP and member of KANUP
    - James H. Robaro, MP and member of KANUP
    - Ernest Gitu Muni

39. Korea (Democratic People's Republic) – Korean Committee for the Solidarity of Afro-Asia
    - Kim Wal Yong, member of the Central Committee of Korean Workers Party (President)
    - Zi Sun Chin
    - Kim, Chong Nam
    - Kim, Pyong Yui, Counselor, Korean Embassy, Havana
    - Lee, Yu Yui
    - Kim, Yung Kun
    - Chong, Te Jien, Attaché, Korean Embassy, Havana
    - Chung, Pyong Chul, Vice President of CRCE
40. Laos – Neo Lao Hak Xat – Lao Patriotic Front
    - Phoumi Vongvichit, Secretary General of Neo Lao Hak Xat (President)
    - Soulivong Phrasithideth
    - Phouthasack Khamlook
    - Thammavongsay Boun Nhum
    - Khamphay Boupha
41. Lebanon – Progressive Socialist Party
    - Farid Jubran, Vice President of the Progressive Socialist Party (President)
    - Georges Battal, member of Communist Party of Lebanon
    - Muhamad Said Kishli, member of the Arab Nationalist Movement and journalist on Al-Hurriyyah
    - Georges Hawi (or Haoui), member of Orthodox (pro-Soviet) CP
42. Malaysia – Malaysian Committee of Solidarity of Afro-Asian Peoples
    - Dr. Lee Siew Chock, Chairman of MPAASC (President)
    - Abdul Rahin Karim, MPAASC
    - Chia Thye Poh, Central Executive Committee member of Barisan Sosialis Party of Singapore
43. Martinique – National Committee for the Conference of Solidarity of the Peoples of Africa, Asia, and Latin America
    - Edouard de Lepine, Martinique Communist Party (President)
    - Marcel Manville
44. Mauritius – Peoples' Progressive Party of Mauritius
    - Teekaram Sibsurun (President)
45. Mexico – National Liberation Movement (MLN)
    - Heberto Castillo Martínez, National Committee of MLN (President)
    - Armando Castillejos Ortiz, member of Independent Workers' Movement

- Manuel Mesa Andraca, MLN
- Maria Antonietta Gascón Córdoba, member of the University Front of Mexico
- Antonio Tenorio Adama, MLN
- Salvador Bojorquez Urias, Trade Union Affairs secretary of the national executive committee of the General Union of Workers and Peasants of Mexico (UGOCM)

46. Morocco – National Union of Popular Forces
    - Hamid Barrada, ex-president of Moroccan Student Union (President)
    - Mohamed Habib Sinaceur
    - Mohamad Horma Babi

47. Mongolia – Mongolian Committee of Afro-Asian Solidarity
    - Chadraival Lodoidamba, Chairman, Mongolian AACS (President)
    - Nauzad Bayarju, representative of AASC
    - Damba Dulamyn, interpreter
    - Pountsan Terentsodol
    - Narhoo Tsogtyn
    - Namsarian Sodnom, rector of University of Ulan Bator
    - Badamtar B. Balde

48. Mozambique – Liberation Front of Mozambique (FRELIMO)
    - Marcelino Dos Santos, Secretary of International Relations, FRELIMO (President)
    - Eugenio Machado
    - Mariano Matshinha, FRELIMO representative in Zambia
    - Pascoal Nhapulo
    - Josina Abiatar Muthemba
    - Madalena Jingo Juvangiro

49. Nepal – Committee of Afro-Asian Solidarity
    - Poorna Bahadur, President of AASC (President)

50. Nicaragua – National Committee for the Conference of Solidarity of the Peoples of Africa, Asia, and Latin America
    - Pedro Ruiz, member of the Communist Socialist Party of Nicaragua (PSN) (President) (possible pseudonym for Carlos Perez Bermudez)
    - José Pedro Rivera Lopez (possible pseudonym for Abdul Sirker Urroz)
    - José López Rivera (pseudonym used by Enrique Orentes Ruiz)

51. Niger – Sawaba Party
    - Abdoulaye Mamani, Sawaba Party (President)
52. Nigeria – Socialist Party of Workers and Farmers
    - Wahab O. Goodluck (President)
    - Salomon Olaloyo Fagbo Martins, Nigerian Youth Congress
    - Elias Dupe Fadipe
    - Johnson O. Ebohom, Nigerian Youth Congress
53. North Kalimantan – Organization of North Kalimantan for the Solidarity of the Peoples of Afro-Asia
    - Ahmad Zaidi Adruce (President)
    - Mohammad Jais Abbas, AASC
    - Mohamad Kasin, AASC
    - Dustan Chong, AASC
    - Ahmad Mohtar
54. Oman
    - Faysal Ali Faysal (President)
55. Pakistan – Pakistani Committee of Solidarity with the Peoples of Afro-Asia
    - Abdul Hamid Khan Bashani, President, National Awami Party (President)
    - Ijaz Husain Batalvi
    - Arif Iftikar
    - Syed Qmaruzzman Shah, lawyer
    - Skaukat Ali Khan
    - A. T. M. Mustafa, lawyer (died in Havana during conference)
    - Miraj Khalid Ras Masud Husain, Secretary AAPSC
56. Palestine – Organization for the Liberation of Palestine (PLO)
    - Ibrahim Abu Sitta, member of Executive Committee of the PLO (President)
    - Husni Khuffash Saleh, Secretary General of General Confederation of Palestine Workers
    - Zuhayr Rayyis, editor of newspaper Palestina, Gaza
    - Abd Al Karim Al Karmi
    - Dr. Salah Heddin Dabbagh, Director of Foreign Affairs
57. Panama – National Committee for the Conference of Solidarity of the Peoples of Africa, Asia, and Latin America
    - Jorge Enrique Turner Morales, Vanguard of National Action (VAN) (President)
    - Francisco Gutiérrez

- Roberto Madariaga Montes
- Floyd Britton, Revolutionary Unity Movement (MUR)

58. Paraguay – National Committee for the Conference of Solidarity of the Peoples of Africa, Asia, and Latin America
- Carlos Valenzuela (President)
- Héctor Gutiérrez
- Jacinto Correa
- Juan Carlos Arza
- Angel Gómez

59. Peru – National Committee for the Conference of Solidarity of the Peoples of Africa, Asia, and Latin America
- Hector Cordero Guevara (President)
- Jesús Masa Paredes, FALN
- Alberto Ramírez
- Jaime Venegas Romero, FALN
- Armando Pérez Carlo
- Elizardo Sánchez Lomba
- Freddy Eyzaguirre Luque
- Jorge Altoriaga Campos

60. Puerto Rico – Pro-Independence Movement
- Norman Pietri Castellon (President)
- Ana Livia Cordero
- José Luis González Coiscou
- Narciso Rabell Martínez

61. Rwanda – National Union of Rwanda (UNAR)
- Francois Rukeba, UNAR (President)
- Nelson Rwagasore, UNAR

62. São Tomé and Príncipe – Committee for the Liberation of São Tomé and Príncipe
- Antonio Barreto Pires dos Santos (President)

63. Senegal – African Independence Party
- Mamadou Keita, African Independence Party (President)
- Thierno Amath Dansoko (or Dankoke), African Independence Party
- N'Dioaque Babacar, World Federation of Democratic Youth

64. Somaliland (French) – Popular Movement Party
- Moubarak Ahmed Moubarak, African Association (Cairo)

65. South Africa – African National Congress
- Alfred Diliza Kgakong, (President), ANC
- Reginald September, ANC
- Yusuf Mohamed Dadoo, ANC
- Mzimukulw Ambrose Makiwane, ANC

- Thomas Titus Nkobi
- Robert Resha, ANC
- Joyce Judith Mesonwa, ANC
- Marie Muthoo Pragalathan Naicker, ANC
- Meinrad Hsimang

66. South West Africa – National Union of SW Africa (SWANU)
- Fanuel Jariretundu Kozonguizi, SWANU (President)
- Moses K. Katijnaongua, SWANU

67. South Yemen (occupied) – National Liberation Front of Occupied South Yemen
- Saif Ahmed Saleh Dhalee, NLF of Occupied South Yemen (President)
- Jaifar Ali Awadh, NFL

68. Swaziland – Progressive Party of Swaziland
- Dingane Dominic Cain Nxumalo (President)
- Ephrain Nbholv, National Congress for Liberation of Ngwane

69. Sudan
- Ali Abdel Rahman, People's Democratic Party (President)
- Muhammed Yusif Bushara, Sudanese Communist Party
- Billghiez Ahmad
- Ali Osman
- Shazali Amin Shazali

70. Syria – Committee of Afro-Asian Solidarity
- Mouffak Haffar, Syrian Peace Committee (President)
- Morris Salibi
- Muhammed Ali Al Khatib, Secretary General, Ministry of Information
- Mustafa Amin, attorney, Communist Party of Syria
- Mohamed Nouri Rifai (or Nuri Haj Rifai)
- Muhammad Zuhdi Nashashibi, secretary to the Economic Committee
- Dr. Muhammed Ali Yusaf Al Khalil, Ba'ath Party
- Joubran Nakkla Majdalani, Ba'ath Party

71. Tanzania – Tanganyika African National Union
- Salim Said Rashid, Deputy Finance Minister (President)
- Amanas Raymond Rowland Swai, AAPSO
- Mohammed Ali Foum
- Lugo Taquwabwa, Assistant Secretary of the African Section, Ministry of Foreign Affairs
- Ali Mahfudh
- Abdulla Said Netepe

72. Thailand – Patriotic Front of Thailand
    - Bhayone Chulanond (President)
    - Suchart Bhumiborikak
    - Siddhicahi Ionaraksa (or Songkarakse)
73. Trinidad and Tobago – National Committee for the Conference of Solidarity of the Peoples of Africa, Asia, and Latin America
    - George Weeks, President of Oilfield Workers Trade Union (OWTU) (President)
    - George Brown, representing Union of Petroleum Workers of Trinidad and Tobago
74. Uganda – Uganda People's Congress
    - Kanyunozi Yonasani (President)
    - Ali Muwabe Kirunda Kivejinja
    - Raiti Omongin
    - Khahid Younis Kinene
    - Henry Nyakairu
75. United Arab Republic (Egypt)
    - Yousef El Sabai, Secretary General of the Conference Preparatory Committee for the UAR (President)
    - Mohamad Kamal Bahaa El Din, journalist, AAPSO
    - Mursi Saad El Din, AAPSO
    - Khaled Mohieddin, member of presidential committee for World Peace Council and secretary general of Egyptian Peace Council (President)
    - Dr. Suhayr Al Kalamawi, AAPSO
    - Madame Amina Ahmed Al Said, AASO
    - Ezzel El Din Ali Moustafa, AASC
    - Dr. Rifat Al Muhjub, Socialist Union
    - Madame Bshuya Karam, AAPSO
    - Mohamed Diab, Socialist Union
    - Sekina Sadat, Reviata Dar El Hilal Monsawar
    - Ahmad Muktar Kutb, AASC
    - Ragua Ramsi El Kholy, TV cameraman
    - Samiba Taher Mustafa
    - Ahmad Rida Muhammad Khalifa, Communist journalist on Al-Ahram
    - Shebl Hefez Mohamed Shalaby, AASC
    - Mohamed Wafaey Shulkamy, AASC
    - Mohamed Owda, AASC
    - Hoda Tawfik
    - Louis Grace

- Anis Mansour, Arab Socialist Union
- Edward K. F. El Kharrat, AAPSO
- Salah El Sayed
- Hussain Rizk

76. Uruguay – Leftist Liberation Front (FIDEL)
- Luis Pedro Bonavita Salguero, President of FIDEL (President)
- Cesar Reyes Daglio, member of FIDEL
- Blanca Silvia Collazo Odriozola
- Edmundo Suarez Netto, Vice President of FIDEL
- Rodney Arismendi Carrasco, First Secretary, Communist Party of Uruguay (PCU)
- Luis Echave Zas, head of student section of FIDEL

77. USSR – Soviet Committee of Afro-Asian Solidarity
- Sharaf Rashidov, alternate member of Presidium of CPSU CC and First Secretary of CC of Uzbek CP (President)
- Anatali Sofronov, Deputy Chairman of Soviet AASO
- Dimitry Gorbachev, AASC
- Boris Gorbachev, Deputy Chairman of AASC, also reported as newsman
- Vladimir Judintsev, AASC
- Rodolfo Chliapnikov (or Shliapnikov), AASC, 2nd Sec., Embassy, Havana
- Yans Vladimirski, AASC
- Timur Gaidar, AASC
- Natalia Berejnaia, AASC
- Alexeyev Mayevsky, Deputy Chief of Latin American Dept., Ministry of Foreign Affairs, and Secretary General of AASC
- Latif Maksoudov, AASC
- Bahadur Abduzazakov, AASC
- Shakham H. Tyuleubekov, AASC
- Vladimir G. Iarovom (Yarovoi, or Yasonov), Vice President of Soviet Youth Committee
- Mirzo Turzan Zade, Chairman of Tadzhikistan AASC
- Zinaida I. Federova, Chairman of AASC and secretary of committee of Soviet women
- Rasul G. Gamzatov, poet, member of Supreme Soviet and Azerbaidzhan AASC
- Fikriat A. Taveyev, member of Presidium of Supreme Soviet of the USSR and of Tatar AASC
- Dimitry Q. Shevliaginu, AASC
- Mikhail I. Kosix (or Kossykh), AASC

- Kanran A. Guseinov, Kazakhstan AASC
- Bizhiinan R. Ramazanova, press secretary of Supreme Soviet, AASC
- Chinguiz H. Aitmatov, writer, Deputy Chairman, Kirgiz AASC
- Zouleikha I. Guseinova, wife of Kanran Guseinov
- Grigori Lovchine
- Vladimir M. Kollontayu
- Tchermychev Viatchislav, AASC
- Sima S. Panich, AASC
- Nikolai I. Bazanov, AASC
- Veniamin V. Migtsev, AASC
- Spartak Tsissanov, AASC
- Ch. Richat Kudachev, AASC
- Y. A. Bochkarev, AASC
- R. K. Miniar Belourchev, AASC
- Victor F. Buzarkov (or Boukharov)
- Valeri Soukhine
- Arnold B. Dobkin, AASC
- Mikhail IL Kovalev, AASC
- Valeri A. Zhizarev, AASC
- Petr I. Nikolaev, AASC

78. Venezuela – National Liberation Front (FLN)
- Pedro Medina Silva, Commanding General of FALN (President)
- Gilberto López, FLN
- Rosendo Menéndez Luz
- Ciro Rodríguez
- Atencio Manrique, FLN
- Gerónimo Carreras, member of World Labor Union Federation
- José Vicente Rangel, leader of the Nationalist Popular Vanguard (VPN)
- Héctor Marcano Coello, FLN representative (resident in Cuba)
- Héctor Pérez Marcano, FLN
- Omar Cárdenas, resident in Cuba
- Moisés Rafael Moleiro Camero, FLN and Movement of the Revolutionary Left (MIR)
- Oswaldo Barreto Miliani
- Jorge Rubio
- Ali González
- Adolfo Gañenego

79. Vietnam (Democratic Republic) – Committee of Afro-Asian Solidarity
    - Tran Danh Tuyen, Vice President of Vietnam Federation of Trade Unions (President)
    - Nguyen Duy Tinh, Vice Chairman of Vietnam Peace Committee
    - Tran Cong Tuong, secretary general of Lawyers Association
    - Nguyen Thanh Le, deputy editor of Hanoi daily Nhan
    - Nguyen La Cou, AASC
    - Bun Le Quang (or Le Quang Ba), Vietnamese Army AF captain
    - Thang Dong Thi, AASC
    - Truong Si Phan, VAASC
    - Doan Dinh Ca, AASC
    - Nguyen Dinh Bin, AASC
80. Vietnam (South) – Committee of Afro-Asian Solidarity
    - Nguyen Van Tien, central committee member of NFLSV, NFL representative in Cairo (President)
    - Tran Van Tu, South Vietnamese member of NFL regional committee and secretary general of SV Committee for Solidarity with Latin American Peoples
    - Kim Nguyen N. Dang, AASC
    - Van Sau Li, AASC, resides in Cuba
    - Le Thi Cao, NFLSV
    - Trinh Van Anh, delegate representing NFLSV and IUS
    - Professor Ba Nguyen Ngoc, President of AASC, Cairo
81. Yemen – Committee of Afro-Asian Solidarity of Yemen
    - Assayed Abdallah Bin Jehir El Alawi, AASC (President)
82. Zimbabwe (Rhodesia) – Zimbabwe African Peoples' Union (ZAPU)
    - Edward Ndlovu, ZAPU (President)
    - Ethan Allen Duba, ZAPU secretary in Dar-es-Salaam, Tanzania
    - David Mpongo, ZAPU
    - Charles Tarehiva Madando, ZAPU
    - Lusaka Amos Ngwenya, ZAPU
    - Arthur Masuka
    - Charles Chikerema
    - Moulawa Noshe Moko, ZAPU
    - Nelson T. C. Sankange, ZAPU

ORGANIZATIONS PARTICIPATING AND NAMES OF OBSERVERS
INTERNATIONAL ORGANIZATIONS
1. World Peace Council (WCP)
    - Enrique Lister Forjan (Cuba/Spain)
    - Alfredo M. P. Valera
    - Omprakash Paliwal (India)
    - Francis Boaten (Ghana)
    - Juan Marinello Vidaurreta (Cuba)
    - Angel Domínguez Santamaría (Spain)
    - William Gollan (Australia)
    - Oldrich Belic (Czechoslovakia)
    - Lucio Mario Luzzatto (Italy)
2. Women's International Democratic Federation (WIDF)
    - Florence Mophosho (South Africa)
    - Helga Dickell (West Germany)
    - Vilma Espin de Castro (Cuba)
3. World Federation of Democratic Youth (WFDY)
    - Eulogio Rodríguez Millares (Cuba)
    - Ctibor Citek (Czechoslovakia)
    - Rodolfo Mechini (Italy)
4. International Union of Students (IUS)
    - Trinh Van Anh (South Vietnam)
    - Kwamena Ocran
    - Zbynek Vokrouhlicky (Czechoslovakia)
    - Felix Rodriguez (Cuba)
    - Cándido Domínguez García (Cuba)
5. World Federation of Trade Unions (WFTU)
    - Satish Chaterjee (India)
    - Mark Shope (South Africa)
    - Jose Bustos (Brazil)
    - Renato Bitossi (Italy)

SOCIALIST COUNTRIES
6. Albania – Albanian Committee of Solidarity with the Peoples of Afro-Asia
    - Foto Cami, Secretary of AAPSO for Albania
    - Sotir Kamberi, President of Afro-Asian Solidarity Committee and Secretary of Central Council of Trade Unions
    - Faik Zeneli, member of Albanian/Latin American Friendship Society
    - Sezai Shyti, student at University of Havana

7. Bulgaria – Afro-Asian Solidarity Committee
    - Zdravko Mitovski, secretary of AASC
    - Elena Gavroilova, on CC of Bulgarian CP
8. Czechoslovakia – Czechoslovakian Committee of Solidarity with the Peoples of Afro-Asia
    - Antonin Vavrus (or Varbuch), AAPSO
    - Vladimir Simek, AAPSO
9. German Democratic Republic – Afro-Asian Solidarity Committee of the DRG
    - Horst Maz Brasch, AASC
    - Edmund Rohrer, AASC secretary
    - Henrich Engebrecht, AASC secretary
    - Heinz Joswig, member of AASO, Berlin University professor
    - Siglinde Ackerman, AASC
    - Freidel Trappan, AASC
    - Heinz Schmidt, AASC Chairman
10. Hungary – Hungarian Committee of Solidarity with All Those Peoples Who Struggle for Their Independence
    - Andras Tardos
    - Eva Koltai
11. Poland – Committee of Solidarity with the Peoples of Afro-Asia
    - Wladyslaw Sliwka Szczerbic, editor of monthly magazine Konpynenty, PAASC
    - Josef Kulesza, Vice President of Central Council of Polish Trade Unions, member of PAASC
12. Romania – Rumanian League of Friendship with the Peoples of Afro-Asia
    - Mircea Radulescu, AASC

AFRO-ASIAN ORGANIZATIONS
13. Afro-Asian Conference of Jurists
    - Shih Sheng Chao
    - Wang Hsien, AASO, resident in Conakry, Guinea (China)
    - Keita Fadialla, Attorney General at Conakry and Secretary General of AASO Jurists Organization (Guinea)
    - S. H. Wiganto, IAASC Lawyers Secretariat representative, Conakry, Guinea (Indonesia)
14. Permanent Bureau of Afro-Asian Writers
    - Nihal Lakshaman Ratnapala (Ceylon)
    - Karunasena Jayalth (Ceylon)

15. Conference of Afro-Asian Journalists
    - Dharmasena Manuweera (Ceylon), representing Afro-Asian Journalists' organization headquartered in Indonesia

AFRICAN ORGANIZATIONS
16. Organization of the Peoples of South West Africa (SWAPO)
    - Peter Mueshihange, SWAPO
    - Andreas Shipanga, SWAPO central committee member and SWAPO representative in Cairo
    - Ewald Katjivena, SWAPO representative in Dar-es-Salaam, Tanzania
    - Emil Appolus, SWAPO
17. Zimbabwe National African Union (ZANU) (Rhodesia)
    - King David Mutasa, newspaperman
    - Simpson Victor Mtambanonqwe
    - Augustine Mombeshora
18. All-African Trade Union Federation
    - Prosper M. Akanni, Convention Peoples Party (Ghana)

ASIAN ORGANIZATIONS
19. Council Against Atomic and Hydrogen Bombs
    - Masaharu Hatanaka (Japan)
20. Economic Bureau of Asia
    - Samuel Díaz Bandaranaike (Ceylon)
    - Theja Gunawardhana (Ceylon)
    - H. M. Packeer Mohideen (Ceylon)
21. Peace Committee of Asia and the Pacific
    - Victor Montgomery Keeling James (Australia)

INVITED GUESTS
1. Argentina
   - Miguel Angel Rubinich
2. Bolivia
   - Juan Carlos Lazcano Henry, member of Spartacus Group of National Revolutionary Movement (MNR)
3. Brazil
   - Félix Athayde, resident in Cuba
4. Cambodia
   - Antonini Helene Toutch Vutthi

5. Chile
   - Juliana de Rojas
   - Luis Eduardo Labarca Goddard, Communist Youth Leader
   - Gonzalo Rojas Pizarro
6. Colombia
   - Marco Tulio Rodríguez Martínez
   - Jorge Zalamea Borda, university professor, leftist poet and author
7. Congo (Brazzaville)
   - Augusti Mahoungou
   - Alice Mahoungou
8. Cuba
   - Antero Regalado Fallón
   - Zenén Buergo, secretary of foreign relations of the Union of Secondary Students (UES)
   - Reinaldo Calviac, member of UES
   - Pedro Montalván, member of UES
   - Asela de Los Santos, secretary general of the Federation of Cuban Women (FMC)
   - Radamés Mancebo, national organizer of the Committees in Defense of the Revolution (CDR)
   - Aleida March, wife of Ernesto "Che" Guevara
   - Juan José León, secretary of publicity of the Association of Small Farmers (ANAP)
   - Dora Carcaño Araujo, production secretary of FMC
   - Francisco Dorticós Balea, secretary general of the Federation of University Students (FEU)
   - Orlando Rosabal Llanes, organizational secretary of university branch of the Union of Young Communists (UJC)
   - Oscar Domenech, member of UJC
   - Lupe Velíz Villavilla, secretary of foreign relations of FMC
   - Leopoldo Ariza Hidalgo, secretary of foreign relations of ANAP
   - Enrique Velazco López, president of technology faculty, FEU, University of Havana
   - Félix Sautié Mederos, member of UJC
   - Roberto Ogando Faz, member of UJC
   - Gloria Aguilera, secretary of foreign relations of CDR
   - Calixto Morales, member of national secretariat of CDR
   - Alejo Carpentier Valmont, Vice President of the National Union of Cuban Artists and Writers (UNEAC)

- Antonio Nuñez Jiménez, President of the Cuban Academy of Science
- Rolando Cubela Secades, physician, comandante in the Cuban Armed Forces
- Nicóélas Guillen Batista, President of the National Union of Cuban Artists and Writers (UNEAC)
- Salvador Vilaseca Forne, Rector of the University of Havana
- Jaime Crombet, President of the FEU
- Justo Guerra, secretary general of Havana of the Cuban Confederation of Labor (CTC-R)
- Agapito Figueroa Barrero, secretary general of the Cuban Steel Workers Union

9. Czechoslovakia
   - Jiri Meisner, secretary general of International Organization of Journalists

10. Dahomey
    - Codjo Azodogbehov, deputy chairman for foreign affairs of the North African Students Federation in France

11. France
    - León Félix, President of the Political Commission of the Communist Party of France
    - Josephine Baker (American entertainer)
    - Ives Fernand Moreau, editor of *L'Humanite*
    - Regis Jules Debray
    - Madame Voisin

12. Guatemala
    - Aurora Benítez

13. Italy
    - Alberto Moravia, writer (novelist)
    - Mariani Dacia Moravia, writer and poetess, wife of Alberto Moravia
    - Joyce Gioconda Lussu, member of Italian Socialist Party and with Italian Newspaper *Il Nuovo Mondo*

14. Mexico
    - Rafael Estrade Villa, MP, PPS deputy but not a member of any official group
    - Ester Blanca Muñoz Cota de Tenorio, MLN
    - Adalberto Pliego Galicia, PPS
    - Alberto Orduña Curbelo, MP
    - Luis T. Córdova Alvarez

- Gilberto Rincon Gallardo Mellis, MLN
- Manuel Stephens García, member of the Popular Socialist Party (PPS)
- Manuel Marqué Pardiñas, Director of *Politica*, a Mexican Marxist monthly magazine
- Arturo Orona Gamez
- Manuel Terrazas Guerrero, member of the Mexican Communist Party (PCM)

15. Paraguay
- José Asunción Flores, writer
- Elvio Romero, poet

16. Peru
- Hilda Gadea Acosta
- Mario Vargas Llosa
- Patricia Llosa Urquidi de Vargas

17. Puerto Rico
- Halinga Linger de Rabell

18. Tanzania
- Lydia Foun

19. United Arab Republic
- Muhammad Faiq, Director of African Affairs at the Presidency
- Nadia Zulficar Sabri, wife of Muhammad Faiq

20. United Kingdom
- Robin Osmond Blackburn, Bertrand Russell's private secretary, representing the BR Foundation for Peace
- Jack Woodis, author

21. USSR
- Jursand Rashidova

22. USA
- Robert Williams
- Rick Rhoads

23. Uruguay
- Aida de Matteis Ventura, wife of Cesar Reyes Daglio, of FIDEL
- Maria Victoria Espinola Cabrera, wife of Luis Pedro Bonavita Salguero, President of FIDEL

24. Venezuela
- Elena Sánchez
- Elizabeth Burgos

FOREIGN PRESS
1. Argentina
    - Diario El Mundo – Juan Lefgovics
2. Belgium
    - Boletín Informativo de Cuba – Hugues Charles Henri Benoy, member of Belgium CP
    - Le Drapeau Rouge – Hubert Jacob
    - Magazine Europeo – Gabriel F. Dannau, Marie Noelle Cloes, Alphonse Roosens
3. Bulgaria
    - Agencia BTA – Todor Steianov
4. Canada
    - Canadian Tribune – Francis William Park, Libbie Campbell Park
5. Chile
    - Radio Minería Ibar Aibar Varas
    - Las Noticias de Ultima Hora – Frida Moda Schatz (Socialist)
    - Periódico El Siglo – Adriana Serle
6. China
    - XinHua – Chiu Ling, Ho Ching, Mu Kuang-jen (correspondent for NCNA), Chin Te-chi (correspondent for NCNA), Ming Fu Ming, Yi Lin Shu (correspondent for Radio Peking), Shei Chong Hsu, Liu Chong Yang, Sun Shon Guia
7. Costa Rica
    - Semanario Libertad – Francisco Gamboa Guzman (also local TASS representative)
8. Czechoslovakia
    - Radio-Difusion Checoslovaca – David Leff
    - Agencia CTK – Jaroslav Boucek
    - Lyternarny Noviny – Martha Dodd
    - Radio-Difusion Praga – Vera Stocickova
9. Denmark
    - Land Og Folk – Jan Stago
    - CBS News – Carl Sorensen
10. Finland
    - Televisión Finlandesa – Antti Kovanen, Esko Haapaniemi, Pekka Makinen
11. France
    - Agencie Intermonde Presse – Pierre Rondiere
    - Nouvel Observateur – Claude Estier
    - Radio Europeo – Francois Phillipe Fetjo
    - Agencia AFP – Sergio Mendez, Ives Doude, Robert N. Katz

- Revue Democratic Nouvelle – Albert Paul Leutin
- L'Entincelle – Genri Herve
- Le Monde – Marcel Niedergang
- L'Express – Edouard Bailby
- Le Partisans

12. Germany (East)
- Das Andere Deutschland – Leonor Veltfort
- Agencia ADN – Dieter Coburger, Wolfgang Meyer, Peter Heinz Junge (photographer)
- Television RDA– Erick Firendlanger, Peter Ctasshke (or Groeschke), Hannelore Coburger
- Deutscher Demokratisher Rundfunk – Manfried Schroeder
- Neues Deutschland – Peter Lore

13. Guinea
- Francois Henri Pieree Maspero
- Prensa de la República de Guinea – Bob Sow

14. Hungary
- Radio y TV Budapest – Laszlo Salgo (Magyar Radio and TV)
- Nepszabadsag Daily – George Kalmer
- Agencia Telegráfica Húngara – Jozsef Haval

15. Iran
- Shahbay – Rahim Namvar (editor of Shahbaz [The Eagle], organ of the Revolutionary Movement of Iran)

16. Italy
- L'Unita – Saverio Tutino, Gaetano Pagano de Melito
- El Mundo Nuevo, L'Astrolabie, Il Ponte – Mario Lana
- Foto Reporter – Antonio Sansone
- Giornale D'Italia – Guiseppe Dall'Ongaro

17. Japan
- NHK Radio Televisora del Japón – Hiroshi Shionosaki, Kyoichi Hoshino, Hirayama Kenaro
- Asahi Shimbun – Bill Watanane
- Periódico Yomiuri – Takeshi Ogawa

18. Korea (North)
- Agencia Central de Corea – Choun Tak, Zi

19. Mexico
- Cuadernos Americanos – Sol Arguedas
- Revista Siempre – Marta Solís, Alberto Gutiérrez Sánchez, Eduardo del Rio Garcia (cartoonist)
- Revista Política – Raquel Rabinovich de Rosen, Carlos Perzabal Marcué

20. Morocco
    - Diario Aklifah – Abdallah Layachi (member of Moroccan Communist Party)
    - Diario L'Avant Garde – Mahamed Tibari (secretary general of UMT Casablanca local union)
21. Netherlands
    - Algemeen Dagblad – Leo Klatser
22. Norway
    - Orientering – Oysteith Pettersen
23. Poland
    - Zicie Warsawy – Aniela Krupinska
    - Agencia PAP – Miroslav Iconowicz
    - Dookola Swiata – Andrezej Binkowski
    - Editory Office Gromada – Henryk Borzecki
    - Polish Presse Panorama Weekly – Maciev Szczepanski
    - Chtopsha Droga – Leszek Mackow
    - Tribuna Ludu – Ludwik Krasuski
24. Romania
    - Ager Press – Victor Stamate
25. Scotland
    - The Week – Alexander Scott
26. Soviet Union
    - Periódico de "Trud" – Guergorgui Tikonev
    - TASS – Aleksey Stuzhm (or Stoujine), photographer, Mikhail Vasilyevich Artyushenkov, Valery Laskarev, Ruslan Knyazem (or Kunzazey)
    - Radio y TV URSS – Sergio Pokin, Vladimir Pugachev
    - Pravda – Yuri Pogosov
    - Izvestia – Vladimir Silatiev
    - Novosti – Valentin Mashkin, Yuri Paporovo, Mikhail Roy
    - Komsomilakaya Pravda – Alexandre Krivopalov
    - Maladai Comunist – Lev Korenechov
    - Literoturnaya Gazeta – Rimma Kazanora
27. Spain
    - Oficina Actualidades Argelinas – Daniel Ortiz de Miguel, journalist for Noticiano Cinematografico Argelino, a Spaniard who works in Algeria
    - Revista Triunfo – Eduardo García Rico
    - Radial Press – Alfonso Sobrado Palomares
28. Sweden
    - Nydag – Karl Staff

29. Switzerland
    - L'Illustre – Luc Bernard Chesex
30. Tanzania
    - Uhuru – Dadu Hamdum Mansur
    - Unión Nacional Africana de Tanganyka – James Gilbert Markham
31. Tunisia
    - Periódico Les Temps Moderns – Rachid Cheriff
32. United Kingdom
    - Agencia Reuters – Michael Arkus, María Isabel Arostegui
    - Sunday Telegraph – Charles Ian Lundson
    - Evening Standard London – Peter Kingsley
33. USA
    - Associated Press Agency – Antonio Ortega, Isaac Flores
    - UPI – Gabriel Badia Diaz, Pedro Bonetti
    - Mid-Week and Weekly Worker – William Allen (Daily Worker)
    - The Worker – Beatrice Johnson
    - Jewish Daily Freiheit – Joseph North
34. Uruguay
    - El Popular – Ricardo Saxlund
    - Semanario Marcha – Carlos Nuñez Gallategui (also Montevideo correspondent for NCNA)
    - Diario Epoca – Manrique Salvarrcy
35. Vietnam (North)
    - Agencia Noticiosa de Viet-Nam – Au Vu San
    - Fafilm – Chong Li, Cuong Hguyen Duy, Nguyen Nhu Ai
36. Vietnam (South)
    - Agencia del Frente de Liberación Nacional – Vo San Ca
37. Yugoslavia
    - Agencia de Prensa Tanjug – Boza Rafajlovic